SOUTH HAMPSTEAD SYNAGOGUE

ArtScroll Judaiscope Series®

Rabbi Nosson Scherman / Rabbi Meir Zlotowitz
General Editors

Raising children in troubled times –

Collected from the pages of
The Jewish Observer
Rabbi Nisson Wolpin, Editor

Parenting
understanding, coping, succeeding

Distributed by
Mesorah Publications, ltd

FIRST EDITION
First Impression … June 2000

Published and Distributed by
MESORAH PUBLICATIONS, LTD.
4401 Second Avenue / Brooklyn, N.Y 11232

Distributed in Europe by
LEHMANNS
Unit E, Viking Industrial Park
Rolling Mill Road NE32 3DP
Jarow, Tyne & Wear,
England

Distributed in Israel by
SIFRIATI / A. GITLER
10 Hashomer Street
Bnei Brak 51361

Distributed in Australia and New Zealand by
GOLDS BOOK & GIFT SHOP
36 William Street
Balaclava 3183, Vic., Australia

Distributed in South Africa by
KOLLEL BOOKSHOP
Shop 8A Norwood Hypermarket
Norwood 2196, Johannesburg, South Africa

ARTSCROLL JUDAISCOPE SERIES®
TIMELESS PARENTING
© Copyright 2000, by MESORAH PUBLICATIONS, Ltd.
4401 Second Avenue / Brooklyn, N.Y. 11232 / (718) 921-9000 / www.artscroll.com

---

ALL RIGHTS RESERVED
The text, prefatory and associated textual contents and introductions
— including the typographic layout, cover artwork and ornamental graphics —
have been designed, edited and revised as to content, form and style.

No part of this book may be reproduced
IN ANY FORM, PHOTOCOPYING, OR COMPUTER RETRIEVAL SYSTEMS
— even for personal use without written permission from
the copyright holder, Mesorah Publications Ltd.
except by a reviewer who wishes to quote brief passages
in connection with a review written for inclusion in magazines or newspapers.

THE RIGHTS OF THE COPYRIGHT HOLDER WILL BE STRICTLY ENFORCED.

The publication of this volume was made possible in part by a generous grant from the New York City Department of Youth and Community Development.

ISBN:
1-57819-510-1 (hard cover)
1-57819-511-X (paperback)

Typography by CompuScribe at ArtScroll Studios, Ltd.
Printed in the United States of America by Noble Book Press Corp.
Bound by Sefercraft, Quality Bookbinders, Ltd., Brooklyn N.Y. 11232

Table of Contents

Publisher's Preface — xiii
Overview / Rabbi Nisson Wolpin — xv

Family

Introduction / *Rabbi Yitzchok Kerzner* — 27
The Role of Women in Bringing the Redemption / *Rabbi Shneur Kotler* — 29
Jewish Families — In Glory and in Crisis / *Rabbi Avraham Pam* — 36
Inner Strength / *Rabbi Noach Orlowek* — 45
The Structure for Family Harmony / *Rabbi Reuven Feinstein* — 53
Harmony in the Home — Keeping It Together / *Rabbi Yissocher Frand* — 61
Mrs. Rosenberg's Yeshiva / *Rabbi Yisroel Miller* — 71
Making Our Family a Mobile Home / *Devorah Greenblatt* — 76
Report From Ground Zero / *Rabbi Yakov Horowitz* — 82
Dear Mom (poem) / *Bracha Druss Goetz* — 92
Washing Dishes (poem) / *Sarah Shapiro* — 94

Raising Children, as Viewed by Great Leaders

The *Chazon Ish* on the Educator's Responsibility to the Weak and Wayward Student / *Rabbi Zvi Yabrov* — 97
Notes on Education / *Rabbi Simcha Wasserman* — 105
Raising a Family / *Rabbi Elya Svei* — 108
Between Parents and Sons / *Rabbi Avraham Pam* — 118

Helping Our Children Do Their Best

Disciple-Discipline / *Rabbi Noach Orlowek* — 127
Foundation for Growth: Self-Esteem / *Rabbi Mordechai Blumenfeld* — 130
The Art of Reproof / *Rabbi Hillel Belsky* — 135
Instilling Good Character in Our Children / *Rabbi Yitzchok Kirzner* — 139
Developing Character: Learned or Experienced? / *Dr. Bentzion Sorotzkin* — 149

Teamwork / *David Mandel*   160
Seminars on Raising Children / *Malka Kaganoff*   168
A Mother's Reflections (poem) / *Shiffy Lichter*   179

⇒ *Chinuch* Concerns

Teacher and Parent: A Spiritual Partnership / *Rabbi Shmuel Dishon*   185
The New Horizon in Education / *Rabbi Shimon Schwab*   191
School and Home: Partners or Adversaries / *Rabbi Yaakov Reisman*   196
Of Growth and Belonging / *Rabbi Ahron Kaufman*   204
Some Kids on the Brink Can Be Saved / *Rabbi Yisroel Wolpin*   214

⇒ Maximum Benefit From Our Schools

Reclaiming Aspiration / *Chana Juravel*   221
When Children Help Children / *Yaakov Astor*   229
Inclusions vs. Insularity: A Symposium / *Rabbi Shneur Aisenstark, Rabbi Hillel Belsky, Rabbi Yoel Bursztyn, Mrs. Rochel Spector, Rabbi Yechezkel Zweig*   238
Only for the Chosen of our People? / *Rabbi Yaakov Bender*   259
When Children's Learning Handicaps Are of Our Own Making / *Rabbi Yitzchak Kasnett*   270
A Teacher's List of Do's (not Don'ts!) / *Mrs. Rachel Leah Frankel*   275

⇒ *Shabbos, Yom Tov*, etc.

Pivotal Precepts in the Building of Our Nation / *Rabbi Zev Cohen*   287
My Father's *Kittel* / *Rabbi Myer J. Schwab*   291

⇒ Meeting the Needs of Special Children

A Parent's Agony / *Anonymous*   297
These Children Are Ours / *Rabbi Abraham Twerski, M.D.*   300
A Special Visitor / *Dovid Greenwald*   302
Reflections of a Parent / *Ephraim Milch*   307

⇒ Dealing With Problem Situations

Short-Term Gifts (a SIDS kid) / *Rabbi Avrohom Y. Stone*   315
An Open Letter to My Questioning Friends / *From That Mother of the Boy on Crutches*   324

Intensive (Care) Reflections / *Ephraim Milch*   329
When Crisis Looms / *Dr. Aaron Twerski*   334

⤖ Combating Negative Influences

The Jewish Home Under Siege / *Rabbi Shimon Schwab*   345
From Station to Station / *Akiva Davidsen*   353
"Plastic Frames" / *Anonymous*   358
Affluence or Attitude / *Rabbi Shimon Finkelman*   362
Landmines Along the Information Highway / *Yoseph Herman*   368
The Time for Perfection Has Come — Are We Ready? / *Dr. Aaron Twerski*   379
The Gift / *Dina Smith*   393

⤖ Dropouts

An Ounce of Prevention / *Rabbi Yakov Horowitz*   399
Dealing with the Dilemmas of Kids At Risk / *Interview with Rabbi Shmuel Kamenetsky*   412
Where Responsibility and Love Intersect / *Rabbi Shloime Mandel*   416
The "At-Risk Child": Early Identification and Intervention / *Dr. David Pelcovitz & Rabbi Shimon Russel*   422
Buying Time / *Rabbi Michoel Levy*   431
Consequential Conversations (Without Being Confrontational) / *Rabbi Ahron Kaufman*   436

⤖ Afterword

Basic Principles of Parenting / *Rabbi Shlomo Wolbe*   451

⤖ Postscript

"Hereby Resolved..." A Father's Resolutions / *Dr. Jerry Lob*   459

Contributors to this volume*
(In alphabetical order)

Rabbi Shneur Aisenstark is principal of the Beth Jacob School of Montreal, Canada.

Yaakov Astor is a published author and a frequent contributor to The Jewish Observer.

Rabbi Hillel Belsky is the principal of Hanna Sacks Bais Yaakov in Chicago, Illinois.

Rabbi Yaakov Bender is Rosh Hayeshiva of Yeshiva Darchei Torah – Mesivta Chaim Shlomo, Far Rockaway, New York.

Rabbi Mordechai Blumenfeld taught at the mesivta level for 25 years, and is currently involved in marriage, family and personal counseling in Toronto and New York. He is the author of Fundamentals and Faith, based on lectures by the late Rabbi Yaakov Weinberg, Rosh Hayeshiva of Yeshiva Ner Israel in Baltimore, Maryland.

Rabbi Yoel Bursztyn is Menahel of Bais Yaakov School for Girls in Los Angeles, California.

Rabbi Zev Cohen is the Rav of Congregation Adas Yeshurun in Chicago and serves as the Mashgiach of Bais Medrash LeTorah in Skokie, Illinois. He is also a maggid shiur in the Daf Yomi Dial-a-Daf program.

Akiva Davidsen is a professional who lives and works in New York City.

Rabbi Shmuel Dishon, Mashgiach of the Bais Medrash of Yeshiva Karlin-Stolin, has been active in yeshiva education for over 25 years. This essay is based on a presentation at a symposium at a national convention of Agudath Israel of America.

Rabbi Reuven Feinstein is Rosh Hayeshiva of Yeshiva of Staten Island and a member of the Nesius of Agudath Israel of America. His essay is based on an address at a national convention of Agudath Israel of America.

---

* Most of the biographical information was culled from the original articles in The Jewish Observer.

Rabbi Shimon Finkelman, a *rebbi* in Yeshiva Darchei Torah, Far Rockaway, New York, is a frequent contributor to *The Jewish Observer.* He is the author of several biographies published by ArtScroll/Mesorah Publications, as well as the collaborative works of *Chofetz Chaim, A Lesson a Day* and *Chofetz Chaim, A Daily Companion.*

Rabbi Yissocher Frand teaches a *shiur* in Yeshiva Ner Israel in Baltimore, Maryland as well as a weekly *shiur* in the Agudath Israel of Baltimore. His essay is based on a fuller treatment of the topic that Rabbi Frand delivered as a lecture. He is the author of *Listen to Your Messages* (ArtScroll/Mesorah).

Mrs. Rochel Leah Frankel has been involved in girls' education on the high-school level for over a decade, most recently as Hebrew Department principal of a Bais Yaakov in Monsey, NY.

Mrs. Bracha Druss Goetz, a published author, lives in Baltimore, Maryland. Her poems include, *A Hellinist Left Standing.*

Mrs. Devorah Greenblatt served as the director of Youth Services for Project YES.

Dovid Greenwald, a *musmach* of Yeshiva Ner Israel, Baltimore, lives in Spring Valley, New York.

Yoseph Herman of Monsey, New York, has used the benign features of Internet on the job for many years. When researching about the dangers of Internet, he uncovered facts that shocked him, which prompted him to write his essay to alert the reader to these problems and to search for options to minimize their effects.

Rabbi Yakov Horowitz is the *Menahel* of Yeshiva Darchei Noam (Monsey, NY) and the director of Project YES.

Mrs. Chana Juravel of Monsey, New York, is involved in girls' education on the high-school and seminary level.

Rebbitzen Malka Kaganoff, author of *Dear Kallah* (Feldheim Publishers), lives in Jerusalem where she teaches in seminaries and writes.

Rabbi Shmuel Kamenetsky is the *Rosh Hayeshiva* of the Talmudical Yeshiva of Philadelphia, chairman of the *Nesius* (Presidium) of Agudath Israel of America, Rabbinic Advisor of Agudath Israel's Project YES, and a member of the Rabbinical Administration Board of Torah Umesorah, the American Society for Hebrew Day Schools.

Rabbi Yitzchak Kasnett was the coordinator of the P'TACH program in Yeshiva Rabbi Chaim Berlin. Presently he is the principal of the Ocean Parkway Developmental Center and managing director of The Center for Research in Applied Theories of Education.

Rabbi Ahron Kaufman is a *rebbi* in Yeshiva of Far Rockaway, New York. He has successfully implemented the concepts expressed in his essays in dealing with teens both in and out of yeshivos.

Rabbi Yitzchok Kerzner, rabbi of Congregation Machzikei Hadas of Clanton Park in Toronto, chaired a symposium on "Preserving the Torah Family" at a national convention of Agudath Israel of America. His introduction to this volume is adapted from the convention address.

Rabbi Yitzchok Kirzner, ל"צז, served as Director of the Citywide Outreach Educational Program of the Jewish Renaissance Center in New York, and authored the book, *The Art of Jewish Prayer*. This essay was prepared for publication by Mrs. Menucha Lev.

Rabbi Shneur Kotler, ל"צז, was the *Rosh Hayeshiva* of Bais Medrash Govoha, Lakewood, New Jersey. His essay was based on an address to a Bnos Agudath Israel convention.

Rabbi Michoel Levy of Lakewood, New Jersey, is a high-school *rebbi* in Torah Academy for Boys in Brooklyn, New York.

Mrs. Shiffy Lichter lives in Spring Valley, New York.

Dr. Jerry Lob is a clinical psychologist in Chicago, Illinois, working with families and teenagers in the *frum* community. He is a *musmach* of Bais Medrash Govoha of Lakewood, New Jersey.

David Mandel is the Chief Executive Officer of OHEL Children's Home & Family Services in Brooklyn, New York.

Rabbi Shloime Mandel is *Rosh Hayeshiva* of Yeshiva and Mesivta of Brooklyn.

Ephraim Milch, a *talmid* of Yeshiva Ner Israel, Baltimore, Maryland, lives in Pittsburgh, Pennsylvania, where he practices law with the law firm of Campbell and Levine. The author acknowledges the contribution of a number of people to the formulation of his essays, most notably, Maier Kutoff of Minneapolis, Minnesota.

Rabbi Shimon Schwab, ז״צל, was Rav of K'hal Adath Jeshurun of Washington Heights, New York. His essay, The New Horizon in Education, is based on excerpts from an address delivered at the national convention of Torah Umesorah, the National Society for Hebrew Day Schools.

Sarah Shapiro is a well-known author, poet and editor who lives in Arzei HaBira, Jerusalem. Her work includes Growing With My Children – A Jewish Mother's Diary (Targum Press) and Of Home and Heart (ArtScroll/Mesorah).

Mrs. Dina Smith is on the faculty of Machon Bais Yaakov Hilda Birn High School of Brooklyn.

Dr. Bentzion Sorotzkin is a therapist with a private practice in Brooklyn, New York.

Rebbetzin Rochel Spector is the Assistant Principal, Hebrew Department of the Girls' High School Division of Yeshiva of Brooklyn.

Rabbi Avrohom Y. Stone, of West Orange, New Jersey, was formerly the Rav of a shul there and gives shiurim throughout the community. He is a frequent contributor to The Jewish Observer.

Rabbi Elya Svei is Rosh Hayeshiva of the Talmudic Yeshiva of Philadelphia, and a member of the Moetzes Gedolei HaTorah (Council of Torah Sages) of Agudath Israel of America. His essay is based on an address at a national convention of Agudath Israel of America.

Dr. Aaron Twerski, a professor of law at Brooklyn Law School, Chairman of Agudath Israel of America's Commission on Legislation and Civic Action, is a frequent contibutor to The Jewish Observer. His essay, The Time for Perfection Has Come — Are We Ready? is based on an address at a national convention of Agudath Israel of America.

Rabbi Abraham Twerski, M.D. is a best-selling author and the founder and medical director of the Gateway Rehabilitation Center in Pittsburgh, Pennsylvania. Dr. Twerski's essay is from his opening remarks at a symposium, "These Children Are Ours," at a national convention of Agudath Israel of America.

Rabbi Shimon Schwab, ז״צל, was *Rav* of K'hal Adath Jeshurun of Washington Heights, New York. His essay, *The New Horizon in Education*, is based on excerpts from an address delivered at the national convention of Torah Umesorah, the National Society for Hebrew Day Schools.

Sarah Shapiro is a well-known author, poet and editor who lives in Arzei HaBira, Jerusalem. Her work includes *Growing With My Children – A Jewish Mother's Diary* (Targum Press) and *Of Home and Heart* (ArtScroll/Mesorah).

Mrs. Dina Smith is on the faculty of Machon Bais Yaakov Hilda Birn High School of Brooklyn.

Dr. Bentzion Sorotzkin is a therapist with a private practice in Brooklyn, New York.

Rebbetzin Rochel Spector is the Assistant Principal, Hebrew Department of the Girls' High School Division of Yeshiva of Brooklyn.

Rabbi Avrohom Y. Stone, of West Orange, New Jersey, was formerly the *Rav* of a *shul* there and gives *shiurim* throughout the community. He is a frequent contributor to *The Jewish Observer*.

Rabbi Elya Svei is *Rosh Hayeshiva* of the Talmudic Yeshiva of Philadelphia, and a member of the *Moetzes Gedolei HaTorah* (Council of Torah Sages) of Agudath Israel of America. His essay is based on an address at a recent national convention of Agudath Israel of America.

Dr. Aaron Twerski, a professor of law at Brooklyn Law School, Chairman of Agudath Israel of America's Commission on Legislation and Civic Action, is a frequent contibutor to *The Jewish Observer*. His essay, *The Time for Perfection Has Come — Are We Ready?* is based on an address at a national convention of Agudath Israel of America.

Rabbi Abraham Twerski, M.D. is a best-selling author and the founder and medical director of the Gateway Rehabilitation Center in Pittsburgh, Pennsylvania. Dr. Twerski's essay is from his opening remarks at a symposium, "These Children Are Ours," at a national convention of Agudath Israel of America.

Rabbi Simcha Wasserman, צז"ל, educated at the feet of *gedolei Torah* of pre-World War II Europe, was from the early 1940's until his passing in 1992 a leading figure in *chinuch* and *harbotzas haTorah*, as well as a pioneer in *kiruv*, in Europe, America, and most recently in Jerusalem, where he founded Yeshivas Ohr Elchonon.

Rabbi Shlomo Wolbe, author of *Alei Shur* and other works, is one of the foremost living educators and *mussar* personalities. His essay is an abridged selection from the book, *Planting and Building in Education* (Feldheim Publishers), which was prepared for publication by Rabbi Leib Kelemen.

Rabbi Nisson Wolpin is the editor of *The Jewish Observer*, Agudath Israel of America's monthly journal of thought and opinion, where the articles in this volume originally appeared.

Rabbi Yisroel Wolpin is a *maggid shiur* in the Yeshiva Gedolah of Midwood in Brooklyn, New York.

Rabbi Zvi Yabrov is the author of *Maaseh Ish*, a three-volume biography of the Chazon Ish.

Rabbi Yechezkel Zweig is *Menahel* of the Bais Yaakov High School of Baltimore, Maryland.

The essays in this book first appeared as articles in
The Jewish Observer, a monthly journal of thought and opinion
published by Agudath Israel of America.

Rabbi Nisson Wolpin, Editor

Editorial Board
Dr. Ernst L. Bodenheimer, Chairman
Rabbi Abba Brudny
Rabbi Joseph Elias
Joseph Friedenson
Rabbi Yisroel Meir Kirzner
Rabbi Nosson Scherman
Prof. Aaron Twerski

Rabbi Yosef C. Golding, Managing Editor

Publisher's Preface

HISTORICALLY, TRADITION HAS HAD SHIFTING MEASURES OF authority. At times and in places, it has been inviolable, and such cachets as "orthodox" or "traditional" were ironclad seals of approval. Increasingly in Western society, "traditional" has become almost a pejorative. Dress codes in schools and offices, Emily Post's code of behavior, old-time morality, conventions of language, respect for authority figures, discipline at home and in school — these are part of a long list of societal pillars (opponents would call them shibboleths) that are under lethal ridicule and attack.

Has society been improved by this demolition of society's edifice of old-fashioned values? Popularizers of newer and looser cultural norms may trumpet the praises of the self-proclaimed "greatest generation," but the fact is that a proven infrastructure of family, school, and neighborhood norms is being undone before a new one is constructed. And what will the new one be? Will there even be one, or will structure give way to anarchy, and at what cost?

This book makes no bones about being a forum for traditional parenting and educating. Although it collects the ideas and advice of Jewish thinkers, scholars, leaders, educators, and mental-health professionals, it has much to say to everyone who seeks to adapt proven wisdom to new situations.

The great medieval sage Moses Maimonides urged, "Accept the truth from whoever says it." In that spirit we feel that the truths of this book will profit a very broad range of people, whatever their background. We call it "Timeless Parenting," because we feel that its comments and suggestions are based on timeless principles that are as valid in the new millennium as they were in the old.

The articles in this volume are anthologized from more than 25 years of the "Jewish Observer," a respected journal of opinion, published by Agudath Israel of America. Recently the Observer sparked international debate with an issue on the burning subject of "children at risk," a topic that generated unprecedented response and prompted two reprints of the issue, not only for sale but for wide distribution in schools and homes. That testifies to the importance of the issues covered in this anthology and to the public's regard for those who address it.

We are gratified, therefore, that the New York City Department of Youth and Community Development has provided considerable assistance to make this publication possible. Thanks to its support, this book will receive wide community distribution, thus enabling countless families and institutions — and ultimately young people — to benefit from its counsel.

⚯ An Overview
Parents and Children

An opportunity for interaction.
A format for fun and fulfillment.
A setting for joy and celebration.
An investment in *nachas* and success.
A link in the chain of tradition.
A mandate to teach and instruct.
A structure for conveying values and ideals.
A burden of responsibility and accountability.
A challenge to patience and forbearance.
A trip wire for frustration and disappointment.
A springboard for blame and accusation.
A cause for fear and despair.

PARENTING IS SWEEPING AND ALL ENCOMPASSING IN SCOPE. It is crucial to one's sense of happiness, and can — when effective — result in a richer life and a better world for all concerned. And when something goes awry, the ramifications can be crushing. Especially today —

Contemporary society seems to be marked by rapidly changing mores, antifamily messages from the entertainment and information media, mounting peer pressure coupled with diminishing parental influence. Kids are described as being "at risk," and so is the family.

And yet parents persist. They dream, hope, plan, strive — and pray — to imbue their children with a sense of values, and a will to live by them. In other words, to raise them as responsible, generous, caring, moral human beings.

A formidable undertaking. When does it begin?

> *A religious couple, blessed with a healthy baby boy, invested him with all sorts of goals for greatness, but were not certain how to lead him there — realistically and effectively. So when the infant reached his first birthday, they approached the young father's mentor from his student days, and asked him, "How can we raise our little Yosi to greatness?" "True greatness?" "Yes. As close to perfection as possible."*
>
> *The sage peered at them over his glasses, and — after a long pause — asked, "How old is your Yosi?"*
>
> *"Today is his first birthday," the father replied.*
>
> *"Then you are twelve months too late," sighed the mentor.*

Parents actively instruct their children in countless ways. But more than teaching them such rudimentary skills as tying shoes, maintaining cleanliness and order, learning to be obedient and to express gratitude, parents exert greater influence on their offspring in a more subtle, yet more potent level, by the way they hold a child, hug him, grab his hand, sing, play, and — yes — scold the child. Messages spoken and conveyed with a look or a touch create attitudes and forge relationships, many times with words or gestures not even directed to the child.

There is a Hebrew word for this kind of communication — *hashpaah*, which[1] is related to the word *shipua*, slanted, as in a *gag shipua* — a slanted roof. When someone seeks shelter from a rainstorm, he will usually find cover under a roof. Should the roof be pitched at an angle, and

---

1. According to Rabbi Yaakov Kamenetsky, late sage, teacher, and universally revered community leader.

the person venture out beyond the roof's edge, he will be showered by the cumulative benefit of all the rain that falls on the roof and rolls down over the edge, to the place where he stands.

In much the same way, a person who is under the wing of another's influence will find himself treated to the full measure of attitudes, values, and trickle-down views and perspectives articulated by the person stretched out over him — articulated by spoken word, facial gesture, or simple act.

Such messages transcend ethnic identity. Clearly, different cultures will adapt universal messages to their own situations — different strokes for different folks — but societies that have succeeded in transmitting their values from generation to generation have much to teach.

Parental actions, choices, decisions can cast long, long shadows that last a lifetime. In the last years of his life, Rabbi Yaakov David Wilowsky[2] (1845-1913) lived in the holy city of Tzefas in then-Palestine. Prior to that, he had been spiritual leader of Slutzk, Poland, and was considered one of the outstanding scholars of his generation.

One winter afternoon in Tzefas, on the anniversary of his father's passing, Rabbi Wilowsky came to the synagogue earlier than usual for the afternoon services. He stood at his lectern for a few moments, meditating, as tears welled up in his eyes.

A close friend asked him, "Why are you so emotional? Your father was 80 years old when he passed away, and that was almost fifty years ago."

"I'll tell you," said Rabbi Wilowsky, composing himself. And this is the story he related:

> "When I was a young boy, my father arranged for me to have the most skilled teacher in our town, a certain R' Chaim Sender, as a private tutor. He charged one ruble a

---

2. He is known by the name of his two classic commentaries on the Jerusalem Talmud, *Ridvaz*, which is an acronym of his name.

month, which was a large sum of money in those days, especially for my father, who was very poor.

"My father made his living building brick furnaces for people. One winter, business was very bad because there was a shortage of bricks, and my father couldn't meet the payments to R' Sender. Three months went by, and then I came home with a note from my tutor that said that if he did not get the money the next morning, he would be unable to continue teaching me.

"My parents were devastated. To them, my daily studies meant everything. When my father went to shul that evening, he heard a wealthy man complain that the contractors building a house for his son and future daughter-in-law could not get a furnace for heating and cooking because of the brick shortage. He offered six rubles to anyone who would get him a furnace.

"When my father came home from shul, he discussed the matter with my mother, and they agreed that my father should take apart our own furnace, brick by brick, and use them to build a new one for the rich man. Then they would have six rubles for my teacher, three for back pay, and the other three for the next three months.

"The winter was bitterly cold and we all froze and shivered. All that, so that I should have the best teacher and grow in Torah."

Rabbi Wilowsky paused, took a breath and continued, "I cried today because I remembered the boundless affection and devotion that only parents can have so that their child should learn our precious studies." (From *The Maggid Speaks* (ArtScroll), Rabbi Paysach Krohn).

Perhaps the Wilowskys never preached to their son about the importance of education. They didn't have to. Their personal example was the most elegant sermon imaginable.

As life becomes more complex, and parents more harried than ever, they are forced to delegate more of their instructional responsibilities to others. Thus enter teachers who are not family members, educating, guiding and molding children. America is proud of having introduced universal education, through the public school, by the initiative of Horace Mann. But he was not the first person to do so.

Actually, universal public education was instituted some 2,000 years ago. The Talmud singles out for praise Yehoshua ben Gamla, a High Priest who lived in Israel during the time of the Second Commonwealth. He is remembered for his great accomplishments (*zachur latov*): Before his time, only children who had fathers capable of teaching them would learn; other children simply remained ignorant. Yehoshua ben Gamla traveled the length and breadth of the land, and established schools for *all* of Israel's children.

It has been pointed out[3] that, contrary to the popular view, Yehoshua ben Gamla's innovation was not a signpost of social progress; it marked a deterioration of the standard Jewish household of those times. The situation can be compared to a middle-American city that boasts that every child born in its hospitals is accommodated with an incubator in their neonatal units. At first blush, one might marvel at the advanced level of medical care in the city's maternity wards. On the other hand, one must wonder: What is wrong with the local population that renders the mothers incapable of carrying their fetuses through to full development? After all, a neonatal unit is meant to compensate for the lack of maturity and self-sufficiency that should have been achieved in the mother's womb. Normally, any child who is carried full term should fend for itself without need to resort to technological life support. Something is remiss.

Similarly, there must have been a deficiency in the standard families (with the exception of single-parent families) if they lacked fathers capable of teaching their sons. The introduction of universal schooling must be seen as the response

---

3. Attributed to Rabbi Yitzchok Hutner, late *Rosh Hayeshiva* of Mesivta Chaim Berlin Kollel Gur Aryeh.

An Overview: Parents and Children

to a social deficiency. Parents seemed to need all the help they could get.

And the expanding assumption of parental role by teachers, seminary deans, and *mashgichim* (ethical supervisors), launched by Yehoshua ben Gamla, continues to this day.

Nowadays teachers are increasingly doing the work of parents — instructing, inspiring, setting examples, conveying values. And, in some cases, teachers are the most dedicated parents imaginable.

The talmudical academies of Eastern Europe were not only institutions of analytic study, but in many cases were the settings for concentrated ethical introspection, hothouses of self-improvement and self-realization. At the head of these academies were devoted teachers and mentors, who were deeply dedicated to in the growth of each student.

> *A gentleman who was visiting one of the classic schools of talmudic research in pre-World War I Europe was fascinated by a young man three rows to the left, deeply engrossed in a page of Talmud. He pointed him out to the head of the yeshiva and asked about his status as a scholar.*
>
> *"Do you mean Aaron Leib?" asked the Rosh Yeshiva. "Ah, yes, an outstanding scholar. He's my ben yachid (only son), you know."*
>
> *A few minutes later, the visitor pointed out a different student — a tall young man engaging in a heated argument on a subtle, abstract matter with his study partner, and asked about him.*
>
> *"Oh, that's Shalom Dov, a very penetrating thinker. Yes, yes, my dear only son."*
>
> *The visitor was taken aback. "I thought that Aaron Leib was your only son!"*
>
> *"True enough. They both are."*
>
> *"How can that be?" he questioned. "How many 'only sons' can one person have?"*

"Two hundred of them, at the last count," replied the dean. "Every young man in this study hall — each one — is my precious one-and-only son. No two at all alike. Each one is special to me."

⸻

At the 1975 Convention of the National Society for Hebrew Day Schools, Rabbi Yaakov Yitzchok Ruderman, dean of Ner Israel Academy in Baltimore, reflecting on the problem of the waning authority in the educational scene, recalled a childhood experience that illustrates in an extreme way perhaps how a parent or mentor earns the right to be an authority figure. We quote:

"I was only 14 (in 1910) when I arrived in Slabodka (an elite school in a town across the river from Kovna, the capital of Lithuania). The Alter (lit. "the elder," used as a reference of endearment to the head of the institution, Rabbi Nosson Zvi Finkel) took special interest in me. When he learned that my roommate had revolutionary leanings and could exert a harmful influence on me, he found some pretext to invite me to stay in his home — a small two-room cottage. (His son, Reb Leizer Yudel, had married the daughter of Rabbi Eliyahu Kamay, and made his home in Mir, where his father-in-law was Rav. The Alter's house was thus empty.)

"One night, he sensed that I was ill. Indeed, I was suffering stomach cramps, and he understood that I was afraid to venture outside to use the primitive facilities — the night was extremely cold and pitch black. The Alter told me to go out while he stood in the open doorway, wrapped in a coat against the biting wind, talking to me continuously, to dispel any fears I might have had. When I returned to the house, I found that he had asked his wife to prepare a glass of tea for me.

"I felt that he loved me as much as any father could love his own child, and he let me know it. Now, I ask you, could there possibly be a question of the Alter's right to assume a role of authority in my life?"

On another occasion, Rabbi Ruderman recalled an animated conversation he had had with the *Alter* in the yeshiva's *beis hamidrash*:

> "I was explaining a chiddush (novel interpretation) on a Talmudic topic I had come up with. He was taking it apart, while I defended my view. In the midst of our exchange, his son, Reb Leizer Yudel, visiting from Mir, entered the Beis Midrash doorway. The Alter hadn't seen him for over seven years, yet he scarcely looked at him, continuing our discussion to its conclusion. He then turned to his son and greeted him warmly, embracing him. I followed him out the door to greet the guest.
>
> "His wife asked him, 'Why did you ignore our Yudel?'
>
> "He answered, 'Because I was talking with Yaakov Yitzchok.'
>
> "'But Leizer is your son!' she protested.
>
> "'So is Yaakov Yitzchok my son,' he replied.
>
> "This was said to his wife, not for my ears, and I knew he meant it.
>
> "— With such a teacher, such devotion, could there have been problems of our accepting his authority?"

―――◦―――

Parenting and teaching, instructing and influencing the next generation — these constitute an awesome responsibility. And in some ways, the challenges seem more daunting than ever. We've absorbed effective approaches and successful techniques from our own mentors, and hopefully we utilize them to pass our values on to our charges. Foremost amongst the astute, experienced mentors are *Chazal* (the wise men of the Talmud) who share their wisdom and insights with all who are equipped to turn to their words for guidance.

In the generations since their ideas were recorded, countless people have tapped into their timeless techniques and shared them with yet others. And so, we somehow have managed to find our way in a constantly changing, dynamic society, benefiting from ancient wisdom, often stored in new casks, decanted from sparkling new carafes, filling our freshly fashioned thirsty cups.

Over the more-than-thirty-five years of its publication, *The Jewish Observer* has regularly featured articles and discussions on the topic of effective parenting and teaching, featuring a blend of timeless wisdom and timely innovation. We are proud to present a sampling of these essays in the pages that follow.

Rabbi Nisson Wolpin

June 2000

Family

Introduction

The Role of Women in Bringing the Redemption

Jewish Families — In Glory and in Crisis

Inner Strength

The Structure for Family Harmony

Harmony in the Home — Keeping It Together

Mrs. Rosenberg's Yeshiva

Making Our Family a Mobile Home

Report From Ground Zero

Dear Mom (poem)

Washing Dishes (poem)

Introduction

The Family

Rabbi Yitzchok Kerzner

THE FAMILY AS AN INSTITUTION IS IN TROUBLE ON THE American scene, as has been well documented. While the Torah society has managed to create vibrant communities that have shielded and insulated themselves from the devastating onslaught of the new morality, it would be a dangerous self-delusion not to recognize that some seepage has taken place into our own homes. One cannot escape the pervasive influence of a materialistic, secular, and hedonistic society.

The Torah describes Yaakov *Avinu's* return to the Land of Israel from Charan with his twelve sons as: "Yaakov returned *shaleim* — complete, perfect." Rashi quotes the Midrash as finding Yaakov "complete in body, complete in material possessions, complete in Torah."

This remarkable achievement has become the goal of every conscientious Jew. It is the sum total of the course of study of every yeshiva; and indeed, it is within our study halls of Torah that this ideal can best be realized.

But there is a world beyond these walls, and it is essential that this tri-faceted perfection be pursued in the broader world, without compromise, acculturation, or accommodation to corrosive values.

The rabbis add that Yaakov's arrival was "at twilight; and

he established boundaries." The implication is that it was a time of ambiguity, when it was difficult to discern between right and wrong — so like our own complex era. Yaakov's task of drawing sharp lines of distinction has been assumed by the yeshivos. Inevitably, however, the point is reached when one enters the world of the marketplace, where one is so subject to the influence of foreign value systems. Here, we do not function in a setting of perfection, but in one of fragmentation and disunity. The tendency is to compartmentalize our values, and assume one mentality in the office or behind the counter, and another in the *beis midrash* or *shul*. It is tragic, indeed, if the criteria for "completeness in material possessions" is from a different source than "completeness in body" or "...Torah." Yet the affluence we are enjoying may well be responsible for some severe problems in our lives, and may have cut us off from the purity and wisdom of the *beis hamidrash*.

All concerned parents surely harbor private anxieties and fears, hopes and dreams for their children's wholesome development; and it undoubtedly will be to their advantage to study the words of two leading *roshei yeshiva,* who offer their insights on how to raise a Torah family in a society that is so hostile to the Torah outlook on life. With their guidance, our goals become clearer, and our chances for success that much more possible.

The Role of Women in Bringing the Redemption

Rabbi Shneur Kotler זצ"ל

JUST AS THE EXILE IN EGYPT HAD WITHIN IT THE SEEDS OF every *galus* the Jews were to experience, so too did the redemption from Egypt have within it the beginnings of every *geulah*. As we anticipate *bi'as hagoel* — the coming of the *Mashiach* — we are actually praying for the completion of the redemption process that began in Egypt 3300 years ago.

Chazal tell us that it was in the merit of righteous women that the initial redemption from Egypt took place. To complete the redemption, we must look to today's women to seize those elements of righteousness that distinguished the generation of the Exodus, and to perpetuate them today. No doubt some are attributes that the women directly imbued into the Jews of Egypt. Others were native to people or implanted in them by their fathers, to be nurtured, developed and preserved by the women in their role of *"beiso zu ishto"* ("his house," referring to his wife). That is, just as in the material sense, furnishings and decorations can make or add to the amenability of a place, yet the spot does not become a house until four walls are erected around it to protect it; so too can the head of a household furnish a family with values and ideals, yet they cannot perpetuate their role as a single unit with like-minded goals and purposes without the women's protective, insulating role as *bayis*.

What, then, were the distinguishing features of the generation that G-d redeemed from Egypt?

The Family

First, it would be impossible to conceive of Jewry emerging as a nation from slave status were there not some cohesive force binding them together. The primary level of such cohesion is, of course, the family unit. Considering that to so great an extent the men were enslaved, it was the women's task to bind together the members of the family and to preserve the family as a viable unit. Without their extra perception and dedication, the *geulah* could never have taken place.

The crucial role of the family must never be underestimated nor permitted to be undermined. This is especially vital in today's world, where values contrary to Torah have gained so much currency, insinuating themselves into the finest of homes; at the same time, now more than ever, the family as a viable unit is suffering, and the women's traditional role as homemaker is under attack from so many quarters. It is thus more imperative than ever that the Jewish woman appreciate her function as *akeres habayis* as a prime factor in meriting the *geulah*.

"Midos" — Positive Character Attributes

Another extremely significant factor in the *geulah* was the exceptional *midos* (character attributes) that the Jewish people had maintained throughout their sojourn in Egypt. A prime example is Moshe *Rabbeinu's* reaction to being told that it would be his mission to lead the Jews to freedom. In their dialogue on the subject, G-d told Moshe to go, for "Your brother Aaron will go out toward you and he will rejoice in his heart." The Midrash tells us that it was essential that Moshe know that Aaron was, indeed, rejoicing in his heart over his assignment, because Moshe had refused to undertake this mission for fear that his older brother would have misgivings, should the leadership role be assigned to him, the younger brother.

Now this might seem strange. Millions of Jews were suffering torture and even death. The time for redemption had finally come. His older brother would surely welcome the redemption regardless of who leads it. No doubt, he would find in Moshe's leadership role a source of pride, even if this pride may somehow be tinged with envy. Yet, Moshe *Rabbeinu* refused to carry out the task of leading the Jews from Egypt if, in some way, this might hurt his brother. Should the redemption of millions be delayed because of one man's misgivings?

The Alter of Slabodka (Rabbi Nosson Zvi Finkel) explained that Moshe *Rabbeinu's* reluctance was not an obstacle that had to be overcome for the sake of the redemption. On the contrary, it was a prerequisite to his serving as redeemer. As is recorded in the *Chumash*, Moshe's first act upon reaching maturity was to step out among his brothers to share their hardships with them, so he could fully appreciate the suffering that they were enduring. As leader and redeemer of *Klal Yisrael*, Moshe had to be sensitive to the individual suffering of each and every Jew, including his brother. Had he not taken into account Aaron's possible misgivings over the role he was to play, Moshe would have been lacking in required qualities for leadership.[1]

In general, a remarkable sensitivity of this sort is not inborn. It is customarily nurtured in the home created and sustained by the mother — in her role of *akeres habayis*.

---

1. The Warsaw Dayan (rabbinical judge) Davidoff once remarked that he would have been a *chassid* of the *Chidushei Harim* (first Gerer Rebbe) had it not been for several statements that he had made. One of them that especially troubled him was a quotation from the Rebbe Reb Bunim of P'schis'cha:

The Rebbe Reb Bunim had said that he was endowed with the power to bring *Mashiach*, but would not do so for one consideration. After *Mashiach's* arrival, a grand *seudah* (feast) would be convened, and for sure all the Torah giants of the generation would be seated at the head of the table, while *"Ich, der blinder Bunim"*

The Role of Women in Bringing the Redemption / 31

A People of Faith

Another way in which the righteous Jewish women of Egypt brought the redemption is alluded to in the signs with which Moshe *Rabbeinu* was to convince the people of his role as leader to the Jews. He was instructed to insert his hand in his bosom and withdraw it, to find it "white as snow with leprosy." *Rashi* tells us that leprosy is generally afflicted on slanderers, and Moshe had indeed slandered the Jews when he expressed doubt that they would believe him. A strange omen, this one! What source of comfort is there to a suffering nation in learning that their would-be redeemer slandered them before their G-d? Why was this chosen as one of the signs to demonstrate that he was selected for this awesome trust?

One mustn't forget that Moshe was the *adon hanevi'im* — the supreme prophet of all time. If anyone, it would be he who could plumb the depths of the Jewish soul to determine how strong their commitment to faith actually was. Yet, he had underestimated them — doubting that they would believe him; only to be reprimanded by G-d Himself, Who assured him that they are indeed believers. Thus, Moshe addressed the Jewish people and said, "Don't underestimate yourselves. You may feel that you don't have the capacity to listen, to invest in G-d's promise, and to have faith in its fulfillment. But you are wrong. You are believers, the children of believers. It is part of you; it has been kept alive in you through the efforts of the heads of your families. Look, I also doubted you — as evidence, my leprosy — but I was wrong."

---

would be in a corner. "I can picture the Apter Rav, 'The *Oheiv Yisrael*,' at the head of the table, turning to *Mashiach* and asking him, 'And who was it that succeeded in finally bringing you here after all our years of prayer and hope?' And *Mashiach* would say: 'It was he, over there, *der blinder Bunim*.' If the Apter Rav would experience even the slightest misgivings, that would be terrible. If it would be so, how could I bring *Mashiach*?"

It was beyond the Warsaw Dayan how such a minor consideration could prevent the Rebbe Reb Bunim from bringing *Mashiach*. The Alter of Slabodka's explanation, however, makes it clear.

Hence, Moshe's leprosy as a testimony to his slandering of the people did not degrade them. On the contrary, it served to show that they should not be disheartened by their lack of faith in their own faith. He, too, had doubted its strength and was proven wrong .... This capacity to believe was instrumental in keeping Jewry worthy of redemption. And, as stated, the merit of the righteous women who stood at the helm of the Jewish families in Egypt preserving their faith was responsible for the redemption.

Narrowness of Spirit

One more point: We are today afflicted with a certain narrowness of spirit that is referred to in Moshe's discussion with G-d: He was commanded to bring his pleas for freedom to Pharaoh, after having failed to gain the attention of the Jewish people. Said Moshe: "But the Jewish people didn't listen to me. How then will Pharaoh?" Rashi refers to this as one of ten cases of *kal v'chomer* (a fortiori arguments) in the Torah.

But one can challenge Moshe's reasoning. The passage before (*Shemos* 6:11) states, "And the Jews did not listen to Moshe because of a narrowness of spirit from hard labor." Here is a refutation to Moshe's argument. Of course the Jews did not listen. They had been burdened with an increased, crushing workload, and were, for this reason, suffering narrowness of spirit. On the other hand, Pharaoh was dwelling in the comfort of his palace. There was no reason why he should not listen to Moshe.

Such, however, was not the case. There are different types of *kotzer ruach* (narrowness of spirit). People who have clear-cut life-goals in mind are not beset by inner turmoil. They may be distracted, at times, from pursuing these goals because of external pressures; but when given the opportunity to repair to more peaceful contemplation, their goals are still vivid before their eyes and they are capable of aligning their aspirations, plans, and actions accordingly. The "narrowness" is gone.

The Role of Women in Bringing the Redemption / 33

This was the status of the Jewish people in their bondage in Egypt. True, they were suffering "hard labor," but when given even the briefest of respites from their workload, they cold return to the peace of their homes and refresh their spirits. They could revive the ideals implanted in them by their father Yaakov and kept alive within them by the women who maintained their homes.

By contrast, Pharaoh undoubtedly suffered from an inner turmoil and narrowness of spirit. He was constantly in pursuit of new sensual experiences, seeking to gratify every desire in ever-different ways.[2] This inner turmoil is an even greater barrier to absorbing the spiritual content of G-d's message than the external distractions of hard labor and physical bondage.

Thus, Moshe's *kal v'chomer* was very much in order: The Jews, who were only suffering a narrowness of spirit that emanates from physical bondage, did not listen to me. How, then, could Pharaoh, who suffers from an internally caused narrowness of spirit?

The affluence we so enjoy today should serve as a source of support for Torah and relieve us of the distracting pressures of poverty. Instead, it serves as a source of new pressures, operating from within, for affluence also offers the means for fulfilling an enormous range of desires and appetites. The mere potential becomes an imperative. So, while modern Jewish society is spared the externally caused narrowness of spirit produced by the circumstances of hard labor, many suffer the narrowness of spirit that comes from within.[3] In today's constant rush

---

2. Commentators have pointed to the paradox of Egypt's wide-open, hedonistic moral code in contrast to the etymological root of *Mitzrayim* (Egypt) which is associated with *M'tzorim*, meaning "walls," or walled in. Here, the relationship becomes clear.

3. Thus we find that תמהון לבב (confusion) is both an aspect of the *tochachah* — G-d's severest punishment of Israel when they err and part of the על חטא confessional. At first glance this presents a contradiction: Is it a condition induced by G-d's wrath or is it an outgrowth of personal weakness?

As תמהון לבב relates to קוצר רוח, one can see how these are two variations of this malaise. On the one hand, an unanticipated rush of events can breed confusion — a punishment from the Heavens recounted in the *tochachah*, from which a person can

and search for instant gratification, people are without time or presence of mind to savor a spiritual experience. Gratification must be instant, for people are without time or patience to await the advent of the experience, or to guide it in its development.

Here, too, it is the task of the Jewish woman to keep ever vivid and alive those overriding spiritual goals that earned for our people the redemption of over 3,000 years ago, and can again earn for us the coming of the *Mashiach*.

---

find shelter and gain inner repose. On the other hand, a headlong pursuit of pleasure and new experiences also breeds confusion, but in this instance man cannot find relief unless he retreats from it, into a confessional introspection — the תמהון לבב of the חטא על.

The Role of Women in Bringing the Redemption

Jewish Families — In Glory and in Crisis

Rabbi Avraham Pam

I. The Rise of Glorious Families

⤖ Why Our Forefathers Suffered

MUCH ATTENTION IS BEING FOCUSED ON THE JEWISH FAMILY as a vital force in insuring our people's continued existence. To fully appreciate the strength of the Jewish family, one should begin with the founding Patriarchs and Matriarchs of our people. It is noteworthy that the *Avos* and *Imahos* — Avraham, Yitzchak, and Yaakov; Sarah, Rivkah, Rachel, and Leah — developed their families in a most unique fashion. These couples were barren and according to the laws of nature, they could not possibly have built families of their own. It was only through Divine intervention that they had children. Why was this so?

The *Gemara* deals with this question.

> Rav Yitzchak says, "Our forefathers were barren because the Almighty desires the prayers of the righteous" (*Yevamos* 64a).

This is truly difficult to understand. It would imply that the Almighty had deliberately caused these righteous individuals to endure immense pain and sorrow — to the point that Rachel exclaimed, "If I cannot have children, then I am as if dead!" And Sarah was willing to suffer the indignity of giving her maidservant to her husband, Avraham, in the hope that in merit of this act she would have a child of her own. And why were they made to suffer so? "Because the Almighty loves the prayers of the righteous"!

If we could but fathom the power of "the prayers of the righteous," we would perhaps approach an understanding of the profundity of Rav Yitzchak's teachings. "The prayers of the righteous" are not like our ordinary prayers. Rather, they flow from a disengagement from physical existence, a removal of one's focus from the daily world of *Olam Hazeh*, a fostering of intense desire within one's soul for spirituality, and a complete identification with the Creator.[1]

From this perspective we can gain an insight into the statement in the *Gemara* that the early *chassidim* would devote three hours to prayer: one hour before prayers, an hour in prayer, and an hour afterwards (*Berachos* 28a). We can understand why these righteous individuals would need an hour for preparation — to rid themselves of inappropriate thoughts, and distance themselves from worldly involvements — so as to focus their thoughts on the Almighty alone, in keeping with the maxim: "Know before Whom you stand"... to enter into another world in which one is only aware of the Creator of the Universe. But why would they also need an hour after their prayer?

When one has left this mundane world for higher spiritual realms, it is G-d's will that we return, and it is no simple task to do so. It requires another hour of introspection to once again become mortals who function in an "ordinary" world.

⇒ The Power of Heartfelt Prayer

This is the essence of Rav Yitzchak's explanation: The Almighty wished to build *Klal Yisrael* as a holy nation, different from every other nation in the world, with its children born through the prayers of *tzaddikim*, of righteous individuals. As

---

1. See Rabbi Chaim Volozhiner's explanation of true prayer in *Nefesh HaChaim, Shaar 2*.

Chana had said, "... and I will pour out my soul before Hashem" (*I Shmuel* 1:15), and from such prayer was Shmuel *Hanavi* born. The Almighty wanted *zera kodesh*, holy progeny. For this reason, Rav Yitzchak teaches us, G-d made the Patriarchs and the Matriarchs barren, for "Hashem loves the prayers of the righteous."

If parents truly aspire to have *zera kodesh*, to merit bringing down a holy *neshamah* from its source, beneath the Divine Throne, one must recognize the requisite level of holiness — from conception, through birth, and on into life — and be faithful to that responsibility. This is reflected in the special prayer recited by the *sandek* and the *mohel* at the *bris* of a Jewish infant:

> "Please, Hashem, send through Your holy *malachim* a holy, pure soul for this child who will be given a *bris* for Your Holy Name ..."

When that holy soul is dispatched by the Almighty, it requires an appropriate spiritual climate for its growth and development. And the proper climate for such a holy soul to grow to be *zera kodesh*, holy progeny, is a home full of holiness and pleasantness, a home that recognizes its responsibility in being the fertile ground for the *zera kodesh*, a home of *shalom bayis*.

A home blessed with *shalom bayis* — where there is only love and concern among husband, wife and the entire family — is a home where the priorities are in order. The central focus of the household is the children, as our Sages say, "*Amaleinu* — our toil — this refers to our children" (*Haggadah Shel Pesach*). Such a home recognizes that its primary purpose is to forge another link in the chain of generations, to be *ovdei Hashem*, the Almighty's servants.

The Steipler ז״ל once said that the spiritual resources necessary to merit "good children" were "50 percent *tefillah* (prayer) and 50 percent *shalom bayis*." The *tefillah* mentioned by the Steipler is not of the ordinary, "catch-as-catch-can," daily habitual variety, but those deep, heartfelt feelings that flow from the realization that the entire purpose of building a Jewish home and of being a Jewish parent, to which all other goals are subservient, is to have one's children grow to be "good children." These prayers, as constant as they must be, provide only 50 percent of the required spiritual merits. The other 50 percent must be *shalom bayis*, to create the climate for this prayer to come to fruition.

II. When Crises Arise

Cause for the Altar to Weep

WITH GRATITUDE TO THE ALMIGHTY, WE HAVE BUILT MANY wonderful Jewish families in America. And from these blessed families come holy, pure children. Indeed, we have homes that exemplify the ideal of being a "*mikdash me'at*, a miniature *Beis Hamikdash*," permeated with holiness, joy, and pleasantness, endowed with *ahavas Hashem, ahavas Yisrael*, and *ahavas habrios*, love for one's fellow human beings. But our joy is not complete. We also have — to our great pain — homes in which there is no *shalom bayis*. And the ones who lose the most in such situations are the children. They may even possess the holiest of *neshamos*, but if they live in a home where they hear only bickering, anger, and worse — even such children will be sacrificed.

The *Gemara* (*Gittin*) says: "When one divorces his first wife, even the Altar in the *Beis Hamikdash* cries for him." One may wonder: What connection is there between divorce and the Altar in the *Beis Hamikdash*? In light of the previous discussion, the insight of our Sages is clear: Although the Altar has a variety of sacrificial objects offered to be consumed by its fires, there is one item that even the Altar cannot accept: a broken household. The result of a divorce — the sacrifice of a broken home and its injured children — is too much for even the Altar. Hence, our Sages say the Altar cries at a divorce, for the sacrifice of a Jewish home is too great for it to bear.

Jewish Families — In Glory and in Crisis / 39

Nor is this the worst of our pain. We also have the problem of *agunos*, of bound spouses, where a marriage is strained beyond the point of repair, but no *get* is in the offing — the result of a cruel, smoldering hatred of one spouse towards another, a stratagem in their private, bitter war.

Before we address this issue, one must understand: These lines are not inspired by any individuals. Rather, this issue requires our attention because it is filled with such pain and suffering. And yet, so often one hears the accusation: "The *Rabbanim* don't care about the plight of the *agunos*." This is a vicious canard, an absolutely false statement, for the *Rabbanim* feel the pain of the *agunos* with unimaginable acuteness.

And what is the suggested alternative? Again, one hears that there is a need to "reform," to "improve" the *halachah*. Or do they really mean: We should find spurious loopholes in the *halachah*!

Further, one hears, "There are no honest religious courts." What a slander against earnest, dedicated Torah scholars! What a defamation of the Jewish people, and the Torah — intimating that justice cannot be found in a *beis din*, but in the secular judicial system!

And then the most unpardonable of arguments: "Religious courts always make compromises; I want all that's coming to me. I need to go to secular courts to get the best deal."

One must take note: The *Shulchan Aruch* states clearly that going to secular courts is a blasphemous act; it is an unspeakable humiliation of the Torah and a *chillul Hashem*, as if one lifts one's hand against the Torah of Moshe.

⟜ A Civilized Approach to *Gittin*

It is, of course, conceivable that a particular match will not "work out," where the marriage is simply not compatible, even after mutual efforts at reconciliation have been made and reasonable steps were taken to bridge the difficulties. But why cannot the task of dissolving the marriage be approached with respect and humanity — with *menchlichkeit*? When two individuals agree — "It would be better for me, it would be better for you. Let's end this relationship" — why can't they set up their plan of action with understanding that "to end our partnership, we must go to honest judges of a respected *beis din*, and they will help us divide the property, the responsibilities, and structure our future relationships with the children"?

All too often, we witness such hatred and cruelty that one can only wonder: "Where did Jews ever acquire such character traits? The pain, the suffering, the cost in dollars and in health to the *agunah*, who may sit for months and even unending years without a solution to the problem — and all with no concern, no sensitivity on the part of the recalcitrant spouse. How did such bitter cruelty ever come to the seed of Avraham — the paradigm of *chessed* and mercy?"

> *Once, in a bygone era, a Jew came to his Rav to divorce his wife. As the Rav had not heard of any marital problems, he was surprised, to say the least. He pressed his visitor, "Can we perhaps arrange a reconciliation? What are your complaints against your wife?"*
>
> *"No," the Jew told the Rav, "all has been discussed and now it's time to arrange the get." As to his complaints, he said, "Since the get is not yet final, she is still my wife. With all due respect, I will not speak evil of my wife."*
>
> *The Rav persisted, "You must have complaints; what claims do you have against your wife?"*
>
> *"As long as she is still my wife," the man resolutely responded, "I will not speak against her."*
>
> *Seeing no alternative, the Rav sadly administered the get.*
>
> *After the divorce proceedings were finished, the Rav approached the Jew with a final question: "Now that the get is completed, will you tell me what your complaints were against your former wife? Why did you want the divorce?"*
>
> *The man answered the Rav, "Since the divorce is final, the woman who was my wife is no longer related to me. She is like any other Jew. Why should I speak evil about another Jew?"*

How far removed is this approach from that adopted by all too many couples — even erstwhile fine, caring couples — in our time. Too often, individuals, who in all other areas of their lives exhibit kindness and compassion, behave with such cruelty, such hatred when it comes to this most difficult of situations, the breaking of a marital union.

If a couple "cannot find an honest *beis din*," it is only because they do not want to find one, each finding fault with the other's suggestions for *dayanim*. Hatred and *lashon hara* abound. How ironic that the Chofetz Chaim writes that one must forfeit his entire fortune not to violate a single negative commandment; yet in disagreements over how to divide property in a divorce settlement, a couple will willfully transgress a host of negative commandments, including bearing hatred, speaking falsely, and *lashon hara*. Worse yet, all of this is compounded by *chillul Hashem*, as the entire spectacle is played out before non-Jewish lawyers and judges, a sin for which no forgiveness is possible until one leaves this world.

Where is the concern and sensitivity for the humanity of the other spouse, the father or mother of one's children? Where, in the entire process as practiced in too many families today, is honor for the Torah, honor for the Almighty? Shlomo *Hamelech* says in *Koheles* (9:6): "Their love, their hate, their jealousy have already perished...." After all is said and done, all of the hatred and jealousy will disappear, and all that will remain will be: "*Lifnei mi atta asid litein din v'cheshbon* ... — Before Whom will you give accounting for your actions in the future? Before the Almighty" (*Avos* 2:1).

If a couple must divorce, why can they not deal with each other with respect and dignity, with concern and sensitivity? One can rebuild one's own life, and help the other person do the same, as well; and in this way lead a meaningful, quality life. Why can't children of divorced parents continue to have a mother and a father — an attitude that would have such an ameliorative effect on their long-term psychological development!

⇒ Living Up to the Model of Our Forebears

We do not need to "reform" or "improve" the *halachah*; David *Hamelech* tells us, "*Pekudei Hashem yesharim* — the Laws of Hashem are just, giving joy to the heart" (*Tehillim* 19:9). Rather, we must cure the corruption in society. We must remember we are *zera Avraham*, the children of Abraham. We need not even go that far back in history. We are all children of holy, pure, righteous *tzaddikim* of two, three generations back, who would never have thought that their children would find themselves in such straits or guilty of such conduct.

When Yisro saw that the Jewish people were besieging Moshe *Rabbeinu*, requesting his guidance from morning to night, he realized that this was a situation that could not last. Both Moshe and the people would be worn out from the unyielding strain. Yisro therefore proposed that a system of judges be instituted. But this was only a partial solution for Moshe and the people — treating the symptom, but not the malady itself. The complete solution was, as Yisro said, "You shall caution them regarding the decrees and the teachings, and you shall make known to them the path in which they should go, and the deeds they should do" (*Shemos* 18:20). Teach them, as the Chofetz Chaim said, the path — the path of Avraham *Avinu*, the path of kindness,[2] of sensitivity for another's feelings.

A Jew should ask himself, "Was I put on this earth to cause pain to someone, to my wife/husband? Was it for this purpose that my mother endured labor pains at my birth, that my parents suffered the tribulations of child-rearing, my *rabbe'im* the effort of teaching me wisdom — to bring an individual into the world capable of such cruelty?" This was Yisro's ultimate solution to the problem he saw: Instituting judges will lessen the problem, yes; but teaching the people to live with *menchlichkeit*, with *chessed*, would solve the problems in their entirety. We do not need to "reform" or "improve" the *halachah*; we need to renew our society.

---

2. From this verse, *Chazal* derive the obligation to do *chessed* beyond the requirements of the letter of the law, i.e. *lifnim mishuras hadin*.

When Avraham parted company with Lot, he told him: "*Im hasmol v'eimina, v'im hayamin v'asm'ila* — If you turn to the left, I will go to the right; if you turn to the right, I will go to the left" (*Bereishis* 13:9). Avraham gave Lot the first choice, and even offered to modify their separation with the word "*v'eiminah* — and I will go to the right.*"* *Rashi* tells us that Avraham had meant that even after the break, if Lot would need him, he would be at his right side, ready to help if necessary — as, in fact, later occurred. Avraham could have taken a different approach, pointing out that all that Lot had acquired was attributable to him. Instead, he gave Lot first choice, and even offered to help him; in short, he was *menchlich*.

All the more so should a husband and wife, who had made a covenant of love with each other on their wedding day, be respectful and considerate of one another. Let them recall how their relatives invoked the blessings of Hashem for them! If only couples entering into a divorce would bring out their wedding album to remind themselves of their mutual hopes and promises!

May Hashem help us remove this humiliating mean-spiritedness from among our people, and replace it with a pleasantness of spirit, inspiring *kiddush Hashem*. Indeed, the Almighty has told us, "I wish kindness, not sacrifice" (*Hoshea* 6:6).

Inner Strength

Rabbi Noach Orlowek

"בא חבקוק והעמידן על אחת"

CHAVAKUK CAME AND PREDICATED them [the rules for a successful life] on one [principle]."[1] As the generations deteriorated,[2] the teachers of the Jewish people sought to distill their lessons for life into successively fewer life principles. I will attempt to follow this principle in presenting what I feel is the basic, underlying obligation of the Torah-guided community in the coming years.

We, the Torah community, have the obligation to protect our children (and ourselves) from a dominant society, which is becoming increasingly hedonistic and immoral. On the other hand, we are obligated to reach out to our sisters and brothers who have not been exposed to Torah, and demonstrate how a Jew who is true to Torah values can function in a modern society. In the following paragraphs, I would hope to present how this dual responsibility can be met.

I would first like to present why reaching out to others must stem from a position of inner strength, and then attempt to offer some suggestions as to how that inner strength can be achieved.

---

1. *Makkos* 24a.

2. It has been taught that the word for generation, *dor*, is a derivative of the word לדרדר — to roll downward. It is an integral part of the course of history that the generations are in spiritual descent. Why this is so and how this descent is expressed is a vital subject, but outside of the scope of this article.

Reaching Outward and Reaching Inward

Rabbi Eiiyahu Eliezer Dessler was critical of those who moved from Torah-true communities to engage in outreach.[3] I merited, for almost twenty years, to enjoy a personal relationship with Rabbi Chaim Friedlander, *Mashgiach* of Ponevez and Yeshivas HaNegev. Reb Chaim was one of Rav Dessler's closest *talmidim* and had a major role in preparing *Michtav Me'Eliyahu* for publication. I once asked him how Rabbi Dessler could be so opposed to going to communities where Torah was weak; wasn't he, as a result, condemning a huge portion of *Klal Yisrael* to spiritual annihilation? Reb Chaim's response was immediate and clear:

> Rabbi Dessler was opposed to *individuals* going out to communities where Torah ideals were weak. If ten *bnei Torah* would go together, however, then the situation would be different. But there is an important condition. That these ten not be ten individuals, but ten who form a single unit. (In effect, they generate their own protective environment, which allows them to reach out to others without the risk of becoming adversely effected by the values of the hedonistic society that envelops them and their children.)

I would suggest that an important principle emerges from this:

While we have a primary responsibility to reach all of our brothers and sisters in *Klal Yisrael*, this must be done from a position of inner strength and conviction, which can then allow us to offer the care, love and patience that are necessary to any *kiruv* effort.

Patience, Torah, and Protection

My Rebbi, Rabbi Simcha Wasserman, put the same idea in a different way: At the time of the return to *Eretz Yisrael* from the Babylonian Exile, the *Anshei Knesses Hagedolah* were

---

3. See *Michtav Me'Eliyahu* vol. 2 p. 169, where he contrasts Lot's going to Sodom to teach with Avraham's remaining in the mountain, in his own environment, and teaching those who came to him. See also ibid., p. 216.

charged with the task of reaching large groups of Jews who had strayed from their heritage. My *Rebbi* [Reb Simchah] postulated from their teachings the guidelines[4] for someone who wants to reach out to *Klal Yisrael*:

First, the *Anshei Knesses Hagedolah* said, הוי מתונים בדין — "Be patient; do not judge others quickly." Those who lead a life void of Torah are not to be judged harshly or quickly. We must feel love and compassion toward them, as we would toward any brother or sister whom we wish to bring back to Torah. Secondly, העמידו תלמידים הרבה — "Teach a vast amount of Torah": My *Rebbi* [Reb Simcha], who was perhaps a founding pioneer of the *Teshuvah* Movement, used to say that Torah is comparable to power-steering in a car. The mechanism does the job, not the person turning the wheel. So too did he bring people to keep Shabbos by learning "*HaMafkid*"[5] with them, for Torah does the job by itself.[6] In short, as we devote energy to teaching much Torah, the Torah itself will do the "driving."

Thirdly, עשו סיג לתורה — "Make a fence around the Torah." If you are going to be involved in a society that could adversely affect you, you must set up "fences" for yourself, extra safeguards to ensure that you retain your Torah perspective and outlook, safeguards that may not have been necessary in a different time and place.

Again, the same principle. We must reach out to others, but only when we ourselves are secure and connected to the ideals that we espouse.

In the beginning of *Avos*, Shimon *HaTzaddik* (who was the last of the *Anshei Knesses Hagedolah*) says that the world stands on three pillars: Torah, *avodah*, and *gemilus chasadim*.

There is significance in the order in which Shimon HaTzaddik *presents* his list: First, people's inner world and

---

4. See *Avos* I:1.

5. The third chapter of *Bava Metzia*, where no mention is made of Shabbos.

6. This is providing that it is authentic Torah, Torah meant to be lived. A person could assimilate such Torah into his/her life. He therefore opposes teaching the laws of Shabbos to someone who was not going to keep Shabbos, since such Torah was not to be likened to power-steering, since it was not תורת חיים, Torah of life, Torah learned with intent to be followed.

their relationship with *Hashem* must be secure.[7] Only then can they embark on a career of true kindliness, both in the material and the spiritual sense.

Where does this sense of self begin, this sense of self-worth and security in what we stand for? I would suggest that it is rooted in the family, in domestic tranquility, in the ability of parents to provide a secure basis for the values that they stand for. In the decades that I have worked with youth, I have rarely encountered someone born in a *frum* family who had trouble with G–d who did not have trouble with parents. Schools can often compound the problems of such children, but schools do not generally create them. The scope of this article does not allow for elaboration, but I believe that anyone working with alienated *frum* youth will support this. Domestic tranquility, both among the parents and between parents and children, is therefore vital if we wish to retain a core of Torah-loyal people who can then be inspired to share what they have with others.

⇒ The Family — The Chariot of the Divine Presence

Rabbi Shlomo Wolbe quotes a passage in the *Gemara* (*Kiddushin* 70b) to support his statement that the family is the bearer of the Divine Presence in the Jewish people.[8]

Rabbi Yitzchok Hutner, 20 years ago this past Chanukah, quoted the *Ramban* (*Bamidbar* 5:20) that whereas we are normally enjoined not to rely on a miracle, there is an exception when it comes to the purity of family descent, which relates to the resting of the Divine Presence; in this regard we do enlist supernatural forces (the *sotah* drinks the bitter waters to test her fidelity). This is because the family is the bearer of the *Shechinah*, which is eternal, hence transcending what we call "nature."[9]

---

7. Both the *Maharal*, in his introduction to *Avos* (and on the above *Mishnah*), and the *Gra*, in *Aderes Eliyahu* (*Devarim* 32:5), refer to Torah as בין אדם לעצמו, *between man and himself*, the perfection of his inner world, This is why, I think, good character must precede success in Torah.

8. מכאן, כי המשפחה היא היא הנושא שכניה בישראל. *Alei Shur*, vol. 1, page 255.

⤖ Our First — and Most Important — Line of Defense

I would therefore humbly propose that we exert great effort to help identify and relieve those "allergens" that have penetrated our camp, which are wreaking havoc in our families. This effort could be expressed in several ways. To offer a few suggestions:

- Elementary schools should see themselves more as an extension of the home, and not primarily interested in teaching information, as vital as that is.[10] The first function of a school whose students are living in an environment that is hostile to the credo of the school is to give the students a sense of closeness to the school, which children can carry with them when they are in the dominant society. Teacher training needs to focus more on how a teacher can build such a relationship.
- Young parents, as a matter of course, need guidance in understanding the problems they face when bringing up children, especially when the family grows, and they must decide how much to protect their children from the dominant culture and how much to expose them. Many couples are fortunate to have parents whom they can turn to, but this cannot be a matter of assumption. Schools should implement parenting workshops, especially for those parents who are enrolling their first child in school.
- The syllabi of yeshivos, high schools and seminaries should include courses on learning to get along with others, with Hashem, and with themselves. The class-

---

9. He tied this to the fact that the Western Candle of the *Menorah*, which was a sign that the Divine Presence rested in *Klal Yisrael* (*Shabbos* 22b), burned the longest, without need for extra oil. Since the *Menorah* is the sign of Divine Presence, we do honor this even in exile, for the Divine Presence is just as real (to use his words, בצאתי מירושלים as it was בצאתי ממצרים) in exile as it was in the *Mikdash*. Lighting the *Menorah* is therefore the only part of the service in the *Mikdash* that we emulate, every Chanukah, even in exile.

10. Rabbi Hutner זצ״ל said that a teacher is a במקום טאטע, a substitute father.

es must be carefully designed and should be given by teachers who teach as much by example as through Torah sources.

- Our yeshivos suffer from a lack of true *rebbi-talmid* relationships. In part, this is symptomatic of a system where, in high school, a student has a different teacher every year, and then, one or two years after high school, goes to *Eretz Yisroel* for two years, to return to America and begin the *shidduch* process. Those that remain in America and prepare to pursue a profession also often fail to develop a *rebbi-talmid* relationship that will see them through the difficult environment of the academic world. An ongoing *rebbi-talmid* relationship must be consciously fostered. A home where the husband has had the opportunity to form a true *rebbi-talmid* relationship, and where that source of guidance is applied to the new family, has a far greater likelihood of developing as a healthy, thriving home.

- We must also strive to establish *shalom bayis* on a national scale, so that we come to accept, and work with, those of the Torah community who do not see things exactly as we do. As Rabbi Shlomo Brevda once commented, "We live in a generation where if you are 1 percent against me, I am 100 percent against you." Although it is true that if you even deduct the smallest part of truth — the א of אמת — you have מת, *death*, this does not imply that any deviation from my particular approach to truth is sacrilege.

I believe that Agudath Israel of America, which during the past seventy-five years has earned the admiration and, above all, the trust of Torah-true Jewry, has a most significant role to play. The direction and unity of our *gedolim* was never more needed to spearhead what could truly be a historic return to Torah values. No communal force in modern Jewish history has been equal to that of Agudath Israel, where *gedolei Yisrael* have been able to, and continue to, give *Klal Yisrael* direction.

A Historic Time, a Historic Challenge

Mori VeRabbi, Rabbi Simcha Wasserman, said that our generation is different from all others in that we see a return to Torah even when there is no blatant anti-Semitic persecution. He would often cite the following incident, to illustrate his belief that our times are truly the era immediately preceding the coming of *Mashiach*:

> *A man had promised his mother, shortly before her death in Rochester, New York, that he would say Kaddish for her according to the Reform "minhag" — for one month. Upon his return to his home in Los Angeles, he went directly to the Reform Temple on Wilshire Boulevard, only to find the doors locked, since it was the middle of the week. From there he proceeded to the Orthodox Beth Jacob, on Olympic Boulevard. He had missed Minchah, but arrived during the break before Maariv. There he heard someone learning Torah with a sweet, haunting melody. At that moment, the man decided that here was something that he had to took into, resulting in the eventual reshaping of his life.*

Rachel *Imeinu* (the Matriarch Rachel) was told (*Yirmiyahu* 31) that not only would *Klal Yisrael* return to *Eretz Yisrael* "from the land of the enemy" (because of anti-Semitic persecution), but *ligvulam,* as children returning to their natural borders. There would come a time when *teshuvah* would not be spurred by terrible persecution, but by a genuine search for Torah,

There is no doubt that we must instill in our people a deep and immediate commitment to reach the masses of Jews who have not been fortunate enough to taste the happiness that Torah living can offer them. We need to take steps now to devote our resources to this cause.

We will see very limited success in our efforts, however, if this work is done only by a cadre of outreach "professionals," as dedicated and gifted as they may be, and as noble as their cause is. Each and every one of us must reflect the happiness that we possess, and then, as *Mori VeRabbi* [Reb Simcha] said, the Torah will provide the power-steering to bring back *Klal Yisrael*, that we may all joyously greet *Mashiach Tzidkeinu*.

The Structure for Family Harmony

The objective voice of halachah has created the contractual obligations of marriage, and within this frame, the feelings of trust love, generosity and appreciation can find full expression.

Rabbi Reuven Feinstein

I: The Invasion of Contemporary Values

⇒ The Internal Assault

MARRIAGE IS UNDER CONSTANT THREAT FROM THE PREVAILING mores of contemporary society, and the assault is not always a frontal one. The invasion sometimes happens because non-Torah values permeate the air, and enter our thought-processes by osmosis. We read about them, hear about them, we talk to our friends about the problems that they have — and the attitudes that spawn these problems enter our minds. I would like to mention several such attitudes, and how they affect our lives.

Society has canonized the concept of unisex. Even the Bible has been retranslated by the Protestants into a form with all references to G-d written as neither male nor female. This approach has trickled down to the point where in many cases, the law ceases to recognize the differences between male and female. By contrast, the Torah states clearly that "male and female, He created them." Each gender has a distinct approach in how to react to things in general, a specific assignment in raising children, and an individual role in setting up a family, as *Chazal* (the sages of the

Talmud) tell us: The father's role is *lelamdo Torah*, to teach Torah to his children. The mother is *mishtadlatu bidevarim,* comforting and encouraging them. The father is expected to be a bit on the stern side, while the mother makes the discipline of Torah study more palatable to the children — encouraging each to reach his ultimate potential, while maintaining emotional stability. This delicate balance in the home has been violated by the unisex concept, which — when carried to its furthest implications — has led to what is commonly called "single-parent families." Indeed, there is a growing willingness among people to raise children as a single parent, with the attitude that parents are like kidneys: Having two of them is great, but with only one, you can do just as well, thank you. And now the courts have given the concept the imprimatur of the law by granting adoption rights to a single girl to raise her child, without the father having either visitation rights or responsibilities.

It does not take much thought to realize that this is an unhealthy trend. A single-parent family will usually limit the optimum development of a child, best realized in the context of the two-parent family; but this does not seem to matter to those in the *avant garde* of social change. As a corollary of this situation, where people accept a limited degree of development, a child that reaches his ultimate potential is labeled an "overachiever." Instead of being grateful for the average child's unusual performance, people wag their heads and bemoan that it's not normal for a child to work so hard and to push himself to do his best. The poor child is "overachieving"!

⇒ Rx for Conflict: "What's in It for Me?"

As the parent generation grows in self-centeredness and assertiveness, men and women lose their interdependence. A "What's-in-it-for-me?" attitude breeds conflict, because each partner in a marriage feels that the other one is taking advantage of him or her. In this age of unlimited horizons and the absence of sex-stereotyping in many fields of endeavor, it is possible for any man or woman to believe himself self-sufficient. After all, any bright person can earn a living. And between restaurants and take-out food emporiums, convenience appliances and maid services on call, each one thinks that he can get along without the other. Marriage is just not that important anymore, and people are not as afraid of facing the world alone as they once were. Add to this how commonplace divorce has become, and even the deterrent of shame of being divorced has disappeared. Such is the climate of our times.

Against this background of social change, the main cause of divorce in the normal household is — as in the past — the absence of *shalom bayis*, but changing attitudes have made it more common. Lack of domestic harmony is usually caused by the perception of being shortchanged. The partner feels, "If I were really loved, he/she would be more considerate. He/she is taking advantage of me, and I'm the loser in this relationship." This unfortunately leads to an adversarial atmosphere of arguments and fights, with each one trying to hurt the other, until the only thing that could work — it seems — is a divorce.

The result is two wounded adults, with children worse off than orphans. An orphan at least has one parent doing his or her best, nurturing favorable memories of the other parent; while in the case of a divorce, each parent competes to get on the child's better side, while trying to negate the influence and values of the other parent. In the end, the child has no real parents, only two slaves spoiling him completely.

II: The Halachic Marriage: A Framework for Harmony

WHEN ONE APPROACHES MARRIAGE FROM THE GUIDELINES of *halachah*, marital obligations will not always flow from constant feelings of affection, or even shared goals. Indeed, just as there are halachic responsibilities in every aspect of life, responsibilities which supersede our desires and emotions, so too does marriage entail halachic responsibilities toward one another that do not necessarily wait for the person's emotions to conform with his or her actions.

This does not at all mean to say that a marriage that honors *halachah* is a marriage free of emotional involvement. That is neither possible nor desirable. Rather, *halachah* creates a structure for the performance of all obligations, from the most perfunctory to the most intimate. Within this framework, there is an opportunity for the full range of human emotions to flourish.

Maintaining a Balance

To gain a better perspective of the halachic framework of the mutual obligations that prevail in a Jewish marriage, it would be advisable to review briefly the history of the emergence of the institution of marriage as we know it today. One could well begin from some abstract point, based on numerous passages in Talmud and Midrash that describe the lack of equilibrium of both man and woman in the single state, and how marriage serves as a means for fulfillment. For our purposes, however, we will start from the factual account of Creation, when Adam and Chavah brought the first child into the world on the very first day of their existence.

After their *aveirah* (sin) of eating from the *Eitz Hadaas* (the Tree of Knowledge), and the subsequent curse that befell mankind, childbearing, childbirth, and childrearing now involve much suffering and pain for the woman. *P'ru u'revu* — fathering children — is man's first *mitzvah*, and since his wife's involvement in bringing children into the world and caring for them incapacitates her to such a great extent, it should be expected that the man will provide for her needs, as the mother of their children. After all, she willingly enters into a condition of high risk, pain, long-term convalescence, and emotional and physical involvement — and, in terms of *mitzvah* fulfillment, he is the prime beneficiary.

Obviously, no one would ever enter such a mutually taxing

arrangement if it did not also entail fulfillment of some strong basic emotional and biological needs, and if both the man and the woman did not achieve a sense of *shleimus* — emotional and spiritual completeness — through marriage and raising a family. And yet, if a man were to provide material sustenance for his wife, and not receive any similar material compensation in return, he would grow resentful. To maintain a balance between the flow of mutual obligations, the wife is required to maintain the house, prepare meals, in addition to caring for the children.

Any number of variables can be introduced into this equation, especially in the context of today's rapidly changing world. A woman may be working, contributing financially to the basic needs of the household budget, which would entail relieving her of some household obligations. Or she may be using her talents and energies to pursue a career, for her personal gratification, which according to *halachah* would not free her from housekeeping responsibilities, yet would provide her with some funds for discretionary spending. ... The specifics are immaterial. What does matter, in this discussion, is the existence of a halachic framework, which tells us that there is an entire body of Torah law that addresses each situation. An objective voice has created the contractual obligations, and within this frame, the feelings of trust, love, generosity and appreciation can find full expression. Changing circumstances need not threaten *shalom bayis*, as long as *halachah* is consulted and honored.

III. In Need of Comment and Clarification

THIS DISCUSSION IS NOT MEANT TO BE A SOURCE BOOK FOR halachic decisions, but rather an attempt to show how *halachah* structures marriage and thus helps preserve *shalom bayis*. There are, however, several areas that are often misinterpreted, and call for comment and clarification.

- If the wife has undertaken the full support of the family for as long as, for instance, her husband is studying in a *kollel* or is continuing his professional training toward a degree, then obviously the husband would be expected to contribute time and effort to domestic chores — as long as (especially in the case of *kollel*) such activities do not interfere with his pursuit of *shleimus*. After all, the woman's reason for sacrificing so much is that it provides her with a share in the *shleimus* he is striving for. She surely would not want him to compromise his potential for growth.

- *Nedunya* is a term that has a negative, old-world connotation, yet in truth, it can be a means of ensuring the happiness of a very contemporary couple when the woman comes from a more favorable economic background than the man. For instance, she may not be accustomed to shopping for bargains, or to postponing purchases to a time when prices are lower, while his limited income may require careful budgeting. If a father wants his daughter to maintain the same standard of living that she was accustomed to without putting an undue strain on the marriage, he obviously has to help the couple by giving them the requisite *nedunya* (financial support) to enable them to do so. This has nothing to with supporting a *talmid chacham* (positive value), nor with "selling your daughter" or "buying her a husband" (negative connotation). It's simply that a young lady not find the adjustment to married life unduly complicated by the introduction of financial tensions.

When a young man is devoting himself to full-time Torah study, it is a rare privilege — indeed an obligation of the highest order — to provide financial support for him as a *talmid chacham*. Even those people who are not in a position to give *nedunya* in its broader sense can help a young *kollel* couple by at least providing them with whatever expenses the parents had when their child was still living in their house before he got married. Even the poorest person in *Klal Yisrael* can participate in this type of Torah support.

- The *kesubah* was designed to be a deterrent to divorce because of the large sums of money to be paid should the marriage terminate. Yet, in America one never hears of a woman collecting her *kesubah*. This is primarily because until recently, divorce settlements were usually determined by the courts. The wife was awarded alimony (in addition to child support, which the father is obligated to pay by *halachah*, whether the court ordered it or not). Over the years, alimony judgments amortized the *kesubah* to the point where no decision could be made to collect the *kesubah* until an evaluation was made of how much money was collected and how much would still be due. Nowadays, new laws have evolved, assigning alimony payments from whoever was earning more, opening up the possibility that, at times, the woman should pay alimony to the man. In such cases, the *kesubah* plays a role, reaching upwards of $50,000. ... Awareness of this would indeed give a discontent husband some pause.

⌛ Halacha, Common Sense, and Restraint

Differences and disputes in one form or another may be inevitable in any long-term relationship, but can be dangerous inasmuch as they might breed anger. For when a person becomes angry, his impulse is to hurt the second party. There are generally three ways to hurt somebody in a marriage. One way is simply by physically striking the other person. Whether the man or the woman is the aggressor is immaterial; whoever raises a hand to strike somebody else is considered a *rasha* — wicked. And the financial liability one carries for hitting a stranger applies obtains for the husband and wife, as well. Yet, since it is done in the heat of emotion, it is the expression of anger easiest to forgive.

On the other hand, if a person insults his or her spouse, the injured party may be willing to forgive the offender, but he will always feel that the other party "really thinks little of me," and the mutual trust that keeps a marriage together inevitably suffers. This, especially, must be avoided.

Worst of the three is rejecting the other person, as a form of punishment. Aside from denying the other person's needs, the sense of rejection lingers on even after the rejecter would be willing to accept a reconciliation, for the person hurt will still be haunted by fears of further rejection.

Anger can also trigger foolish behavior, which sets into motion a chain reaction that cannot easily be stopped. In my *Chumash shiur* in the yeshiva, I once commented that when a person is ill tempered, he can pick a fight with his wife on the most trivial point — for instance, because she squeezed toothpaste from the middle of the tube instead of from the end. The boys laughed at my ridiculous example, so I made a mental note never to use that example again ... until a phone call I received several years later.

A *talmid*, married for several months, called me to report on how he had had an argument with his wife on what he thought was a serious matter. When he went into the bathroom to brush his teeth before retiring, he picked up the toothpaste and found the cap missing — worse yet! — the tube was squeezed in the middle. He was about to shout some verbal abuse at his errant wife in the next room when he remembered how he had once laughed at the possibility of a marriage slipping on a toothpaste tube. He began to laugh out loud at his own folly, and then, in response to his wife's curiosity, shared the humor of the situation with her.

Anger is dangerous, and can make fools out of the best of us, if we do not exercise caution and restraint. *Chazal* took all the weaknesses of the human condition into account, and even anticipated the various scenarios that are confronting us today, and created the halachic structure for a successful marriage. This framework guides a person to override sentiments of anger and fear of rejection, and to give healthy emotions of gratitude, acceptance and love an opportunity for full expression, making *shalom bayis* a reality for those who live by the Torah laws

Harmony in the Home — Keeping It Together

There once existed the premise that a marriage must last, and that would help temper the attitudes of husbands and wives towards divorce. But today there is no assumption of permanence

Rabbi Yissocher Frand

⟶ A Good Topic for Discussion

THE READER'S INTEREST IN A DISCUSSION ON "*SHALOM bayis*" does not necessarily indicate that he's having problems at home. Quite the contrary! It says that he is no better than Rabbi Isser Zalman Meltzer.

Rabbi Isser Zalman Meltzer was the father-in-law of Rabbi Aharon Kotler and the author of the classic work on the *Rambam, Even Haozel,* which is recognized as a key text in understanding the *Rambam*. Rabbi Isser Zalman Meltzer was a gaon and a *tzaddik*, and by any account, an exceptional person. He certainly did not have *shalom bayis* problems.

And yet ... one time Reb Isser Zalman happened to enter a *shul* where the famed *tzaddik* of Jerusalem, Rabbi Aryeh Levin, was delivering a *shmuess* (lecture) on the subject of *shalom bayis*. Afterwards, Reb Isser Zalman thanked Reb Aryeh, "You truly helped me in my attitude on *shalom bayis*."

Rabbi Aryeh Levin responded in astonishment, "You, Reb Isser Zalman, need a *shmuess* on *shalom bayis*? You could give the *shmuess* on *shalom bayis!*"

Reb Isser Zalman explained, "When I was writing the *Even Haozel,* the printer couldn't read my poor handwriting. I asked my wife, Baila Hinda, to copy the *sefer* from my manuscripts so the printer could decipher it. But when I would read the proofs and find that occasionally my Baila Hinda failed to copy exactly what I wrote, I would lose my patience with her. Now, Reb Aryeh, I see my fault. *Yeyasher koach* for strengthening me in my awareness of *shalom bayis*."

No less than Reb Isser Zalman, we can all benefit from giving thought to improving our marriage.

There is, however, a second point: We dare not bury our heads in the sand. We must face the tough issues that plague us, and tackle them. And lack of *shalom bayis* is one of the severest issues facing *Klal Yisroel* today. We live today in what can be called an age of divorce. Statistics indicate that the divorce rate in this country is approaching 50 percent. It wasn't always that way. And the Jewish community has always been even stronger in this area. I recall an incident when I was a 9-year-old boy. My mother and my father had a wonderful marriage, but they must have raised their voices at each other, and I asked my mother, "Are you going to get a divorce?"

My mother told me a "fact" that I carried with me for many years: "Jewish people don't get divorced." And that was true for many years. But as I grew older, and times changed, I had to modify my mother's sociological principle. Jewish people may get divorced, but "*frum*" people don't. After a time, *frum* people have joined the trend; they, too, are getting divorced. This tragedy occurs among *yungeleit* and middle-aged couples, *chassidim* and *misnagdim*, in yeshiva communities and in every sector of the "*frum*" world — it's universal.

⛝ Behind the Splitting Tendency

There may be any number of reasons for this tendency. Firstly, there existed the premise that a marriage must last, and that would help temper the attitudes of husbands and wives towards divorce. But today there is no assumption of permanence.

This may be part of our contemporary "throw-away society."

People use paper dishes and then throw them away. And it goes beyond paper goods. Have you tried to have an appliance fixed recently? You go into the repair shop and say, "Here, I just bought this phone a couple of months ago. Could you please fix it?"

"Fix it?" comes the incredulous reply. "It doesn't pay to fix."

This attitude permeates our society. It does not "pay" to fix things anymore: not telephones, not toasters, nor marriages.

Furthermore, the ease with which people resort to divorce is a social disease that feeds on itself: The stigma that was once associated with being divorced no longer exists. Twenty-five years before Ronald Reagan was elected president, we could not have had a president sitting in the White House who was a divorcé. Today we can.

The most significant cause of divorce and the lack of *shalom bayis* in our community today, however, may well be a pervasive lack of love, for love is one of the two pillars of the *bayis ne'eman* — the home built on Torah principles. The *Rambam*, based on a *Gemara* in *Yevamos*, writes, "*Ohavah k'gufo* — one is to love his wife like himself; *umechabda yoser migufo* — and to honor her more than himself" (*Hilchos Ishus* 15:19). "Love" is widely discussed today, but much of what we hear and read about love reflects a warped understanding of the concept. Rabbi Eliyahu Eliezer Dessler explains that the only way to create love is by giving. The more one gives, the more he (or she) will love the recipient: "The strongest bond between man and wife results from a giving relationship. Then their love will not end, and their lives will be filled with everlasting happiness" (*Michtav Me'Eliyahu* I).

In fact, parents love their children so much because they are constantly giving to them. They get up for them in the morning, they get up for them at night, and they are constantly giving to them — which generates their vast love for their children. If you want to love someone, be giving toward him.

Love in a Jewish Marriage

To be a giving person, one must be selfless, but we live in a selfish society, where "me" is number one. "My" needs are paramount. A society that is selfish allows no room for true love. Indeed, Rabbi Dessler wrote thirty years ago that an acquisitive society will ultimately promote small families — our present statistical families of 2.2 children. Rabbi Dessler, unfortunately (or fortunately), did not live to see what has been dubbed (appropriately) "OINK," which stands for "one income no kids." Or "DINK" — "double income no kids." This lifestyle is endemic to a society that structures its life around ideals promoted in beer commercials, not by *maamarei Chazal*. We live in a society where "you can have it all," ... but in truth you can't. A society that is selfish and ungiving is a society where there is no true love, a society that will be plagued with *shalom bayis* problems. ... And, then, what does one really have?

Thank G-d, the Torah community is not overcome by the malaise of small families, and once again the blessing of large families has become the rule rather than the exception. But that does not mean that we are impervious to other selfishness-related sicknesses. We are as addicted to conspicuous consumption as everyone else. And like others, we too are affected by the illusion that happiness comes with a designer label. ... When "me" is the most important personal pronoun, there must inevitably be a lack of love between people, and then marriages come apart.

In introducing the *parsha* of *get* — divorce — the Torah uses an expression that is most unique: "*Ki yikach ish ishah u'v'alah* — when a man will take a woman and he will live with her" (*Devarim* 24:1). Marriage is discussed in various places in the Torah, but no other *parshah* speaks so starkly. Not surprisingly, the passage ends with: "*V'hayah im lo simtza chein b'einav* — and it will come to pass if she will not find favor in his eyes." The Torah tells us that if one enters a marriage in a spirit of self-gratification, that marriage will culminate with a *get*.

One cause of *shalom bayis* problems today, then, is a warped concept of love. A person may sigh with ecstasy, "I love steak!" But that does not mean that he truly loves steak. It means "I love me." The steak is merely an object. In such a society people also become objects to one another, with "love" a self-centered emotion, leading inevitably to divorce.

⇝ A Society Without Respect

The second pillar of successful marriage — that of *kavod* (respect) — has been dislodged by yet another flaw that we have absorbed from our contemporary society. *Kavod* is foreign to all that surrounds us, in our casual, egalitarian society. We lack a frame of reference for approaching *kavod* — we do not even know how to honor our parents properly. And certainly we do not honor our spouses adequately.

Rabbi Avraham Pam commented, "If only people would speak to their spouses with the care that young men exercise when speaking to their prospective *kallahs*!"... I have boys of marriageable age in my *shiur* in Yeshiva Ner Yisroel in Baltimore. If a fellow is absent on Sunday, likely as not, he'll be in to see me on Monday, to tell me about his meeting with a young lady. And he will want to discuss: *How should I ask her to take the next step? Should I call? When should I call?* We sit and plot just exactly how the *bachur* should phrase something to his *kallah*, or to his prospective *kallah*. ... "Things would be vastly improved, if even one tenth of that care would be invested in the way one speaks to his wife!" said Rabbi Pam.

Of course, we are familiar with our wives, we are intimate with our spouses, and the formality that exists between *chassan* and *kallah* would be out of place. Nonetheless, there surely is a place for respect when talking to one's spouse.

Wives usually do the cleaning and cooking for the household, the type of duties that maids perform. How is one to determine whether a wife is indeed a maid, or a queen, as she should be? This is determined by the husband, when he acknowledges those very actions, appreciates them, and expresses gratitude for them, elevating her actions into the realm of majesty, out of the realm of servitude.

This is not a one-way street. "Similarly," says the *Rambam*, "the Sages made it incumbent upon a wife to honor her husband excessively, and that she view him like an officer or a king" (*Hilchos Ishus* 15:20). The husband is not just a money-making machine. In a Jewish household, respect between husband and wife must prevail.

⇢ Homes Without a Tradition

In addition to the invasion of foreign values into our communities, the Jewish home is faced with yet another problem — resulting from the Jew's status as a creature of *golus*. In our wanderings, we have forgotten much of our *mesora* — our chain of Tradition. In the process, our homes have become spiritual vacuums. There was a time when we had *rabbeim, rabbanim,* and *admorim* to instruct us and to serve as role models for us. We knew which *sefarim* to consult for every occasion and every situation, and we knew what they said. But this long and bitter *galus* — especially its most recent, devastating *churban* in Europe — has robbed us of so much of that precious *mesorah*.

I recently heard a story of a *Yid* in Russia who makes *Kiddush*, but does not know what to do with the *kos* (wine cup) while he says the words. *Do you hold the cup, or do you leave it on the table?* The *Shulchan Aruch* does not specify, yet we all seem to know what to do, for everyone of us saw his father pick up the *kos* when he made *Kiddush*.

We here in America have the *Shulchan Aruch*, and we have experts and knowledgeable people to tell us how to perform *mitzvos*. But we are impoverished in our own way: We do not know how to conduct ourselves in a Jewish home. We do not know what actions reflect Torah values and which violate Torah values. People who are well intentioned think that their actions represent *daas Torah*, but their conduct may be contrary to Torah.

For instance, the Torah recognizes that monotony can invade and destroy a marriage. If husband and wife are always available to each other, their relationship might suffer, for familiarity breeds contempt. In other words, the Torah is concerned that there be freshness and regeneration in the sacred marital relationship. Rabbi Shlomo Wolbe writes that today husbands and wives should go beyond the directives of *halachah* in seeking to insure that their marriages do not become stale and they do not become contemptuous of each other. How? There is no universal prescription. I know of a couple that studies *Midrash Tanchuma* on Friday nights; that is how they spend their special time together. ... It is not against *daas Torah* for a husband and wife to step out occasionally to get away from the pressures of the children and the workplace. To the contrary, that is consistent with *daas Torah*.

The *Gemara* says (*Bava Metzia*) that when the *malachim* visited Avraham *Avinu*, they asked, "Where is Sarah your wife?" Even though they knew that she was in the tent, they asked the question to make Sarah more dear and more precious in the eyes of Avraham *Avinu*, highlighting the fact that she was a *tzenuah*, always in the tent. Did an Avraham *Avinu* really require their "*l'chavevah al baalah*" — an extra word to endear his wife to him? Apparently Avraham *Avinu* did benefit from it, and so would we. Is the prescription for endearment the same for everyone? No. But the need is universal.

⤖ United in Marriage

Furthermore, there must be *achdus* — a sense of unity — in a marriage. The *tenaim* (contractual agreement to marry) includes the phrase: "And both will control their possessions equally and neither will keep secrets from the other." This does not refer only to monetary affairs; *achdus* must embrace all aspects of their lives. As Rabbi Wolbe writes, "You have to work on being 'one'." Communication between husband and wife should not merely deal with who is going to take car pool and who is going to pick up the dry cleaning. If a spouse's day consists of diapers and dishes, then that too should be shared. If the boss "did it again," then the partner should listen and share the agony. If busy schedules do not leave enough time, then time must be made to talk about meaningful things. A couple that shares their days will share their lives. The Chazon Ish writes in a letter to *chasanim*, "When you leave your house in the morning tell your wife, 'I'm going to do this, I'm going here or there.'" Apparently, the Chazon Ish made a practice of telling Rebbetzin Karelitz, "I'm going here; then I'm going there." His Rebbetzin needed the verbal involvement in his life. We certainly need it.

⌛ Learning From the Previous Generation

The first time I delivered the contents of this article as a lecture, I asked my *Rosh Yeshiva*, Rabbi Yaakov Yitzchok Ruderman for guidance.

The *Rosh Yeshiva* replied, "Tell them the story about the Chofetz Chaim and Rabbi Nochum Horodno." Of all the stories the *Rosh Yeshiva* knew, and as vast as his knowledge of *Shas*, *poskim* and *teshuvos* was, he chose this particular story.[1]

> Reb Nochum was an *ish tzaddik* whom the Chofetz Chaim visited from time to time to learn from his personal conduct. One Chanuka, Reb Nochum did not light the *menorah* in the *l'chatchilah* (preferred) time, waiting until his wife's arrival instead.
>
> Afterwards, he explained to the Chofetz Chaim simply: "My wife derives pleasure from watching when I light *neiros* Chanuka. It's worthwhile to give up on the *l'chatchilah* of lighting the *neiros* early for the sake of *shalom bayis*." Reb Nochum then brought proof from the *Gemara* in *Shabbos* (24b) that states: "*Shalom bayis* supersedes *neiros* Chanukah."

Those who knew Rabbi Ruderman would not wonder why he chose this story over all others, for this was typical of our

---

1. This story appeared in a fuller treatment in the biographical appreciation of Rabbi Ruderman in *The Jewish Observer* of November '87.

Rosh Yeshiva's concern for educating us properly. He personified a constant evaluation of the various options that a situation presented, and then determined what is of greater importance and what is of lesser importance. To the *Rosh Yeshiva*, *shalom bayis* was of the greatest value, and he made certain that we knew it.

⇒ A Matter of Top Priority

Indeed, the more one observed the *Rosh Yeshiva*, the more one learned of his concern for *shalom bayis*, and it is worthwhile dwelling on this for the sake of the lessons to be learned:

His Rebbetzin regularly prepared chicken fricassee for his Friday night *seudah*. On one occasion, she apologized to the *Rosh Yeshiva*, "I'm sorry, I forgot to make the fricassee."

The *Rosh Yeshiva* told her, "I'll tell you the truth, it's not my favorite dish."

Astounded, she asked, "Rabbi Ruderman" — I never heard her call him by his name; in the presence of visitors, she always addressed him as "Rabbi Ruderman" — "I've been making this same fricassee for twenty years. Why didn't you ever tell me that you don't care for it?"

"I was aware of the trouble you took to prepare it and I always ate it with relish to show my appreciation," he replied.

I will never ever forget how the *Rosh Yeshiva* always approached *Mussaf* on *Rosh Hashanah*. The awe and fear of what *Mussaf* on *Rosh Hashanah* represents was apparent on the *Rosh Yeshiva's* face. Anyone who had the privilege of being in his presence cannot easily remove the imprint of how his face reflected total *eimas hadin* and *pachad* — awe, fear, and reverence for the approaching judgment. This same *Rosh Yeshiva*, who used to tell us that the whole year rides on this *Mussaf*, once forgot to leave a *Machzor* at home for his Rebbetzin, who was not feeling well that *Rosh Hashanah*. And this same *Rosh Yeshiva* who had that awesome *eimas hadin* over what *Mussaf* on *Rosh Hashanah* entailed, missed *tefilla b'tzibbur* (praying with a *minyan*) on that *Rosh*

Hashanah to bring the *Machzor* home for Rebbetzin Ruderman.

That is the compelling nature of *shalom bayis*. It is thinking about your spouse, and putting daily life in perspective, and realizing that there are not many things in this world that are more important than *shalom bayis*.

Life is very short, life is tough, and it is filled with many *tzaros* (problems) — some that we cannot control. There is one "problem area" that we can control, and that is *shalom bayis*. It is essential to happiness and to a fruitful, successful existence.

Mrs. Rosenberg's Yeshiva
Where little scholars grow in a carefully controlled atmosphere combining the best elements of Kelm, Slabodka, and Novardok

Rabbi Yisroel Miller

IN THESE DAYS OF WOMEN'S LIBERATION, I KNOW THAT A woman isn't considered "fulfilled" unless she's a bank president, astronaut or congressman (congressperson?). Still, I'm sure you'll understand my cousin Miriam's not opting for any of these. When still an idealistic teenager she read a short biography of Rav Aaron Kotler, and the story of his fight to build Torah and yeshivos in America. She became inspired by the idea of training young people in Torah, *yiras Shamayim* (fear of G-d) and good character, and by the thought of actually making a yeshiva a "*mikdash m'at*," a place of holiness for the Divine Presence ... the *Shechinah*.

Today, still idealistic (though no longer a teenager), Miriam — now Mrs. Rosenberg — has made her yeshiva. The work is hard, like that of every *Rosh Yeshiva*, but she has the rewards that come from true accomplishment, and from seeing one's dreams come true.

The yeshiva is small — only four students — but she's more concerned about quality than quantity, and is kept pretty busy as it is. There's Dovid, 5 years old; Esther, 2; Shaindy,

6 months; and of course the oldest, who also helps in running the place, Shlomo, who's 31.

Mrs. Rosenberg is also *Mashgiach* (spiritual supervisor and counselor) in her yeshiva, and the day begins early. Like Rav Elya Lopian, she personally awakens her *talmidim* (except for Shaindy, who usually gets up even earlier), encouraging them to look forward to a wonderful Torah day. An enthusiastically sung "*Modeh ani,*" a *shiur* (class) in correct *netilas yodayim* — washing (2-year-old level), and a brief talk on the joy of *tzitzis*-wearing — all punctuated with a general air of optimism and *joie de vivre*.

Breakfast Session

The *shiurim* continue through breakfast, though more by example than by precept: A child who hears an audible *brocha* tends to make one as well, and no better way exists to teach "saying thank-you to Hashem" than to do so wholeheartedly oneself.

Like every good *rebbi*, Mrs. Rosenberg is equally concerned with her *talmidim's* physical well-being. She chooses food for her dining room and mattresses for her dormitory with careful deliberation, knowing that these are *mitzvos* to compare with presentation of any *shiur*.

Lessons in *mitzvos* "between man and man" are an integral part of the curriculum. Kindness, courtesy, taking turns and sharing are taught not as necessary peace-making compromises, but as ethical principles; and, like any good *Mashgiach*, Mrs. Rosenberg teaches without overly moralizing, intimidating or boring her listeners.

Opportunities for teaching basic Jewish *hashkafah* (worldview) are also not missed, again without sermonizing. When a child sees that a broken vase arouses parental disapproval, while slanderous *lashon hara* does not, the lesson is not lost as to the relative importance of the two. The wise teacher makes the proper adjustment in her reactions (not to mention her conversational topics), preferring a smashed vase to a smashed character.

Outdoor Learning

As Mrs. Rosenberg bundles Dovid up for the trip to his "other" yeshiva (she cheerfully admits Rabbi Goldstein's superiority in explaining *Chumash*, and readily sends Dovid to better-equipped *rebbei'im* for a good part of the day), she notices that it's begun to rain. Rather than teach Dovid that life is one vast panorama of human suffering ("Raining again? My new hair-do — my day is ruined!"), she tries a different tack. "Isn't it fun to walk in the rain? And Hashem is giving us water to drink, and making the flowers grow," etc. With a bit of forethought this *shiur* can be said with real sincerity, especially if one practices by learning it for oneself. And even if Dovid does not get a full appreciation of the wonders of Creation, he at least escapes the fate of most people, who feel doomed to misery at the slightest change of climate not to their expectation.

Just Like in Kelm

The next few hours, given over to dishwashing, bed making and meal preparing, are also special training for two-year-old Esther, instructing her in needed skills and a sense of responsibility. As in the great European yeshiva of Kelm, all the *talmidim* do their share of housework, and consider themselves honored to have a share in the yeshiva's upkeep.

Mrs. Rosenberg is also in charge of the purchasing department, and plans her shopping carefully. Although Shlomo is executive director and chief fundraiser (he views his 9-to-5 real-estate job in a light similar to that of *Roshei Yeshivas'* fund-raising trips), she, in charge of the budget, fully feels the importance of not wasting the yeshiva's income on extravagances of little benefit. Of course, the little pleasures needed for happiness and a relaxed atmosphere are also given their due, just like any other *mitzvah*.

Included in today's shopping is the search for a living-room couch. After consideration of the issues ("Do we really need it? Will it make guests feel more at home? How much shall we spend?"), inspection of the potential purchase is made with all the scrutiny of a professional *esrog* dealer ("Is it too ostentatious? Does it add a feeling of warmth?"). Likewise in buying a new record ("Is this *Jewish* music? Will it give over something beneficial to the children?"') or a wall decoration. According to the importance one gives one's sanctuary, so is the importance attached to details.

⇥ Supper, Slabodka-Style

Comes suppertime, and Shlomo returns home. Tired though she is, Mrs. Rosenberg remembers reading how the *Mashgiach* of the Slabodka Yeshiva worked two years on "greeting every man with a smiling countenance" (*Avos*), and she hides her own troubles, to listen instead to the troubles of others.

Listening, sympathizing, comforting and counseling, she helps Shlomo forget the hard day at the office, and gives him the encouragement and incentive to go off to his nightly *Gemara* class. She would like to have his company, of course, but she willingly trades it for something higher, sublimely sweeter.

And retiring at day's end, she emulates Rav Yosef "Yoizel" Horvitz, of Novardok, thinking of each *talmid* before going to sleep, trying to help each one with a plan, a thought, a blessing and a prayer. With a concluding "*Shema*," another link is quietly added to the eternal Jewish chain.

Mrs. Rosenberg's yeshiva isn't famous, and she herself speaks at no conventions, makes no headlines. But glory does not interest her, and she feels too full inside to have need of the applause of others. Praise just embarrasses her, and I had to change her real name in writing this article. But you'll recognize her, I'm sure; if she's not seated at the head table, it's because she'd rather be taking the guests' coats and making them feel comfortable.

Like Rav Nosson Tzvi Finkel, the Alter of Slabodka, she

has no official title, even in her own yeshiva. But she's always there; taking care, keeping things running, bringing the *Shechinah* into the hearts of her *talmidim*, and daily thanking Hashem for her lot, portion and inheritance — that of a Jewish wife, and a Jewish mother.

Making Our Family a Mobile Home
Mrs. Devorah Greenblatt

⚯ When the Shtetl Walls Crumble

THE WORLD IN WHICH WE ARE RAISING OUR CHILDREN IS utterly different from the one that we grew up in. When I close my eyes and try to peek at that world through the eyes of my children, there is not much that I recognize.

One of the most radical differences is in the way in which we define our own homes. There was a time, not so long ago, when each member of the family could clearly recognize what was "home," which dimension was sacrosanct, where the space was private. When one physically crossed the threshold of one's home, it was understood that they were stepping into another domain, a *reshus hayachid*, the domain of the family. What was outside had to remain there, unless invited to cross the threshold with you. And like the age-old concept of *bayis*, a *bayis* contains, encompasses, surrounds, at the same time that it stands as a physical symbol excluding that which must remain outside its walls.

It was not so long ago that many of our grandparents lived in a *shtetl*, protected by a double lock, that of the home and that of the community. Just as when the *shtetl* wall crumbled, and we faced new challenges that required new responses, so too, as the protective wall of *bayis* is penetrated, a new response is required.

Rabbi Hutner once remarked, "Don't think you will protect your children from the *gasse* (street). Your children will be exposed to more *tumah* (defilement) going to the corner to buy a soda than your grandfather did his whole life in the *shtetl.*" There are children from every community, every type of Orthodox upbringing, whose *frum* homes and yeshiva education have not been a sufficient barrier against the ills of society. What is the solution?

> *Recently, several yeshiva students went one night to daven at the kever of a great tzaddik. As the group reached the cemetery, one of the boys held back. Realizing he was a kohein, his friend came up with an ingenious solution. Finding a discarded refrigerator box on the street, he pried open the top, and fashioned a handle on either side. Voila – the bachur was in his portable bayis within the cemetery.*

While I certainly cannot comment on the halachic viability of this scheme, the image is valuable. We are all like that *kohein* whose mission requires him to separate himself from *tumah*, and yet finds himself in the cemetery.

This must be part of a two-pronged response. First, we must fortify the walls of the *bayis* that our children carry with them by strengthening all of the relationships within the home. Second, we have to teach our children how to deal with failure. All the protection in the world cannot prevent a problem, but if children know how to put their own mistakes into perspective, then the problem does not have to evolve into a catastrophe.

⤞ Overcoming the Pull of the Street

In seeking to foster the relationships within one's home, we must realize that today it is not sufficient for things to be just OK. To fight the glamour, glitz and pull of the street, we must have an alternative that is real and more enticing.

That alternative is passion, and our children must see our passion. Take commitment, sprinkle it with devotion, warm it on the flame of emotion, and you have passion. Rabbi Wolbe says in his *sefer, Planting and Building in Education*, that one half of the formula for success with children is *Shalom Bayis*. Though the love between husband and wife is private, it spills over and warms and envelops the other family members. Rabbi Wolbe refers to this feeling as the warmth of the home, a necessary atmosphere in which the children can flourish.

Do our children know we are passionate about them? Not just about what they should not do, but also what they mean to us, how much we enjoy being with them, how much we believe in them. Do our children ever see our passion for *Yiddishkeit*? Do they see us cry? Do we shed tears when we are move by a *shiur* or by a righteous person we have met? Do we ever shed a tear of sadness for the plight of another Jew? Or a tear of joy for a fellow Jew's *simcha*?

⇒ On the Same Team

Parents have a natural influence over their children. During adolescence, that is challenged. One way to maintain that influence, necessary if we are to guide them, is to convince them that we are on the same team as them. As long as the relationship is adversarial – if you win, I lose – there are no winners. Once our children come to believe that their success is our success, and their setbacks are ours as well, having nothing at all to do with what the neighbors will say, we can exercise influence over our children and give guidance to them.

There are other factors that can lessen our ability to influence our teenage children. We live in a world in which the concept of "*kavod*" (honor) has been lost. There is no position or person whose honor is not challenged. *Kavod* is the ability to feel the weightiness of someone because we maintain a vision of the whole person. Our ability to diminish another person sets in when we fragmentize them: the way they look, dress, etc. rather than who they are as a whole person. We learn this from *Chazal* when we are taught "Judge *kal ha'adam* (lit. every man) favorably" – as long as we view him as *kal ha'adam, all* of the person, we can maintain a focus on what is positive. An adolescent (particularly a girl) starts to see herself as fragmented. Her body image, her peer relations, are now seen as who she is rather than as aspects of her self. We need to help our children maintain their own vision of themselves as whole, thereby reducing the influence of any of the singular "parts." This is done through interacting with *kavod* with our children.

When we must criticize, the *Rambam's* laws of *tochachah*[1] must be applied. The three conditions are: (1) We may never criticize in public. (2) The words and the tone must be soft. And (3) we must convey to them that we want what is best for them, not what is best for us – and believe me, they know the difference. A young person, who sees *kavod* modeled in the home in all the relationships there, learns *kavod atzmi* – self-respect – which is a protective shield that a person takes with him/her into all situations.

Since all our best efforts cannot put our children in a protective cocoon, and difficulties will inevitably come their way, it is essential to teach our children how to deal with failure. *David Hamelech* says, "*Vechatasi l'negdi samid* – My sin is always before me." I once heard an insightful explanation in the name of the Satmar *Rebbe*. "*Tamid*" is usually translated as continuously. The Satmar Rebbe, however, said that *tamid* means "always at the appropriate time." We must always remember our wrong actions at the appropriate times, whether it is on *Yom Kippur Kattan*, during the month of *Elul* or *Aseres Yemei Teshuvah*. The rest of the time, we need not remember; we must forget, to allow us to move forward.

---

1. *Hilchos Dei'os* 6:7

⟜ There Is a Road Back

One of the saddest things that I encounter at Project YES are girls whose perception of themselves is that they are not *frum*. One of my first Project YES cases was a 14-year-old Bais Yaakov girl who had been asked to leave her school in the fall of ninth grade. She had a difficult personal situation, and when I spoke to her, she related her story stoically and in a monotone. In over two hours talking, she cried only once, as she told me the following: One Friday night, desperate to get out of her house, where she had been locked in for a week, she climbed out of a ground-floor window, thereby turning on the light on the alarm panel. "Now I am a *mechalleles Shabbos*," she sobbed. She certainly made a serious mistake. The question is, *What is our message to her? Is there no road back?*

How do our children see us deal with our own failures? Do they see us struggle trying to grow in our *Yiddishkeit*, and in that process sometimes having setbacks for which we have remorse? We want our children to "become" committed Torah Jews. Are we also in the process of "becoming," or are we finished products? To be alive is to struggle. It is good to let our children in on that ongoing struggle. They may be motivated to struggle also.

Finally, we must teach our children not only to be *frum*, but to actively cultivate a relationship with הקב״ה. Too many teens say to me, "Why should I be *frum*?" They see only an external set of rules and miss the essence entirely. We must teach our children through our own behavior, not through lecture, that our Creator is *tov u'mativ*, that He loves us no matter what. To teach them that "we cannot get through one day without His direct guidance" is indispensable. Knowledge of *Hashem's* presence and love is life-sustaining nourishment.

> At the recent *levaya* of a *tzaddeikes*, her son-in-law spoke of the impact of entering her kitchen late one night, after the house had long gone to sleep. He saw his mother-in-law at her kitchen table deep in conversation. Not wanting to disturb her, he paused in the doorway. He realized that

there was no one else in the kitchen, and the telephone was resting in its cradle. "Please, Hashem," she was saying, "watch over my children. Please help me to raise them as yirei Shamayim, devoted to Your Torah."

All of this while she was still well, before the two-year illness which claimed her life. If her son-in-law was forever changed by this encounter, need we speak of the effect on a son or daughter?

Report From Ground Zero[1]

Rabbi Yakov Horowitz

Al Regel Achas ... On One Foot

IF WE ARE GOING TO HAVE AN IMPACT ON THE FRIGHTENING trend of young men and women abandoning the teachings of our yeshiva and Bais Yaakov system, we will need to improve the overall quality of our home life. There is a common inclination to lay the blame for these problems on families in crisis. This type of thinking, however, does not do justice to such a difficult and complex issue. We must avoid the tendency to attribute all of the blame on the "broken homes," and work to minimize the tension levels in *all* of our homes.

Several years ago, at an Agudath Israel National Convention, *Mori VeRabbi* Rabbi Avrohom Pam quoted the Steipler as having said, "*Hatzlachah mit kinder* (success with one's children) is 50 percent *shalom bayis*, and 50 percent *tefillah*."

One thing is painfully clear. Our home life is under assault. It is not merely the unraveling of the moral fabric of secular society and its effect on (even) our insular community. *Our homes are under assault.* Longer work hours for both spouses, the exponential increase of our *simchah* schedule and

---

1. Ground Zero refers to the epicenter of an explosion – the exact spot where a bomb explodes.

social obligations, and the increased burden of providing *parnassah* for our growing families are taking their toll on the tranquility and *simchas hachayim* (*joie de vivre*) of our home life. Many of us are able to maintain this juggling act and keep all of these balls in the air at once. Many, however, are finding it very, very difficult.

Those who deal with at-risk teens almost unanimously agree that the greatest factor that puts children at risk is lack of *simchah* and *shalom bayis*[2] at home.

Yes, some children just seem to be born "difficult." Some have an ornery disposition. Others have an innate propensity to challenge authority. Some are extremely restless and simply not cut out for a ten-hour school day. Many have significant learning disabilities.

Experience has shown, however, that children from warm, loving homes have the best chance of overpowering these difficulties and becoming well-adjusted adults despite having risk factors[3].

But children can never get used to bickering, stress, unhappiness, negative comments, emotional abuse. These create unhappy, distracted children who are unable to concentrate in school. They develop an intense distrust of authority figures, and harbor a simmering rage at an adult world that cannot seem to get its act together and provide them with a peaceful environment in which to grow up and thrive. This holds true for all households – including two-parent ones.

So, a short response to the frightened parents who ask – *al regel achas* – what they can do to "protect" their family from the ravages of the counterculture that threatens their boys and girls is the poignant comment of Rabbi Chaim Pinchas Sheinberg, *Rosh Yeshiva* of Torah Ohr,[4] that the

---

2. As the *Gemara (Shabbos 23b)* clearly indicates, the phrase *shalom bayis* is not limited to harmony between husband and wife (or lack thereof). I refer to the overall sense of tranquility and *simchas hachayim*.

3. It is important to note that there are children who have none of these factors, who come from warm, loving homes, and slip through the cracks nonetheless.

4. Rabbi Sheinberg said, "Dovid *Hamelech* says in *Tehillim* (119: 111), 'Nachalti

most important thing that parents need to maintain in their home is a sense of happiness, *simchas hachayim*.

As vigilant as we must be to shield our children from the influences of secular society, ultimately, our greatest defense against this onslaught is to create a happy and stable home life for our children. We must keep our eye on that goal and do everything possible in our power to see to it that the quality of our home life is as good as possible.

A Time for Action

IT IS NOT THE INTENT OF THESE LINES TO DISCUSS THE BROAD-based issues related to the topic of at-risk teens. We do, however, need to implement some initiatives and solutions that relate to the topic of this article – the improvement of our home life.

1. *Shalom Bayis* Classes

During *shanah rishonah* (the first year of married life) when a young couple is at the critical stage of developing their relationship, it should become the accepted societal norm[5] for *both* spouses to attend a series of four, six, or perhaps eight classes on *shalom bayis*. Although the newlywed couple may not think so, this is the ideal time to do this. Young couples have a reasonable amount of discretionary time, and can begin

---

eidosecha l'olam ki s'son libi heimah – I am in eternal possession of your statutes, for they are the joy of my heart.'"

Rabbi Sheinberg commented that there are two levels of happiness. *Simchah* is an internal contentment with one's position in life. *Sasson* is when the inner peace manifests itself in a display of external happiness. He explained that when raising children, it is not merely enough to attain that ever-elusive goal of inner peace, *simchah*. A sense of happiness and *simchas hachayim, sasson,* must emanate from the home in order to create the optimum environment in which to raise happy, well-adjusted children.

5. If our community succeeded in instituting the premarital screening test for the dreaded Tay-Sachs disease – as part of the outstanding Dor Yeshorim program – we can marshal our energy and collective talents to initiate *shalom bayis* and parenting classes to eradicate the more common epidemics of divorce and drop-out teens.

to prepare their home to be a resting place for the *Shechinah* and a nurturing environment for their children to thrive in.

Many young men and women lack proper role models for establishing a relationship based on mutual respect and trust, or simply were not exposed to the positive influence of the parents' home during crucial years. Training helps. Education helps. More so, a good mentor will provide an opportunity for young couples to seek guidance when the inevitable bumps[6] will occur. Many couples are uncomfortable going to their parents for direction at this critical stage in their lives.

2. Parenting Classes

Here, too, education is the key. It would be naïve to think that any one person has all the answers to the difficult questions that parenting requires. Many, many parents, however, have told me how their home life was immeasurably improved as a result of attending parenting workshops.

> *At a recent symposium, Rabbi Shmuel Kamenetsky related the story of a young woman who was experiencing significant difficulty at home and in school. Professional counseling was recommended. After several sessions, a remarkable improvement was noted by all. Reb Shmuel related that the therapist told him that he had instructed the mother to take her daughter out of school for lunch in a restaurant and spend at least one hour together, conversing, prior to each session. This, the therapist felt, was far more effective than his time with the young woman.*

Similarly, it is great training for a young couple to spend time together growing as parents and sharing in the raising of

---

6. Several mental health professionals have mentioned to me that the birth of the first child, and financial pressure after parental support for the young couple is eliminated, are great sources of stress in young married couples. At that point, however, there is less time for the couples to work on improving their marriage.

7. Many yeshivos and day schools have initiated a series of parenting workshops that the entire parent body is required to attend. In fact, a yeshiva in the New York metropolitan area actually offers a tuition discount to parents who attend the entire workshop series.

their children.[7] The practical tips and skills that are imparted at these sessions greatly improve the quality of the home life as parents are trained to deal with the many issues and challenges that they face on a daily basis.

Yes, our parents seem to have done a decent job raising us without attending lectures or reading books, but times have changed and our children are faced with temptations that we never had.

Good parenting skills do not always result in wonderful children. Effective parenting, however, can significantly improve the likelihood that a difficult child will grow into a well-adjusted, productive adult.

3. Strengthening the *Kehillah*

A woman approached a colleague of mine at a public gathering. She had been recently divorced and asked him to arrange for someone to take her school-age sons to *shul* on Shabbos. He related to me that his initial reaction was that a situation like this would be unthinkable in a small town, or in a *kehillah*-type *shul* setting. *People often speak about children falling through the cracks. The reality is that all too often, it is the families that are falling through the cracks.*

In large metropolitan areas, where most Orthodox Jews live, one can *daven* in several *shuls* throughout the week without being a member in any of them. Although this may be very convenient for the individual *mispallel*, the family – lost in the anonymity of city life – forgoes the unique protection that the *kehillah* has to offer. An involved Rabbi and Rebbetzin guide young couples and their children through the inevitable difficulties that they will encounter. They are there to notice troubling tendencies in *shalom bayis*, the *chinuch* of the children, or any one of a host of issues.

It is critical in the development of a Torah home that the family belong to a *kehillah*, attend *shiurim*, and above all, to actively nurture a relationship with the Rabbi and Rebbetzin of the *shul*. Doing so will add many strands to the communal safety net that we so desperately need.

4. *Simchah* Schedules

People are always asking what has changed so dramatically (regarding the at-risk-teen issue) in the past decade. There are some obvious answers – and more subtle ones. One of those that fall into the latter category is that we are more "stressed out" than any generation ever was. Please allow me to rephrase this. *We are not home enough.* Our family life is unraveling. We are working longer hours in more stressful situations. Perhaps much of this is unavoidable, with the enormous pressure to provide *parnassah* for our growing families. One area, however, where significant improvement is not only possible but absolutely necessary is our *simchah* schedules.

Our *gedolim* have – for years now – been requesting that we limit conspicuous consumption at our *simchos*. Although there are some exceptions, as a group, we have been reluctant to take their advice.[8] If we cannot or will not bite the bullet for the sake of a lifestyle of *tzeniyus*, then *asei lemaan tinokos shel beis rabban* – let us do so for the sake of our children.

Every evening that we dress up after a busy workday and travel a half-hour to wish a young couple *mazel tov* at a *lechayim* (to be followed by a *vort*, wedding,[9] and *Sheva Berachos*), we are depriving our own children of desperately, desperately needed quiet time with us.

While I am not recommending that we all become social dropouts and refuse to attend any *simchos*, it is clear that we need to limit our time away from home. Our primary obligation, after all, is to raise and nurture the children that *Hashem* blessed us with and whose upbringing He has charged us with.

---

8. A must-read is Professor Aaron Twerski's article, "Are Things Bubbling Over?" (*JO*, Feb. '96).

9. One area that is in critical need of improvement is the outrageous 60-90-minute picture session following the *chupah* that has unfortunately become the norm at our *simchos*. Proper planning of weddings must take place to eliminate this needless delay.

5. Shabbos and Yom Tov – an island of tranquility… hopefully.

Shabbos Kodesh. A time for spiritual and emotional rejuvenation. A time for children, relaxation, and family. No telephone calls, no appointments, no distractions. Your children can now get your individual attention as you – and they – unwind from the pressure-filled week. *Me'ein Olam Habba.*[10]

Sadly, the hectic nature of our lives is unfortunately spilling over into the last bastion of our home life – *Shabbosos* and *Yamim Tovim.* After a forty/fifty-hour school week, when most children would treasure some downtime with their parents and family, or simply the luxury of being left alone to unwind, many are subjected to long Shabbos meals with company present, where they are expected to behave in a picture-perfect manner. This despite the fact that the entire conversation at the table is geared to the adults.[11] Children who are naturally shy are pressured into reciting *divrei Torah* in front of strangers. Parents go *Kiddush*-hopping until well past noontime – with the unrealistic expectation of coming home to a clean home and relaxed children; or leave their children[12] with friends or relatives to attend weekend *Bar Mitzvas.*

It is of great importance that we pause and take stock of our objective for our *Shabbosos.* We must strive to create – at least once a week – this zone of *menuchah* (tranquility) in our homes so that our children can relax and look forward to this special day with their family.

---

10. Comparable to the World to Come

11. I often tell parents that if they wish to get a sample of what they are subjecting their children to – long conversations that are meaningless to some of the participants – they should have one of their teenage children invite a dozen of their friends to the house for a meal. Then both parents should sit quietly for one hour listening to *their* conversation.

12. Parents should never, ever leave their teenage children at home for Shabbos without adult supervision. In today's climate, it is a recipe for disaster – especially in large metropolitan areas.

The "Broken Home" Component

ALLOW ME TO STATE THE OBVIOUS. CHILDREN'S NEEDS are best served growing up in a two-parent household. *Chazal's* comment that the *mizbei'ach* "sheds tears" when a couple divorces needs no elaboration.[13]

Having said that, divorce in and of itself does not consign a child to a bleak educational and social future. While statistically, children from broken homes are in a high-risk category, it is only so, in my opinion, when there is strife and unhappiness in the child's life. Children can adjust to the painful reality of growing up in a single-parent household – when *both* parents maturely put their own feelings aside for the sake of the children.

Please allow me to share with you two incidents regarding children from broken homes that I am currently involved with.[14] With the help of Hashem, I am confident that the first child will mature into a self-confident, well-adjusted young woman. I hope that I am wrong, but I do not share that optimism about the teenager in the second story.

> *Aviva is a bright 6-year-old girl attending first grade in a local Bais Yaakov. Her parents divorced four years ago. Aviva lives with her mother, and spends most weekends with her father, who lives in the same community. Her parents are both very involved in her chinuch and secular education, even attending Parent-Teacher Conferences together. Recently, Aviva went through a difficult week when she was quite rude to her mother. Her mother's response was to call her ex-husband and discuss the matter with him. Twenty minutes later, the doorbell rang. It was Aviva's father. He took Aviva for a drive and discussed with her the importance of treating her mother with respect. Throughout the following*

---

13. A noted therapist recently mentioned to me that he is like the *mizbeiach*. The *mizbei'ach*, he pointed out, was singled out as shedding the tears, since the *mizbei'ach* seeks *korbanos* everyday.

14. Names changed to protect the identities of the children and their families.

week, Aviva's parents conversed nightly with each other to monitor the situation.

Yossie's parents divorced three years ago. It was a messy divorce, with endless litigation about joint assets, custody and visitation. Yossie's father threatened to withhold a get until he would receive favorable conditions in the asset distribution. Yossie, then 13 years old, and his three siblings were made to appear before a judge to respond to highly personal questions about their relationship with the two parents.

This past Yom Kippur was not on the father's court-mandated visitation schedule. (All nine days of Succos were.) Yossie's father asked his ex-wife for permission to spend Yom Kippur locally (he has since moved away from his former community) and meet Yossie in shul for the davening so that "Yossie shouldn't be the only child in shul without a father." This reasonable request was refused, and he was informed that any attempt on his part to follow through on this plan would result in court action.

Yossie is currently a bitter young man who has been in several yeshivos in the past two years. He spends his nights "hanging out," and has a strained relationship with **both** *his parents.*

It is of paramount importance that in the event of a divorce, all parties design a plan of action that will provide the children with the most pleasant home environment that is possible under the circumstances.

The Third Partner

For the record, I do not think that children from orphaned homes are included in the high-risk category. Aside from the pledge of the *Ribbono Shel Olam* – the *Avi Hayesomim* – to watch over his special children, anecdotal evidence would indicate that the overwhelming majority of *yesomim* grow to become well-adjusted, very often outstanding, young men and women. Fired in the crucible of the pain and loneliness of losing a parent, they often outgrow the inevitable "Why me?" phase, mature earlier than their peers, are more sensitive human beings, and become exceptional spouses and parents, having learned at an early age to appreciate life to its fullest. And yes, they usually develop an incredibly close relationship with the surviving parent who raised and nurtured them under such difficult circumstances.

Ma Tovu Ohalecha Yaakov

IT IS INTERESTING TO NOTE THAT THE INITIAL ATTRACTION TO *Yiddishkeit* for many *chozrei b'teshuvah* is not a beautiful *d'var Torah* or deep thoughts of *hashkafah*, but rather their participation in the warm atmosphere of a Jewish family sitting around the Shabbos table. Throughout the generations, our homes have always been the anchor in our lives and one of the primary sources of the transmission of our *Mesorah* to future generations. And it is in our homes – down in the trenches – that our generation's *milchemes hayeitzer* (battle for spiritual survival) is being fought.

May the *Ribbono Shel Olam* grant us the wisdom and *siyata diShmaya* to create the type of home life for our children that will inculcate them with Torah values and prepare them to transmit our timeless *Mesorah* to yet another generation.

Many young men and women lack proper role models for establishing a relationship based on mutual respect and trust, or simply were not exposed to the positive influence of the parents' home during crucial years. Training helps. Education helps. More so, a good mentor will provide an opportunity for young couples to seek guidance when the inevitable bumps will occur.

Dear Mom

Bracha Druss Goetz

Dear Mom, Shalom! How are you? I hope you're feeling well.
Thank G-d everyone is fine. And I have some news to tell.

    It's hard for me to write you, these words which should cause joy.
    Soon we will have, G-d willing, a brand new girl or boy,

Already I can picture your look that's on your face,
Daughter dear, must you produce the whole human race?

    I'm thinking of your health, you'd say with genuine concern.
    You want to save the Jewish People — but give someone else a turn.

Your body needs a rest, my dear, why can't you take a break?
If you will not listen to me--do it for the children's sake.

    Until you gave me my first grandchild, I could hardly wait.
    But every year you're giving birth — and now it's number eight!

Of course I love each little face. I treasure every one.
But don't forget you're still my child — and I'm worried about you, hon.

    Physically, emotionally and financially too,
    Children are very draining. What will be left of you?

And then come your closing words — Mom, they always pierce through me.
Just remember: what's important is quality, not quantity.

    The other arguments never swayed me — but this one would sting,
    Quality — -not quantity — that does have a good ring.

Your words never leave me, Mom, they won't go away.
But this time as I write to you, I now know what to say.

> *Better quality than quantity, which one must I lose?*
> *Who says that you can't have both? Who says I have to choose?*

I don't see why I should settle and sell myself so short.
I'm trying to make good human beings — this isn't merchandise I've bought.

> *This job would be too much for me if it all fell on my shoulders.*
> *Their father and I do our parts — yet it is G-d who grows them older.*

You're worried if we'll have enough — but can't you see my wealth?
I am glowing from my diamonds and these children give me health.

> *Do you think more pleasure will drain me? Then let me say one thing —*
> *All that I can give to them does not compare with what they bring.*

Why don't you understand me? Really you're the one to blame.
You filled my life with so much love, Mom, I want to do the same.

> *I'll keep wishing you will share my joy — I hope someday you'll see*
> *All my children are an expression of all the love you put in me.*

Dear Mom / 93

Washing Dishes

Sarah Shapiro

*Washing dishes, watching the dishes,
not really seeing
her hands wash the dishes,
because it's always like this, and the sun
        lengthening along the floor.*

    *One,
      two o'clock,
   and then she's done
the laundry. Get the baby crying, Oh, sweet baby.*

        *Because.
      There is no because.*

*But one day the sun hits a frying pan in soapy water
and she's holding a rainbow.
The thought flashes through her like lightning:
"G-d's creating light!" and she sees
all this,
the light, the water, her hands, herself,
are miracles.*

Raising Children, as Viewed by Great Leaders

The Chazon Ish on the Educator's Responsibility to the Weak and Wayward Student

Notes on Education

Raising a Family

Between Parents and Sons

The Chazon Ish on the Educator's Responsibility to the Weak and Wayward Student
Principles and Vignettes[1]

Rabbi Zvi Yabrov

⇒ The Requirements of an Educator

THE NECESSARY PREREQUISITE TO INFLUENCE ONE'S students, the Chazon Ish told Rabbi Michel Yehuda Lefkovitz, is a genuine love of people. He based his view on the directive of *Chazal* (*Avos* 1:12) that one must be "*oheiv es habriyos u'mekarvan laTorah* love people and draw them closer to Torah." These are not two unrelated commands. They are rather cause and effect. Only one who loves others can draw them close to Torah.

He once requested that a certain individual be appointed as *mashgiach* in a particular yeshiva, despite the fact that the candidate was not a great *talmid chacham*, nor renowned as an exceptionally great *tzaddik*. (Today the man works for the *Chevra Kadisha*.) "He has a good heart," the Chazon Ish explained, "and he will make every effort to help the boys through their pain." That character trait sufficed. He rejected the other candidate as "too tough."

---

1. Every situation is unique, and one cannot assume that the Chazon Ish's directives in the examples cited here can be freely applied to specific cases that may appear to be similar (*halachah lemaaseh*). They do, however, serve to illustrate the extent of a *mechanech's* responsibility and *achrayus* for each and every *talmid*.

The ideal educator, in his view, must be of elevated character. A *mechanech* of deficient character causes a double tragedy. Since his actions do not match his words, his students will not learn Torah from him, and even worse, they learn from his behavior (*Emunah U'Bitachon* 4:16). A student emulates his teacher. And if a teacher is of imperfect character, his *talmid* will learn bad *middos* from him.

⇥ The "Weaker" Student

"*Chanoch lenaar al pi darko* — educate the lad according to his way," the Chazon Ish insisted, does not mean to withhold the possibility of becoming a *gadol baTorah* from one who seemingly lacks that capability. We have to ensure that every child has the opportunity to be that "one out of a thousand," however improbable that seems. Hence, a yeshiva must never devalue any student, for it is impossible to know which young *bachur* will one day be the *gadol hador*.

Rabbi Shlomo Lorincz once asked the Chazon Ish if it would not be beneficial to create a different kind of yeshiva, emphasizing *pshat* and *halachah* (literal meaning and practical application), rather than *lamdus* (abstract probing), for less gifted boys. Since such boys have no hope of becoming *roshei yeshiva*, and will eventually become *baalebattim*, Rabbi Lorincz wondered, would it not be better to emphasize the skills necessary to understand a *daf Gemara* and learn *halachah*?

The Chazon Ish was vehemently opposed to the suggestion. "Our *chinuch*," he said, "must be based on the assumption that every boy can be a *gadol*. One who does not seem blessed with great intellectual gifts can turn the corner one day and be blessed with formidable intelligence. Suddenly all the wellsprings of Torah open up to him and he is recognized as a considerable *baal kishron* (intellectually gifted)."

The Chazon Ish buttressed his view with the story of a contemporary *gadol* who was considered slow as a youth. Even at the age of 18, he asked the Chazon Ish to explain a *Rashi* that any third grader could understand easily. "Yet," he told

Rabbi Lorincz, "that person is now one of the great Torah luminaries of our times."

A *talmid* who felt he was not cut out for learning once informed the Chazon Ish of his plans to master a trade. The *gadol hador* invited the young man to learn with him, and they spent a long time learning *Gemara* together. When they were finished, the Chazon Ish asked the young man, "Don't you see that you are capable of learning?"

Good Children

"Make sure that you learn with them every day," was the Chazon Ish's advice to a father who wanted to know how to help his sons become *talmidei chachamim*. He often shared with fathers, who asked for a blessing for their children's success in learning, the reply of the Chofetz Chaim to a similar request: "You do not educate your son by collecting *berachos* for him, but only by being willing to sell the pillow under your head to pay for his tuition."

Becoming a *gadol baTorah*, the Chazon Ish often said, is as dependent on the tears and *tefillos* of the boy's grandmother as on his intellectual gifts.

The Difficult Student

When asked how a yeshiva should treat a troublemaker, the Chazon Ish responded, "It is better to put up with him and draw him as near as possible. The function of the yeshiva is to provide wisdom to the weaker ones and understanding to those who go astray. One cannot blame the unruly student. That is the nature of children. We must make every possible effort. Sometimes the right hand must push away while the left hand draws closer. And sometimes we must draw them near with both hands" (*Kovetz Igros* 1:81).

A boy was once expelled from a yeshiva for joining an inappropriate youth group. The Chazon Ish arranged for him to be accepted in an out-of-town yeshiva. Once again he joined a proscribed youth organization. The boy was sent to talk to the Chazon Ish. The latter spoke to him at length without ever mentioning the youth club. After the meeting, the one who arranged the conversation with the Chazon Ish expressed his surprise: "I brought him here with the hope that the *Rav* would convince him to sever his ties with that group. But the *Rav* did not even mention it!"

"He obviously derives satisfaction from his membership in this group," the Chazon Ish replied. "Before you take something away from someone, you must first give him something else in return. This *bachur* isn't yet ready to taste the sweetness of Torah and it won't affect him. So I was nice to him and invited him back next week. I'll speak with him in learning again, and he will begin to enjoy it. And when his eyes light up in Torah, the darkness will disappear on its own."

⇢ Expulsion – a Matter of Life and Death

Sending *bachurim* away from yeshiva, he often said, is tantamount to *dinei nefashos* (capital punishment). Accordingly, he often refused to decide the issue. "Yeshiva _____ says that I'm ruining their yeshiva by not allowing them to expel their students," he once admitted. "But what can I do? I can't be the one to decide that they should send them away. Hopefully, Heaven will have mercy and these boys will leave on their own."

Rabbi Yehoshua Yogel once came to the Chazon Ish with the following dilemma: In his yeshiva were several problematic students who would deteriorate if sent away. On the other hand, if allowed to stay, they might have a bad influence on others. The Chazon Ish's initial response was that this was a difficult life-and-death issue. He then asked Rabbi Yogel how he had handled similar situations in the past. Rabbi Yogel replied that he had indeed expelled several students. As a rule, though, the hard cases left on their own and as a result the others succeeded in straightening out. Thus, in his view, experience had shown that when the hard-core troublemakers left the yeshiva, the others improved greatly.

The Chazon Ish interrupted him: "Experience does not overrule the *Shulchan Aruch*. One may not expel a student. You don't have to court him, but if he wants to stay you have no right to send him away. You must rather dedicate all your strength to educate him and to supervise his behavior."

"I don't know if I have the strength," Rabbi Yogel responded.

"Hashem will give you the strength," was the reply.

A yeshiva student was once caught stealing, and the yeshiva's dean asked the Chazon Ish whether the boy should be expelled. "Did you ever speak *lashon hara*?" he asked the questioner. "Did they throw you out of the yeshiva as a result? What difference does it make what *aveirah* he did? Surely he is not *chayav mesah* (liable for capital punishment) for these actions."

When asked how a school should deal with a child in the class whose parents are *mechallelei Shabbos*, he replied that one must never disgrace parents in the eyes of their children.

On one occasion, the Chazon Ish decided that a student should be expelled from his yeshiva. Nevertheless he made the expulsion contingent on several conditions. The *Rosh Yeshiva* was required to first establish a regular learning-*seder* with him.

"First begin learning with him," the Chazon Ish insisted, "and only afterwards can you notify him of his expulsion. And you must continue learning with him thereafter, as well. In this way, he will be able to deal with the trauma of expulsion and will be in a learning framework until he finds a new yeshiva."

The *Rosh Yeshiva* involved related that that student became a great Torah sage and *Rosh Yeshiva*. And the once wayward youth admitted that if his *rebbi* had not drawn him near, he does not know if he would even be Jewish today.

The Chazon Ish followed the same approach with girls' schools. Asked about the possibility of expelling of a girl from school, he replied. "Capital cases require a *beis din* of 23 judges."

In those instances where he permitted the school to expel the girl, he stipulated that the school find some other arrangement for her to ensure that she not land in the street. "Nowadays," he told Rabbi Avrohom Wolf (founder of the Bais Yaakov high school of Bnei Brak), "as a result of the influence of the street, all girls, even those who have parents, are like orphans. And one doesn't throw orphans into the street."

⇒ The Mechallel Shabbos Child

When asked how parents should treat their children who have gone "off the *derech*," he responded that they should try to draw them closer with bonds of love and not to push them away. A youth who became a *mechallel Shabbos* later asked his father to buy him a car. The father agreed on condition that he promise not to drive on *Shabbos*. The son refused to promise and the tension between father and son rose sharply. The Chazon Ish, however, advised the father to give his son the car without any conditions, for in that way he would have much more influence over him.

⇒ Our Obligation to Every Jewish Child

Any child who does not receive a proper Jewish education was in the Chazon Ish's eyes an orphan, and accordingly, there is a *mitzvah min HaTorah* to take pity on him and provide him with a Torah education.

The Chazon Ish was once asked if students who frequented inappropriate places were in the halachic category of a *talmid she'eino hagun*, to whom it is not permitted to teach Torah (*Yoreh De'ah* 246:7). The Chazon Ish replied, "That *halachah* does not apply today. In previous generations, Torah study was for the entire community. The *Rav* gave *shiurim* in the *shul* and everyone understood that they had to attend. Of course there were always a few degenerate individuals who had no desire to learn and came only because of societal pressure. It was those whom *Chazal* classified as ones to whom one should not teach Torah. But the youth of today, who come on their own free will and seriously want to learn, even though they do not yet keep all the *mitzvos*, are not considered to be *talmidim she'einam hagunim*. One should teach them Torah."

Like Putting on Tefillin

The obligation to help weaker *talmidim*, the Chazon Ish held, is not only the province of the educator. It extends to every *ben Torah* as well. On the basis of "talking in learning" with students of Ponovezher Yeshiva, the Chazon Ish came to the conclusion that many younger *bachurim* were getting lost there, and felt despondently alone and helpless. He requested Rabbi Yaakov Eidelstein, then studying in Ponovezh, to organize the older *bachurim* to learn with younger ones. "If they refuse with the excuse that they have no time for anything but learning," he told Rabbi Eidelstein, "ask them how they have time to put on *tefillin* every day. Tell them," the Chazon Ish continued, "you put on *tefillin* because it is a *mitzvah*. Well, helping younger *bachurim* is no less a *mitzvah* than putting on *tefillin*.'"

The Ultimate Zechus

A *ben Torah* whose father died came to the Chazon Ish for advice. He wanted to establish a free-loan fund to perpetuate his father's memory. The Chazon Ish responded that while it would be a great merit for the deceased to establish a free-loan fund in his memory, it would be an even bigger *zechus* to learn with a weaker student, build him up and put him on his feet, and help make him into a *ben Torah*. When that young man marries, his children will also be *bnei Torah*, and their children as well. Establish a free-loan fund, and you will benefit a limited number of people. But if you build a weak boy into a *ben Torah*, the potential merit is limitless and will sustain your father's *neshamah* for eternity.

The Chazon Ish had a powerful love for every Jewish child and his actions and activities were an outgrowth of that love. He once told his nephew Rabbi Shlomka Berman that *Roshei Yeshiva* are generally concerned primarily with the good of the public, with what's good for their yeshiva or for the Yeshiva World as a whole. But what is right for the yeshiva is not necessarily beneficial for the individual student. "I look at it differently. To me every individual is an entire *Klal*.

Notes on Education
Rabbi Simcha Wasserman

AN IMPORTANT LIFE RULE TO REMEMBER IS THAT A PERSON can never be successful if he has more than one aim in what he is doing. It follows that if you want to succeed when teaching a *talmid,* you cannot have one aim for the *talmid* while having your own interests in mind, as well. (This seems to be the reason that it is forbidden to teach Torah for remuneration. When teaching *bechinam* — without pay[1] — then the very act of teaching is solely for the benefit of the *talmid*).

Chazal[2] tell us that *talmidim* are called their teacher's children. It would seem that any teacher training must therefore be of secondary importance, for if it were of primary importance, then every parent would have to undergo a special training program.

The Rambam states:[3]

> "Just as a man is obligated to teach his son, so too is he obligated to teach his grandson, as it says:[4] 'And you shall make them [the words of Torah] known to your children and grandchildren.' Not only to his son

---

1. *Nedarim* 37a.
2. *Sifri, Devarim* 6:7.
3. See *Rambam: Hilchos Talmud Torah* I, 2.
4. *Devarim* 4:9.

and grandson, but it is a mitzvah for every Jewish scholar to teach all students, even if they are not his sons, as it says:[5] 'And you shall teach them [the words of Torah] to your sons' [and it has been taught] by the Oral Tradition[6] that 'your sons' refers to your talmidim, for talmidim are called 'sons,' as it says:[7] 'And the sons [i.e. students of] the Prophets went forth.'"

The *Rambam* seems difficult to understand. If a *talmid* is only called a son after being taught, how can the *Rambam* use the *pasuk* of "*Veshinantam levanecha* — and you shall teach to your children" as a source to obligate a scholar to begin teaching?. It must mean that the *Rambam* understands that the *pasuk* is indicating an obligation to make him your son.

In truth, however, another point can be made. Unless he is my son, I cannot teach him. "*Veshinantam levanecha — eilu hatalmidim*"— is because the teaching is always with your son, it follows that you cannot teach him until you adopt him. So making him your son is part of the *mitzvah* of "*Veshinantom.*"

If your son enters the kitchen Friday afternoon while you are preparing a *cholent* and you tell him to leave because he is disturbing you, this is anti-educational. A parent should be concerned only with how his child develops. It would be good *chinuch* to send him out of the kitchen so as to teach him to avoid being a nuisance to others when they are busy, rather than to do so for the parent's own convenience.

"*Ben chacham yisamach av* — A wise son will cause his father to rejoice."[8] This is not to be misconstrued as a double aim — the son's wisdom and the father's happiness. Rather, the *nachas* that the father enjoys is an outgrowth of

---

5. *Devarim* 6:7.
6. *Sifri* ibid.
7. *Melachim II* 2:3.
8. *Mishlei* 10:1.

his child's development. But, on the other hand, if a father teaches his child because he wants to have *nachas* from him, the result will be imperfect. When he teaches his child because he wants the child to mature into a correct person, the *nachas* comes as a matter of course.

This is the foundation of all *chinuch*. The *talmid's* welfare is my only concern. In this way, and only in this way, does my *talmid* become my son and my son my *talmid*.

Raising a Family

Rabbi Elya Svei

⇌ The Family — a Keystone of Civilization

WE ARE CONCERNED ABOUT THE STATE OF THE FAMILY, and for good reason. Before entering a discussion on the issue, however, let us first examine the Torah perspective on the topic.

The family structure involves a number of *mitzvos*, notably teaching one's children and honoring one's parents. These are not, as one might think, a Torah reaction to the existence of the family: grandparents, parents and children living together, often under one roof. Rather, because the Torah contains the *mitzvah* of honoring one's parents, the world was created with each person having a father and mother. As the *Zohar* says:

"G-d looked into the Torah and then created the world." Torah is the blueprint of the world.

What, then, was the underlying reason for the world to be set up in such a manner? No living creature except man has an ongoing family life. This is surely of significance.

Man is different in yet another way — he is utterly helpless at birth. It takes him many years before he develops any degree of strength, intelligence, and independence. By contrast, all other creatures are born with their potential in evidence. As the *Gemara* says: A day-old ox is also called an ox. This is also a factor of importance.

The family structure — the sharing of lives and interests by members of different generations — is closely connected with the concept of *mesorah* — the passing on of our heritage from generation to generation, which is one of the very foundations of our belief. The *mesorah* began when 600,000 Jews witnessed the revelation, at Mount Sinai, heard "*Anochi* ...," the first of the Ten Commandments, and passed on the essence of this experience from generation to generation. For a child to accept and believe in this tradition, he must develop loyalty to his parents. How is this nurtured? The child is born helpless, and relies on his parents for virtually all his needs. And the parents are *moser nefesh* — extend themselves beyond all considerations of comfort or convenience — for the sake of the child, engendering a loyalty in him. Then the *mesorah* can be transmitted. This concept of *mesorah*, by the way, is not limited to Jews, but applies to all of mankind. Non-Jews also have *mesorah* — the seven Noachide commands — which emanate from G–d's instructions to Noach right after the *Mabul* (the Flood).

The condition of contemporary society, then, is easy to understand. After one generation of a weakened family structure, where in many respects transmission of *mesorah* has ceased to function, the level of society's morality has tumbled and general decency has sunk beyond any foreboding. Primarily, this is because we must rely on the health of the family to uphold the world, and the family itself is failing.

⤜≡ Parental Cooperation

Yet another aspect of man's uniqueness is underscored by the *Ra'avad* in the introduction to his *sefer Baalei Nefesh*, and this, too, is a significant feature of family life. Whereas in all animals, the male and female were created as separate entities, in mankind woman was created as an integral part of man; later, when separated, Adam described Chavah as "bone from my bone, flesh from my flesh," and they still maintained a special bond. There is a reason for this unique feature. Had the male and female been created separately, then they would be like animals in that no relationship would exist between the two other than that of male vis-à-vis female — to mate, for the perpetuation of the species. But human couples must share a spirit of cooperation, working together for a common purpose that goes beyond bringing a new generation into the world — to pass on the *mesorah* which they had received. There must be a relationship whereby she is the *eizer kenegdo* (helpmeet) and he views her in terms of "his wife is like part of himself."

⚷ The "Tznius" Element in Mesorah

Yet another feature of human nature, also exclusive to mankind, is the sense of modesty and privacy, with the capacity for shame, known as "*tznius*."

This, too, was implanted in the human personality —especially in the woman — as part of the Divine plan.

Chazal point to the term that describes G–d's creation of woman — "*vayiven* (and He fashioned)" as related to *hisbonen* — contemplated. That is, G–d (*kaveyachol*) had to consider (*lehisbonen*) which limb to select for the purpose of creating the woman. Had He created her from Adam's eye, this faculty of vision would be dominant, and women would have a compulsion to gaze, even where one should not; if from the ear, she would tend to hear too much, even that which one should avoid hearing; if from the mouth, she would be endowed with a tendency to talk too much ... for that limb or organ would have been her very essence. G–d chose to fashion her from Adam's side, a part totally hidden from view, so that the woman would be a *tzenuah*, modest. This feminine factor — her very essence, as interpreted by *Chazal* — is essential for the existence and successful function of the family, to facilitate the family's role in perpetuating our *mesorah*.

The Talmud refers to this in taking note of the decision of Rachel, the daughter of Kalba Savua, to marry Akiva, a decision that seemed something of an enigma. Her father was one of the three wealthiest men of Jerusalem who had helped support the city's populace when it was under siege. She could have had her choice of the finest of men as her husband, yet she selected a 40-year-old, poor shepherd who was an *am ha'aretz* — an illiterate. What did she see in him? — his *tznius*, we are told — an attribute that is a binding prerequisite for Torah. With the necessary character traits, he was able to study Torah and grow in scholarship for forty years, and then teach Torah for another forty years, and became the *Rabban Shel Kal Yisrael*, a key link in the chain of *mesorah*.

The *Gemara* interprets the phrase חמוקי יריכיך in *Shir Hashirim* as equating the thigh with Torah. Both require concealment, for Torah is only acquired with *tznius*. Thus, woman — who is the *eizer kenegdo*, and whose province is the family which transmits the *mesorah* — was created from a hidden part of Adam, for this is an essential requirement of Torah.

⇒ The Family Under Siege

Smugness and complacency are dangerous, for they breed a lack of awareness to threatening problems. Proud as we are of the outstanding educational institutions that we have created in our communities, we dare not take our blessings for granted. The morrow is never secure. By the same token, we take pride in the relative stability of our families. But complacency is a trap, and we dare not rest on our laurels. This very element took its toll in the "first family" of Jewish history: Yaakov *Avinu* and his family... the Twelve Divine Tribes, who in their perfection provided the foundation of *Klal Yisrael*.

One incident regarding Yaakov's children begs for clarification. How could this family, in its glorious perfection, suffer the degradation of Dena's violation by Chamor the crown prince of Shechem?

One of the explanations offered by *Chazal* is derived from the *pasuk*: אל תתהלל ליום מחר, "Do not rejoice over the morrow." *One may be sure of today's situation, but one can never be certain of tomorrow's.* Yaakov apparently failed to honor this principle when he told Lavan, "And my integrity will answer for me tomorrow" (*Bereishis* 30:33). A harmless enough statement, yet Yaakov was faulted for saying it, for with these words he indicated a certainty in his integrity to which no one is entitled; he expressed a lack of self-doubt in regard to his future standing as a righteous man, when one must forever question himself in this respect. As confident as Yaakov was, Dinah proved the vulnerability of the family to outside assault.

⇨ Watching for the "Tznius" factor

Our concern for our families and their integrity should make us question ourselves, even when our motives are honorable — especially in areas that touch on *tznius*. With this in mind, we must examine a pressing problem in the educational scene. Young women helping in the support of their *Kollel* husbands find drawbacks in careers in education. Teaching salaries are too meager, and positions are in short supply in the geographic areas where the men are studying. So even when the girls are yet single, they gravitate to "a clean and simple profession" such as computer programming, which they can continue to pursue in any location, after they are married.

Their argument seems reasonable, but it does not take into account that element of *tznius* which is so crucial to the Jewish family. Again we have a precedent from the first Jewish Family, that of Yaakov *Avinu*: Another factor of weakness pointed to as a cause for the breach in Yaakov's family is Dinah's outgoing nature. The very words describing her excursion into Shechem just prior to her violation — "And Dinah *went forth*" — are used to describe her mother's action when "Leah *went forth* [toward Yaakov]" to inform him that he was to spend the night in her tent instead of Rachel's. The Midrash describes Dinah as "One who goes forth, the daughter of one who goes forth," implying that

Dinah's outgoing tendencies that invited trouble were inherited from her mother.

This is puzzling to say the least, for as a result of the initiative of "and Leah went forth," she conceived her son Yissachar, and Yissachar more than any of the other sons of Yaakov came to personify Torah study. In fact, the term Yaakov uses in his blessings to describe Yissachar, as "a donkey ... ," is a reference to the donkey Yaakov rode, coming in from the fields; Leah heard the donkey bray and then stepped out to greet him. When Yaakov praises Yissachar's forbearance, as "he bends his shoulders to carry the burden," he is referring to his total submission to G–d — as the braying donkey shoulders his burden. This admirable trait was inherited from his mother: Stepping forth to tell her husband, "I have engaged you... [from Rachel] with my son's blossoms," was not a simple matter for her; it was an act of self-negation, to submit to what she perceived as G–d's will ... as the braying donkey shoulders his burden. It was this that Yaakov found so praiseworthy, and singled out as Yissachar's strength. Yet, how ironic: The very same "And Leah stepped forth" that earned Yaakov's praise was the source of the trait that made Dinah a victim of Chamor, prince of Shechem. A most laudable attribute — the ability to step forward — has its inevitable built-in pitfalls and demands caution.

When planning a career, a young lady will undoubtedly think in terms of financial compensation, and for the best of motives. But at the same time she must not lose sight of the *vateitzei* ("and she went forth") factor. A young lady teaching little children in a yeshiva or day school is not only in a protected environment; she is functioning in one that promotes personal growth, as well. By contrast, can one say that when a girl is working in an office, her *tznius* (personal modesty) is totally unaffected or her sense of refinement is as wholesome and innocent as it was the day she left seminary? Granted, her reason for choosing office work is a good one: a case of "and Leah went forth" for a good cause — she wants to enable her husband to study, to have a "Torah home." But one cannot overlook considerations of *tznius*, which is a requisite for Torah, for the existence of the family, and for the perpetuation of the *mesorah* — an essential ingredient for ascertaining that one's children will grow up to be *bnei Torah*.

⤏ Who's Responsible for the Family?

An unprecedented burden is being placed on our young people as wives and mothers, as husbands and fathers, but there are reasons for this.

Family life in our own generation is significantly different from that of previous generations. In the past, "family" referred to the extended group of father, mother, grandparents, aunts and uncles, great-aunts and great-uncles. In those days, it was possible for both parents to be involved in a business venture and the child would receive *mesorah* directly from his grandfather — who sat and learned, went to his *Rebbi*, and generally linked the child to Sinai ... while the girl received her *mesorah* from her grandmother, who was a *tznuah*, and wise in the facts and nuances of her tradition. But today's generation is nurtured only by parents; they — the father and the mother — must play the role of parents, grandparents, and the entire constellation of relatives to properly transmit the *mesorah*.

Parents cannot make verbal demands of their child, and rest their case on that alone. The child must *see* whatever his parents demand of him in their conduct. When he witnesses the *mesorah* his parents had received from *their* parents as a vibrant reality in their own lives, then he can accept that *mesorah* from his parents. This will make a deep and lasting impression on him, and then they can expect him to be an ideal yeshiva *bachur*, to their pleasure and satisfaction. This is in keeping with the purpose of the family — to transmit the *mesorah*. To be sure, this means that the parents have to make sacrifices for the sake of their child, involving inconvenience and even hardships so they can serve as effective role models in their daily life; but this is essential if their children are to grow up as they should.

⤖ Links in the Generation Chain

Young people must conceive of themselves as links in the chain of *mesorah* — not only as parents of the next generation, but as teachers as well. Both the women and the men must appreciate this and prepare themselves accordingly.

A young lady may decide that as far as she is concerned, entering the world of commerce, or computers, or whatever area, is worthwhile (in spite of the "*vateitzei* factor") because in this manner she will be helping her husband grow into a *gadol b'Torah*. Nonetheless, she must also consider the needs of *Klal Yisrael* at large. *Mechanchim* are alarmed that the best products of the Bais Yaakov schools — those most qualified to become the teachers of the next generation — are instead seeking employment in other areas. We all must share this concern over who will train the girls of the next generation so that they too will want to marry *bnei Torah*. This is a problem that requires careful consideration, and no young lady should make her decision without consulting her mentors. If our best teachers — those who would be worthy of transmitting the *mesorah* that they received — seek careers in other fields, our future is bleak indeed.

The men, of course, have their share of the responsibility, too. As the *Gemara* in *Megillah* explains, *Klal Yisrael* is able to face the worst of circumstances and survive — only because of the Torah giants of each generation:

> *Chananyah, Mishael, and Azaryah in Bavel. . . Mordechai and Esther in Modai (Medea). . . Mattisyahu and his sons, and Shimon Hatzaddik in Galus Yavan (Greek domination) . . . And today (asks the Gemara)? By virtue of Rabbi Yehuda Hanassi and the contemporary giants do we manage to surmount the impossible pressures of galus.*

There was no other way for *Klal Yisrael* to survive, nor is there today. Everyone capable of assuming a leadership position is truly obligated to aspire for such a role and to prepare for it. Now some argue that "A thousand enter school to study Scripture, and one emerges as an authority in *halachah*." What need is there to go beyond the traditional ratio? But so very, very few are entering our yeshivos, that we simply have no right to accept a similarly smaller number of authorities to serve as our elite leadership. Our needs demand far more than one per thousand out of the meager thousands that enter yeshivos in the first place.

It is also wrong to sidestep the issue, as many of us do, by rationalizing: "My family was always only merchants; they were never *rabbanim* or *roshei yeshiva*, and nonetheless they found time to study Torah. I'm pleased that my children are learning now, and I'll even permit my son to continue his studying a year or so after his marriage, but then he'll go into business."

Klal Yisrael simply cannot exist without the *Chachmei Torah*. If G–d grants us the gift of a talented child, one who is endowed with the capabilities and the character attributes requisite to being a *marbitz Torah* (disseminator of Torah) or a *gadol b'Torah*, or to being an *eizer kenegdo* (helpmeet), then that child should be encouraged to pursue this goal; and the parents should recognize their good fortune, that G–d had endowed them with such riches — a child worthy of serving as a key link in the chain of *mesorah*.

↦ The Resident "Priest"

The goal of every Jewish household is implicit in the *viduy maasaros* — the so-called confessional declaration made periodically (every three years) in the time of the *Beis Hamikdash*: "*Biarti hakodesh min habayis* — I have removed the sacred from the house" — to the effect that all priestly gifts and tithes have been emptied from the house and duly delivered to the appropriate individual (*Devarim* 26:13). The *Seforno* questions the use of the term "*viduy*" — confessional — to describe this declaration, for nothing improper is being confessed to here. He replies that it is a sad situation when the "*kodesh*," the sacred is removed from one's house. There was a time when every home had its own resident "priest" in the person of the *bechor*, the firstborn, and there was no necessity to remove the "*kodesh*" from the house; for initially (until the incident of the Golden Calf) the firstborn son in every household served as the *kohein*. Not having a resident *kohein* in the person of the *bechor* is a reminder of the loss from the time of that tragic incident from which *Klal Yisrael* has never fully recovered.

All is not completely lost, however, for today every household can still have resident members that devote themselves to spiritual pursuits and even have the status of belonging to the priestly tribe of Levi. This is in keeping with the *Rambam's* description of anyone who devotes himself to Torah study, dissemination of Torah, or community service, as possessing the rank of *Levi'im*. It should be the goal of every family to have its representative among the *Levi'im*; someone who has the talent and the special sense of commitment to become involved in such sacred endeavors should be encouraged, guided, and supported in realizing his quest. And the other members of the family should feel fortunate that one of theirs will be one of the perpetuators of our heritage, for the benefit of *Klal Yisrael*. As a result, the entire family will be on a higher spiritual plain.

The strength of *Klal Yisrael* has been described as the rock of Israel — *evven Yisrael,* אבן ישראל. The word *evven* consists of two components: *av* and *ben* — father and son (אב/בן).

The interrelationship of father and son, both promoting goals of strengthening Torah, bring *kedushah* into the home. This inspires a similar relationship between G–d our Father, and us, His children — a transcendental Father-son relationship — fulfilling the command of "Make for Me a sanctuary that I might dwell within them" — not within *it*, the sanctuary — but within *them*, the people. Our families become an *evven*, the cornerstone of a revitalized *Klal Yisrael*, serving as a sanctuary for G–d's Presence.

Raising a Family / 117

Between Parents and Sons
Rabbi Avraham Pam

⟜ The Ultimate "Tachlis"

Family life — so crucial to Judaism — consists of several different aspects. The following lines will deal with one of them — the importance of a healthy relationship between father and son.

In the yeshiva, one often encounters a phenomenon that brings about a breach in family life, causes anguish to parents, and ends up perplexing the *bachur*. As with most problems, it roots begin early in life:

When a boy is born, everyone extends his blessing to the parents: "May the child grow up to be a *gadol b'Torah*," and the parents second the blessings with a hearty "Amen!" ... At his *Bar Mitzvah,* the speakers all stress the same theme — that they hope that the young man will grow up to be a *gadol b'Torah* ... If the boy is gifted and progresses in his studies, he brings his parents a bounty of joy and *nachas* ... All is well until the boy approaches the end of high school. Then the problems being to surface: *What will be the tachlis?*[1] *What kind of future lies in store for him?* Then come the conflicts, the arguments, the years of controversies. The *bachur* is in a

---

1. Literally: "ultimate purpose." In the vernacular, it refers to means of earning a livelihood.

dilemma. He has tasted the joys of Torah study to the point that "his soul yearns for Torah." His awe and his reverence are directed toward *gedolei HaTorah* and he wants to follow in their footsteps. But his parents are concerned about his earning a living and they are impatient for him to apply himself to secular studies.

Now, the young man is aware that Torah study does not fall in the purview of the requirement to honor one's parents: He could continue to devote himself fully to Torah study in spite of his parents' views. Nonetheless, he doesn't want to hurt his parents by opposing them. So he is in a quandary. It affects his learning and soon his *rebbe* becomes aware of the problem.

> *A father once consulted the Chofetz Chaim about this very same problem: "Shouldn't a person concern himself with tachlis? Is it wrong to be concerned about the future?" The Chofetz Chaim answered, "Of course, you must think about tachlis! What kind of a question is that? Bereishis — In the beginning G–d created ... [the Midrash says] For the sake of the Torah, which is called 'Reishis' did G–d create the world. The world was created for tachlis and that tachlis is Torah. Of course one must keep in mind his 'tachlis'!"*

On another occasion, the Chofetz Chaim said, "G–d is a provider for all. Is it possible that He will care for everyone except His most beloved children — those that are completely immersed in Torah?"

Perhaps concerned parents are really worried about luxuries. When we say, "*Dorshei Hashem*... — The seekers of G–d will not miss the good things of life," it does not mean that they will have all luxuries. The meaning is that they will not miss them, because they are not really important to them — in the spirit of Yaakov *Avinu's* declaration: "*Yesh li kol* — I have everything."

Children who are willing to forgo life's luxuries, and are not concerned with their level of material achievements, whose burning desire is to lead a life of Torah — such children are a gift from G–d. How blessed their parents should feel!

When a father complains to me that his son wants to forgo a secular education to devote himself more fully to Torah study, it brings to mind the lament of the Jews in the wilderness: "We have nothing but the manna!" (*Bamidbar* 11:6). At this point the *pasuk* adds a description of praise, "And the manna was like coriander seed, etc.," *Rashi* explains that these are G-d's words, implying: "Look at what my children are complaining about when the manna is so wonderful!" (ibid. 11:7).

Indeed, mothers since time immemorial have shown special appreciation for their sons' growth in Torah study, as the Midrash says in regard to Rivkah and her love for her son Yaakov: "The more she heard his voice [engaged in Torah study] the more her love for him increased." She never found his learning excessive. We must emulate her and demonstrate our appreciation to our children for their devotion to Torah, and encourage them. How often the Shabbos and Yom Tov table — the only time the family gets together — becomes converted from a setting of domestic harmony to a battleground over *tachlis*! And the poor *bachur* becomes torn between the urge to set the record straight and a reluctance to appear to be insolent to his parents.

Jewish men and woman always prayed for children, as did the *Avos* and *Imahos* (Patriarchs and Matriarchs) so their families might be building blocks in the formation of the glorious edifice of *Klal Yisrael*. More than bringing children into the world, this also entails guiding them so they might assume their places as leaders, rabbis and teachers — *gedolim, manhigim, mechanchim*. When sons and daughters aspire for a significant place in this magnificent chain of *mesorah*, the parents should find this as cause for justifiable pride, rather than quibble over "self-deprivation and loss of career opportunities." In such cases, the children have actually selected the major "*tachlis*" of their lives, and are to be encouraged to pursue it.

The *Mechilta* on *Beshalach* states that in the future, Eliyahu *Hanavi* will return the jar of manna that had been hidden away at the time of Hoshiyahu *Hamelech* prior to the destruction of the first *Beis Hamikdash*. In *Tanach*, however, we see the role of Eliyahu as that of heralding the advent of the *Geulah* and uniting children with parents in *Avodas Hashem*. The message of the manna, however, is an eternal one: Just as it is a basic tenet of our faith to believe that Torah is *min haShamayim* (from heaven), so too is daily sustenance ordained in heaven.

Indeed, it was to demonstrate this point that Yirmiyahu *Hanavi* had displayed the manna. When he had reprimanded the Jewish People for not devoting more time to Torah study, they explained that they had to earn a livelihood. In response, he took out the jar of manna, to show how even under the most impossible conditions — during the forty years of wandering in the wilderness — G–d provided for His People. Many are the ways of G–d to provide sustenance for those who adhere to His word. The returning of the jar of manna is thus very relevant to the assignment of Eliyahu *Hanavi* (as expressed in *Malachi*) of bringing harmony in the family, between parents and children on the issue of *tachlis*, by revealing the jar of manna and demonstrating its message: Those who are dedicated to Torah will not be deprived of their livelihood.

⤏ Toward Tolerance, Restraint and Consideration

When discussion relationships between parents and children the focus is usually on children's obligation to honor their parents. However, parents, too, are obliged to follow the guidelines of the Torah concerning general human relationships in dealing with their children; for instance the *issur* (negative command) of "*Lo sonu ish es amiso*" — which prohibits speaking to a person in a manner that will cause him pain and misery. This certainly applies to parents speaking to their children. Likewise the *issur* of "*Lo sisa alav chet* — Do not bear a sin because of him" — embarrassing a person — applies to parents as well. Even a small child is susceptible to shame, and it goes without saying that the teenager is especially sensitive to it. If a child feels insulted or hurt by a word from his father or mother, it can do great damage to his personality. These are matters that affect family harmony, and all concerned must be keenly aware of their obligations — the child to his parents, and the parents to their child, to uphold the child's honor and self-respect.

Very often parents are impatient with their children for becoming excessively *frum* — exhibiting more zeal than is necessary or even desirable in *mitzvah* performance. This becomes a point of contention and strains the relationship between parents and children. Sometimes it is wiser for parents to accept this in the general context of youthful exuberance and not be worried by it. It certainly does not warrant insult or mocking on the part of the parents.

Even when a child's conduct is suspect, he is entitled to respectful treatment, as *Chazal* say: "Honor him and suspect him." When, for instance, the parent suspects the child of not telling the truth, he should not accuse him of lying, and certainly should not label him as a liar. It is far wiser to give him the impression that you have faith in his good character. Moreover, to accuse the child of something he may not have done can inflict such a terrible hurt on him that it may drastically affect his attitude toward his parents.

If a father wants to admonish a child in order to improve his learning or behavior, he is likely to achieve better results by encouragement, rather than reproach.

> *The father of one of my students was an accomplished talmid chacham, and was very concerned about his 16-year-old son's progress in Torah. When the father asked about his son, I told him that he was a bright boy, but was not applying himself to his studies. He immediately called his son over, and I was sure that he would lash out against the boy. Instead he spoke in a soft friendly tone: "Your rebbi says that you're doing quite well ... just a little bit more effort on your part is needed. Please apply that little more and it will be excellent."*
>
> *The boy left feeling very pleased and began to learn much better. Eventually, he grew up to be a Rosh Yeshiva in a well-known Mesivta ... This is tochachah (reproof) — with honor.*

My mother once told me of an incident that took place when she was 8 or 9 years old: She had wanted to fast on the Tenth of Teves, as grownups do. She knew her parents would not permit her to do this, so she spent the day at homes of her friends, and did not come home until nightfall, when it was time to eat. The Dayan of Shedlitz, where my grandfather was Rav, happened to be at my grandfather's house when she came, and he was aware of what had taken place. He was very angry at the child, and insisted that she deserved punishment. "She must be taught a lesson!" he demanded. "Oh, would I give it to her — the 'fasterke'!"

My grandfather remained silent. The child was given her supper, and went off to her room to sleep. My grandfather followed her to her room, took her in his arms, and said to her: "Mein kindt, you wanted to do a mitzvah; you should know that if one is commanded to fast, and he fasts, it is a mitzvah. But when one doesn't have to fast, it is not a mitzvah to fast. One should not torture the body unnecessarily. Im yirtzah Hashem, when you'll be Bas Mitzvah — 12 years old — then you will fast, and it will be a real mitzvah. Now, you must be very tired, so go to sleep, and sleep tight. Good night!"

The words warmed her heart as long as she lived, beyond the age of 90.

Let us always bear in mind that the primary purpose of the family is to bring up a Torah-loyal generation. Everything else is of minor importance. All energies should be concentrated towards achieving this end. This will promote a pleasant and wholesome climate in the entire family: among parents, between parents and their children, among the children themselves.

Helping Our Children Do Their Best

Disciple-Discipline

Foundation for Growth: Self-Esteem

The Art of Reproof

Instilling Good Character in Our Children

Developing Character: Learned or Experienced?

Teamwork

Seminars on Raising Children

A Mother's Reflections (poem)

Disciple—Discipline

A Concept to Consider on the Festival of "And You Shall Tell Your Children ..."

Rabbi Noach Orlowek

⊷ Pleasure as a Requisite for Learning

MY FATHER TAUGHT ME THAT THE WORD "DISCIPLINE" IS A derivative of the word "disciple." A disciple is a student, someone who learns from a teacher. Just as learning cannot be forced, but must result from the student's *desire* to learn, *true discipline must also stem from the desire to follow.*

Learning cannot be forced. As the Gaon of Vilna states in his famous letter to his family, "Learning is retained only through gentleness." Rabbi Yitzchok Hutner, in *Pachad Yitzchok, Shavuos, Maamar* 15:6, expressed this concept: "Just as the ears hear through the medium of sound waves and the eyes see by responding to light waves, the mind also has its medium through which it connects to information. That medium is *pleasure*. The mind learns what it *wants* to learn, what it enjoys learning." Hence *Chazal* (the rabbis of the Talmud) tell us that a person should study what he finds pleasurable (*Avodah Zarah,* 19a). For this reason, the *berachah* on Torah study contains the phrase, — and make sweet Your Torah in our mouths." This is as true with true discipline as it is with the development of a true disciple.

"Discipline" that has its roots in intimidation will evaporate as soon as the student or child is freed — or frees himself — of his fears. Then, more often than not, enmity and rebellion will appear, with the "disciple" unwilling to obey even the simplest and most reasonable of requests.

Rashi tells us that when the Torah says "to take" a person, it refers to convincing the person to come with you. How? "With beautiful words"![1] The Alter of Kelm, Reb Simcha Zissel Ziv, put the major elements of discipline into sharp focus:

> A student must know two things about his teacher, which will inspire him to accept his lessons with joy and willingness. One — that his teacher is wiser than he is and knows better than he does what is for his benefit.
>
> Two — that he *very much* [italics mine] seeks his [the student's] good and not his own, or *any other* [italics mine] intention.[2]

With regard to parents, the *Alter* continues by saying that the major factor that causes a child to fail to love his father fully is because "he thinks that his father does not know what is best for his (the child's) benefit."[3]

⇥ Trusting One's Parents

Sometimes more than a lack of love can result from a child's thinking that a parent does not know what is best for him. We have today a worldwide malady known as the "Generation Gap." Children feel estranged from parents. As my *Rebbi,* Rabbi Simcha Wasserman, put it: " 'My son the doctor' is the cause of the generation gap." When children feel that parents' expectations and the advice and direction they give may not be with an eye to the child's best interest, but as a result of other considerations, then poor — or no — communication will result. Far more than discipline is lost.

---

1. *Rashi, Bereishis,* 2:15. See also *Rashi, Bamidbar* 27:18,22 and *Devarim* 1:15. See also *Kiddushin* 22b.
2. *Chachmah U'Mussar,* Volume II, *Maamar* 225.
3. ibid.

On the other hand, parents who convey to their children that only the child's best interest is at the root of whatever advice they give will find that their child's love and respect toward them will continue to grow in step with the child's emotional and intellectual maturity. A clear expression of this can be found when parents from weak or even nonreligious backgrounds enroll their children in Torah-oriented schools. Such parents are concerned solely with what type of education will benefit their child most. Any fear that what the child would learn in school would detract from the respect accorded the parents is soon discovered as being totally unjustified. If anything, quite the opposite happens. As the child matures, he finds himself thinking, "My parents care for me and want what is best for me. They understand life and people, and are worth turning to experts for advice on how to live successfully."

Good discipline is rooted in the ability of the mentor to imbue in his child (or student) the desire to follow his parents' lead. The child must know that the parent feels positively about him, and has the good judgment to direct him on the path to a successful life. Learning to lay the groundwork for this type of relationship, and pinpointing and dealing with the problems which are likely to hamper the development of such a relationship, are the basic elements needed for successful discipline.

Foundation for Growth: Self-Esteem

Rabbi Mordechai Blumenfeld

⚯ Few Words, Great Impact

"Thinking back, it's hard to believe that so few words could have done so much. The memories are so painful, it's difficult to recall exactly what happened.

"I know I had asked a lot of questions, perhaps too many. I know my Rebbe had seemed irritated that day. I now know how ill prepared I was for his sudden outburst. But his words were words I will never forget. They ring in my ears as if I heard them yesterday. You think you know how to learn? You don't know how to learn, and you will never know!"

ON THAT DAY, THIS YOUNG MAN LEFT HIS YESHIVA HIGH school, never to return. There was nothing his parents could say to prevail upon him to stay. There was nothing they could say to convince him that he had not wasted many years of his life. He was certain that he had been living in a world of illusions and that all his hard work was in vain.

When Rebbi [Rabbi Yehudah *Hanassi*] was told that Elazar bar Shimon, who had recently died, had a wayward son, he immediately went and ordained him. He then sent him to learn. Every day the boy would beg to be sent back to the street life he had become accustomed to. His Rebbi would say to him: They have made you a sage, spread over you a gold-trimmed cloak [at the ceremony of ordination] and designated you a Rabbi, and yet you want to leave!" Eventually he became a great scholar and joined Rebbi's Yeshiva (*Bava Metzia* 85a).

There are many who would have had harsh words for the son of Elazar bar Shimon and the corrupt life he was living. Instead, he was won over with respect and honor. He was persuaded to live up to the status he was given — a model for all future generations of how to win the confidence of a wavering disciple.

Rabbeinu Yonah says at the very beginning of his *Shaarei Avodah*: "The first step for the individual who seeks to serve *Hashem* is to know his own value, to be aware of his greatness, and the greatness of his ancestors; their eminence, importance, and endearment to their Creator." If you feel insignificant and unimportant, how can you possibly relate to G-d? You are a nobody. What difference can it make if you do the *mitzvah* or not do the *mitzvah*? Furthermore, you also cannot relate to others. If you do not respect yourself, why should anyone else respect you? If you don't like yourself, why should anyone like you?

It is extremely difficult to escape the influence of the secular world that paints man as a mere speck in the cosmos or an irrelevant creature who descended from the ape. There is a tremendous payoff to the secular world in supporting this position. What would one expect from a mere speck or the great-grandson of an ape? What a convenient way to avoid responsibility! Many of our talented youth are crippled because they fail to appreciate how important they are.

Implied in the *pasuk* "Love your neighbor as you love yourself," is the concept that one loves oneself, which means to respect oneself, appreciating what it means to be created in the image of *Hashem*. It means to have confidence in one's potential. It means to feel good about oneself, knowing the love and concern the Almighty has for each and every individual.

Foundation for Growth: Self-Esteem

The Basic Need for Self-Esteem

Self-esteem is necessary for growth and maturation. We are all born with a basic need to feel our self-worth. When this need is met by warm and loving parents, when the child feels concern and caring, encouragement and praise, a positive feeling of self-worth is created.

When this basic need of the child is not satisfied, however, because parents are too involved with their own problems to adequately give to their children, or worse yet, when the child faces criticism and perceives himself as being unwanted, or worst of all, when the child is simply ignored, this basic need goes totally unmet. The child sees himself as being without worth, and searches and grasps at any means of validation. Obsessively, he craves the approval of others. His self-worth is like a badly sunburned arm where the least pressure is painful. There is a great need for healing.

The resulting self-perception of being different, the self-perception of not being as good as others, paralyzes the child as he focuses completely on himself. The destructiveness of his self-centeredness is, in a remote way, akin to the "*lo tov*" of Adam *Harishon* ("It is not good — *lo tov* — that Man dwell alone" — *Bereishis* 2:18) before he was given Chavah. As a self-contained entity, Adam *Harishon's* status was "*lo tov*" because he lacked the *opportunity* to intimately relate to something outside of himself. A self-centered individual lacks the *capacity* to intimately relate to anything outside of himself. He is stunted in the maturation process, and his world, too, is void of "*tov*."

The role of parents in affecting a child's sense of self-worth is obviously critical, but there are many other factors that can contribute to the presence or absence of self-esteem. In our present educational system, the struggle to achieve a healthy self-esteem is a difficult one, with high risks. The extremely competitive world of the yeshiva sees many casualties where fragile feelings of self-worth make many good boys vulnerable to a chance slight that can be deeply wounding. It is well known that a critical father or an overbearing mother can destroy the natural confidence of a child. It might not be as well known that a "put down" from a *rebbi* or another significant figure in a child's life can also be devastating, as in the opening anecdote. (To be sure, many children can be motivated through a negative comment, but its success is dependent upon being offered in a context of love rather than anger or irritation, and, most important, upon the keen discernment of the *rebbi* who knows and understands the child.)

⤖ An Essential Component in the Curriculum

Our *mesivtos* and *yeshivos*, like our girls' schools, concentrate on their primary purpose: the all-important tasks of presenting Torah in an attractive, understandable way, and developing important learning skills in their students. Few appreciate how much energy and talent is invested to succeed in these vital areas. Yet, there is another dimension to *chinuch*. The *Rebbi* and teacher must remember that he and she are significant figures in the lives of their students. A word of encouragement, a word of praise, or a mere demonstration of concern for a student can make a world of difference to him (or her). A *Rebbi* should try to be aware of which students are struggling with issues of self-esteem, and then devise strategies to deal with these problems and reduce them. Sometimes a *Rebbi* might direct a particular student to a specific area where he can excel. Often the cause of the student's sense of diminished self-worth is so insistent and incorrigible, the *Rebbi* must explore it, better to understand it, and relate to it judiciously. Critical parents must be made to understand the extent of the harm they can cause, and when necessary, family counseling should be encouraged.

Competition creates pressures. Some children and adolescents thrive on these pressures. They become *masmidim* entering the world of learning with ambition and drive. Others do not. It may seem unfair to ask the *Rebbi*, who may already be overwhelmed, to address this other dimension of the learning process, especially since he must devote so much effort and creativity to kindling and firing ambition in his students. Yet, it is he, and only he, who commands so much influence and power.

According to the *Gemara* (Bava Basra 21a), our formal educational system was developed for children who had no fathers to teach them. Until that time, education was solely a matter between father and son, as is mandated in the Torah. Surely the neglect of orphans only affected a very small percentage of the children, and yet it precipitated nothing less than a revolution in *chinuch*. Nowadays, we are beset with a greater crisis, for a far greater percentage of our youth are ill equipped to deal with pressure and competition, and might become victims of our educational system, as it is currently operating. We must do what we can to meet the needs of our youth for confidence and self-esteem, to enable them to flourish as *bnei* and *bnos Torah*.

The Art of Reproof
Rabbi Hillel Belsky

⇒ Who Is Capable of Reproof?

AS A LONGTIME READER OF *THE JEWISH OBSERVER*, I HAVE been treated to an ongoing series of articles that endeavor to define the weaknesses of the Orthodox community. Certainly, nothing described in these articles is inaccurate; yet I am invariably left with a profound sense of sadness after each attempt to again explore where precisely we are failing. And each time I feel the urge to defend.

Any attempt to communicate to the public where they have failed puts us into a relationship of *tochachah* (reproof) — the writer as the *mochiach* (accuser) and the reader, hopefully, as a *mekabel tochachah* (recipient of corrective advice). Rabbi Yitzchok Hutner offered clarification of the Talmudic statement that in the time of Rabbi Tarfon the era of *mochichim* (those capable of reproof) had come to an end (*Eruchin* 16b). He explained that the *mitzvah* of *tochachah* requires that the *mekabel* not be left with a sense of hopelessness, *yai'ush*; rather, that he be able to accept the criticism and still preserve an optimism about his *avodas Hashem*.

I am reminded of a conversation that I had some years ago with a prominent member of the *Eidah Hachareidis* in Yerushalayim. "After the Six Day War there was a tremendous *hisorerus leteshuvah* (inspiration to return to Torah)," he remarked, "whereas after the Yom Kippur War, there was not. Do you know why?" he asked me. "It is because we won the Six Day War dramatically and the Yom Kippur War we did not. The problem is that we no longer understand a *potch*."

At first I was taken aback by his remark, but then I realized that his comment merely illustrated what I believe Rabbi Hutner had meant, and what I am sure Rabbi Avraham Pam had intended to convey in an article published in The Jewish Observer some years ago (See "Between Parents and Sons, p. 118).

Rabbi Pam told of a *talmid* who was doing poorly. His father had come to speak to the *Rebbi* and received the less-than-glorious report. The father asked to see his son, and told him that the *Rebbi* said he was doing very well, but that with a little more effort he could really excel. This child, reported Rabbi Pam, grew to be an outstanding *talmid chacham*. The reproof was cushioned in love and encouragement. The boy was not brow-beaten. He was lifted up and then challenged, and he responded.

So too did *Klal Yisrael* respond to the events of the Six Day War, but not to the Yom Kippur war.

⇥ In Pursuit of — What? — and Why?

We live in very difficult times. There is much emphasis on materialism and there is much emphasis on our emphasis on materialism. I am not sure that, as has been postulated many times, the alien culture is entirely to blame. I am not sure that *redifas hamamon* (as it is called in these pages) is because of the *goyim*. It seems as though one must be *rodeif mamon* to hold his head up in the *frum* community. Tuition, *tzedakah* for *mosdos* all over the world, support for children in *Kollelim*, *kein yirbu* (not to speak of "getting a good *shidduch*"), hiddur mitzvah, *simchos* (yes, even the minimum), housing in cities that are Torah centers — these all make it impossible not to be overly conscious of money. This is only one of the challenges with which we struggle.

Every *frum* home today is, in some measure, wrestling with the impact of the feminist movement on the women of our community. (Rabbi Hutner wrote in his introduction to *Sefer Mitzvas Habayis* that any movement that envelops a generation will affect everyone, regardless of his or her efforts to resist it.) A secular, professional woman whom I know was invited to a *simchah* attended by over three hundred very *frum* women. She had not seen any *frum* women since dimly remembered memories of her aged grandmother's era. She commented that these women were not "traditional women," but rather women who on some level had struggled with integration into broader society. For instance, they were multitalented, represented myriad jobs and professions, were articulate, and current with contemporary styles, in addition to their expertise at homemaking and childrearing.

Yes, we are wrestling with the problems of the culture, but materialism is not the worst of them. We are facing an unprecedented divorce rate, with its breakdown of families. We live in a world that is not immune to abuse, alcoholism, drugs and other ripples from the host culture. And within all this, our men and women are attempting to create a Torah life, a Torah environment for the children. In spite of the pressures of the *tirdos hazman u'mikreihem* (the pressures and distractions of contemporary society) and the effects of the frequent economic necessity for two incomes (with the dual set of demands on the wife/mother, and the dual set of demands on the husband/father to earn and learn), they are striving to offer their children the best *chinuch* (education), the best *sevivah* (environment), and the best examples that they can make of themselves. All this is usually taking place without their having witnessed firsthand the implementation of the lifestyle they are seeking to create, for the parents of today's *bnei Torah* were by and large *baalei battim* — pillars of their communities, perhaps, but far more integrated than we are trying to be.

At some level we are all the child in Rabbi Pam's story. When a child feels that he has failed, he continues to fail.

Only the hope of success motivates and challenges a child to succeed. I feel that instead of focusing on where we are guilty, we need to provide *chizuk* for our beleaguered families. We must stop suggesting that our problems stem from the self-indulgent parents that we are. In answer to "Where are the parents?" I would say that, for the most part, the readership of *The Jewish Observer* is out there trying to survive and to meet economic commitments that have become the standardized membership dues in a contemporary *frum* society. And even if we have strayed, I believe we need to acknowledge the pressures on the young families. Perhaps by offering them *chizuk*, we will free them to recognize areas in which they can rise above their own limitations.

Instilling Good Character in Our Children

Rabbi Yitzchok Kirzner זצ"ל

The Divine Factor in Character Development

SHADCHANIM PRAISE IT. TEACHERS STRESS IT. *ROSHEI Yeshiva* emphasize it. *Gedolim* personify it. Most of all, it is the crowning glory of parents — a child with *middos tovos*, admirable character traits. The rare nobility of *middos tovos* and all that they encompass calls for an analysis of the subject.

We tend to think of *middos tovos* as they relate to two distinct categories: *bein adam lechaveiro* — interpersonal affairs — and *bein adam laMakom* — between man and G–d. Yet, they are not separate entities, but integral parts of one another, with a tightly woven interplay between the two.

Pirkei Avos, the primary source of *middos* development in the Oral Law, is introduced with the statement, "Moshe received the Torah from Sinai...." *Chazal* point out that only in *Pirkei Avos,* where character traits are discussed, is the element of *mesorah* — transmission of Torah — stressed, to underscore that *middos tovos* emanated from Hashem, together with His Torah.

We might wonder why this is so. After all, a saintly human being could conceivably be capable of authoring a reasonable text on social ethics!

Another puzzling aspect of the opening verse is that there is no mention of Hashem's Name; the emphasis seems to rest on the word "Sinai" — an omission that certainly needs explanation.

These difficulties can best be resolved in the context of *Chazal's* explanation that our ultimate goal in the world is to plant, nurture and develop within ourselves an ever-deepening relationship with Hashem. We develop our connection to Hashem through seeing His all-encompassing presence in the midst of our mundane activities — in moments of grief, in times of tension, in spurts of joy — and, ultimately, perceiving the Hand of G–d in all that occurs in our lives, feeling gratification and even joy for our awareness of His constant presence.

For this reason, Shmuel *Hanavi* is aghast when *Klal Yisrael* approaches him in request for a king. He appeals to Hashem in pain, and Hashem replies, telling him that in actuality, they had not rebuffed him, they had rebuffed G–d. They were solely interested in a king for their social and political well-being. As far as the *shefa Elokai* — the enhanced spirituality that the *Navi* and the *Sanhedrin* nurtured in *Klal Yisrael* — that was of lesser concern to them!

Similarly, when we strive to instill *middos tovos* in our children, it should be with a clear focus: Do we simply want a "well-mannered," socially acceptable person who graces the scene with proper etiquette? Or do we want a child whose *middos tovos* are a springboard for ultimate growth to a close relationship with G–d? Since Hashem authored the criteria for good *middos*, there must be an element of G–dliness inherent in them.

That Divine element manifests itself in a person, who by virtue of his *middos*, is inviting Hashem's presence into his life. And Hashem, so to speak, looks at the person with positive *middos*, and is thoroughly pleased. The person becomes a delightful place for Him to dwell.

Thus, the passage stresses Sinai, the lowliest of mountains, as a symbol of humility, to emphasize this vital prerequisite for absorbing Hashem's Torah in its fullest sense, that the receiver of Torah and *middos* would better absorb and accept these teachings "from Sinai" — from a place of humility, a place where ego does not create a barrier between the person's will and G–d's will. Only then can he be connected to Hashem, the Giver of Torah at Sinai.

The Degree of Interrelations

REB TZADDOK HAKOHEIN, THE FAMED 19TH-CENTURY Chassidic thinker, elaborates on how the spheres of *bein adam lechaveiro* and *bein adam laMakom* are actually a single, unified field. He begins by addressing the mystery of what precisely causes an "impurity" of the body, as, for example, *tzaraas* (Biblical leprosy). We commonly believe that when a person is overcome with a negative trait such as jealousy, he succumbs to *lashon hara* (slander), and as punishment is stricken with *tzaraas*. Not so, points out Reb Tzaddok. The body, as long as it is nurtured in harmonious union with the *neshamah*, remains pure and healthy. But when the body adopts negative *middos*, it tears itself away from the *neshamah*. Once it is depleted of its source of pure spiritual nourishment, the body becomes vulnerable to impurity, which is then physically manifest in the form of *tzaraas*.

Ultimately the two ailments are very much linked to one another. For, to the degree that a person is ravaged with character flaws in an interpersonal area, to that degree is he tearing his body and *neshamah* apart, effecting a most certain personal alienation from his *neshamah*, and ultimately Hashem.

Instilling *middos tovos* in our children, then, is *not* simply a matter of training a "well-mannered" child. Rather, it is part of the intense desire that, with healthy *middos*, the child should be connected with the ethereal *neshamah* with which he was blessed.

The Steps to Take in Advance

ARE THERE ANY MEANINGFUL STEPS THAT WE CAN TAKE, SO as to equip our children with *middos tovos,* so that they blossom into spiritually healthy people who will embrace Hashem, who will include Him in their lives, under all circumstances? The following is but a partial list — certainly not all inclusive of suggestions that could help us begin working at this formidable task.

⤙ Pure Motivation in Raising Children

The *Chovos Halevavos* in *Shaar Habitachon* discusses the delicate balance between *hishtadlus* — the efforts a person expends towards a goal — and *bitachon* — his ability to refrain from further effort, and to stand back and rely on Hashem. In regard to raising children, the *Chovos Halevavos* addresses the dilemma of determining the limits of *bitachon*: How *do* we know that we have already done our utmost in raising our children, at which point we can then plead for Hashem's compassionate intervention?

A parent (the *Chovos Halevavos* states) is nothing more and nothing less than a responsible *shaliach,* an emissary of Hashem, designated for the lofty purpose of raising his child to grow into an *eved Hashem,* a person whose essence embodies one overriding desire: a yearning to grow close to his Creator by understanding, knowing, and doing Hashem's will. In keeping with the ruling that a *shaliach* in a sense embodies the powers of his designator, parents as true emissaries of Hashem become infused with strength from the One Who has entrusted them with His mission.

That deceptively simple statement of the *Chovos Halevavos* alludes to a myriad of possible ulterior motives that might interfere with a parent acting as the ideal emissary in raising children. Parents, though instinctively loving their children, might unwittingly push their child to succeed in areas where they themselves had failed. Or, a parent who, having suffered from a domineering parent in *his* home, is no longer the hapless victim, and is now delighted to have his chance in the powerful role of despot. Or, parents might nurture their children as insurance for caring for *them* in their old age.

All these motives, says the *Chovos Halevavos*, and many, many more, are all different facets of the same element: that of ego. A parent, in communicating honestly with a child, need not fear "bad chemistry" between them if the parent's rebukes to the child are not laced with ego. In expressing concern to the child about negative behavior, the child will not respond favorably if the parent is acting in a self-serving manner, i.e., a good part of what the parent is concerned about is, "What shame this child is causing for me!" Leaving the "me" out in raising children indicates clearly that our children's negative behavior upsets us only because it will create obstacles in their ultimate quest for Hashem.

If letting go of our ego is our primary concern in raising children in general, how much more so does this apply in regard to instilling *middos tovos* in our children. If we react to children out of self-gratification — the child's inappropriate behavior will embarrass "me," what's it going to look like for "me," what's in store for "me," how well will their accomplishments reflect on "me," how will people look at "me," what will my friends and relatives think of "me" — then what is the subtext of the message we are transmitting to the child? One resounding word: "ME." The child has to be concerned with "ME"!

Besides picking up messages of ego through parent-child interaction, children also sense ego involvement when watching parents communicating with each other. Do they witness their parents struggling with choices, basing their decisions solely on saving face? Or are the parents negotiating with a sense of humility, bending towards what is essentially right and true? Ego, in this context as well, can speak volumes to our children.

Either way, a child absorbing "me" messages will grow up with an unhealthy sense of ego — a sense of the world at large being at his beck and call. What will happen to this child if later in life he is faced with inexplicable circumstances? Circumstances where, in order for his *emunah* to survive, he must yield and bow to Hashem's will even though he may be resisting it with every fiber of his being? Who can say whether he will overcome these enormous *nisyonos* (tests) in *emunah*? *Middos tovos*, or lack of them, actually equip, or handicap, the child in eventually handling all the emotional highs and lows intrinsic to a healthy relationship with G–d.

⤖ Functioning Through Selflessness or Selfishness?

Another factor in inculcating good *middos* in our children is a matter of how we relate to *ourselves*. The revered *Mashgiach* of prewar Mir, Reb Yerucham Levovitz, would decry selfishness as being the root of every *aveirah*. Inevitably, when parents convey selfishness, they are creating an almost insurmountable spiritual handicap to the child.

In communicating selfishness, appearances can be very deceiving. There are, for example, mothers who seem selflessly dedicated to their families. That devotion — as an exclusive obsession — is simply not enough. Since family members are, in a sense, an extension of oneself, a child might interpret family dedication as another form of self-service. Additionally, the child assumes that "Mommy thinks I'm the center of the universe, so it must be so!" People involved in *Klal* work, selflessly and purely giving to others, are commonly confronted by the query: "Doesn't your family suffer from all your time away from home?" The answer is rather straightforward. Children who see their parents selflessly devoted to the benefit of others (devoid of ulterior motives, such as honor, monetary benefit, etc.), are constantly learning a crucial lesson in *chinuch*: that of selflessness.

At a slightly different angle, the issue of selfishness must also be considered when we pamper our children. We oftentimes do a great disservice to our children when we indulge them — be it in the form of money always jingling in their pockets, constant sugary snacks, or the like. Overindulgence is likely to develop one overriding trait: that of self-centeredness. A parent must be clever in exercising discretion in setting boundaries in this area, charting the middle course — a very fine line, indeed. Otherwise, an egotistical child will harbor only one constant thought: "What's in it for me?" Everyone, at all times, will have to yield to his wishes, his needs, his opinions.

On a deeper level, this "me" attitude will spill over into how a child will relate to Torah and *mitzvos*. An egotistical child, for example, may also perform *mitzvos*, but with a marked difference. The root of his actions will not be to serve G–d first and foremost, thus forging a bond between him and his Creator, but rather, unfortunately, to serve himself in the forms of monetary gain, honor, esteem, approval, or some other variety of self-service.

While two people may seem, superficially, to be doing the same *mitzvah*, their motivating roots bear drastically different results. To be sure, both will gain a certain level of reward for the performance of the *mitzvah*, but the person whose motives are "Hashem-oriented" will grow immeasurably in his spirituality, deepening his understanding of Hashem as his nurturer. By contrast, the person performing the *mitzvah* out of self-service will undermine the very purpose of a *mitzvah*. Instead of drawing closer to Hashem, he will draw closer to himself.

The Slonimer *Rebbe* portrays this concept most vividly. He describes *middos tovos* as *kanfei ha'avodah* — the wings of serving Hashem. Everyone performs *mitzvos*, everyone *acts* in serving Hashem, but the determining question remains: How much will the *mitzvah* elevate the person? How high will he soar? What permanent change will the *mitzvah* indelibly imprint on the person? All these depend upon the roots, the motivations that lurk beneath the surface of the simple performance of the *mitzvah*.

➣ The Intellect Directing the Emotions

We commonly perceive mankind as consisting of two basic components — intellectual and emotional. We sum up the intellect as being our potential for processing information intelligently, while we see our emotional aspect as a naturally flowing function, beyond our control.

All our *sefarim*, from *Sefer Bereishis* through *Sifrei Mussar* and *Sifrei Chassidus*, teach the co-existence between intellect and emotion. *Hashem* created within the human personality the potential to use his *seichel*, his intellect, to influence and cultivate wholesome, productive emotions. We can appreciate this concept through the following tale:

> It was Simchas Torah, a time of sheer joy in celebrating with our most precious gift: the Torah. In the Rebbe's court, all eyes were riveted on two Chassidim fervently dancing, clutching the Torah close to their hearts. Their dancing increased in tempo, seemingly ad infinitum. People began speculating as to who would tire first. Curious, they turned to their Rebbe, wondering about his thoughts as to the ultimate winner in the dance-a-thon. The Rebbe indicated his choice, offering no explanation as to his decision. Eventually, one of the dancing men began showing signs of fatigue as his steps slackened, until he finally stopped... as the Rebbe had predicted.
>
> Intrigued, the Chassidim sought an explanation from their Rebbe for his intuition. "When both of these people were dancing, thoughts fueled their emotions, their drive to dance. One person was joyously celebrating the Torah that he had already learned while the other was exhilarated for the Torah that he would still absorb. After all is said and done, Torah that has already been learned is finite. Torah yet to be mastered is unlimited. I therefore knew that the person dancing with an unlimited vision in his mind would outlast the one with limited motivation."

Another aspect of using the mind to channel the emotions is taught by the Alter of Novaradok, Rabbi Yosef Yoizel Horowitz. The Alter advises that the only method by which a person can permanently cultivate healthy *middos* is by focusing one's mind on the unadulterated truth in every instance — to seek not a personal truth, but an objective truth as expressed in the Torah. Inevitably, good *middos* will flow from such thought-out Torah perspectives.

For the mind to steer the emotions, however, calls for time. We live in a fast-paced world where slow-moving reactions are derided and delayed responses are deemed inferior. But if a person's good *middos* are to take root and develop, a person must be patient with himself. A person needs to allow himself the time to *think* before reacting to any situation. One needs time to assess what has occurred, and what the Torah response should be.

Consequently, crucial in implanting *middos tovos* in our children is for parents to exemplify this lesson: *Think with a Torah perspective before reacting:* Would Hashem be pleased with my reaction? Does the Torah sanction my response? Children, by osmosis, absorb their parents' attitudes. Teaching them this basic concept of "thought before action" can determine the entire spectrum of their *middos tovos* ... or lack thereof.

⇒ Supply the Mind With Wholesome Nourishment

Another means of instilling good *middos* in children is to fill their minds with nourishing, wholesome ideas. A child's mind is not a void; its supply lines need constant replenishment. The more that parents provide it with positive, healthy *hashkafos*, the healthier the child's *middos* will be.

Each child should be addressed at his or her own capacity and age level. Sermonizing is usually counterproductive. Telling inspiring stories, and sharing incidents and observations are much more effective.

Character traits, *Chazal* teach us, are directly related to the level of one's thinking. A person aspiring to superficial, petty things in life will lose his temper over minor annoyances. The higher one's aspirations, the less likely will his temper be triggered by petty things. And yes, children too can aspire to big things, to lofty ideals. One just has to tune them in to a higher frequency.

Tzenius in the Home: A Blessing for Having Children With Inherently Good Middos

In *Shir HaShirim,* Shlomo *Hamelech* says, "As chaste as a garden locked is my sister, my bride; a spring locked up, a garden sealed" (4:12). This verse depicts the beauty and sanctity of *tzenius* in the Jewish home. Personal modesty reigns between parents; and in the home, in general, modesty in behavior, in thought, in speech and in dress express the quality of the person's inner being — in contrast to flashy externals. The element of *tzenius*, reserving one's beauty for the one that it was intended, will result in fulfillment of the promises of the verse that follows: "Your least gifted ones are a pomegranate orchard with luscious fruit" (ibid, 13).

Inevitably, where *tzenius* is honored — where parents do not relate to glitzy externals, but identify with the purity of the *neshamah* within — the natural outgrowth will be children who reflect that very concept of the privacy of inner beauty over emphasis on externals, children with *middos tovos* ... our ultimate wish.

Developing Character: Learned or Experienced?

Dr. Bentzion Sorotzkin

WHEN THE TALMUDIC SAGE HILLEL WAS ASKED TO summarize the Torah in one sentence, he proclaimed: "*Di'lach sani, lechavrach lo savid* — What is hateful to you, do not do to your neighbor; the rest is commentary."[1] This is the minimum level of *chessed* (loving-kindness): Do not harm others. A higher level is expounded by Rabbi Akiva in his famous statement: "'*Ve'ahavta lere'acha kamocha* — Love your neighbor as yourself'; this is the great principle of the Torah."[2] It is clear from this that the violation of *mitzvos bein adam lechaveiro* (*mitzvos* that govern interpersonal relationships) are at least as objectionable as those *bein adam laMakom* (between man and *Hashem*). Parents who are sensitive to this point put in a great deal of effort to teach their children *middos* (ethical character traits). It is the purpose of this essay to determine the most effective means by which we can develop positive character traits in our children.

⇝ How Are Middos Taught?

Clearly, the importance of *middos* has to be stressed as part of formal instruction both at home and at school. The

---

1. *Shabbos* 31a.
2. *Yerushalmi Nedarim* 89, 4, See *Michtav Me'Eliyahu* III p. 88.

deleterious effect of living in surroundings where "everything goes," and a culture that fails to uphold even minimal standards of moral behavior, can be observed in contemporary Western society. At the same time, by stressing formal instruction, we run the risk of overlooking other avenues of indirect influence that can often have a stronger and more lasting impact than direct instruction.

The most powerful form of indirect influence is the example parents set by their own behavior, especially in their conduct toward their children. "Children learn by example" has become a cliche as unassailable as motherhood and apple pie. In practice, however, few parents or teachers are truly comfortable relying on this "indirect" method of instruction.

> Recently, a young father came over to me at a simchah and asked, "At what age should you start disciplining a child?"
>
> "Discipline starts when a child understands the words 'yes' and 'no'," I responded.
>
> Realizing that this was not likely to be a purely academic question, I asked him how old his child was.
>
> "Four," he answered.
>
> "What is your specific need for disciplining him?" I asked.
>
> "I need to teach him to say 'please' and 'thank you'," he explained.
>
> "Then it is a matter of instilling middos, rather than disciplining," I answered. "And in that case, I would ask: Do you say 'please' and 'thank you' to your son?"
>
> He was taken aback by this question, but gave it some thought.
>
> "I'm not sure, but probably not," was his honest response.
>
> Although he seemed to understand my point, he could not fully accept the idea of forgoing the use of direct instruction or any degree of pressure, and to have faith in the power of setting an example.

⇒ Learning by Living

It is difficult to have faith in the indirect influence of setting an example. Many parents feel they are being derelict in their duty of being *mechanech* (educating) their children if they are not actively and forcefully instructing (or perhaps they are not confident in the example they are setting). From the words of *Chazal* (our sages), however, we see that indirect influence is the *most effective* means of educational influence.[3]

The *Midrash* states that Moshe had ten names: "Yered" because he brought down the Torah to the world; "Chever" because he united the children with their Father in heaven, etc. Hashem told Moshe that He will call him only by the name given to him by Basya, the daughter of Pharoah, i.e., Moshe.[4]

Rabbi Chaim Shmulevitz asks: Why did Hashem choose to call Moshe by the one name that seems to least reflect his greatness? In fact, this name does not even reflect something that Moshe did. Rather, it relates only to what Pharaoh's daughter did, "*Ki min hamayim mishisihu* — For I drew him from the water."

Reb Chaim explains that since Pharaoh's daughter saved Moshe with *mesiras nefesh* (at the risk of her life), this character trait of being devoted to others became part of Moshe's personality.[5] It does not say that Moshe received lessons in self-sacrifice, nor is there evidence that he won first prize in a "devotion to others" contest.[6] The major contributing factor was that *he himself* was raised with self-sacrifice.

Likewise, Reb Chaim continues, the *Talmud Yerushalmi* states that we learn that Jews have the character trait of compassion for others from "*Veshamar Hashem Elokecha*

---

3. See also Rabbi Matis Roberts, "Whisper Above the Roar: Making the Case for Subtlety," *JO,* April '98.

4. *Midrash Rabbah, reish Vayikra.*

5. See *Sichos Mussar* (5732:25): "Whenever one person endows another with a *middah*, the recipient becomes enriched beyond any reckoning."

6. As indicated above, it is not my intention to question the usefulness of these teaching tools; rather, it is to emphasize the importance of setting an example in addition to direct instruction.

Developing Character: Learned or Experienced?

lecha es habris ve'es hachessed — Hashem will safeguard for you the covenant and kindness that He swore to your forefathers."[7] The *Torah Temimah* asks the obvious question: How can you learn about a characteristic of the Jewish people from a verse describing how Hashem treats them? Here, too, Reb Chaim explains that since Hashem treats the Jewish people with kindness, this virtue becomes absorbed in their national character. By treating His children with kindness, Hashem is, in effect, presenting them with this character trait as a gift.[8]

We also see from *Chazal* how people (and even nations!) develop negative traits by being treated negatively. The apathy of *Amalek* is attributed to the coldness with which Timna, the "mother" of *Amalek*, was rejected by the *Avos*.[9]

From this we can conclude that the primary means of instilling the attribute of kindness in children is not by training them to say "thank you," etc.! Rather, one *treats them* with kindness (perhaps by saying "thank you" to them), and that instills this trait into their essence.[10] In a recent business article, the successful owner of a chain of restaurants describes his version of a trickle-down "*middos*" program: "My goal is to perfect a model of hospitality *that starts with the way I treat my staff.*"

⇨ Teaching by Example

Some schools (and parents) pride themselves in "teaching" *middos* by using contests, essays, prizes and even

---

7. *Devarim* 7:12; *Yerushalmi Sanhedrin* 6:7.

8. Since, as Reb Chaim points out, attributes such as feelings of love can be instilled even into inanimate objects, it is obvious that this process is of a *ruchniyus* nature rather than a cognitive one.

9. *Sichos Mussar* (5731:31). A well-known *Rosh Yeshiva* was once asked at a meeting for parents and educators in regard to rebellious youngsters: "How can these youngsters have no consideration for the pain they are causing their parents?" He responded, "Apparently, these parents showed little consideration for the pain they caused their children."

10. These words of *Chazal*, as explained by Reb Chaim, should reassure those parents who become excessively worried that being "too nice" to their children will cause them to become spoiled.

punitive measures (!) to promote and encourage polite behavior. How effective are such tools if a teacher in one of these schools is not sufficiently careful to exemplify *middos* when he or she speaks to a student? If he insults, "puts down" or embarrasses a student in front of others? Or if he "just" fails to treat his students with respect? Here again, while everyone knows the cliche that "Do as I say and not as I do" is an ineffective means of instruction, this knowledge is not always internalized.[11] One reason for this may be the fact that some adults are convinced that the Torah laws regulating interpersonal relationships do not apply to how an adult treats a child (especially their own child, or student). This idea is clearly contrary to *halacha*.[12]

Rabbi Pam spoke recently for the Chofetz Chaim Heritage Foundation on the subject of *onaas devarim* (hurtful speech). Making it clear that this Torah prohibition also applies to teachers and parents, Rabbi Pam said: "Many children can be turned off from *Yiddishkeit* because of verbal mistreatment, either from parents or from teachers if they use sarcasm or public insults in class.... This is all included in the prohibition of *onaas devarim*, which is part of the same negative prohibition as *lashon hara* (gossip, slander)."

Similarly, Rabbi Moshe Feinstein was asked if a teacher is permitted to ask his students to identify the student who misbehaved (to "snitch," in the vernacular). Reb Moshe responded that for a teacher to do so would be repulsive, since it teaches the students to take lightly the prohibition of speaking *lashon hara*.[13]

Some educators were not comfortable giving up this well-used, direct "educational" tool. They wrote to Reb Moshe

---

11. See *Orchos Ish* p. 142 regarding how students absorb more from their *Rebbi's* actions than from his lectures; p. 143 for comments regarding the negative results from punitive demotion. Also: According to Rabbi S.R. Hirsch, "Demanding honor and obedience from our children without granting them respect and dignity in return is doomed to failure" *Yesodoth Hachinuch*, Vol. 1. — cited by C. Juravel, see "Reclaiming Aspiration," (p. 223).
12. See *Choshen Mishpat* 420:103; *Minchas Chinuch, mitzvah* 328; *Sefer Chassidim* 565.
13. *Igros Moshe* Y.D.II 103.

Developing Character: Learned or Experienced?

questioning his ruling based on their contention that the teacher's intention is to influence the student to stop transgressing. It seems that they could not understand how an educator could forgo a direct and "certain" educational tool (exposing and punishing the culprit) for the sake of what they perhaps saw as a dubious gain, i.e., setting an example of not encouraging *lashon hara*.

Reb Moshe responded in no uncertain terms that the concern of setting a negative example outweighs any other "educational" consideration.[14] Reb Moshe makes it clear that setting the right example takes precedence over the teacher's desire to "instruct" or reprimand the student. Unfortunately, due to the zeal with which some teachers and parents approach their task of teaching an offending child to behave properly, they become oblivious to the damage they are causing by the example they are setting. Telling a child to speak *lashon hara* will *inevitably* cause the child to become insensitive to this *aveirah* (transgression). The teacher's intentions and justifications have no mitigating effect on this negative influence.

Similarly, Reb Moshe comments on the *Midrash* that is critical of Avraham *Avinu* for sending his son to get water for his guests instead of getting it himself. Asks Reb Moshe: Perhaps Avraham was trying to train his son in the *mitzvah* of *hachnassas orchim* (hospitality)? To this Reb Moshe answers that if someone wants to educate his son in a *mitzvah*, the *most effective* method is for the son to observe his father performing the *mitzvah*, rather than having the father instruct his son to perform the *mitzvah*!

---

14. In a conversation with the author, Rabbi Dovid Feinstein (*Shevat* 5759) indicated that there are situations where Reb Moshe would have permitted asking students to inform on their peers, (e.g., to find out which child has been playing with matches). Even in such a situation, however, every effort should be made to minimize the damage of asking children to speak *lashon hara*. He suggested having the *Rebbi* speak to the whole class about the problem without asking for the name of the culprit, or asking the *talmidim* to try to convince the perpetrator to come over on his own to the *Rebbi* to discuss his problem (perhaps by promising not to punish him). These suggestions obviously work best when the *Rebbi* establishes a close, non-threatening, warm relationship with his *talmidim*.

⤘ Teaching Children to Daven

Another arena where the conflict between setting an example and direct instruction is often played out is in parents' attempts to teach children to *daven*. An all-too-common sight in many *shuls* is a father raising his voice, reprimanding, or even hitting his son to get him to *daven*, or perhaps "only" directing his head toward the *Siddur*, in an effort to be *mechanech* him in the importance of *davening*.

This approach has been severely criticized by many *gedolim*. Rabbi Hillel Goldberg relates an incident involving Rabbi Yitzchok Hutner. He had observed a father "disciplining" his son to *daven*. Every time the child would get up or divert his attention, the father redirected him. It was a battle.

"What are you doing?" Rabbi Hutner asked the father.

"I'm teaching my son to *daven*!" answered the father.

"No, you're not," said Rabbi Hutner. "You're teaching your son to grow up to tell his own son to be quiet, to sit down, to pay attention.... If you want to teach your son to *daven*, then *daven*!"[15]

Similarly, Rabbi Shlomo Wolbe is critical of parents who force a child to *daven*, thus inducing a superficial form of devotion devoid of any emotional connection. "These parents will be held responsible for making *davening* a burden for their child," cautions Rabbi Wolbe.[16]

In spite of this criticism — notwithstanding that anyone who bothers to investigate the matter can clearly see that this approach is counterproductive — it remains widely practiced. Why? I would suggest the following reasons.

1) The parents who use this approach tend to be poor *daveners*.[17] They are therefore, paradoxically but predictably,

---

15. *The Jewish Parent Connection,* Vol. 3, No. 5, 1995, p. 14.

16. See Rabbi Wolbe's *Zeriah Ubinyan Bechinuch,* p. 46: "*Tefillah* should be a Jew's *neshamah*. If one forces a child to *daven* in a superficially habitual manner, perhaps striking the child if he doesn't *daven*, he makes him despise *tefillah*. Ultimately, he will feel no inner connection with *tefillah*, and the fault will lie with his parents who forced him to *daven* before he was ready."

17. See ibid. p.30.

more intolerant of normal deficiencies in their children's *davening (kol haposel be'mumo posel).*

I was in a *shul* during *Kabalas Shabbos*. A man behind me was loudly discussing the stock market with his neighbor. This man noticed his 11-year-old son, who was sitting a few rows ahead, exchanging a few words (quietly) with his friend. The father emitted a shout, demanding that his son sit next to him so he (the father) could make sure that his son *davens* properly! What is even more amazing is that after the son took the seat next to his father, and the father made sure that his son had his eyes on his *Siddur*, the father resumed his conversation with his neighbor!... I am fairly certain that if the father reads this article, he would have no idea that I am describing *his* behavior.

2) People who tend to see things superficially think that as long as they get their child to act properly (e.g., to *daven* or to act politely), then it does not really matter how he feels about the matter. They are also unable to appreciate the indirect and subtle influence of setting an example.[18]

3) The lack of appreciation of the process of natural development causes some parents to overreact to what is essentially normal (mis)behavior for the child's age.[19] Some

---

18. This approach is often defended by quoting the *Sefer Hachinuch*: "A person is influenced by his actions." However, it is clear that this is effective primarily when the gap between the behavior and person's true level is not too wide.

Another frequent objection to the "indirect" approach is from the *pasuk* in *Mishlei*, "*Chosech shivto sonei bino* – He who spares the rod hates the child. An extensive and very enlightening explanation of the true meaning of this *pasuk* can be found in the *Alei Shur* (Vol. 1, p. 261) and in *Zeriah Ubinyan Bechinuch* (pp. 23-27) from Rabbi Shlomo Wolbe. From his discussion it is clear that the *pasuk* is criticizing those who refrain from disciplining their children due to neglect or lack of interest. The *pasuk* is not recommending a specific form of punishment, which would depend on the infraction, and the age and temperament of the child. Rabbi Wolbe states that, in his congregation, one is not permitted to hit a child over the age of 3. (See also *Pardes Yosef, Beshalach* p.120, and *Atara L'melech* from Rabbi Pam, p.176). In *Shimusha Shel Torah,* Rabbi Shach states that success in *chinuch* is primarily due to a positive relationship between a student and teacher. The *mechanech* must exert himself to find the way to be loved by his students, says Rabbi Shach (p.148). The point here is certainly to find the most effective means for achieving our chinuch goals.

19. Rabbi Wolbe (ibid. p.16) criticizes parents who demand that their young children sit at the Shabbos table throughout the long meal. "This is impossible for a young child," declares Rabbi Wolbe. Some parents, however, interpret their child's resistance to remaining at the table as a sign of rebelliousness, etc.

Recent studies (e.g., Z. Strassberg, *Journal of Abnormal Child Psychology,*

parents are not cognizant that a happy, well-adjusted child who is not pressured, and who sees his father *davening* solemnly, will in due time also develop the ability and inclination to *daven* seriously. Instead, they fear "If I don't put a stop to it [e.g. not *davening* seriously] now, he'll *daven* this way when he's an adult!"

4) Another factor is the lack of appreciation for the damage being caused by their own behavior toward their children. They are unaware that they are inculcating in their children negative attitudes toward *davening*, and that they are harming their relationship with their child, which is the basis of all *chinuch*.[20]

In addition, they are setting an example of embarrassing someone (in this case, their children) in public, and other harmful *middos*. Even if there was some benefit to this method of discipline, it would certainly be a case of *yatza secharo behefseido* (losing more than one gains). This problem is exacerbated by the attitude of some parents that when dealing with their own children, their proprietorship rights exempt them from the usual obligations of *middos* that apply to their interactions with others. It is as if they say to themselves, "It is only my own wishes, interests and needs that matter. My children must subordinate their needs to mine without resentment. In fact, it must be their pleasure to do so."[21]

1997 [25], 209-215) indicate that aggressive children tend to have parents who are excessively punitive. This behavior on the part of the parents is often prompted by inaccurate and overly harsh judgments as to how noncompliant their child actually is. If a parent tells a playing child to prepare for bed and the child merely politely requests additional playing time, the parent will interpret this request as reflective of *chutzpah* and noncompliance. But an even stronger factor influencing their reaction is their tendency to attribute negative intent to the child's behavior. So the child's request for additional playtime is attributed to defiant intentions ("He wants to be in control, he's being manipulative") and/or to retaliatory intentions ("He's trying to get even with me").

20. See Rabbi Wolbe's *Alei Shur I,* p. 260: "Parents specifically establish bonds between their children and Torah. Only the deep connection between parents and children direct children on the *derech Hashem* (Divine path)."

21. See *Zeriah Ubinyan Bechinuch* by Rabbi Shlomo Wolbe, p. 28: "We frequently find parents who take action toward their children, ostensibly for educational purposes, when in fact, the true motivation is purely egoistic. At times the parents act toward their children with totally unacceptable *middos*, behavior that would be considered reprehensible in any other interpersonal context... i.e., jealousy, hate, anger,

5) Even when there is a need for direct intervention and direction, they are unaware of, or not willing to avail themselves of, more effective means of instruction. One can use a glance, a gentle comment, or a friendly pat on the cheek to redirect a child's attention to his *Siddur* without creating negative feelings.

⇥ Middos or Politeness?

A related problem is when we evaluate a child's level of *middos* development by external criteria — e.g., politeness.

A young man related how he proudly told his Rosh Yeshiva about the efforts he invested in teaching his children to be polite. To his dismay, the Rosh Yeshiva was not impressed. "The Nazis ימ״ש were also polite," he reminded the father.

When we try to develop *middos* in our children (or in ourselves, for that matter), we need to have a clear understanding of the essence of the *middos* and not focus merely on its external manifestations.[22]

For example, some people agree to do extraordinary acts of *chessed* even when they strongly resent having to do it. They

---

pride and especially the need for power. [The parent feels] 'My child is my possession and I am entitled to rule over him in an absolute manner. He is my 'object' and his mission in life is to serve my needs.'"

In addition, see *Sefer Habris II* 13:16: "There are people who are careful not to hurt anyone's feelings; in fact they treat everyone with love. Yet they hurt their own children's feelings. They say that 'this behavior isn't sinful since Hashem put them in my hands and He compelled them to accept my discipline — as it says, 'Honor your father...', and my intention is to discipline them in the ways of the Torah." But, in truth, their words are neither logical nor according to the Torah, for why should their children not be included in the commandment of "love your neighbor as yourself"?... The truth is that ... one is punished more severely for hurting a relative, and therefore one who unjustly causes pain to his own child will be punished more harshly" *(Sefer Habris).*

22. See *Ohr Gedalyahu* (*Moadim* pp. 28-31) from Rabbi Gedalia Schorr: Both Shem and Yeffes did the same compassionate, respectful deed of covering Noach. Yet Shem was rewarded with the promise of Hashem's Presence, while Yeffes was only rewarded with the external beauty of art and culture. This is because Yeffes was motivated to cover his father by external factors, e.g., "What will the neighbors say!" and so his reward was external. Shem, by contrast, was motivated by intrinsic reasons and so was rewarded with a gift of intrinsic value. Rabbi Schorr emphasizes the destructiveness of beauty that is only external. In a similar vein, Rabbi Yissocher Frand (in his very insightful tape on the root causes of *lashon hara*) quotes the *Shem MiShmuel* that if you criticize someone because of an "external" fault, it shows where you yourself are holding, i.e., in a status of superficiality.

feel compelled to do so in order to gain approval in the eyes of others. This compulsion is especially strong in those with poor self-esteem. This can cause them to resent the person they are doing *chessed* for, which undermines the whole purpose of doing *chessed*.[23] True *chessed*, on the other hand, comes from the expansion of a satisfied self to include others,[24] as we see by the *Ribbono Shel Olam*, Who is a *tov, virotzeh leheiteiv* — the essence of good, and wants to do good.

A person who feels deprived, either for emotional reasons or because his environment is under the influence of *middas hadin* (the attribute of justice), will find it difficult to attain true *chessed*.[25] A child who has difficulty sharing, in spite of being raised in an environment where sharing is an important value, is more likely an unhappy child.[26] Conversely, if we treat children with kindness, we make it easier for them to treat others with proper *middos*. When parents set an example of respectful interpersonal behavior in their relationship with their children, the positive impact of their formal instructions in *middos* is tremendously enhanced.

---

23. See *Birchas Peretz* (*Shemos* 15b), wherein the Steipler Rav cautions us not to be impressed with external manifestations of *chessed*, since it may not reflect true inner feelings of *chessed*. (In fact, extreme examples of *"chessed"* behavior, as in the incident the Steipler referred to, may mask underlying negative feelings.)

24. See *Sichos Mussar* (5731:23); *Alei Shur* I p. 255; *Michtav MeEliyahu* I p.37, and II p.89.

25. See *Michtav MeEliyahu* I p. 236.

26. Rabbi Yissocher Frand (in the tape cited above) points out that the main victim of *lashon hara* is the speaker, since it makes him into a negative person who always sees the bad in others and in events. Such a person, Rabbi Frand continues, is also likely to be very critical of his children, since he also only sees the negative in them. I would add that this phenomenon of being critical of children is not only the result of being a negative person, but also the cause. As Rabbi Frand points out, the reason there is such a *yeitzer hara* (evil inclination) to speak *lashon hara* is because it helps insecure people with low self-esteem temporarily feel better about themselves. A child who is always being criticized by a negative parent will become insecure and develop poor self-esteem and will, therefore, also grow up with a strong *yeitzer hara* to speak *lashon hara*.

Teamwork

David Mandel

WHAT IS THE RELATIONSHIP AND RESPONSIBILITY THAT parents, students, the *rebbi*, teacher and the yeshiva have in raising a child? It is important to develop this relationship early on and strengthen it in order to yield the best results. At the same time, when a problem develops or when a crisis occurs, this "team" can work together in the best interests of the child.

⌛ Team

Team is a much overused word that describes the deliberate and coordinated action by two or more people to accomplish one goal. Examples of teams abound in the home, school, playground and office. It is logical then to emphasize that one of our most important teams comprise the child, parents, *rebbi*, teacher and yeshiva. Count the hours, days and years this team will be together and it comprises the most elaborate, consistent group of people in a child's entire life. If you knew right now that you would spend at least thirty-five hours a week, fifteen hundred hours a year or twenty thousand hours over the next twelve years with a group of people, you would surely want to know and understand the other members of this group. Consider, then, whether you as a parent, as a *rebbi* or *morah*, as a teacher, have a good working relationship with the other members of your child's/*talmid*'s team.

It is an understatement that school is one of the most critical transitions in the life span of an individual. It is also fair to state that a greater amount of time, effort and resources are needed so that the members of this team involving the student, parents, *rebbi* and teacher can collaborate to achieve the maximum potential of each child. As long as these issues remain unresolved, we will continue to experience the "blame you" syndrome when problems occur, of parents blaming the yeshiva, the yeshiva pointing to the parents and the child struggling in the middle.

⇒ Yeshiva System vs. Home System

Learning theory is based on a concept called generalization. We apply what we learn in one setting to a variety of other situations. We learn a set of values, we learn *Aleph-Beis* and a,b,c, basic arithmetic and so on, and we generalize from these basic concepts to formulate our everyday activities.

A fundamental concern of *chinuch* is whether the values and concepts taught in yeshiva are reinforced at home. The yeshiva, after all, is open and you can "see" what is taught and how. You can ask for a daily schedule or curriculum, you can "interview" the *rebbi/morah*, you can observe a classroom, you can go to parent-teachers meetings, and a variety of other examples permit you to learn a great deal about the important members of your child's team.

The reverse is not true. Parenting is done mostly behind closed doors. This same *rebbi, morah* or teacher does not have similar opportunities to observe the parent/child interaction at home. They don't know how much time you are spending at night supervising homework, how you are teaching *mitzvos*, what Torah values you are instilling, what magazines enter your home, how many parenting workshops you attend.

Our need to emphasize the value of our team is only underscored by the very long days children are spending in school. Couple this with the numbers of mothers who are working today, not by career choice but out of financial necessity, and you have a compelling reason to ensure that the key players in a child's life are working together towards a common goal.

⇌ Prevention

We have too many children who have entered the risk pool. We, all of us, professionals and lay people alike, have done a disservice to our youth lately by affixing so many labels to them. "Off the *derech*," "youth at risk," "in the *parshah*," "troubled youth," are all labels that serve to stigmatize more than to heal. We tend to speak in shortcuts rather than to take a moment and describe what the problem actually is. It comes to a point where a child is walking down the street with a certain look and we too quickly assume he or she is "one of them." He might actually be the best in the class or just returning from *a Tomchei Shabbos mitzvah*, but he has that look so he must be "one of them." Our first form of prevention is for all of us to look inward and stop categorizing and labeling people.

Early investment in the team of people who will be spending the majority of their waking hours with our child will yield benefits whether the child becomes an *illuy* or, *chas v'shalom*, if he/she develops learning or behavior problems. Every parent has the desire for his/her child to behave normally and to be the brightest in school. Parents' expectations of the yeshiva is to make their child a genius and turn him into a *mentsch*. But what if yeshivos told you that they required you to spend fifteen minutes every night with each one of your children? Only fifteen minutes with each child, every night whether he is 6 or 16 years old. This investment of time early on will reap great dividends. How many parents, mothers **and** fathers, can honestly say they are spending fifteen minutes every evening with each and every child? *How was your day? Did you do or see anything that you like, that you don't understand? What are your plans for tomorrow?*

This team can jump into action early on when a problem is

identified. We need not go into a discourse here on the benefits of remediating a learning disability or a behavior problem at the earliest possible age. Much has been written on the subject and it is well understood by educators and parents alike. Suffice it to say that an undiagnosed or untreated learning problem will likely translate into a future behavior problem from the frustration experienced by the child, that he/she can't keep up and is labeled as "dummy."

We are all familiar with the adage there is no "I" in team. When everything is going ב"ה fine, the team members may have little interaction. But when the child begins to have problems, no amount of "I" can do it alone. The entire team will need to coordinate their efforts.

⇢ Intervention

The real test of our team will occur when a child is deemed to be out of sync with the yeshiva. We are not discussing here that small percentage of children who have psychiatric symptoms that require professional treatment and medication management. Nor are we including children with a diagnosed learning disorder that is addressed in a resource room, special education class or remedial tutoring. Rather, we are focusing on those children likely to develop into a 12-to-15-year-old who is disinterested in school, who lacks a focus, who is behaving "*nisht Yiddish*," who the *rebbi* feels is having a bad influence on others. If you, as a parent, invested yourself in the yeshiva system and you developed a partnership and this team was working together all these years, you and your child are likely to reap the benefit now when you may need it most. Similarly, a *rebbi* who invested his time developing this relationship with parents of his *talmidim* will also reap the benefits.

Every workshop and seminar on the youth-at-risk issue today, and there are many of them, includes a discussion on expulsion from yeshiva. Yeshivos have a right and an obligation to establish policies that will be in the best interest of the overwhelming majority of students. Parents pay substantial

Teamwork / 163

tuition for education and they do not want their child to be "ruined" by boys and girls who speak and dress differently, whose interests in music and recreation are anathema to their upbringing. But then again, throwing a child out of yeshiva has had deleterious effects on that child and his family. We have not yet developed a system where a yeshiva obligates itself to hold the child until a transfer is made to another yeshiva or an alternate plan is in place. (In the Far Rockaway–Five Towns community, a program called TOVA has succeeded to a large degree by organizing ten yeshiva high schools to participate in a shared transfer system. (See *The Jewish Observer* Nov. '99.)

Recommended Solutions

The yeshiva system should continue to underscore to parents the value of joining and being active members of the team. Parents should understand that the time invested in this team partnership when the child is 6, may well reap its rewards when he is 16. And, *chas v'shalom*, if your child develops behavioral problems that place him/her at risk in yeshiva, your years of teamwork will now pay off.

Our *chinuch* system is being challenged daily by external forces that are *mashpia* on our children in ways we could not imagine several years ago. Forget television, *Roshei Yeshivah* today are telling parents not to have computers in their home or to keep them under lock and key when not used under adult supervision. Orthodox Jewish men are peddling drugs to our children inside some *shuls* and yeshivos. Orthodox Jewish men are arrested for offending our children in our *shuls*, our parks and our yeshivos. These are devastating issues to deal with that our *mechanchim* who came to these shores from Europe did not have to contend with.

Our *mechanchim* need to understand these complex issues so they can identify at-risk factors at the earliest age to know how to respond and to understand when they need to call for help. This will involve additional training that many of our *mechanchim* have expressed a desire to have.

It has been suggested by many principals that parents be obligated to attend several parenting workshops every year. This is a good idea. It will not only help to clarify the role of the parents and the yeshiva, but it will strengthen the teamwork your child needs for him or her to be successful.

The approach to this could be for a school to assess parents an extra fee, which the school would return to parents attending the workshop(s). The money retained by the school from parents not attending these workshops would be used to enhance *rebbi*/teacher training. Alternatively, every yeshiva would require this training for a child to be registered so that no parent could find a way to avoid the training.

We must recognize that certain teenagers will require professional help. When we are dealing with a child who has an eating disorder, who is constantly angry or depressed, who is a habitual truant, who has lost interest in yeshiva, who is using drugs or is *mechallel Shabbos*, a mental health professional should become part of the team. We as a *frum* community and a yeshiva community have too long averted this for fear of stigmatizing the child or the yeshiva. We have also heard from our *gedolei hador* who have clearly stated the obligation parents have to involve a mental health professional when the child's problem appears to exceed the capability of the parent, *rebbi* or *Rav*. A parent's reluctance to involve a mental health professional may be understandable given the stigma our community attaches to this. The other members of the team should encourage the parents to seek and accept this help and assure them that the yeshiva will be an active partner.

OHEL social workers, for example, have become active members of such teams. When a child displays serious behavioral or family issues, the *rebbi* and parent find such a mental health professional to be helpful and at times it is part of a negotiated agreement to keep the child in yeshiva.

When a child has a problem, the members of the team have to know the same story, the entire story. Otherwise, well-intentioned people will be responding in the wrong way and be counterproductive. This means that we have to confront and deal with the issue of confidentiality amongst team members so the entire team will work to help the child, the family and the yeshiva.

It has been commonly suggested by our *gedolim* that every yeshiva should designate a *mashgiach* to relate to these children who display risk factors. This *mashgiach* also assumes the important role of mentor/Big Brother with the ability to discuss a wide range of Torah and worldly issues. It is common to hear from even those teens who are seriously involved in *chillul Shabbos*, drugs and *pritzus* to refer to their "Rabbi" in a positive tone.

The Special Parental Role

Rabbi Yisroel Reisman in his *Motzaei Shabbos Navi shiur* on February 5, 2000 (Help, My Son is a Teenager) references his discussion with Rabbi Pam on what is the secret to raising children. The *Rosh Hayeshiva* answered simply, "It is role modeling by the parents." What does the child see at home, what consistent message does he or she hear, what Torah values are instilled? This is an issue that mother and father, who together make up one of those very important teams, should discuss, agree on, and be consistent in their message to their children.

It may be convenient for us to blame the bad behaviors our children learned on their friends, but if you spend enough time speaking and listening to them, their words also point to an inconsistent message heard at home and their frustrations and inability to deal with it. The concept of generalization we discussed earlier that applies to educational concepts also applies to behaviors. We learn one set of behavior at home and we apply it elsewhere in school, in *shul*, with friends and later in life in our own home and business.

One size does not fit all in the classroom. We have, ב"ה, 150,000 boys and girls in our yeshiva and day-school system throughout the country. We know that a certain percentage of these kids will not have the "*zitsfleish*" to sit in a classroom from 9 a.m. to 6 p.m. or longer. That does not mean they are bad kids. We have to develop a response for them that meets their needs without necessarily telling the parent their child cannot meet the demands of this yeshiva, to try another yeshiva, which the child is then interpreting that he is a dummy.

⌒ Teamwork

The message here is simple. Teamwork is an essential aspect of raising a child.

There are no complex or hidden messages in this concept. Your child's team will have to involve different people over the years but the consistent members are the parent(s) and child who form the nucleus. Invest time early on in kindergarten and every single year thereafter in formulating this team. Develop that action plan with more time, energy and interest than virtually anything else conceivable to you. Every member of the team brings knowledge and strength but must also recognize at times their limitations and seek information, training and support. No one member of the team will be equipped with all the ability and resources to deal with the most complex issues. With *emunah* and *bitachon* we will all be *zocheh* to raise our children in the *derech hayashar*.

Seminars on Raising Children
An Idea Whose Time Has Come

Rebbetzin Malka Kaganoff

Yossie is a bright 10-year-old. Maybe a bit too bright for his own good. Whenever he is asked to do an errand by one of his parents, he responds with a wisecrack. Exasperated, Yossie's parents raise their voices and snap at him day after day. How many times will this pattern repeat itself? Does Yossie realize that his parents really love him when they seem to be constantly berating him?

Shani Levi arrived home from nursery school wearing a cute beaded necklace. When her mother inquired about the trinket, Shani explained that it belonged to her classroom, but she wanted it so she had taken it. Mrs. Levi was horrified. Her daughter a thief? Where had she gone wrong as a parent? What should she do?

Purim was approaching, and costumes were the talk of the day. Four-year-old Mendy wanted to be a policeman with a real gun. His older brother bluntly informed him that he would not be getting a real gun. "But I need a real gun," Mendy stubbornly insisted.

"Why do you need a real gun?" everyone asked Mendy, quite amused by the prospect of a 4-year-old with a gun.

Their amusement changed to horror as he answered, "I want to kill people."

A Common Phenomenon

CHILDREN ARE OUR GREATEST TREASURE, AND WE ARE entrusted with the awesome responsibility of raising them to be productive members of *Klal Yisrael*. At times, the job seems overwhelming. Can we rely on our intuition, instinctively reacting properly to the challenges we face? Will we make mistakes that might have severe consequences? We read wonderful books on childrearing, but they do not address our unique children and our specific situations. What can parents today do to fortify themselves to fill their *tafkid* (life-mission) as primary educators of their children?

As a relative newcomer to *Eretz Yisrael*, I became aware of a fascinating development that can be found in English-speaking Torah communities here – ongoing *chinuch habannim* workshops and *shiurim*. In many *frum* neighborhoods in Israel, it is common to have several such workshops or *shiurim* available for women. Men too are encouraged to attend *shiurim* and reinforce their parenting skills. The lecturers are well-known *mechanchim* and *mechanchos* or licensed workshop leaders,[1] and parents of children young and old flock to these courses.

"Since I have been going to my *chinuch* classes, I truly feel that my life has changed. It isn't that I wanted to make mistakes in childrearing, but my eyes were not open. To become a doctor, one goes through years of training, but people usually become parents with very little prior preparation, thinking that it all comes naturally. I had to face the fact that I had much to learn. I now realize that I am not doomed to experience difficulties. I have been able to incorporate the lessons I've learned into my life, and I see the fruits. My life and my children's lives have become more pleasant," says M.E., Neve Yaakov resident and participant in a *chinuch habannim* workshop of Rebbetzin Sima Spetner.

Attending a *chinuch habannim* course is seen as an indication of an interest in being the best parent possible, and not a

---

1. More about this license later.

confession of weakness or incompetence. Mrs. Yehudis Salinger, who has an MA in Special Education, is a proud student of Rebbitzen Spetner and is involved in guiding parents, both in workshops and via a hotline. An acquaintance once told her, "You don't seem the type to go to a parenting workshop," insinuating that she did not seem to *need* training as a parent.

Mrs. Salinger responded, "I *daven* every day, but I would eagerly go to a *shiur* that could help me improve my *davening*. Why wouldn't I want to go to a *shiur* that helps me master parenting?"

Variations in Format

THE EXACT FORMAT OF THE CLASSES VARIES, BUT THERE ARE common threads. Participants make a commitment to attend a series of classes on *chinuch habannim*. (Some of these last for ten sessions, while others are once a week for a year or more.) Most classes seem to be organized for mothers, but there are courses for fathers or couples as well. Principles of *chinuch* are presented and discussed, with an emphasis placed on real-life situations and problem-solving techniques. The participants bring up practical questions and feel that they can contact their teachers with more personal situations.

Rabbi Zecharya Greenwald, principal of Me'ohr Bais Yaakov Seminary in *Yerushalayim*, has presented a number of ten-session *chinuch habannim* classes to couples in a separate-seating format.[2] "When there is a problem, everyone comes running," says Rabbi Greenwald, "but here we have parents who come because they are interested in learning the skills of the *chinuch* profession. These couples experience a positive change in the home environment and *chinuch* becomes more of a focus. In general, parents are so busy that they don't discuss *chinuch* strategies; but once they invest time in a series of *shiurim*, they begin to discuss childrearing more."

---

2. Rabbi Greenwald has recently prepared a series of ten tapes titled "Preparing Your Child for Success," available through Feldheim Publishers.

Rabbi Noach Orlowek is another *Yerushalayim* resident who has long been in the foreground of education for parents. He is the author of *My Child, My Disciple,* among other works, and serves as a consultant and guide for many parents. He conducts an eighteen-session parenting class for men, requiring their wives to hear the tapes of all the sessions and come to every fourth class in place of their husbands to discuss what they learned from the tapes. Rabbi Orlowek's sessions are run like workshops, involving role-playing and problem-solving. He believes that these workshops "encourage parents to believe in their own capabilities to handle most situations." Rabbi Orlowek is also in the process of organizing a new project to promulgate these workshops.

Rebbetzin Fruma Altusky and Rebbetzin Sima Spetner each give many workshops weekly for women. They are both education professionals and experienced mothers. (Rebbetzin Altusky is a grandmother and great-grandmother, as well.) Although they have different styles, they both present *hashkafos* and also practical situations, stressing that solutions do exist and guiding their participants to finding these solutions based on the principles they have learned. The need to strengthen *bitachon* and to *daven* for *siyata diShmaya* are underlying themes of all the sessions, and the participants value these classes and their teachers, viewing them as role models and resources available for questions. Rebbetzin Spetner has also created an organization called *Toras Emecha* that has several experienced *mechanchim* available to answer questions by telephone on many topics.

A Successful Workshop

REBBETZIN ALTUSKY HAS A LOYAL FOLLOWING WHO ATTEND her *shiurim* year after year. Rabbi Orlowek fills his sessions quickly, and Rebbitzen Spetner has a long waiting list to join her workshops. Wherein lies the success of these workshops?

Seminars on Raising Children / 171

Word spreads that these *chinuch habannim* classes bring success, giving parents proper focus, instilling confidence, presenting concrete principles that they can integrate into their lives, and creating a support system. Parents see that their problems are not unique. After attending a workshop, either they can find solutions to their problems on their own or they have access to resource people who can help.

Focus

People often react automatically without focusing on the consequence of their actions. Parenting is a responsibility that warrants much thought and deliberation, not just automatic reactions. Rabbi Wolbe (in the introduction to his *sefer, Building and Planting*) calls education a science that "cannot be mastered after a bit of casual consideration or by depending on one's hunches."

> *If wise guy Yossie's parents had been to a chinuch habannim workshop, they might have realized that they were responding to Yossie with annoyance instead of working to improve the situation. Hopefully, they would take the time to discuss Yossie's behavior. How long had this been going on? What would motivate Yossie to comply with his parents' wishes? Was his behavior a ploy to attract attention? Focusing on Yossie and their reactions to his behavior will bring his parents to more productive interactions with their son.*

Confidence

Rebbetzin Altusky feels that many women lack confidence in themselves as mothers. The overwhelming task of childrearing becomes less frightening when tools are presented and situations are openly discussed. Rebbetzin Spetner prefers to begin with parents of small children, to help them start off right, but she stresses that it is never too late to learn new patterns.

> *If acquisitive Shani's mother had been to a parenting class, she would have not felt threatened as a parent just because her three-year-old had not yet learned the concept of property. She would calmly return the necklace the next day with an apology to the teacher, with her confidence as a parent intact. No one's child is perfect!*

Principles

Hearing principles of proper *chinuch* enunciated week after week and seeing how to integrate them into daily situations is beneficial to any parent.

> *Policeman Mendy's mother was able to cope with her son's alarming pronouncement. She remembered Rebbetzin Spetner saying again and again, "Talk to your children. Find out what they mean, and why they are acting in this fashion." When Mendy expressed a desire to kill, she asked, "Mendy, why do you want to kill people? Do you know what 'kill' means?"*
>
> *Mendy very innocently admitted that he had no idea what the concept of murder meant. He just knew it was something that policemen did, and he wanted to be a policeman. Mendy's mother allowed herself a smile as she sighed in relief and thankfulness that she had the tools to deal with the situation.*

Support System

We live in an age of isolation. Gone for many are the multi-generational family networks with grandparents and extended relatives as Torah role models sharing their experiences. People tend to struggle alone with the challenges that come their way, involved in their own lives, and not sharing with others. The workshop leaders become sources of encouragement and advice, but in addition to that, the members of the group become a support system for each other. Sharing situations and hearing that others have dealt with similar struggles and survived to tell the tale is a comfort. The give-and-take of the group setting allows parents to benefit from the experience of their peers, and enables them to give advice to others as well.

> Toby had come to dread Shabbos. She knew intellectually that Shabbos was meant to be the day of rest, but she could not look forward to much rest with four lively pre-school-aged children. Shabbos mornings in the wintertime were particularly difficult since her husband was in shul and the children grew restless in their small apartment.
>
> She shared her problem at a chinuch habannim workshop, and she soon found that she was not alone. She was tipped off with a few plans of action — all provided by group members and not the group leader. Toby herself came up with a few ideas once she began to see that she was not trapped in the current situation.
>
> In addition to new strategies on how to entertain her children, Toby picked up a new attitude. Her friend Miriam, whose children were a bit older, assured her that things would improve, and her oldest would begin entertaining the younger children before she knew it. Every Shabbos morning Toby woke up and said to herself, "Miriam said this stage will pass." This comforting thought, along with a few ideas to structure activities for the children, helped lift her mood and made the time pass more quickly.

The Teachers

WHILE THE CONCEPT OF A *CHINUCH HABANNIM* WORKSHOP is new, the concept of turning to *chachamim* for guidance and advice is integral to our heritage. The source of the success of these workshops is in the personality and knowledge of the educators who have systematically worked through the Torah concepts in the topic of *chinuch habannim,* and all their teachings are solidly rooted in *mesores avoseinu.* They turn to *gedolim* for clarification and the participants know that they are hearing proper *hashkafos.* The educators are seen as experts in the field of *chinuch habannim* and satisfied parents spread their name. The enthusiasm of parents is their best *haskamah* (endorsement).

The Ministry of Education in Israel has recognized the benefits of workshops and has even created a license called *"manchah horim."* *"Manchot,"* parenting workshop leaders, are trained in special institutes. They go through a structured course of four years of study, five hours a week, which focuses on the concepts of parenting as well as in workshop leadership. In addition to the secular Israeli institutes, there is one institute that trains *frum* women to be *manchot* – *Machon Hachareidi L'hachsharat Manchot Horim* (The Chareidi Institute for Training of Parenting Group Leaders).

Mrs. Devorah Speyer, recent graduate of the Institute and current workshop leader, attributes her ability to successfully lead workshops to the training she received in the Institute and its unique series of courses. They taught her to help foster in a mother "a responsible confidence in her own motherly strengths." In Mrs. Speyer's words, the workshops help a woman "look inside herself and develop her own unique pattern, as she simultaneously finds the strength and understanding needed to carry it through."

Other workshop leaders, such as Rebbetzin Spetner, have not gone through training at the Institute. She perceived a need to begin giving workshops when neighbors came to her and pleaded with her to share from her expertise in *chinuch habannim.* Since she had many years experience in *chinuch,* as well as professional educational training, she was able to glean from her experience and knowledge and formulate a course in a workshop format.

Rebbetzin Altusky is herself one of the earliest graduates of the Institute, and she has continued training in various areas of specialization with the Institute over the past twenty years, even as she employs her own unique style of presenting a *shiur* on the *parshah* with emphasis on *hashkafos* which relate to parenting.

The Participants

PARTICIPANTS IN WORKSHOPS COME FROM A VARIETY OF backgrounds. Many of them are graduates of our finest Bais Yaakovs and *yeshivos*. They are parents of children age 2 to 20, learning techniques for dealing with every age child.

In addition to his other workshops, Rabbi Greenwald has organized a *chinuch habannim* class for the students of his seminary, believing that it is not too early to give young women the basic tools necessary to be a parent. "Believe in your children, show them that you love them, pay attention to your children, find a balance between structure and freedom, never discipline through anger...." These and other concepts are covered throughout the year, with the hope that these students will integrate these principles into daily life when they become parents.

The Teenage Years

EVEN EXPERIENCED, CONFIDENT PARENTS ARE OFTEN TAKEN by surprise when their pleasant child becomes a teenager. They need to hear that their challenges are not unique. How do you deal with *chutzpah*? When should you come down with a strong hand, and when should you ignore an infraction? What is your child really trying to convey with his behavior? Is he or she only testing and how do I deal with it?

Most of workshops are for parents of small children, but often parents of teenagers need guidance, too. At this stage, hopefully parents have already internalized the basic tools of parenting and have confidence in their abilities. They know to listen to their children and can help them through their teenage years. Still, parents should feel they have someone they can turn to for clarification.

Rebbetzin Cohen thought that it was more than a coincidence that she was asked about the same topic twice in one week. The women who approached her were very different indeed, but they had one thing in common – they were both parents of daughters. Mrs. Aronoff was a divorced *baalas teshuva,* while Mrs. Schwartz was happily married and of a well-established rabbinic family. Their question: How should I deal with my daughter and *tzenius*? Where do I put my foot down and where do I let her be like her friends? Mrs. Schwartz had an 11-year-old and wanted to be a proactive mom, and Mrs. Aronoff was facing some real challenges with her 14-year-old. Rebbetzin Cohen, after *davening* for *siyata diShmaya* that her advice would be beneficial, gladly gave of her time to discuss teenagers and *tzenius* with each of these women, stressing the importance of instilling pride as a *Bas Yisrael,* recommending that the mothers help their daughters realize that they were up against a difficult test, and encouraging the mothers to be their daughter's ally and support and not to jeopardize her relationship with their daughter.

Rebbetzin Cohen was truly gratified to hear, over a year later, that Mrs. Aronoff's daughter was "doing beautifully." Mrs. Schwartz, too, expressed appreciation for the guidance and guidelines.

New Tools

WHY IS THERE SUCH A CONCERTED EFFORT TO EDUCATE parents in this current age? Our great-grandparents were never encouraged to sit through parenting classes.

Rabbi Greenwald points out that modern life is full of challenges that did not exist years ago. Families are larger, with less multigenerational support systems. The school systems have become more competitive and demanding, and the pressure to succeed is intense. Stresses of modern life, economic and otherwise, and negative influences from the outside world are overpowering. Is it any wonder that parents need more tools to raise their children when the external society is totally contrary to our value system?

Rebbetzin Spetner, quoting Rabbi Wolbe, explains that the situation today is different than in previous generations. People have less ability to tolerate a strong approach than they used to, and more focus must be given to building a relationship between parents and children.

There is a need to educate parents in the use of new, productive tools, and give them the confidence to raise the next generation of *Klal Yisrael*.

The *chinuch* of our children is our privilege and our responsibility. In Torah communities in Israel, parents who perceived the need to learn more about their crucial *tafkid* asked *mechanchim* for *shiurim* on *chinuch habannim*. These *chinuch shiurim* and workshops are now attended by hundreds of parents who wish to properly equip them to raise the next generation of *Klal Yisrael*. What about Jewish parents in the rest of the world? There are qualified resource people and *mechanchim* in every Torah community who can offer the same types of *shiurim*, *shiurim* which will benefit all those who care about their children's futures.

A Mother's Reflections

Shiffy Lichter

I brace myself as I stand
At the entrance of my children's land
They call it playroom—but to me
It's a corner for confessions, and I'm the returnee.

The room's empty, now—and I sigh
Not for the work ahead
But for another day gone by.
And you children now sleep so peacefully
while I'm picking up the pieces—not mechanically,
'Cause my heart now aches for those tiny wisps of time
The millions of moments that never reached their prime.
Every minute I heard you—yet I didn't hear
'Cause I didn't pause to show you
How much I really care.

Like when you, my precious four-year-old, so perfectly pug-nosed
Another silly question to your harried mother posed.
How amazing that I can so clearly recall.
"Why did Tati pick the green and purple ball?"
The answer I gave you came so flat and dry.
"Probably that was the only one left to buy."
 Now I hear you so much better, now I'm tired no more,
Now your whole being fills mine with awe.

I could've then taken the moment—don't I have the art
To put smiles in my little boy's heart
With words like "Tati must've decided to buy just such
Because he knows his little boy
Loves those colors so much?"

I can say it now but you're asleep
And cannot hear
And I didn't pause to show you
How much I really care.

Now I'm throwing the green and purple ball into its box
And it's so heavy, like I'd be lifting rocks
Because my heart aches for the tiny wisps of time
The millions of moments that never reached their prime

I bend down for a crumpled piece of creation
That should have brought my little girl untold elation.
I'm making it out now—I see hands, feet and eyes.
Oh, if I'd have told you, "Sweetie, this picture could win a prize."

I can say it now but you're asleep
And cannot hear
And I didn't pause to show you
How much I really care.

In the corner of the room, so humble and ashamed
A green and white notebook lies as if it's sad and maimed.
Inside this little book more precious than pearls
Are endless rows of A-B-C's—and it's my little girl's.
I was frying onions when you flung this in my face
And I said, 'I'll see it later," with so little motherly grace.
I didn't stop to tell you that I'm more proud than ever
'Cause every single letter looks so crisp and clever.

I hug your notebook now, gently make the pages smooth.
But you, my precious one, may never know this truth
Because although I say it now, I know you cannot hear
And I didn't pause to show you then how much I really care.

The phone screamed for attention exactly when
We were together playing our favorite one-to-ten.
Your faces dropped when I reached to say Hello,
And your laughing eyes suddenly lost their glow.
It seems so simple now to think clear and straight
And say, "When I'm playing with my kinderlach, everything must wait."

I can say it now but you're asleep
And cannot hear
And I didn't pause to show you
How much I really care.

So now you sleep so peacefully, and dream the sweetest dreams
And precisely here, and precisely now—to spite me, it seems
I'm fully awake — really ready this time
To make a million moments reach their prime.

⇸ *Chinuch* **Concerns**

Teacher and Parent: A Spiritual Partnership

The New Horizon in Education

School and Home: Partners or Adversaries

Of Growth and Belonging

Some Kids on the Brink Can Be Saved

Teacher and Parent: A Spiritual Partnership

Rabbi Shmuel Dishon

⇌ The Basis of the Partnership

THE GOAL OF *CHINUCH* — TORAH EDUCATION — IS, TO PUT IT simply, to prepare the Jewish child for a life that exemplifies "*Yisgadal V'yiskadash Shmeih Rabba*" — the sanctification of G–d's Name. The Torah is quite specific in directing us in how to achieve this: "*V'shinantom livanecha* — and you shall teach them (i.e., the words of Torah) to your sons" (*Devarim* 6:7). The Talmud derives from this passage that it is incumbent upon every father to teach his son Torah. The mother's role is to create an environment in the home that nurtures commitment to Torah encouraging the child to maintain whatever Torah instruction he receives.

For generations this system worked, but during the time of the *Mishnah*, it became apparent that some children were falling by the wayside: some who had no fathers, and others whose fathers were incapable of teaching them Torah. To deal with such cases, Rabbi Yehoshua ben Gamla established a *cheder* in each city. This became so accepted amongst Jewry that a community that fails to establish a *cheder* to instruct the young is subject to *cherem* — excommunication.

If for some reason all the *melamdim* would decide that they are no longer going to teach, the *halachah* would demand that no father go to work, but instead teach his son Torah. Today's system, then, is one of partnership — a partnership that results from the father establishing the *rebbi* as his *shaliach,* his agent, to perform his task of educating his child.

⇥ Parent by Proxy

A friend and I were discussing issues in *chinuch*. In the course of the conversation, I asked him (he is in home construction), "How do you go about building a house?"

He answered that first a contract must be drawn up, and for that purpose each party brings his own lawyer.

I interrupted him, "Why do you need a lawyer? You know the owner — he's your friend! You both attended yeshiva and studied Torah together. Don't you trust each other?"

He answered, "Building a new house can be a matter of a half a million dollars. You must read all the fine print in the contract. You can't just sit down and sign an agreement."

I then returned to our earlier subject, and asked him, "Do you know how your son is doing in yeshiva? Did you see your son's *rebbi* this year?"

He replied, "Well, PTA is next week."

This man has entrusted his son to a *rebbi* for six hours a day, every day of the week, and should they pass each other on the street, they may greet each other, without either realizing that the one is the other's *shaliach* — his emissary to equip his son for a life of Torah and *mitzvos*. Never mind engaging a lawyer to read the fine print!

Now, a parent generally recognizes that he has neither the time, the energy, nor the expertise to perform his G–d-given tasks of educating his son the way the *rebbi* is doing it for him. He should also realize that a *rebbi* leads a different type of existence, in both his *bein adam lachaveiro* (affairs between man and his fellow), and his *bein adam lamakom* (service to G–d). His actions, hopefully, even in the innermost chamber of his home, are elevated because he knows that he is charged with carrying the Torah within him, and that he is serving as a modern-day counterpart to Moshe *Rabbeinu,* teaching Torah to his generation's children. As such, he should earn the father's trust, and if so, the father should be deeply indebted to him.

➣ Trouble in Paradise

Unfortunately, real life does not follow this idyllic scenario. First of all, we are all victims of World War II, which has brutally cut us off from earlier generations and the immediacy of their experiences. So here we are, in a country with no *mesorah* (no precise tradition) of its own and yet a multitude of *mesoros*. Each *mesorah* — real or perceived — pulls in a different direction. On the first day of school in a typical *yeshiva ketanah*, a *rebbi* looks at the twenty-five children (if not more) in his classroom, assuming the role of *shaliach* for twenty-five sets of parents, each with his (and her) own vision of how the *talmid* should develop. In the small *shtetl* of old, regardless of any problems, at least everyone — the father, the *rebbi*, the *rav* — were all adherents of the same *derech*... a far cry from the standard American yeshiva, where if the *rebbi* is serving one set of parents faithfully, he might well be "betraying" twenty-four others (and some times twenty-four-and-a-half).

Moreover, most *rebbis* are also surrogate fathers, for it is in them that children confide, sharing their problems and joys. Most parents do not really know their children. The pressures of life today are so great that in more homes than ever before both parents are forced to work, and the first to feel the pinch of the demands on their time are the children. Some parents appreciate whatever the *rebbi* does for their child, and recognize when he's doing even more than is required of him. It is he (or she) who is *melamed Torah*, and often it is he (or she) who is creating the environment to foster Torah growth — both assignments that devolved originally upon the parents.

Consequently, something quite normal will often take place. The father who has such high hopes for his son suddenly realizes that he is slowly losing control over him. He states an opinion, or a *pshat,* and the son protests, "But that's not what my *rebbi* said...."

The father thinks, *What do you mean "your rebbi said"? Where am I in this scene?* An air of competition sets in, for the parent feels that the *rebbi* has usurped his control over the child. His feelings are understandable. But so is the situation. Compare the father who spends (at most) an hour a day with his son, with the *rebbi* who is with the *talmid* six hours a day, teaching him, guiding him, and — if he has a touch of charisma — exciting him over his own *derech* — his own approach to serving G–d! This can breed tension and trigger serious problems. Instead of permitting this potentially adversarial relationship to fester, it should be defused, and cooperation should be fostered.

For starters, parents should become more involved with their children, discuss the day's events and share their opinions with them. Some homes, even with only a few children, can suffer from a lack of communication. Staggering under the pressures of daily life, many parents cannot muster the patience to listen to their children... . All the more reason to appreciate that the *rebbi* does manage to cope with his twenty-five charges!

⇒ Defusing Tension Through Communication

The starting point in any cooperative venture is communication, and the relationship between the parent and the *rebbi* (teacher) is no exception. As a matter of fact the *rebbi's* (or teacher's) specific task with each child could be more clearly defined to the benefit of all concerned, if the parents make a point of meeting the *rebbi* before the term starts, and maintain regular contact throughout the schoolyear. When the *rebbi* is apprised of any special situations, problems can be avoided, or at least be dealt with successfully. When the father and the *rebbi* appreciate that they both are working for the same goal, the spirit of competition tends to fade away. In addition, the child will see their concern over his welfare, and will try to measure up to their expectations.

Since family backgrounds are so divergent nowadays, differences between the school and the home are almost inevitable. Through open channels between the home and the school, these differences will be better understood, and if not resolved, they will at least be treated respectfully — and after all, the father and the *rebbi* know each other as real people, not as phantom figures.

Open disagreement, then, will also surface; but often, not enough thought is given to how and where these opinions should be expressed. When the child comes home and says, "The *rebbi* said...," and the father takes exception to that approach, he should not state his opinion to the child. It would be far more proper and productive if he were to call up the *rebbi* and ask him what he had said, and discuss it with him personally. By the same token, if a *rebbi* hears the child report, "My father said...," instead of reacting then and there, he would be wise to contact the father and speak to him directly. The problem would thus be mitigated rather than blown up out of proportion, as is so often the case.

The Unspoken Messages

Another factor in promoting harmony between the school and the home is *hashpaah* — indirect influence, in contrast to *chinuch* — teaching. *Hashpaah* comes from the word *shipuah* — slant. Just as rain falling on a slanted roof will then pour down on whoever is standing beneath its edge, so too do parents' attitudes rain down on those beneath their "eaves." In past years, fathers imbued their children with a sense that their life's goal was to be an *ehrlicher Yid*. Without hearing one word spoken on the topic, the child saw how his father was *moser nefesh* for Torah, how he worked heart and soul for the yeshiva he attended. In out-of-town communities, this type of devotion is still evident, for committed parents work with supreme sacrifice and dedication for their local yeshiva. Parents in larger communities, however, tend to take their yeshivos for granted. Worse yet, a father may boast within earshot of his children how he was able to run circles around the tuition committee and avoid its "outrageous demands." The children receive a host of spoken and unspoken messages, and will either follow their parents' lead and not take a serious interest in their school, or reject their parents' values and influence. It becomes a matter of either/or.

The school and the house are meant to be partners. Through effective and open lines of communication — talking to each other, understanding each other, and working together — they can be true *shutfim* in one of life's most important missions: raising a generation dedicated to Torah and *mitzvos*.

The New Horizon in Education

Rabbi Shimon Schwab זצ"ל

⤖ Parents and Schools — Mutually Dependent, Mutually Enriching

EVERY JEWISH CHILD HAS THE INBORN RIGHT, THE DIVINE privilege and the inherent need for the *D'var Hashem* (word of G–d), whether he or she was born into a *shomrei mitzvah* family, or not.

The Torah entrusts the teaching of *Yiddishkeit* to father and mother, but even the best of parents cannot do a complete job and carry out their sacred mandate without a Torah school and capable Torah teachers. Parents who expect the best kind of education for their sons and daughters can do very little without the proper school. Yet even the best school will accomplish next to nothing without the cooperation of the parents. A day school, a yeshiva or Bais Yaakov School can impart knowledge and, if it is a good school, the *rebbei'im* and *mechanchim* and *mechanchos* (teachers) could and should serve as role models inspiring their students with *yiras Shamayim* and *middos tovos*, but only as long as the parents do not interfere. If they do, the most devoted *mechanech* or *mechaneches* is rendered helpless and his or her influence borders on impotence. There is an oft-quoted saying: "One flippant remark can negate a hundred words of reproof"—

meaning in our case, that one off-color joke, one foul and unclean word, one *apikorsische* remark from the mouth of a father or mother can undo hundreds of hours of Torah learning and inspiration towards *yiras Shamayim*. Unfortunately, not all parents are equipped with the requisite knowedge to help their children, nor are they all sensitive to what should be said and what utterances would best be left unsaid.

What we urgently need, then, is to add a new dimension to our *chinuch* system, that we may call, for lack of a better term, *Chinuch Hahorim*—parents' education.

⤏ A Syllabus for the Frum Family

For the sake of clarity, we first must differentiate between children from Torah-observant families, and those who were not born to that privilege. As far as *frum* parents are concerned, their education would entail the following agenda (advancing from the simple to the more complicated):

Number 1. A *shiur* for fathers once a week to prepare them to *farherr*, or examine, their sons on the blatt *Gemara* and/or the *parsha* of *Chumash* that they are studying. The same applies to the *Mishnayos* and *Nach* that they currently are studying in school.

Number 2. It is most essential that a series of *shiurim* for parents in the *halachos* of *mitzvos shebein adam lechaveiro* (interpersonal commands) be scheduled. The bookstores are full of excellent *sefarim* in Hebrew and English that could be recommended, such as *Kitzur Hilchos Lashon Hara*, by Rabbi Kalman Krohn, or *Halichos Olam—Kitzur Dinim Bein Adam LeChaveiro*, by Rabbi Avrohom Ehrman, and Rabbi Zelig Pliskin's classic books, among many others.

Number 3. The syllabus should include a friendly, but soul-stirring *mussar shmuess* once a week on such subjects as *Emes* vs. *Shekker, Hakaras Hatov* vs. Ingratitude, the various aspects of *gemillus chessed,* and the avoidance of *lashon hara* (gossip) and *sinas chinam* (baseless hatred). Most important, parents should periodically hear *divrei hisorerus* (inspirational talks) to help them develop a reverential attitude towards *limud haTorah* (Torah study) and *lomdei haTorah* (Torah students); *hisorerus* to *yiras Shamayim* in general, and *kavanas hatefillah* (the meaning of prayer) in particular. If fathers and mothers rise to a higher level of spirituality, it cannot fail to rub off on their children.

Number 4. The most complicated subject in this syllabus is the science of "parenting": how to be parents. This means instruction by an expert on pedagogy, who will impart the skills and share the wisdom needed to become understanding parents to one's children. Remember, these *shiurim*, or lectures, are recommended for *frum* families. The result would be a generation of respectful, courteous children, without *chutzpah*, without arrogance. As we said before, this is only one side of the picture.

⇢ For Families of More Modern Bent

A completely different approach is required for fathers and mothers who are either ignorant of Torah altogether, which is usually not their own fault, and for parents who may call themselves "Modern Orthodox," ranging from those who just abhor the black-hatted *"Yeshivishe"* atmosphere, to those who are filled with doubts on *emunah* in general, and on *emunas chachamim* in particular, and whose minds are infected with attitudes that are alien to the concept of *daas Torah*.

While the first type of *chinuch hahorim*, geared for *frum* parents, should be under the tutelage of a *talmid chacham*, the second type, which we are discussing now, calls for a competent, experienced *kiruv* professional, who must be a *ben Torah* also, and a strong *yorei Shamayim*, but also must be imbued with unlimited *savlanus* (patience), and possess a heart overflowing with *ahavas Yisrael*.

This second type of parental instruction would begin with the teaching of basic halachos of *Shabbos, Yom Tov, Kashrus*, and so forth. This would be followed by discussions on fundamental *hashkafos*, such as *Torah min Hashamayim, s'char v'onesh* (Divine reward and punishment), *Yud Gimmel Ikrim* (Rambam's Thirteen Principles of Faith), and so forth.

Thirdly, it should include rudiments of actual Torah learning, which means portions of *Kitzur Shulchan Aruch*, *Parshas Hashavua*, some *Mishnayos*, and so on.

⤖ Reaching for New Horizons

This syllabus probably sounds too ambitious to be taken seriously. It means that every yeshiva, or every Jewish day school would have to add a "Parents' Department" to its structure—most probably in the form of evening sessions. And the staff would include a professional "Parent Outreach Coordinator," ranking equally in importance to the *rebbei'im* and the principal, with the primary assignment of working with parents. Parents Outreach is indeed a new horizon. Concern would reach beyond the school days of the week. Very often, parents would be invited, together with their children, to join faculty members or Outreach Professionals for *Shabbos* meals. It would also mean that the school have a hand in selecting summer camps for their students. And it would entail similar efforts to win the parents over to a commitment to Torah, especially employing personal visits to the parents, and an ongoing contact with them on a one-to-one basis.

Everybody knows that this is a strange world in which we live. Among other things, we are part of a generation in which, on the one hand, parents lose their children, ח"ו, as we read in the *Tochachah*: "You will have children, but they will not belong to you." On the other hand, we have the very opposite situation in which children excel over their parents in Torah knowledge and *dikduk bamitzvos* (care in *mitzvah* performance). We all know that the parents of our generation have lost much of the authority that the senior generation took for granted when we were young. And very often children have gained power and influence over their parents, contrary to our experience in the past.

This new shift of power need not be an unmitigated disaster. For argument's sake, if a child refuses to join his parents in viewing television, the parents will eventually have to pull the plug from the *klei mashchis* (destructive influence) for the sake of the child's company. If children refuse to enter a *shul* that lacks a proper *mechitzah*, the parents, albeit reluctantly, will give in eventually. But this is only feasible if the parents are systematically disengaged from their ingrained attachment to their assimilated lifestyles, and from the distorted ideas that they constantly absorb from controversial teachers, from the wrong books and periodicals, and from the so-called Jewish media. We believe that parents who send their children to a Torah school deserve something better than the anti-Torah blitz to which they are subjected. This means to be enlightened "*b'meor haTorah*"—with the light of Torah. We also believe that Torah Umesorah, whenever possible, should provide these services. If we strive to make our youth become *ovdei Hashem*, we must first conquer the hearts of their fathers and mothers.

Let us not forget that Eliyahu *Hanavi* does not come only to return "*lev banim al avosam*—the heart of the children to the fathers," but also "*lev avos al banim*—the hearts of the fathers to their children (*Malachi* 3:24)."

If we so will it, all this is not just a dream. If we so will it, Torah Umesorah's "Parent Enrichment Program" could plant a seed.[1] And if we do mean it seriously, we will be *mispallel* that this seed will take root and sprout, grow and bear fruit.

---

1. At this writing, forty-five communities across the continental United States have launched some form of host Parent Enrichment Programs, directed by Rabbi Eli Gewirtz of Torah Umesorah.

School and Home: Partners or Adversaries?
Rabbi Yaakov Reisman

⇝ Choosing — Conforming

THERE ARE DIFFERENT TYPES OF YESHIVOS, DIFFERENT TYPES of homes, different communities with different people from different walks of life, each with a unique style, its own strengths and weaknesses.

In most large metropolitan areas, parents have a choice as to which school to send their son or daughter. So they carefully question friends and neighbors about the schools their children attend. They speak to *menahalim* and *rebbei'im,* principals and teachers, generally selecting a school that most closely reflects their goals and values, a school that will project and reinforce those values to their children, and shield them from corrosive influences. For instance, some schools will not accept children from homes that have televisions. Some prohibit the student body from attending sports events or going to the movies. Some prohibit the student body from reading library books and popular magazines. On the other hand, some schools do not screen applicants but seek to influence their students to be selective on their own. But each school does set a standard that it seeks either to enforce or to imbue its students with.

Having carefully researched and then chosen the school

that best reflects their commitment, parents expect the teachers to instill in their children the sensitivity and commitment that will guide them, and protect them from negative influences. This is what parents expect and should get from the school. And if the school does not deliver, there are, generally, channels through which they can register their disappointment. But what about the home?

The home could be a place of reinforcement, or it might be a source of conflict and confusion. For instance: What will the child think when his parents, or anyone else at home, violates restrictions he was taught to honor in school? What does a daughter think when she picks up the novel her mother is reading, which would make Mommy blush if she knew that it was found? What does a son think of his father who skips a *shiur* (Torah class) or fails to *daven Minchah/Maariv* in *shul* because he must watch an "important" program on television? The very things he was taught not to do.

A girl is taught a standard of *tznius* (personal modesty) both in the physical sense — to dress properly at home and away and in the abstract sense — to be refined and subdued in both manner and dress. What does she think of her mother who seems oblivious to the rules she must abide by?

The son is taught *zehirus b'mitzvos* — care in *mitzvah* observance: not to talk during *davening*, to have *derech eretz* for *talmidei chachamim*, awe for *gedolim, rebbei'im, menahalim*. What does he witness when he goes to *shul* with his father? What are his father's topics of conversations en route to and from *shul* — or *in shul*? How does he speak about his *Rav* or the "other" *Rav*, or about *Roshei Yeshiva* and *Rebbes*? Should there, indeed, be a sincere difference in *shitah* (ideology) between different leaders and their groups, is the child mature enough to understand it as such? Does the father speak about his son's yeshiva, *menahel* and *rebbi* with deference?

Admittedly, parents may be aiming higher for their children than they do for themselves. But the question still must be asked: In sum, do parents' actions reflect the standards of the school, or do they challenge them? How do the children perceive the two, as partners or adversaries?

Black Stains, Whitewash

The parents' mode of conduct can have even further ramifications in terms of how it influences their children. Human nature is such that one never views himself as having done wrong. The *yeitzer hara* (evil inclination) somehow provides us with a rationale for everything we do. "In this situation," "under such circumstances" it's really permitted.

Parents may thus find easy justification for the occasional trip to the movies, "selective" use of VCR's, a junket to Atlantic City (glatt Kosher, of course), all sorts of books and magazines, missing *tefillos* in *shul*.

But what is the message the young, astute mind gets? Compromise? Excuses? "I do what I like and don't do what I dislike"? Attitudes like these can be carried further into *kashrus*, as well as other areas of *issur* and *hetter*, the prohibited and the permitted, and children will infer that not every command is meant for all people at all times.

Furthermore, parents can teach children to be dishonest, without ever uttering a false word. This is a message implicit in a *Gemara* in *Succah*.

> Reb Zeira said, "One should not tell a child, 'I will give you something,' and in the end not give it to him, for this will come to teach ... [the child] to lie. As the *pasuk* states, 'You will teach their tongues to speak lies.'"

On the surface, this *Gemara* seems puzzling. Is it only prohibited to break a promise *to a child*? Are broken promises *to an adult* permitted? In addition, why does the *Gemara* cite a *pasuk* in *Tanach* (Prophets) to prohibit teaching lies, ignoring the *pasuk* in the Torah: "*Midvar sheker tirchak* — Distance yourself from falsehood"?

One might assume from this that the *Gemara* is not dealing with an outright lie. A promise spoken, but not fulfilled, is not yet a lie. Since no falsehood was said, or even implied, "*Midvar sheker tirchak*" does not apply. [Or perhaps we are dealing with a type of lie that is permitted.] Reb Zeira teaches us that even in such cases, it is possible to be teaching our children to lie, by not yet having delivered on a promise. And imparting this type of message, even through indirection, must always be avoided. Yes, inconsistencies between implicit teachings and open behavior can teach a child dishonesty.

⇒ From the Subtle to the Overt — All That Money Can Buy

Until now we have mentioned subtle, passive ways that parents —by their actions or by their lack of them — can set examples for their children, contrary to what they have been taught by both the school and the home.

But there are other — more direct — influences.

As of late, *Klal Yisrael* has prospered and as a whole has become much more affluent than it has been within memory. This has brought with it a new set of lifestyles — and *nisyonos* (challenges): how we dress, how we live, what we eat, what we drive, and where we go on vacations.

Most of us would agree, at least in private, that these lifestyles have made tremendous inroads into our *Yiddishkeit*. We gradually have become more occupied with our material status than with our spirituality. We would welcome the school's intervention to vend off these alien lifestyles, but often fail to realize that, at the same time, we negate the school's teachings by the clothes our children wear, the cars we drive, the homes we live in.

To focus on one aspect of this affluence and its consequence: A debate is now in progress as to whether two full months of vacation in the summer is necessary or even healthy for our children. (A similar debate is currently taking place in some public school systems.) The consensus among *mechanchim* (educators) is that summer vacation is in fact too long and even detrimental to the children. But we are at the mercy of a host culture that designates July 4 to Labor Day as free time. The most we can do for our children is enroll them in summer camps, which is a stop-gap measure at best. Economic conditions limit the amount of time and the number of campers accommodated in this limited summer educational system.

We have yet to resolve this summer problem, while slowly we find creeping upon us the midwinter vacation. Spurred on by newfound affluence, people fly south for several weeks during the winter, and take their children with them. The direct impact on the child is missing school. The new things he will pick up there — Disney World, mixed swimming (Florida is not known for its separate beaches), a rich diet of happy hours in empty days — all will remain with the child for a long time. Even after he returns to the school physically, some time will pass before his mind will be there with him. These impressions, along with the message that school is expendable, will last a lifetime. At the same time, we have the distinction of introducing into *Klal Yisrael* a new trend and lifestyle, something we might be sorry for ever having started. Comes December, are school and home partners or adversaries?

The problem of extracurricular trips — whether or not approved by the school — is not confined to extended vacations trips, but includes all other expeditions and visits where parents directly violate school policy, regardless of their nature, whether entailing a visit to Bubby's house during schooltime, or a late-night *tisch* that results in a tardy arrival to school the next morning.

Unless the parent writes a note stating the truth, he has actively taught his child to be dishonest And should he write the truth, he teaches his child that school policies are made to be broken. The only exception is when the school genuinely believes that at certain times, for certain children, some activities are more important than routine classroom.

One would hope that the parents view the school's policies and attitudes as expressing their own attitudes as well.

⤳ Less Reward Than Effort

So far we have discussed important issues of *dei'os* and *middos* — attitudes and character — but have not touched on the learning process. Here, too, much can be said about the parents helping or hindering their child's scholastic achievement.

Consider: A *rebbi*/teacher trying his/her hardest, virtually giving of himself to teach your child. But your child is not responding either to your satisfaction or to that of his *rebbi*/teacher. The *rebbi*/teacher continues with his/her greatest effort. What is your reaction? Do you express your appreciation to him for his attempts at reaching your child? Are you being objective about your child? Or do you succumb to the subjectivity that parents tend to have for their offspring? *What! My son/daughter is not the best in the class? Can't be! Both I and my wife were at the top of our classes!* Or, *How could he be doing so poorly? All of his brothers and sisters were honor students! How could my nephew be doing better than my son?* Or, *How could my neighbor's son be better than my son? After all, I'm so much more intelligent than my neighbor — and a bigger talmid chacham, to boot! It must be the rebbi's/teacher's fault!*

It can take some parents quite a while before they finally recognize that perhaps nobody is at fault. Every child is different.

Consider, too, when a child is found to be learning disabled. Do parents realize how much *mechanchim* and *menahalim* research the child's capabilities and performance before arriving at such a conclusion? This is followed by the agony of facing parents and informing them. Once parents are told, their immediate reaction is, "*Can't be — not my child!* (That's not what I ordered!) How will I tell Zeidy and Bubby?" etc. But once the truth has had time to sink in, do the parents see to it that the child is taught whatever he or she can and should be taught, or do parents tend to ignore the stark facts (hoping they will go way), all this time putting their child through unnecessary hardships and difficulties to preserve their own endangered egos? Are they thankful for an honest evaluation, which can be helpful to their child, or are they quick to blame the school and staff for bumbling incompetence, and finding "an easy way out"?

When the parents and the school are partners, it is for every contingency.

More Than Money Can Buy

And then there is the Almighty Dollar. We want the best for our children. No compromises. That's how we were brought up and we wouldn't have it any other way with our children. The best of both worlds: The best Torah education along with the best secular education — and the best teachers for both. The building should be a half-decent structure, maintained well, with clean bathrooms and uncluttered corridors. We recognize that all this costs money, and we are willing to pay our share. *Or are we?*

After we return from that midwinter vacation, we decide to visit the school and make a reckoning. But on the way, we have to stop at the car dealer, because the old '84 doesn't look like it'll make it through another winter. And "I definitely have to keep my promise to my wife to redecorate. After all, it's already five years now with the old furniture. Besides, our older children will begin *shidduchim* soon, and the house must be presentable. Sure, I'll pay my share in tuition. But I just don't have the money, just right now."

Meanwhile. While you were away for two weeks, and then, on return, deeply involved in the pains of shopping and redecorating, a crisis developed in school. The cash flow got even tighter than before, and the yeshiva fell another month behind in payroll. Your son's *rebbi*, now two months behind on his meager salary, finds that he can't make ends meet. He exhausts all *gemach* (free loan) connections and comes back to the *hanhalah* (school administration) for help. The *hanhalah* assures him that they will rectify the situation as soon as possible, but the prime movers in the parent body have not returned from vacation.

Your son's class isn't covered for two days and the grapevine has it that his *rebbi* could not hold out any longer, and left suddenly.

Now you really fume: "What! This *rebbi* for whom I've waited for three years so my son will finally have him, gets up and leaves right in the middle of the year! Where is *yosher* (justice)? Where is *mesiras nefesh* (devotion)?"

You promise yourself, come what may, this Sunday you're going to visit the yeshiva to get to the bottom of this.

Sunday arrives, and you go to the yeshiva, directly into the *menahel's* office. You sit down opposite the *menahel* and look him straight in the eye, and declare, "This place is falling apart! And do you know why this place is falling apart? Because you can't hold on to good talent even when you have it!"

And so the parent has leveled with the school.

We have touched upon a number of points, which are perhaps unique to a large-city elementary school. High schools and out-of-town day schools and *chadarim* have their own peculiar challenges, which can be examined as parallels to those enumerated here, or can wait for their own day in the spotlight In any case, successful education is based on a partnership. And to be worthy partners, our home must be a *makom Torah*, a place of Torah. The Torah says: "Make for me a *mikdash* — a sanctuary — and I will dwell in *their midst*" (*Shemos* 25:8). *Chazal* point out that it does not say "in *its* midst" referring to the building, but rather "in *their* midst" — in the midst of each and every one of us. Ideally, the home should be the *makom mikdash* — a veritable sanctuary, and the school should be challenged to strive to keep up with the standard set by the home. Then the two will be partners, not adversaries.

Of Growth and Belonging

Rabbi Ahron Kaufman

A Unique Phenomenon

THE PURPOSE OF THIS ARTICLE IS TO IDENTIFY THE ROOT OF our dropout problem from the perspective of a yeshiva *rebbi*, and offer a practical approach to solving it.

In truth, the dropout problem is not confined to our youth. Everyone is at risk. The difference is that adults tend to be more set in their habits, and their lack of devotion is masked by habit. They will continue to go to *shul* and observe many *mitzvos*, but without putting their hearts into it. This is not what the Torah wants. A continuous and ongoing dedication is required of everyone, and these "observant" Jews actually serve as a microcosm of the dropout phenomenon. Judaism demands growth from people of all ages. It demands it, and it also nurtures it, because its very essence is growth. Therefore, anyone who departs from this – regardless of whether he is 7, 17, 27, or 70 – is at risk of dropping out.

What are the causes of the dropout phenomenon? Exposure to immorality, to alien cultures and values, and the overwhelming power of the mass media are some culprits. Certainly the overwhelming power of television, movies, and the Internet as corrupting forces cannot be ignored. But these are not the direct cause. In fact, after discussions with many teenagers, I have found that they are not rebelling against the Torah in favor of some other culture, as did the Hellenists. Rather these diversions have the power to fascinate and occupy them, intensifying their fall.

What, then, triggers this catastrophe? Some attribute this problem to dysfunctional, broken homes, feelings of oppression and depression. These can be causes of many problems, but do not on their own bring about rebellion against Torah. Historically and logically, these forces usually inspire people toward spiritual search. Thus the question is strengthened.

The question is further highlighted by a unique phenomenon: Never before as a people have we had so many individuals coming close to Torah, while at the same time, others are abandoning a Torah life. The remarkable *baal teshuvah* movement is growing every day. Paradoxically, the number of people growing up in religious homes who are walking away into emptiness is also increasing. What factors are present in our contemporary society that people could both be attracted and repelled at the same time?

"FOB" Vs. Genuine Judaism

THROUGHOUT THE *SIDDUR* — INDEED, DISTINGUISHING EVERY *tefillah* — is the phrase *"Elokeinu V'Elokei Avoseinu."* But nowhere do we find this phrase in its chronological order. Why is "Our G–d" placed before "The G–d of our fathers"? Where does my understanding of G–d come from, if not from the vast and resonant heritage that came before my arrival to this world?

"Elokeinu" is stated first because we cannot rely on those who came before us. If I stand smug and complacent – relying on the achievements of others – then I am not a participating Jew. The Torah wants it to be *"Elokeinu"* – my own G–d. My relationship to Hashem must be through my own journeys, my own struggles, my own discoveries, and my own accomplishments. My relationship to my Creator must be discovered, rediscovered, and reintensified on a daily basis. It must be my

own *avodah*. Only after I extend myself can my inheritance come to me. If I add my own work to the work of my fathers, then the achievements of my fathers will have relevance to me.

The common description of one who grew up in a religious household is "*Frum* From Birth," FFB. To be satisfied with one's Judaism simply as a lifestyle inherited from one's parents is not being "FFB." Rather it is "FOB," a Fact Of Birth. But this is not Judaism. *Hakadosh Baruch Hu* does not want genetically produced robots. To be raised by *yirei Shamayim* is indeed a great gift, but it is only meant to provide a boost to one's own achievements, not to replace them. To the contrary, living in the valley of habit is a great drawback to growth as a Jew. We are all familiar with too many people in our own circles who are mechanical Jews, performing *mitzvas anashim melumadah*. "*Elokeinu*" must precede "*Elokei Avoseinu*."

The reason why the *baal teshuvah* movement is expanding so prolifically is because the bankrupt, empty life in the secular society is driving the *baal teshuvah* to fill an inner void, to find a purpose and a need for his existence. This vacuity is anathema to him, and it becomes a spark that lights a fire, and that fire drives him ever onward.

Filling the Void

UNFORTUNATELY, WHEN SOME PEOPLE FEEL A VOID, THEY seek to fill it with things; with money, with possessions such as magnificent homes, luxury cars, designer clothing, state-of-the-art electronics, and (*Hashem yeracheim aleinu,*) with girls, drinking and drugs. People turn to these diversions because they do not know how to fill the void within. When a person is complacent in his Judaism, when the *davening* is by rote, and his *mitzvos* – and yes, even his Torah learning – are formulae punched in with the same level of involvement as a bank card's PIN code, he perceives himself as Jewish, but he has the urge to look elsewhere to find meaning, to find a reason to live.

How many of us or our children understand the meaning of

our *tefillos*? *Prayer without understanding cannot be prayer with heart. It will not bring any real connection with Hakadosh Baruch Hu.* How many of us or our children truly follow and understand *Krias HaTorah* and *Haftarah*? Is *Tanach* merely a handbook for *vertlach* and *drashos*, or is it the very basis of our existence?

Why is *Lashon Hakodesh* a foreign language? Our children sing *Zemiros*, whose words they don't comprehend. Is it a wonder why English music attracts them? Are we more excited about our vacations and do we derive more pleasure from our *divrei reshus* (religiously neutral activities) than from performing *mitzvos*? What confusing message are we sending to our children? Do we really comprehend the meaning of *Shabbos* and *Yomim Tovim* on a higher level than a grade-school child? Do we genuinely experience *oneg Shabbos*? Is our *Motzaei Shabbos* an honorable escort to the departing *Shabbos* or the antithesis of *kedushas Shabbos*? Can we logically convince an irreligious person to observe *Shabbos* or perform *mitzvos*? If we can't, is it a wonder why our children don't? So many American Jews are surviving Judaism, not living it.

This, then, is one of the causes of the crisis gripping our young people. They live in the shallowness – or, better said, the shallows – of American Jewry. They cannot understand their Judaism. If they do not understand, they cannot appreciate. If they do not appreciate, they cannot be enthusiastically involved, and it is not meaningful to them. If it is not meaningful, they are on their way to dropping out. *Dropping out is not our main enemy; superficiality and ignorance are.*

The Need to Belong

THERE IS ANOTHER SIDE TO THE COIN. EVERY HUMAN being has an extreme need to belong. It is a need that reaches deep into the human soul, and it grasps even at the most introverted of personalities. Yet, it does not even register in one's mind in an intellectual way any more than being hungry or tired, and therefore it frequently escapes conscious analysis. It is there, and it pulls at man, and it does not let go.

In the past, even nonreligious people identified themselves as being Jewish. They felt part of something greater than themselves. When a person does not find identity in his Judaism, he will look elsewhere. The *baalei teshuvah* realize that they have no identity in their original society, and therefore they seek their identity in the Torah. The painful reality today is that there are people in our own society, the society that *baalei teshuvah* are joining, who do not have this crucial need addressed in their lives and they look elsewhere.

Jewish identity can only come from feeling secure and comfortable in one's Judaism. If a person is not comfortable with being a Jew, or where he is as a Jew – in whatever community he lives, or yeshiva he attends – he loses a sense of identity and he will always seek to replace that loss. The popularity of national sports teams across the country can be attributed to this phenomenon.

These two forces – the lack of meaning and the lack of identity – feed off each other. If my life in my society has no meaning to it, I feel detached from that society, and I am no longer bound to it. On the reverse side, if I lack an identity in the society in which I live, then it will eventually become meaningless to me, as I seek to find a place where I feel I belong.

Many accurate points have been made regarding children who do not feel accepted by their parents, their peers, or their *rebbei'im*. A strong correlation exists between children from broken homes and dysfunctional families, children who are not part of the "in" crowd, children who were ejected from the classrom, and children who grow into adults and leave us. This lack of acceptance is real, and it is deadlier than can ever be imagined, but it is not the direct cause of the dropout problem. If a person is secure in his identity as a Jew, then he will not stop being a Jew because one segment of the Jewish populace does not accept him. While it is true that a lack of acceptance can cause a lack of identity, it is the lack of identity that causes the dropping out, not the lack of acceptance.

The Remedy

⤖ What it is not...

BEFORE OUTLINING A REMEDY, WE MUST RECOGNIZE WHAT the remedy is *not*. "Fun," in and of itself, in or out of yeshiva, will not solve the problem. In general, fun activities help us relax and temporarily forget our problems; they can even provide the basis for bonding, which offers a format for further *hashpaah*. But fun activities do not bring happiness. Happiness is an outgrowth of accomplishment, which comes as a result of effort — sometimes painful effort. Watering down Torah learning, making success easier and painless, is the dumbing down of our Judaism. Good PR cannot replace substance, and a person's *neshamah* will sense the difference. Merely telling someone that he is a good boy, and that you like him, without giving him basis to believe that you mean it, is a false injection of temporary self-esteem, and a cosmetic cover for a deeper problem. The voids of meaning and identity continue to plague him.

Among the numerous, unmotivated, and even motivated teens with a broad range of problems whom I've met, one common denominator is this lack of understanding of basic Judaism, its depth and warmth. They frequently ask, "What do I gain in this world from Judaism?" "How do I benefit from being *frum*?" They fail to feel secure in their Jewish identity and to realize that their existence matters. They yearn to be understood and long to understand as their souls' craving for meaning cries out deep inside them. When these issues are addressed, these teens' directional signal changes from downwards to upwards, and subsequently, their other obstacles can now be successfully dealt with.

⤖ ... And what it is

How can one find meaning, freshness, and vitality in actions that are repeated every day? The answer is through growth. In order for my Judaism to be new every day, it has

Of Growth and Belonging / 209

to be greater every day. It has to be something to which I can apply myself and can constantly feel attainment.

Growth is achieved through setting goals. When a person aspires towards something greater, his life has meaning. When he is part of something greater, his life has identity. *Those goals must be in Torah, for that is the essence of being Jewish.*

A teenager with goals in Torah, who identifies with a yeshiva or community, is protected from the obstacles of the world. He spiritually nourishes himself from the wellspring of Torah. A teenager without these goals will become a teenager without growth, and eventually without identity. Such a life is spiritually empty, and is the breeding ground for the rebellion and misery of our troubled youth. A sense of true purpose and value is what will give meaning to our children and will keep them from the emptiness that fills their world. (Of course, we can insert the word "adult" in place of "teenager," and "ourselves" in place of "children," and the above paragraph will be equally true.)

We have to imbue our children with the recognition that we are the "*Am Segulah.*" We are special, and therefore different. We must convey to them a deep feeling of Jewish pride. There is no greater loss to the son of the king than robbing him of his identity – that is, not explaining to him who he is, his responsibilities and privileges. *Mitzvos* take on a different dimension when we view them in this context. They are opportunities to be utilized and cherished. Torah becomes life's handbook. For years, the *Sefer HaChinuch* and *Taamei HaMitzvos* were taught to children at the *Shabbos* table, teaching them the reasons for *mitzvos*. Understanding leads to appreciation.

There are many areas to discover and learn, and the excitement and fufillment generated by *Chumash Be'iyun, Navi, Kesuvim,* Jewish History, *Hashkafah, Halachah, Mussar,* and other topics are real, and true to the essence of Torah. Many successful *bnei Torah* in *Beis Midrash* allocate time in their daily schedules to learn these topics. We should encourage our children to discover these topics earlier, to spend their free time exploring them. It is fertile ground for building up Jewish pride and understanding, and it fills free time with stimulating and engrossing challenges.

Crowding the Schedule, Touching the Source

OUR TEENS ARE FACED WITH MUCH UNSTRUCTURED TIME. IF their time is not filled with something positive, it will be filled with negative influences. Friday afternoon, *Shabbos*, *Motzaei Shabbos* and Sunday afternoon allow too much freedom. The momentum of the previous week's growth is lost and they begin a new week at a deficit. It is worthwhile to implement a system whereby older *bachurim* spend time with younger boys. It benefits both groups. The younger boys have an opportunity to learn and gain from older role models. They will relate and open up to them, providing positive peer pressure. At the same time, older *bachurim* learn and grow as they guide others. Nothing creates a sense of self-satisfaction like being needed and giving to others: The greatest gift that one can give and *chessed* that one can perform is teaching Torah and helping another develop into a *ben Torah*. Everyone gains from this situation. Done properly, this has been proven to have an overwhelming success rate.

One of the most effective tools of motivation and, therefore, prevention is *iyun tefillah*. Spending one half-hour daily, learning the purpose of *tefillah*, its explanations and its depth, guiding students in concentration in *tefillah* allows our students to be acutely aware of *Hakadosh Baruch Hu* and our purpose and mission in life. Classes in *tefillah* become a basis for many *hashkafah* and *machshavah* discussions, both in and out of class. *Tefillah* is engaged in three times daily, so they are aware of the constant results of these sessions. It opens lonely, vulnerable hearts to reach out intimately to The Infinite Creator. *Tefillah* is designed to put us into a frame of

Of Growth and Belonging / 211

mind to be touched by Hashem. It opens our hearts to introspection, to understanding, to warmth; and stimulates growth and motivates us to learn further.

A Sacred Partnership

WHEN A *REBBI* MAKES INVESTMENTS IN HIS *TALMIDIM*, stimulating their growth, he is clearly communicating his love and respect for them, conveying his confidence in them. He thereby cultivates an influential and even intimate relationship with his *talmidim*, which stimulates further growth. Nevertheless, only when parents work together with the *rebbi* can the child's full potential be achieved. After all, *Chazal* describe parents and *rebbei'im* as partners.

While the parental role emphasizes making the child successful in *Olam Hazeh*, and the *rebbi's* primary focus is *Olam Haba*, these areas of focus are not mutually exclusive. Mandatory parenting groups under the auspices of our yeshivos are vital for nurturing this partnership.

Avoiding a Double Misconception

WHEN A PARENT QUESTIONS THE INTEGRITY OF A *REBBI* or *menahel*, and accuses the *hanhalah* of making its primary concern the reputation of their institution or their egos, and of not working with *mesiras nefesh* and concern for the welfare of the child, they are damaging the relationship between the child and *rebbi*, between *talmid* and yeshiva. A child whose attitude becomes negative towards his yeshiva will not absorb the goals of the yeshiva. Moreover, the above parent will not inform the *rebbi* of situations and problems within the home that may influence the child's behavior and performance in the classroom. A child also senses this, and feels uncomfortable communicating his feelings to people in authority, or asking questions about topics that trouble him. This will cause the *talmid* to seek identity and support amongst peers outside the yeshiva, whom he mistakenly perceives to be friends who care.

Only when parents and *talmidim* realize that we are all on the same team can all of these issues be successfully resolved.

Some Kids on the Brink Can Be Saved

Yisroel Wolpin

⇒ A *Rebbi's* View

As a *REBBI / MAGGID SHIUR* for the past seven and a half years in a yeshiva that has many *bachurim* on the fringe or at risk (we've also catered to many who were not), I found your November issue right on target.

To put the blame on the system in yeshivos and *mechanchim* is unfair and inaccurate. Yeshivos like Lakewood, Brisk and Mir in *Eretz Yisrael* are bursting at the seams, as are many top *mesivtos* and *yeshiva gedolos* in America. That does not result from a failing system.

Some *bachurim* claim that they went down because of their powerful *yeitzer hara*. Everybody is endowed with a strong *yeitzer hara*, but they muster the willpower to fight. A person who is negative about himself because of family problems or other reasons will sometimes lack the willpower for the struggle. The triumph of the *yeitzer hara per se* is the result, not the cause of his succumbing to pressures.

I have found boys leaving Torah and slipping in *Yiddishkeit* because of what they perceive to be a lack of success in learning. They don't enjoy pursuing an endeavor at which they are doomed to fail. Learning becomes an unyielding pressure, and they seek to escape from it. The *yeitzer hara* sets in because there is no Torah to fight it.

Several incidents illustrate this point. A few years ago, an article described some 200 boys hanging out on *Simchas Torah* doing things unbecoming of *Yiddish kinder*. One former *talmid* said that he was there, as were a number of boys who had been in his class in elementary school. I asked him if any of them were from the top part of the class. His answer — they were all from the bottom. Apparently, the top part were being catered to, and felt good about themselves.

> *Several years ago, a very lebedig, elaborate niggun played in my mind. I was trying to place it. Then I realized that I had gotten it from a bachur who had been my student that past summer. Even though he had applied himself to his studies during the winter, he was becoming shaky in the summer. I called him over to speak to him in learning. As part of the conversation, I mentioned that he has a good head.*
>
> *"Who says I have a good head?"*
>
> *"Rabbi...., your next-year maggid shiur told me this week."*
>
> *"Really, he said that?"*
>
> *The bachur continued to learn b'hasmadah for the next two hours. A couple of Shabbosos into the next year, I walked into the Beis Midrash to daven Minchah. This bachur rushed over to me to say Shalom Aleichem. He started telling me how much he loves his new rebbi and his shiur, and he was therefore chazering shiur all afternoon on his own time.*
>
> *I had davened Maariv in his yeshiva several times after that. This bachur was always singing this happy niggun to himself. His Rebbi thought of him as having a good head, and he had to prove it. The more he tried, the more successful he was, and the happier he became — until he was singing a cheerful, leibidiger niggun on his way to learning. That's how this niggun stuck in my head. Again demonstrating that success in*

learning promotes further learning; lack of success can ח"ו cause someone to drop in Torah and mitzvos.

⇥ Focused Tutoring Can Make a Difference

When a boy is not doing well in class, his self-esteem usually goes down, and with it, often, his willpower to fight his *yeitzer hara*. An experienced tutor or *rebbi* could diagnose this boy's learning problem. Most weak students aren't weak in every area. Some are not good listeners, but have good comprehension and ask astute questions. Or, they may have good retention, or other pluses, but can't keep up with the pace in the classroom. An effective tutor could boost a boy's self-confidence, and as a result, he'll start learning better, and of course his *Yiddishkeit* level will begin to soar. A good, experienced tutor is expensive. In many cases, however, you can't afford not to hire one. As a bumper sticker put it: "If you think education is expensive, try ignorance."

Five years ago, a *rebbi* in a chassidic yeshiva tried to convince the father of a sweet, young *bachur* that his son could benefit from tutoring. The father was not interested. Said the *rebbi* to the father, "Your son is now an *ehrlicher bachur*. What would you say if by the end of the year he begins combing his hair and trimming his beard?"

"Not my son."

"You never know what one more year of accomplishing nothing in learning can do."

The father relented, and the *rebbi* engaged a tutor for the boy. He learned with him for the next two years, bringing out his strengths in learning, making him feel better about himself. He is currently a *chassan* and plans on learning in *Kollel* after he gets married. There are countless similar cases where focused tutoring thwarted the root causes of someone going down.

⇥ Tailor-Made Environment

Another possibility is a special yeshiva environment, where success is promoted through focusing on the *bachur's maalos* (strengths) in learning. When a *bachur* enters the yeshiva where I teach (Yeshiva Gedolah of Midwood), there's a good chance that he wasn't successful previously. The *talmid* is not told, "Don't you dare get up from your seat for the next two hours." Scolding and pressuring has failed with these boys. Instead, a *talmid* is told, "Let's see what you can accomplish in the next two hours." Usually, the boys get into learning little by little, until they learn intensively enough for "*Hame'or shebo machaziro lemutav,* The light of Torah makes them into better human beings." This can be a slow process. With patience, however, it can work.

Does it work for everyone? Of course not. A number of years ago, we came up with a list of the boys who had been in our yeshiva three years earlier. Eighteen of the twenty-five students were either learning in *Kollel*, or a yeshiva, or are *ehrlicher baalei battiim* who set aside time for Torah. To be sure, a number of these eighteen were quite strong to start with. Someone who is fully succeeding in a high-pressure yeshiva should continue there. Someone who is a *mechallel Shabbos*, or beyond the fringe in other ways, is too far gone for this approach. In addition, there is a risk that he might exert a negative influence on others in this type of yeshiva. This solution is possible only for boys who are starting to fail, for this approach is the easiest for them to feel successful.

In short, the problems often begin with lack of accomplishment in Torah study. The prevention and possible solution can also come through Torah, if it's presented correctly: the right amount in the right way.

The *Gemara* says in *Bava Basra*, "*Barasi yeitzer hara, barasi Torah tavlin.*" *Hashem* says, I created a *yeitzer hara* and created Torah as a medicine. Torah is the best medicine; studying Torah is the best therapy.

Maximum Benefit From Our Schools

Reclaiming Aspiration

When Children Help Children

Inclusions vs. Insularity: A Symposium

Only for the Chosen of our People?

When Children's Learning Handicaps Are of Our Own Making

A Teacher's List of Do's (not Don'ts!)

Reclaiming Aspiration
Instilling a Healthy Self-Image in Our Students

Chana Juravel

Much attention is being focused on adolescents drifting from our schools and our values, and rightfully so. In addition, it would prove worthwhile to address those youths still in our ranks, to curb future statistics. There is, in the words of a seasoned mechanech I spoke with recently, a "dark cloud" over our schoolchildren, now more than ever. In a recent workshop I gave to one group of high-school girls, they unanimously labeled their most pressing problem: "I don't like myself." Many suffer from a low self-esteem, contributing to a lack of simchas hachayim — joie de vivre. These, again, are not the adolescents who have fallen out of our system — they are our system, and it behooves us to address them. Not to simplify the myriad of problems in homes and avoid approaching each situation individually, but perhaps to emerge with a redefined, positive attitude toward students within the classroom, as well as help them master crucial life skills, which could help even those with severe maladies cope more effectively.

"Y'HI CH'VOD TALMIDCHA CHAVIV ALECHA K'SHELACH." May the honor of your student be as dear to you as your own (*Avos* 4:15). According to Rabbi S.R. Hirsch: Demanding honor and obedience from our children without granting them respect and dignity in turn is doomed to failure (*Yesodoth Hachinuch,* Vol. 1).

Children thrive on acceptance, on feeling unconditionally loved and admired as people. They have a strong need for their educators to be *machshiv* (respect) them, to be motivated to grow. This respect should stem from an overall recognition of their essential goodness and potential. In *Yeshayahu* (49:1), the Jews despairingly express their sense of loss: *"Azavtani Hashem v'Hashem shichechani —* G-d has abandoned me and forgotten me." *Hashem* then reassures them, replying, *"Anochi lo eshkacheich —* I will not forget you!" Rabbi Yitzchok Kirzner explains this as G-d's reminder that, regardless of circumstance, we all have a core that is immutably pure. We all, through the Sinai experience and acceptance of His commands beginning with *"Anochi,"* became extensions of Him. That aspect of each and every Jew — the *Anochi,* so to speak — is what *Hashem* views as their constant potential, and *that* will never be forgotten.

Rabbi Zev Leff of Moshav Matisyahu elucidates this, pointing out that the one time Moshe *Rabbeinu* was punished irrevocably for a wrongdoing followed his referring to the Jews as *"morim —* rebels." Interestingly, that was the only time that Moshe labeled the people rather than merely their wrongdoing. Actions, when negative, should strike us as incongruous with what we believe to be a student's essence, and that is the message we should convey.

> *Faced with a student inappropriately dressed, a teacher regained her composure after the initial shock and smiled at her. Privately, she asked the girl, "How do you see yourself, forty years from now, discussing this stage of life with your grandchildren?"*
>
> *The look of relief on the student's face was obvious; someone viewed her as more than a young girl at this stage of life.*

> *A boy was wandering around his yeshiva high-school campus after graduation, unsure of his self-worth. He*

had decided not to pursue a track of full-time learning. A former rebbi approached him and, as if reading his mind, said, "You can be a baal habayis and still be a talmid chacham."

The man, now in his 30's, has pursued that goal with a daily kvius b'limud (scheduled time reserved for Torah study) ever since.

Acceptance yields growth. Students need to feel that their teacher is rooting for them, liking and respecting them as people through their growth process. This attitude must preclude any advance labeling, as well. Students deserve the benefit of a fresh attitude, without preconceived expectations based on reputation.

⤏ Self-Fulfilling Prophecies

There is a story told of a young teacher thanking her principal for keying her in on her students' potential. "Those I.Q. scores you penciled in next to their names on the roster have proven to be right on the mark."

The principal was puzzled. "I.Q.'s?" he asked. "Those were their locker numbers!"

Teachers' rooms, too, unfortunately, can sometimes be breeding ground for many self-fulfilling prophecies, albeit well meaning.

A teacher was frustrated by questions posed by a difficult student that were, she felt, coming from a negative attitude. "How could she ask a question like that about Sarah Imeinu? It just proves that she has no respect for what our Imahos stand for." Luckily, rather than fueling her fire, another teacher tactfully pointed out how many of the mefarshim deal with just that question. The teacher reentered the room, armed with a new attitude. The student was elated over the attention given to her issues.

I once heard a noted lecturer define the ultimate level of *simchah*. The letters of the word that we define as happiness can, with different vowels, be read as *she'machah*: the ability to erase. True happiness comes, after all, from being granted a clean slate. We can all benefit from others through the gift of erasure, the opportunity to move on without previous labels and wrongdoing defining us.

⤖ A Matter of Channeling

There are, however, behaviors and attitudes that are difficult to accept and tolerate, and that warrant discipline. How to view those manifestations of seemingly negative *middos*?

Middos are relative. One who is unaware of his shortcomings, Reb Yisroel Salanter told his students, is compared to one who is sick, the "illness" spreading to devastating ends without his attention. One who is unaware of his virtues, however, is like one who is dead. Only an awareness of our virtues gives us the tools to overcome our faults. Interestingly, one's virtues and faults can be one and the same — it is a matter of appropriate channeling. Rather than assuming the form of verbal castigation, discipline should ideally incorporate constructive channeling techniques, leaving the student hopeful rather than defeated.

> *A teenager, artistic by nature, looked forward each year to the one thing she enjoyed about school: being in charge of makeup application at her high school's concert. One day, not long before the concert, she came into class wearing more makeup than appropriate. Her principal, after verbally castigating her for the infraction, meted out her punishment: no longer could she deserve to be involved with makeup at the concert.*

What an opportunity lost! What a chance for an educator to remind a dear *neshamah* of the fact that, shortly, there would be an appropriate channel available for her useful talent! To even add, "And someday you'll make *kallos* shine on their wedding day!" Not only was the opportunity lost, the young woman was lost to *Yiddishkeit* for many sad years, remembering this incident bitterly as a turning point.

⌐≡ Accentuating the Positive

We often preach *anivus* (humility) to our students, forgetting to differentiate between true humility and low self-image. The girls I spoke to in the aforementioned workshop feared that truly liking themselves would lead to *gaavah* (pride). How misguided! We have to be aware of our strengths and be humbled, in turn, by the gift, and by the obligations inherent in recognizing their G-dly source.

> *A young teacher, seeing a talented student showing signs of being "high on herself," began her own campaign to stem her charge's budding ego. She ignored her raised hand in class and didn't list her name when thanking all involved in a class production in which the girl starred. The student's self-confidence took many years to rebuild.*

How much the girl could have gained had she been complimented on her G–d-given talents, encouraging her to make Hashem proud with them in a way that only she could. That attitude could have yielded true *anivus*, rather than crush her self-image. The girl was left questioning her worth as defined by one whose opinion she valued and whose acceptance she sorely needed.

Students I spoke with told me they have no problem liking their friends — to the contrary! But, I asked, "Don't the same things that stop you from liking yourselves make it difficult to totally accept friends' imperfections, not yet having reached their potential — impure motives, less-than-ideal activities and thoughts, not being all that attractive—?"

"Sure!" one girl replied. "But you realize that you can love them even though they're not perfect. You love them for who they are."

How wise. We're told, though, that *"V'ahavta l'reiacha kamocha* — to love one's fellow man like *yourself,"* and infer that to love others, the healthy basis of loving yourself must exist; the obligation toward *"reiacha"* necessitates love of *"kamocha."* "That unconditional acceptance should apply to you, too," I suggested.

Reclaiming Aspiration

"It's different," a second young woman said, after thinking. "You expect more from yourself."

True, but students need to love the fact that they *do* expect more from themselves; to love themselves as works in progress.

⚯ Evaluation — Based on Potential

Rabbi Dessler asks why there is a need for Rosh Hashanah, if its exacting judgment is only to be overruled come Yom Kippur. One doesn't preclude the other, he answers. Rather, on Rosh Hashanah Hashem judges us based on our actual deeds: who we *were* that year. Yom Kippur, on the other hand, is meant to judge our yearnings: who we *want* to be, once defined and crystallized through the *teshuvah* (repentance) process. That being the case, we find Hashem overlooking the former in judging us by the latter, which He sees as our true self. Self-image can, in turn, be based on the recognition that I, in my unique way, am striving to grow and express a level of G-dliness like no other.

> *A student's self-esteem was shattered. She had become involved in an intolerable relationship. "How," she tearfully asked her teacher, "can I get out of this?"*
>
> *Her teacher soothingly asked, "Could you have imagined yourself in this awful situation two years ago?"*
>
> *The girl shook her head.*
>
> *"So perhaps you can't imagine now what you could grow to be two years from now."*

Presently, courses abound aimed at targeting self-image and developing coping strategies so sorely needed on all levels. Perhaps it would be worthwhile for us to incorporate a *hashkafah* "life skills" program for impressionable 8th-11th graders, drawing on the wealth of Torah teachings accessible to us, aimed at arming them with skills to effectively yield greater results in handling a complicated time of growing up, and offering solid ground in building an all-encompassing relationship with *Hakadosh Baruch Hu*. A sample curriculum could include:

- **Accepting Myself:** my family, talents, weaknesses, my situation...as channels enabling me to grow to my potential as an individual within the Torah world. Rabbi Hutner צז״ל described us as infinite points on a circle, each unique, but sharing a common center.
- **The Need for Help in Growing — Finding a Mentor:** We often wait until we're "finished products" to confidently present ourselves to those we admire (even to Hashem). What we don't take into account is needing their help to get to that point!
- **Decision-Making:** Youngsters need to be guided in the concept of "opportunity cost" — the immediate gain of any decision vs. the long-range effect. This leads to an awareness of the "bigger picture," and controlling difficult situations.
- **Goal-Achieving:** establishing realistic goals that are challenging yet achievable, as stepping-stones to a long-range aspiration. The ability to meet manageable standards does wonders for self-image and provides the impetus needed to take on more.
- **Achieving a Level of Spirituality Within a Mundane Existence:** This seems rather sophisticated, but students are interested in coming to terms with how to apply lofty standards to their "regular lives — now." Students need to view ideals presented as being relevant and applicable.
- **Time- and Stress-Management Skills:** learning to prioritize tasks realistically, viewing overwhelming situations as temporary and ultimately worthwhile.
- **Self-Worth Independent of Peers' Evaluations:** handling rejection, recognizing peer pressure that is potentially detrimental, "people pleasing" vs. the gratification found in making Hashem proud through our actions, once properly thought out and weighed.

This list is merely a springboard. These ideas can be brought up tangentially within the framework of other classes (*Pirkei Avos,* for example) or in a "rap-session" type of setting.

In either case, it is essential to offer enough input while assisting students to arrive at insights on their own. We all, after all, act in a more effective manner when spurred to growth through our own desire to grow, and self-recognition of the need to do so.

> *Walking into a room and feeling the tension following a difficult exam given in the previous period, the teacher put down her books and smiled. "I was having such a rough day," she confided, "but having you girls always picks me up. You have no idea how much I look forward to your class."*
>
> *She went on to teach her best class ever.*

An educator once wrote, "As a teacher, I possess a tremendous power to make a child's life miserable or joyous. I can be a tool of torture or an instrument of inspiration."

We collectively have the ability to inspire and encourage students to the point of getting that dark cloud to pass after all, bathing our youngsters in the sunshine that will herald light in the truest sense.

When Children Help Children
How One Class of Children Made a Difference in the Lives of Other Children Stricken With Cancer

Yaakov Astor

AHUVA*, A SPUNKY, TOP-OF-THE-CLASS 11-YEAR-OLD GIRL from the New York area, was having the time of her life. It was a school trip. She and her friends were free to roam the amusement park and just have fun. With nothing to worry about except which ride to go on next, they talked and laughed and in general acted silly, as responsible yeshiva girls are wont to do now and then.

When Ahuva came home, she felt unusually tired and nauseous. "Probably from that roller-coaster ride," she thought.

The fatigue and nausea persisted, so her parents brought her to a doctor. One test led to another. Finally, the doctor had the results: cancer. The news hit Ahuva and her family like a thunderbolt.

Malky[1] had been diagnosed with a concerous brain tumor when she was 4. Fortunately, the operation to remove the cancer had sent it into remission. Suddenly, at the tender age of 6 something seemed to be amiss with Malky. Her parents brought her back to the doctor. After

---

1. A pseudonym. All the names and nonessential details have been changed for the sake of anonymity. Contact with "Mrs. Winter" can be made through the author or the editorial office of *The Jewish Observer.*

some testing, they received the dreaded news. Malky's cancer had returned.

What Ahuva and Malky did no know at the time was that during the upcoming year they would be recipients of a most unique *chessed,* to be initiated by Mrs. Breindy Winter[1] of Monsey, New York. Over the next year, the lives of Ahuva, Malky, and three other girls who were diagnosed with some form of life-threatening disease would intertwine with the lives of Mrs. Winter and the 28 girls of her seventh-grade class. And before the year would be over, all would be touched and rewarded by the experience in a way they could never have imagined.

I. The Class

BREINDY WINTER HAS BEEN TEACHING FOR 20 YEARS. SHE knows her lesson plans like we know our street address. One summer, on vacation in upstate New York, she was neighbors with Mrs. Chumie Bodek, founder of "Caring and Sharing," a support group for parents of cancer patients. Mrs. Bodek lent Mrs. Winter the book, *Times Of Challenge,* a collection of true stories of difficult life situations various people had to face. It started the wheels turning.

Mrs. Winter asked her new friend, "Why don't you connect me with some of your sick children? Maybe my seventh graders can do something with them."

Mrs. Bodek responded, and connected her with five seriously ill girls from the tristate area.

When she began, Mrs. Winter divided her class into five groups, each group responsible for one particular girl. She told them the specific situation and encouraged them to write letters, make telephone calls, and come up with project ideas (like a Succos party, a Chanukah *chagigah,* a *siyum,* surprise visits) to give the ill girls hope, friendship — life.

Generally, all the letter writing, phone calls, etc. were done outside of class time, for "homework." Thus, on the average, Mrs. Winter spent no more than ten or fifteen minutes a day of class time on the project, and then only to update her students or give them encouragement by telling them how well received their letters and phone calls were. At the beginning, Mrs. Winter reviewed her students' letters before they were sent. By the end of the year, though, it was unnecessary, for her students had developed the proper sensitivity.

The same was true with making phone calls. "They were guided when to call, how to call, what to say, and what not to say," Mrs. Winter said. "By the end of the year, though, they knew that if a girl had received chemotherapy, they had to wait a day or two before calling."

Mrs. Winter organized a *Tehillim* committee for her class and the other seventh-grade class, dividing the assignments among the students as well as the teachers. (Counted together, they would recite all 150 psalms daily.) *Tzeddakah* was collected to fund gifts and similar needs.

Across the board, from the beginning of the year to the end, her class responded beyond her best imaginings. "They gave these children a life," she stated.

II. Ahuva

"WHAT'S THE PROGNOSIS?" AHUVA'S PARENTS, WITH impossible-to-deny trepidation, asked the doctor.

"I think we caught it in time, and if all goes well she should make it. But your daughter will need chemotherapy treatments over the next few months, and it will take everything out of her."

Ahuva was an honors student and looked forward to even greater success in school. Her hopes were dashed when she learned that she was going to miss class time because of the chemotherapy. Then they told her that the chemotherapy was going to make her hair fall out. That devastated her. How would she face her classmates? Ahuva's family, too, was at a loss as how to react. Instead of being in a world full of children, laughter, and a bright daughter's success stories, they found themselves in a world of sterile hospitals, doctors, and social workers.

The therapy started and things went from bad to worse. Ahuva began missing school (she would go for two or three weeks and then be out for six or more). She wore a wig after her hair began falling out, but there was no way to hide the fact that something was seriously wrong. Soon word was out that she had cancer. Unfortunately, her classmates (except for her best friend) virtually disowned her. No one called her. No one came by. Whatever the reason, suddenly it was as if Ahuva had no almost friends.

Unfortunately, the reaction was no better from the children's parents. Suddenly, acquaintances and friends who always greeted Ahuva's mother inexplicably crossed the street to avoid her. "Should I talk to her? Should I ask her?" they seemed to be struggling with in their minds. Invariably they decided that the only way to react was to deny it. Even a childhood friend of Ahuva's mother would change the subject every time she tried to open up and express her fears.

"So, did you hear about so-and-so's wedding?"

"But I really want to share this with someone."

"No. Let's only talk about *simchas*. We are only going to discuss good things."

Ahuva and her family felt totally cut off. Just when things seemed the worst, Ahuva's parents received a call.

"Hello, my name is Mrs. Winter. I am a teacher in Monsey. This summer I was speaking with Mrs. Bodek and she told me about your daughter. I am calling to ask if you would mind my class writing letters and making phone calls to your daughter."

Ahuva's life changed almost instantly. With the arrival of the first letters and individual phone calls, her spirits were lifted. There were people who cared!

"They Really Care About Me!"

Of course, Ahuva still had her ups and downs. One day, two or three days after a chemotherapy treatment, she was home feeling lonely when the phone rang.

"Ahuva, is that you?"

"Yes."

"This is Mrs. Winter."

"Oh, hello."

"I know it's lunchtime, but we got this crazy idea to squeeze all 29 of us into this little office in our school and say hello to you." Not only did Ahuva get the loudest hello she ever heard in her life but they then sang to her as well. And then afterward, many of the girls spoke to her individually.

"Wow! They really care about me," Ahuva thought.

Periodically the entire class would call her in this manner (in addition to regular individual calls and letters). "Who are these girls?" Ahuva thought. "I wish I could get to know them personally."

The class's involvement dramatically changed Ahuva's outlook — rather than focusing exclusively on how depressing her situation was, her life began to revolve around the next letter, the next phone call. One night, while Ahuva's mother was in the kitchen she heard Ahuva laughing hysterically in her room (even though she had sores in her mouth from the chemotherapy, which made it painful to laugh).

"What's so funny?"

"I was just thinking about today's conversations. I was wondering what surprises the girls would pull off next."

⇢ Sibling Rivalry

When a child comes down with cancer, she is not the only child in the family who needs uplifting. Ahuva's older married siblings took the news hard, but they had lives of their own. Her 9-year-old sister, however, had to deal with the unbelievable stresses of the upcoming months, including the fact that her parents would hardly be around for her, shuttling back and forth as they were between home and hospital every day. Although Ahuva was the sick one, at least she was getting all this attention.

Heightened jealousy, sibling rivalry, and then guilt over having such feelings are natural to the dynamics of a home where a child has a serious illness. Armed with that knowledge, Mrs. Winter had the needs of the entire family in mind.

"If we were going to give gifts Chanukah time, for example, we would buy presents for the girl who was sick as well as for all her young siblings. If a student of mine had a younger sister, she was encouraged to write to her. In fact, my 10-year-old daughter and Ahuva's 9-year-old sister became best friends."

Mrs. Winter too found herself forming a genuine bond of friendship with the mothers. She found herself calling just to say hello. After the return "hello," their entire day would pour out — All their ups, all their downs; the humorous moments and the fearful ones. And Mrs. Winter listened, not out of obligation but as "family."

Although by early spring everyone felt like close friends, they had never actually met. Then Mrs. Winter invited Ahuva to their Purim play to meet her class face to face for the first time. "We were anxious and nervous. Ahuva was anxious and nervous. The moment she walked out of the car she just stood there. We also stood there for a moment."

The emotion was palpable. Then one of the girls approached her and said, "Hi, my name is so and so." Then another said, "Hi, my name is so and so." Intimately familiar with everyone's personality through the letters, it was as if she were being reunited with a long-lost sister. Once she connected the name with the face, she automatically felt a special relationship with this "stranger" standing before her.

Most important of all was that by year's end Ahuva not only completed her treatments and received a clean bill of health, but she even managed to catch up with her class.

III. Malky

MALKY'S CANCER WAS IN REMISSION BUT SHE COULD ONLY go to school for a couple of hours a day. That was her condition when Mrs. Winter and her class became involved. Suddenly, a couple of months into the new year Malky relapsed. The girls in Mrs. Winter's class were frightened.

"But she is only 7 years old. What's going to become of her?"

"G-d willing, she will recover. Until she does, though, we have to step up our efforts and send her even better cards, write more letters, say our *Tehillim* more fervently."

Although Malky walked to the class's *siyum* at the beginning of the year, she could only make it to the Chanukah *chagigah* in a wheelchair. (After that, Mrs. Winter videotaped events so Malky could feel part of the class.) Mrs. Winter visited her as often as she could (she was teaching only three days a week, and usually reserved Wednesday and Sunday for visits).

"I would sometimes bring a couple of students with me (after receiving permission from their parents) and would try to make Malky laugh by putting on puppet shows or reading stories." During the visit, Malky would often let out a laugh because of someone's joke. That little laugh would warm everyone's heart.

Malky quickly accepted Mrs. Winter and her retinue. More than once she would be lying in bed with her eyes closed, apparently asleep, when she would hear Mrs. Winter or her students knock at the front door. Then, unlike with other adult visitors, she would somehow manage to wake herself up, muster energy from some hidden reservoir, and tell her mother to let the visitor in. And no matter how bad she felt, her entire demeanor would change with their arrival.

As Malky's condition was worsening, Mrs. Winter informed her class so. They had a month off for *Pesach* and she told her students that they could call her whenever they wanted an update. And call they did.

As with the other sick children, Mrs. Winter's class maintained the flow of letters, cards, and phone calls to the sick child's siblings. "I am me," a sibling in that situation feels. "I am not Malky." They too need to know that somebody cares and that they are a separate identity. The class filled those needs.

Malky was eventually admitted to a hospital. At that point Mrs. Frost stopped taking her students to visit. "I knew Malky

When Children Help Children

would not have benefited from it," she said. "Plus, seeing her connected to all those tubes would have been too much for them. But I continued to visit her myself."

Malky entered a semicoma state and lost complete use of one hand. When Mrs. Winter visited her in that state she would stroke the paralyzed hand. At the end of one such visit, she said to the semiconscious girl, "OK, Malky, I'm leaving now."

Suddenly, the little finger of Malky's hand wrapped itself around one of Mrs. Winter's fingers. The eyes of the nurse on duty bulged. Five minutes passed. Ten minutes. The nurse then said, "Malky, Mrs. Winter has to go home now."

The little finger grasped even more firmly. Mrs. Winter stayed by her bedside for the next two hours while that little finger remained firmly wrapped around hers.

Malky's condition worsened and early one Friday morning, Mrs. Winter received a phone call: "Malky passed away this morning."

Mrs. Winter immediately called every mother in the class. There was no school that day, but she told each parent that she would be in school that morning if anyone wanted to talk about it.

Every single girl showed up.

And everyone cried. They spoke about Malky as if she were their little sister. It was a type of *shivah*. Mrs. Winter told them, "We did everything we could. We can feel proud that we knew her and that we stuck by her to the very end. And she knew it."

IV. The Bottom Line: Children Helping Children

THE MEMORIES OF THE SCHOOL YEAR ARE EMBLAZONED forever on the hearts of all those involved: on Mrs. Winter's, on each of her 28 students', on the hearts of the families of the ill girls, and, most of all, the hearts of the sick girls themselves.

Mrs. Winter received this letter from Ahuva:

Dear Mrs. Winter:

Hi. I don't have the words to thank you. First of all, for coming all the way from Monsey and for spending the day over here. Thank you so so much for the great, adorable, stunning, exquisite, outstanding gifts. Thanks a million, billion, trillion, zillion gallons, tons and most of all for being you.

Can the efforts be measured? Surely not. Looking back over the year, almost all the mothers involved felt their daughters learned and matured in ways they never had before and never could have otherwise. Many of them personally expressed the deepest gratitude to Mrs. Winter.

Still, it would be wrong to think that such a project can be taken up without careful consideration. A person might legitimately ask, "Why expose 12-year-olds to this?" Mrs. Winter admits that it is a very delicate subject. And certain people, rightly or wrongly, might have emotional difficulties no matter how well the project is handled. To any who might consider replicating her ideas or who find their younger children involved in such a project, it is not an endeavor to be taken lightly. Parents and teachers have to be very tuned in to the emotional needs of the children helping out.

"After all is said and done, though, it was the most rewarding year I ever had," Mrs. Winter states.

Perhaps, then, the most important consideration to keep in mind is that there is a certain emotional support that only children can give children. There are some ways in which professionals, parents and even responsible older children cannot affect another child like a peer. And the child who gives is sure to receive at least as much as the child who receives.

Children helping children. Perhaps the greatest *chessed* an adult can do is set up a situation where children help each other.

INCLUSIONS VS. INSULARITY
A SYMPOSIUM

How inclusive are our schools? Should the students of our yeshivos, Bais Yaakov schools and Hebrew day schools be more open and more welcoming to children of different backgrounds?

Fire Drill

A Contemporary *Chinuch* Challenge: Preparing For Inevitable Encounters

Rabbi Shneur Aisenstark

⇢ The Way It Was — And How It Became

ABOUT FORTY-FIVE YEARS AGO, WHEN A BOY BECAME *BAR Mitzvah* in America, he could look forward to receiving a variety of gifts — a pen, a tie clip, a watch, or some kind of clothing. Today, a boy will prepare for his *Bar Mitzvah* by buying a *sefarim shrank* (bookcase) in which all the anticipated *sefarim* will be arranged. Forty-five years ago, a boy was hardly familiar with the names of the *mesechtos* in *Shas*, and certainly was not able to make a *siyum* at his *Bar Mitzvah*. Now, ב"ה, the average boy makes a *siyum* on a *mesechta* in an impressive and competent manner. In the yearbook photos of a *frum* school published forty years ago, one can find most girls wearing bobby socks with portions of the lower leg uncovered. Today this is highly improbable ב"ה. The typical teenager of yesteryear was preoccupied with the choice of a future profession. If an average graduate from our modern yeshiva/day-school system were asked about his or her goals for the future, the boy would most likely answer that he aspires to become the biggest *talmid chacham* he can be, while the girl would probably reply that she would like to marry the greatest Torah scholar available to her.

One could continue with examples of how, in America, Torah and *yiras Shamayim* have grown by leaps and bounds. This incredible progress is due, in no small measure, to Torah Umesorah, which spearheaded the day-school movement and improved professional standards in Jewish education through teacher-training programs, publication of resource materials and general promotion of the broad field of *chinuch*. Viewed from the perspective of the left, the right or the center of the Torah spectrum, the report card on progress in *chinuch* is quite good.

There is, however, one area in that same report card that shows a major failure — our ability to function as an *am echad b'lev echad* — one nation, of one heart in service of the Almighty. Despite all our growth in Torah knowledge and *yiras Shamayim*, we have become increasingly factionalized and divided in many aspects of our lives. For example, we now have schools that cater only to *Shomer Shabbos* parents; we have schools that do not accept children from homes with TV; we have schools that do not accept students whose *"tchup"* (hair) is a bit too long, or whose mother does not cover her hair.

⇒ Diversity or Fragmentation?

In some Jewish communities, within a radius of a few blocks, one can find a dozen *minyanim*, many of them competing for the "tenth." If this burgeoning of *minyanim* were due to *harbei d'rachim laMakom* (the multitude of paths in service of G-d), it would be admirable; when it is due to a feeling that the other *minyan* is not only different, but less worthy, then the rapid growth is less than impressive. I know two brothers, belonging to two different Chassidic sects, who do not eat in each other's homes, since the *shochet* of one is unacceptable to the other. In a similar vein, when a *shul* moved from the old neighborhood to a new one, a former *mispallel* swore that he would not enter that *shtiebel* in its new location because it had moved "uptown." It seems that we have neither the time nor the inclination to teach tolerance of and respect for legitimate differences.

Another point: One of the aspects of the *mitzvah* of *hochei'ach tochiyach es amisecha* — reproof — is being *mekarev* those less fortunate in *Yiddishkeit* than ourselves, reaching out to them; this responsibility devolves on those who are already *shomrei Torah umitzvos*. We *"frum"* Jews, however, often shirk this important obligation because we fear that our children, in engaging with others to strengthen their *emunah* and *ahavas Hashem,* will risk their own. We assume that their *yeitzer hara* will lead them to emulate our less fortunate Jewish brethren. Because of this fear, we take the easy way out and segregate ourselves, saying "This is *asur,* that is *asur,*" and make *Shabbos far zich*.

If success is measured by the number of *pesukim* and *parshiyos* our students cover, but we do not trust them to visit with someone whose hat is not the same color as ours, then we must re-evaluate our goals in *chinuch*. One can always rejoice when more kosher facilities are needed, more schools are established, and more *shtieblach* open. When the need for them develops only from a sense of superiority or lack of trust, however, one should feel considerably less happy. Our *achdus* seems to be disintegrating to the point that we will need forty religious parties in Israel instead of the four we now have.

⇥ Sensitivity or Insularity?

Our increasing fragmentation has resulted in our inability to deal with anyone not exactly like ourselves with any sort of sensitivity. Several years ago, for example, we tried to organize a convention of all Beth Jacob Seminaries in Canada and America. One *menaheles* told me very clearly that if a certain seminary were invited, her students would not participate. Upon inquiring as to the reason, I was told that "those" seminary students are not of the same "type" as hers.

I argued that the convention would last for only one Shabbos; what possible harm would they suffer? (We were talking about 18- and 19-year-olds.) Her retort was that she feared one of "her" students befriending one of "theirs," resulting in a lifelong friendship.

Another incident: A class of girls was invited to a birthday party of a classmate of a different ethnic background. Because the students feared that the *kashrus* standards in this home would not be the same as their own, they took their full plates and hid them under the sofa, to the horror of the mother who found the congealed food the next morning. My question is not what the girls should have done, but what we, as the school, should do to see that such a thing does not happen.

A final example: A teacher was asked by a student, "My mother bought me a blouse with sleeves that are a bit short. What should I do?" The teacher's reply was simple, "You don't have to listen to your mother."

My question is: Why did the seminary not train the teacher to respond appropriately to such questions? Would we hire a teacher who is illiterate? Why engage one who is illiterate in sensitivity?

⇒ Mutual Understanding, Not Capitulation

The *Ribbono Shel Olam* created us to be different from one another and to have distinct *kochos* and abilities, all of which merge into a mosaic glorifying Hashem. "*K'shem she'ein partzufeihem shavim kach ein de'oseihem shavim* — As their facial features differ, so do their personalities."

Hashem fashioned us, a nation, into twelve different tribes, each with divergent and contrasting innate qualities. *Chazal* tell us that each *sheivet* (tribe) had a unique *tzinor* (conduit) for their *tefillos* to *Shamayim*. The distinct individuality of each *sheivet* was accentuated by each having its own specific flag, place of encampment, and parcel of the land in *Eretz Yisrael*.

Yet, "*tachas hahar*" — at the foot of Sinai — they were

Inclusions vs. Insularity: A Symposium / 241

k'ish echad b'lev echad, like one man, with one heart. This is a call for understanding, not capitulating. Tolerance and acceptance of legitimate views can be upheld without moving one inch from *minhag avoseinu beyadeinu* — our ancestral heritage.

⟜ The Road to Mutual Respect

How can we, as responsible *mechanchim,* train the next generation to respect instead of reject others, by being *mekarev* instead of alienating? When the academic year begins, the school posts fire-drill instructions in every classroom, which the teachers read to each class. Yet after this, fire drills are still held. When an English teacher teaches letter-writing, she explains the format of the letter — its salutation, body and closing. Yet after this instruction, she still has her students practice letter-writing. For a month before his *Bar Mitzvah,* a boy dons his *tefillin* and removes them. He has learned all of *Hilchos Tefillin.* Why month-long practice?

Similarly, we can teach children all about proper behavior, *middos,* and the *halachos* of honoring parents, and still fail dismally in the world of action. Apparently teaching about behavior, even by a teacher who is an excellent and enthusiastic pedagogue, is not enough. May I suggest that we must teach correct behavior by having the student practice his behavior in class, with simulated activities. We must write a curriculum of all possible scenarios that we may encounter in our *bein adam lechaveiro* (interpersonal) dealings. For example, we must have a practice birthday party showing students how to sensitively handle problems such as different standards of *kashrus.* Our seminaries must offer classes and workshops on how teachers can create activities and situations that will promote the growth of social skills and sensitivity in our students.

Or for young men: When a man is confronted with a lady who extends her hand in greeting, one has two alternatives: either to ignore her gesture and busy his own hand with some other task, or to explain pleasantly, in a *safah rakah, b'nachas* — softly, pleasantly — that an Orthodox Jew is not permitted to have such contact with the opposite sex and that no personal affront is intended. Let the young man learn to choose the response that combines sensitivity and *frumkeit*. The key thereafter is practice, practice and practice.

Torah Umesorah is actively promoting an excellent program called "Derech" (the brainchild of Dr. and Mrs. A. Aberbach of Toronto), which teaches *"Hilchos Derech Eretz"* on different levels with various materials. Knowledge of the material, however, is not enough. A fighter pilot is trained on a simulator for many, many hours before he is given his wings. We, too, must train our students — not just theoretically, but practically — through simulated real-life scenarios. Students should voice their opinions of what *they* would do in various situations, and explore how these situations can possibly be ameliorated thereby improving themselves in the process.

⇒ A Curriculum of Emphasis, Discussion, and Practice

This article may give the impression of being a critique of the more right-wing type of educational system; my purpose is not at all to criticize, but to sensitize the educational community and heighten its awareness. I am certain that the examples of insensitivity I cite are equally true of all types of educational institutions, with only minor variations.

As a proud member of the Torah-true educational network, I wish to be neither apologetic nor critical. I *do* want to suggest an intensification of the precept that we practice with our students what we preach, and keep on drilling, recounting, relating, prepping and repeating, until our students have internalized a sure sense of themselves as *frum Yidden* who can model the *derech* of our *chachamim* and inspire others to follow.

With emphasis, discussions, and practice, we will succeed in producing a generation of people who know how to talk to each other, to be tolerant of one another, to respect legitimate differences, and, most importantly, who will feel strong enough in their *emunah* to tackle whatever challenges life puts in their path. Secluding oneself and hermetically sealing oneself can only lead to factionalism — the opposite of *achdus*. A pipeline through which water is turned on full strength will not allow the entry of alien matter. Similarly, if our children become a *tzinor* — a conduit for transmitting every fine behavior, every deep expression of our *Yiddishkeit* — then no harmful outside material will gain entry. By training our students to promote our heritage among their peers, their own *emunah* and growth in *Yiddishkeit* will ultimately be strengthened.

The Lab and the Safety Yard

Two Views

Rabbi Hillel Belsky

THERE IS AN OLD ANALOGY THAT IF YOU WANT TO HELP SOMEone see in the dark, you can either give him a candle or train him to be sensitive to seeing in diminished light. The difference between the two emerges when dawn breaks. The candle has outlived its usefulness. The sensitivity to see in diminished light, however, remains integrated within the person and will serve him in future situations of challenged vision. In broad terms, this analogy translates into two hypothetical models of Jewish education. Both claim goals of limud haTorah and character development, but one is solution oriented, the other is gen-

erative or skill based.

We might call the first model the safety yard and the second the laboratory. It is important to distinguish between the models, their goals, the risks inherent to each, their definition of success and the types of mechanchim that distinguish them. These models rotate on different views of childhood, and differ in terms of parental expectations, as well.

⇌ The Safety Yard: Protection Against Hostile Environment

The safety yard has as its distinguishing feature a protection against the hostile outer environment. As such, it is distinguished by its emphasis on standards of behavior, contrasted with the unsavory behavior of others. A WE/THEY emphasis is common. The definition of "we" derives from Torah, of course, but takes its more immediate flavor from contrast. Thus it weaves back and forth between "we" and "they," and acceptable is defined in part through the unacceptable. Success is measured by the ability to feed back in word and deed the formula that has been conveyed for avoidance of pitfalls.

In this model, the *mechanech* is a safety patrolman, one who guards the gates from unwelcome intrusion. In this day and age, there is so much to object to that the *mechanech* is occupied in keeping the gates, in presenting in well-defined terms the contrast between good and evil. This *mechanech* takes charge, might soothe anxious parents with reassurances that he will safely conduct the children to the other side of the stormy sea of childhood, even onward into a "good *shidduch*." But how? It's a great challenge.

Could any *mechanech* have made this promise to my parents or yours when we were young? But many parents do not want to be reminded of their past; they fear the tendencies of youth. The *mechanech* puts much effort into discipline, appearances, normative behavior, conformity and, as stated, the careful rejection of negative behavior.

⇀⇒ Authority, Security — and "Perfection"

An advantage of this model is the sense of security it imparts, the goal of the safety-yard model. During the confusing years of adolescence, students may feel secure in the confident authoritative environment of their teachers. Parents may feel they can finally relax in their struggle to communicate the spirit of *Yisrael Sabba*. Unacceptable behavior is extinguished, everyone is clear about rules. On the other hand, this model suggests homogeneity, simplicity and a suggestion of perfection in a world in which none of these quite exists. A student may feel his individuality is compromised in the group effect. He may doubt both the reality of his own strength and the ability of the simplistic explanatory system to live up to the complexities and pressures he is already aware of.

And now a word about perfection. Children know they are not perfect. They wonder how the imperfections of the children outside the safety yard are not okay. Some will deny their imperfections or become ashamed of them. Students learn to distance themselves from their weaknesses rather than making friends with or taming them. This model tends to stifle rather than encourage a student's questions or successive approximations of the teacher's lessons. Thus it promotes rote learning, which is faster and has more demonstrable results. Some children will learn to criticize those outside the circle, since in part their identity or esteem derives from the contrast. It is not that loving others is omitted, but that keeping negative definitions clear is more crucial. Here no one would denigrate *achdus,* but *achdus* is simply not emphasized. Clarity is desirable in confusing times, but in an attempt to maintain clarity, even variations in *minhagim* become a source of WE/THEY distinction, making it harder to promote *achdus*.

⇀⇒ The Lab as an Ongoing Process

We call the second model the lab because it acknowledges that education is a process, a work in progress. No student is expected to be "finished" at 10, 12 or 15 years of age. Rather, they are expected to understand their own patterns of strengths and weaknesses as a basis for lifelong commitment to learning and development. The *mechanech* is zealous to guard the gates from the awful corrosion in the secular culture, but his emphasis within the gates is on cultivating the individuality, expressiveness, talents and, yes, problems of each student. If each student is prized as an individual, then the emphasis is on mutuality, respect and *achdus* as a living example. In an atmosphere that is tolerant of strengths and weaknesses, students will learn to imitate their teachers, to empower each other's abilities and strive to channel weaknesses.

If the identity of the previous model is exclusion, the WE/THEY, the identity of this model is inclusion, the WE/WE. Identity is not based on specific measures of behavior so much as it is based on effort to grow. The reality is that some students start off on a lower or higher level, some have more fortunate home backgrounds, some less so. No one is exempt. If parents want an anesthetic to their anxiety, the *mechanech* in this model may not always oblige them. Rather, he attempts to help parents mature by encouraging them to acknowledge their children's past successes and exude positive hope, faith and trust in their continued ability to navigate the sea of adolescence.

In this model, as the students struggle with good and evil, we might not always like the stages they go through, the questions they ask, the way they weed out wrong from right, or even the students they identify with. There is no promise of immediate gratification here. The *mechanech* in this model is not a mechanic. (A good mechanic is expected to remove a malfunction or fix it.) He is a gardener. Some plants are hardier than others, some slower growing.

⇥ Tolerance, Patience, and Growth

Patience is needed in an impatient world. Poor behavior is met with demands for conformity (to *halachah*), but is accompanied by a series of interventions designed to help bring the student to a higher level of acceptance.

If the *mechanech* determines that it is appropriate to allow himself time to accomplish this process, the interim may look less successful to outside observers or even parents. In this model, adults are expected to tolerate process, a work in progress. In this model, adults are expected to supply the reassurance to themselves and to the children; children not fully mature are not expected to supply the reassurances by looking good for us. It is understood that children (people) learn from their mistakes.

Learning in this model is skill based, designed for offering students both Torah answers and Torah means of inquiry. This learning takes longer than rote learning, may at times be too complex to reduce to simpler forms of feedback (multiple-choice test, for instance), but this learning has lasting effects and offers the patient adult much *nachas* for the high level of logic, understanding and *ruchnius* gained. (I am reminded here of the late Rabbi Godlevsky, revered teacher in the Bais Yaakov movement, who used to ask his students only one "test" question: What is the *tachlis* of a person?) The student's *ruach* is never left behind in this model.

The risk in a WE/WE model is that if students do not reach their potential, they may absorb weaknesses of others. Therefore the *mechanech's* emphasis must always be keenly directed toward making sure that each student is focused on his potential. This system may flounder if the teachers themselves lack maturity or dedication. It is not that the *mechanchim* in this model are fearless, it is that they regard fearfulness as detrimental to growth. When the gardener sows seeds, he tills the ground, weeds, sweats, prays, then waits in faith. Trust is certainly a great risk; but when well handled, it offers students trust in their own readiness for adult responsibilities, trust in *Hakadosh Baruch Hu* who helps us achieve our efforts, and the key to himself, *gam ki yazkin lo yasur mimenu*.

⟜ Two Models

Two models have been presented. They are not by any means mutually exclusive. Every effort must be made to expand our ways of thinking for the benefit of our students, to incorporate the best features of each educational model.

Chazal tell us the Yaakov *Avinu* was punished for withholding Dinah from Eisav, for she might have inspired him to do *teshuvah*. Although Yaakov did what he must do, the *baalei mussar* indicate that he did not experience sufficient anguish (on the *chut hasaarah,* hairbreadth's level) for this lost opportunity. Every *mechanech* I have admired demonstrated a great share of pain. May this Jewish pain always lead us to helpful formulations for our students.

Knowing When and Where to Draw the Line
Rabbi Yoel Bursztyn

WHENEVER DEALING WITH AN ISSUE, THE DEEPER YOU delve, the more it becomes obvious that there is more than meets the eye. One must not be simplistic in his thinking. *Chinuch* is very complex; setting rules cannot be the only source of guidelines. Decisions may vary between elementary schools and high schools, between *chinuch* for *banim* (boys) and for *banos* (girls), between "in-town" schools and "out-of-town" schools, etc. Therefore, any response to Rabbi Aisenstark's statement is לפלפולא בעלמא — purely academic — and not be relied upon for *halachah lemaaseh* — as a practical guide.

Ahavas Yisrael can be a misguided slogan when inappropriately applied. Just as one would not be deemed as lacking *ahavas Yisrael* for not considering an unsuitable person as a candidate for marriage, so too may denying acceptance to a student be the correct thing to do. For example, admitting a student with a *"tchup"* (example cited by Rabbi Aisenstark) into a *Chassidishe cheder* may cause this particular student to feel out of place, thereby affecting his learning, his social standing, and his overall confidence, and it may also cause others to do the same. The Gerer Rebbe once said, "There are Jews in Germany who are as fine as we are, who dress modern; but should one of us in Poland dress that way, he would be an outcast."

Ideally, there should be no criteria for acceptance into a Torah institution other than "Will this child benefit from being enrolled here?" and "Is this child at least not a detriment to the school?" This would require quite a bit of research on the part of the *hanhalah*. It also would create confrontations. Many schools have therefore instituted guidelines such as "no TV homes" because — just as *Shabbos, kashrus,* and *taharas hamishpachah* differentiate between a *frum home* and a non-frum — TV has become the touchstone for differentiating between a Torah home and a non-Torah home.

Although *Kiruv Rechokim* — outreach to less-committed Jews — is a very noble activity for our schools, most of our institutions were founded to be *mekarev kerovim* — enhance the knowledge and status of the religious children — and that should not be compromised. If, however, *kiruv* could be accomplished without lowering standards, by all means *rechokim* are to be accepted with open arms.

My dear *chaver,* Rabbi Yisroel Shneur Aisenstark, isn't it true that you yourself have standards, and you would not send your students to certain conventions, even if they were run by *frum* Jews, because you may feel that the participants don't quite live up to your standards? In the same vein, why should we — you and I — be so upset if schools who have different sensitivities don't want to send their students to our convention? We all draw lines somewhere — are we only to be tolerant of people who have standards lower than ours? Let's think about it.

It's almost eighteen years now that I live 3,000 miles away from the center of *Yiddishkeit* in the United States. Every time I go back to the East Coast, I am overwhelmed by the beauty of having so many *batei knessios* and *batei midrashim* on each and every block. Most *shuls* exist not because "I would not daven in the other *shul*," but rather because a person feels more comfortable with people his type. Some *shuls* exist because the *Rav* or *Rebbe* needs a position. In the first case, we all benefit by it. In the latter case, it is also an asset, as long as it does not cause undue hardship to other *shuls*.

Who says that by being separate means *pirud* — divisiveness?

May we all in our individual *mosdos* be united in being *marbeh k'vod Shamayim* and be *zocheh* to ויעשו כולם אגודה אחת לעשות רצונך בלבב שלם

Contemporary Chinuch:
A Balancing Act

Mrs. Rochel Spector

↦ Meeting All Obligations

IT IS TRUE, AS RABBI AISENSTARK STATES, THAT OUR GENERATION has made great strides in certain areas of *Yiddishkeit,* mainly *bein adam laMakom* (between man and the Creator), yet we need to re-examine and re-evaluate our growth and accomplishments in the area of *bein adam lechaveiro* (between man and his fellow).

I would like to address Rabbi Aisenstark's point that we religious Jews lack the tolerance of and respect for legitimate differences among individuals who are all part of *Klal Yisrael*. First of all, I am proud to say that I am associated with a school whose *menahel* is sensitive to and aware of the calling of this generation, to educate and be *mekarev* the children of the families emigrating from Russia, Iran, etc. In fact, my father, Rabbi Menachem Manis Mandel tells these children: *We waited for you so for so many years; we davened so much that you be allowed to come and join us!*

Many of these children, who need special attention, have been registered in our regular classes. (Unfortunately, we have no empty rooms or funds for special classes.) Even though the number of children with special needs is limited in each class, some parents are questioning if the ratio between these children, who are not yet fully committed to Torah, and their own children, who are, is unbalanced. They have a point; we did have the experience of a class where those that needed *kiruv* had a negative influence on some of the other students. To avoid the danger of negative influence (albeit unintentional), perhaps we should deal with this issue as we deal with our incomes. Just as we give 10 percent to charity, so too should we allow up to 10 percent of the student body in any one class to come from homes that do not conform to the expected standards of the yeshiva (i.e., they own a TV, the mother does not cover her hair, or they are generally not fully observant).

The Escalation Process

Another problem in accepting students newly arrived from Russia or Iran is that our level of learning is totally out of reach for these newcomers. They would do better in a school that specializes in meeting their needs, such as Be'er Hagolah, Nefesh Academy, or Sinai Academy. When the principal of a transitional yeshiva assesses that a student is ready to be mainstreamed, he/she should approach the various schools in the child's neighborhood. Each school should be given an equal opportunity for this *mitzvah* and challenge. For the benefit of all involved, these new students should be equally divided among our neighborhood schools.

Many of these students progress, and give tremendous *nachas* to the *Ribbono Shel Olam*. One girl who comes to mind, was born in Russia and came to America at age 12. She spent six months in Be'er Hagolah, four months in a special class containing only seven students in Sara Schneirer, and was then enrolled in Yeshiva of Brooklyn. She was placed initially in a class with children three years her junior, caught up, was able to graduate with students her own age, and was selected to speak at the commencement. After a year of study in *Eretz Yisrael,* she returned to America with her *chassan* (her seminary principal introduced them to each other). Today he is studying in a *Kollel* and she is teaching in our pre-school department. Clearly, the extra effort expended on this girl was worthwhile. So too, in ways we cannot always see or measure, is the effort we put into all our students we are *mekarev.*

⇥ Yeshivos: Not Always at Fault

A second point of Rabbi Aisenstark's article that deserves comment: Are all problems to be laid at the door of our yeshivos? A yeshiva is not a foster home. As it is, parents expect way too much (for way too little) from a most overworked staff. It is time to retrain parents as to the responsibilities that *Hashem Yisbarach* has placed upon them by blessing them with children. Who is supposed to teach our children tolerance and respect? Shouldn't this sort of training come from the home? Has parenting become obsolete? Shouldn't parents prepare their child to deal with situations such as how a woman should react to the male who offers her a handshake?

Also worthy of comment is that when married siblings eat different *shechitas* in their respective households, it is not indicative of dissent. When tolerance and understanding coupled with a large dose of respect are present, the difference does not spell disaster.

Also, when *shtieblach* sprout like mushrooms and stores dot the avenue in a continuing string, it is not bred out of insensitivity to others. Let us be optimistic (is our glass half full?) instead of allowing pessimism to set in (thereby making our glass half empty). Namely, our numbers have ב"ה increased, and so have our needs. *Am Yisrael kedoshim heim.* We need not assume that expanding facilities is done to gouge the competitors' eyes out, *chas v'shalom.*

In short, although we must try to strive for more, I feel many yeshivos are coping as well as can be expected with the difficult balancing act of reaching out to those who need *kiruv* and bringing out the best in children who were brought up in uncompromising observance of the Torah.

The Ramifications of Selectionism and Rejectionism

Rabbi Yechezkel Zweig

WHILE THE QUESTION OF BALANCING THE DANGERS OF exposure to a harmful atmosphere against the potential gains of *ichud haam,* the oneness and unification of the *klal,* is certainly not new, perhaps it is timely for us to take a fresh look at the issues.

Those who would separate and insulate children hailing from homes whose standards reflect an uncompromised stance in all areas of *Yahadus* from "lesser" homes are addressing legitimate concerns—and often responding to real dangers and risks. Does the *Rambam* not teach us *(Hilchos*

Dei'os Ch. 6) that it is inherent in human nature for man to be affected by his environment, and does this not dictate that a Jew should choose for himself and his family an environment that will exert a positive *hashpaah* rather than one whose influences may be detrimental to growth and flourishing? Can we easily ignore insights from *Chazal* that teach us of the dangers of exposure to an environment deficient in ruchnius? (See *Michtav Me'Eliyahu I,* "*Hashpa'as Hasevivah*" for a fuller discussion on this topic.)

While the claim of "*Eilu ve'eilu divrei Elokim chayim* — These and those are words of the living G-d," can be submitted as a sound basis to insist on tolerance and respect among *Sefardim, Ashkenazim, Misnagdim,* and *Chassidim,* is it in any way legitimate to apply this premise when considering ideas, movements, or groups that are not guided and endorsed by *manhigei Yisrael?* Certainly not.

On the other hand, the equation is not so cut and dried — we do not live in a world of absolutes. Yes, on a practical level it is feasible for those who so desire to exclude from schools those who hail from homes with televisions, whose mothers fail to cover their hair, who frequent movies and the theater, or whose beliefs may not always be consistent with established Jewish custom. But does doing so constitute a definitive separation of good from bad, pure from impure, and *kadosh* from *chol?* In short, are we certain that the atmosphere — which permeates our schools, once one excludes those considered to have deviated from an ideal — is more "rarefied," and will lead to greater growth and flourishing for those left after the *"selektion"?* This is questionable for there are many other considerations:

- Does *ahavas Yisrael* really remain unaffected once schools have excluded those considered deficient in their commitment to pristine *ruchnius* goals? *Reality:* In most cases, real levels of *ahavas Yisrael* are lessened (deadened?), and many children too easily dismiss from their attention and concerns those considered to be inferior in their pursuits of *ruchnius.* In short, "out of sight, out of mind."

- What happens to the character development and *middos* of our children when we exclude those whose *Yiddishkeit* does not "measure up"? *Reality:* All too easily, our students may turn smug, having (unconsciously) judged themselves to be better than those "others." Too easily overlooked is that our own service of Hashem is often no more than *mitzvos anashim me'lumadah*—more reflexive than inspired. In fact *S'forno* (*Nitzavim* 30:2) expresses the notion that this will be the nature of much of our *mitzvah* performance before the final *geulah!*

- What is the whole truth about the *discomfort* we and our children feel in the proximity of those whose adherence to high levels of *tzenius* and *ahavas v'yiras Hashem* seem to be less than ours? We tend to assume that these feelings are *in and of themselves* an expression of *yiras Shamayim tehorah*. But is it not possible that they may *also* reflect a subtle level of self-centeredness, an *unwillingness* to function in an atmosphere that lacks "*heimishkeit*"? If the feelings of discomfort would be born solely of *yiras Shamayim*, how is it that "villains" abruptly turn into heroes when, if they have "made it," and we need them for our *mosdos*, we suddenly set aside our discomfort when we honor (!) and fete the selfsame individuals at our dinners and programs? If our anxiety stems exclusively from *yiras Shamayim*, why does the same "fear of Heaven" not create discomfort within us when exposed to individuals (sometimes ourselves) who miss time at the workplace by arriving late, shmoozing on the phone—and the multitude of other forms of *Choshen Mishpat* trespass?

- Is it perhaps the case that in defining differences between ourselves and others, we are mired in a set of mental labels that describe a *mitzvah* performance scorecard, while overlooking other qualitative personality aspects that in fact might be cherished by the *Ribbono Shel Olam* — and exposure to which our children might grow from? In considering whom to "exclude," are considerations of personality traits such as compassion, sensitivity, generosity, *ehrlkichkeit,* etc. also given their due? Might we consider that the young man or woman who frequents hangouts or whose appearance may at times be inappropriate (not that improper *conduct* or *appearance* should be accepted) may in fact possess character traits that, if properly cultivated, can serve as a *berachah* for both the individual and the *klal*? Indeed, Rabbi E.E. Dessler, in quoting from the *Talmud Yerushalmi,* presents the profound story of a Jew who earned his livelihood in an unseemly manner, but whose unknown personal worth rendered him more suitable to supplicate Hashem for desperately needed rains than all other members of the community! *(Michtav Me'Eliyahu I, "Hatzne'a Lechess...")*

⇒ A Higher Level of Spirituality: Generosity of the Spirit

Talmidim of the late *Rosh Hayeshiva* of Ner Israel, Rabbi Yaakov Yitzchok Ruderman, carry a thought that he imparted, which characterized an important dimension of his approach to *avodas Hashem. Chazal* tell us that Rabbi Shimon bar Yochai entered a cave with his son, Rabbi Elazar, to escape Roman persecution. He emerged after thirteen years, but was unable to countenance a world given over to mundane pursuits. The piercing stare of his uncompromising eyes brought about destruction wherever he looked, so that he was admonished by a *bas kol,* "Did you leave [the cave] to destroy the world?" He returned to the cave and emerged after an additional year, when he was able to live in peace with the reality of a spiritually feeble and mortal world.

Should not the additional year of intense Torah study have brought these two Torah giants to even greater levels of uncompromising heights? The *Rosh Hayeshivah* explains that herein lies an important lesson: At very high levels of dedicated service to Hashem, we may become uncompromising and unable to countenance that which is imperfect.

However, the yet higher level is that which enables one to function at supreme levels of *kedushah* side by side with those who come up short in their *madreigos* (levels) and aspirations. Indeed, the most supreme levels of *avodas Hashem* may enable us to develop a generosity of the spirit that allows us to see the strengths in others—and perhaps be more honest about our own shortcomings.

Parents may sometimes find themselves liking certain characteristics in one child more than those of another. But the *love* that parents naturally feel for their children is so pervasive that likes and preferences barely register. True, abiding love far overshadows all else. No, we cannot declare as wrong those who wish to create an environment free of tangible dangers to one's spiritual growth. On the other hand, in a very imperfect world, perhaps *our* abiding love might allow us to humbly note and acknowledge our own weaknesses while seeing the potential within each member of *Klal Yisrael* to rise to the *gedulah* (greatness) that is possible for all *Bnei Avraham, Yitzchak and Yaakov.*

Only for the Chosen of Our People?

Rabbi Yaakov Bender

⇥ Chessed for All — But Our Kids

- "Chanoch *lanaar al pi darko* — educate the child in his own way" — a *pasuk* in *Mishlei* quoted again and again.
- *V'chol bonayich limudei Hashem* — and all your children will be students of Hashem's Torah" (*Yishayahu* 54:13). Another *pasuk* heard repeatedly.
- Rav Preida taught each lesson to a slow student 400 times, until he mastered it. On one occasion, the student still did not comprehend it, so he reviewed it an additional 400 times ... earning *Olam Haba* for his entire generation by virtue of his dedication to this unresponsive *talmid* (*Eruvin* 54b). Which *Rosh Yeshiva* or *menahel* has not quoted that famous *Gemara* to his *rebbei'im* or faculty members hundreds of times?

SUCH *MAAMOREI CHAZAL* (QUOTATIONS FROM THE TALMUD) and *pesukim* from *Nach* (passages from Scripture) are the substance of *shmuessen* (inspirational discourses delivered to us in true sincerity. How often have we *mechanchim* (educators) been galvanized at professional conventions to return to our schools and work with our *talmidim*, sometimes under the most difficult conditions, to teach Torah to one and all *bederech Yisrael Sava,* in keeping with our sacred traditions. None of us has ever doubted the Torah-truth of these noble words. Yet something seems to get lost between accepting the conviction and carrying it out. We would like to think that we practice what we preach, but too many of us turn a deaf ear to hundreds of children who want to learn Torah but cannot, without some kind of encouragement and help.

This is paradoxical, for beyond doubt, we are living in an era distinguished by *chessed,* possibly unparalleled in recent history. And yet, judging by the evidence, it would almost seem as though our educational institutions are conspiring to disenfranchise large numbers of our children.

⤏ A Few Case Histories

A few case histories can illustrate this crisis situation (and I use the word "crisis" advisedly):

1. In a discussion with the principal of a highly successful yeshiva, we touched on the topic of the weak student. The *menahel* blithely informed me that if a child cannot read in the first grade, he is transferred out. I asked, "Isn't it your responsibility to take care of all your *talmidim*?"

"Certainly not," he responded. "When we accept a child for kindergarten, we inform the parents that he will be a student in our school only as long as we are able to service him. Otherwise, we cannot accommodate him."

"Why don't you set up a Resource Room to help these unfortunate children?" I asked. (A Resource Room is a facility where specially trained teachers help children overcome learning disabilities within a mainstream environment.)

"We do not have the space availability, nor is our school set up for such children."

The *menahel* then mentioned a neighboring school that does accept such *talmidim.*

2. Not long ago, I received a phone call from a parent of an 8-year-old child who is wheelchair bound, with a difficult case of cerebral palsy. While suffering slight learning disabilities,

he tested with an I.Q. of over 160, is sweet, well behaved, and has wonderful *midos*. But no yeshiva will take him.

Who gave this child cerebral palsy? It was not self-inflicted. The *Ribbono Shel Olam,* in His infinite wisdom, decreed that this child should have cerebral palsy. Can we contest that ruling?

Accepting such a child into a conventional school will surely tax the school's facilities. For instance, someone will have to wheel the child to the rest room, or to the ballfield for a little fresh air and entertainment. That does not frighten me, for if my son were the one to be given this assignment, I am certain that he would *shtieg* (grow) immeasurably from the task, as he would were he to learn *b'chavrusa* with his young man. Must we run away from every situation that does not fit into a safe mold, tried and tested in the past?

3. Last year, a parent came to enroll "Avi," an 8-year-old, in our school. My first encounter with Avi was in the hallway. While introducing myself to him, Avi noticed "Berel" — a former classmate who now attends our yeshiva. Avi turned to me and said: "This crazy kid is in your yeshiva? We all knew Berel was crazy!"

Apparently, Berel was viewed as "off the wall" in his former yeshiva, and was therefore shunned by his peers. He is presently a wonderful student in our third grade, albeit with certain learning disabilities.

4. For years and year, we prayed that *Acheinu Bnei Yisrael* would be released from their bondage in the Soviet Union. Others took their hopes to the streets and demonstrated. Now that they are here, how many yeshivos (with the exception of those especially geared to them) are willing to accept Russian children? Hagaon Rav Yaakov Kamentzky had called on all institutions to include at least 10 percent Russian children in their total enrollment. What can it possibly mean when we beseech the *Ribbono Shel Olam* to release them, only to abandon them when they arrive on our shores? Is it the fate of the children of refuseniks to *be* refused forever more?

5. Some ten years ago, when the Shah of Iran was over-

thrown and Khoumeini took over, there was a sudden influx of Iranian children to this country. Our yeshiva accepted some thirty Iranian boys, as did other schools. Most of them were from non-Orthodox homes and their parents were not always supportive. Yet we persevered and we were ב"ה very successful in inculcating them with Torah and *yiras Shomayim.* Upon graduating, they were neither scholastically nor emotionally prepared to go to out-of-town yeshivos; their goal was simply to attend yeshiva high schools in their communities. In many cases, their applications were refused. Considering their family backgrounds, their ultimate enrollment in public high schools was all but inevitable, as is the fact that many of them are today *mechalelei Shabbos* and *ochlei neveilos.* Who is accountable for this?

6. The *menahalim* of Mesivta high schools often call for the list of our eighth-grade graduating class. (We do not have a high school.) These *menahalim* always mention, "Please indicate which are the better students in the class." Aren't the average and below-average students entitled to a Torah education?

7. Routinely, yeshiva high schools send out rejection letters to applicants who have done everything right. There are few things in life more callous and cruel than these rejection letters. Picture the feelings of an eighth grader — who works very hard, and learns *behasmadah rabbah* (with great diligence) — when he receives this offensive letter; his friend who is not serious in class, but is gifted with exceptional intelligence, receives a letter of acceptance. The first fellow did everything that was expected of him. He has but one problem: He is missing that all-important ingredient so desired in today's high school — champion capabilities. (Our yeshiva attempts to make arrangements with Mesivta high schools whereby acceptance letters are sent to all applicants. Actual acceptance and rejection is conveyed from *menahel* to *menahel.* Weaker boys are then told, "Yes, you were accepted, but I believe you'd do better in school X.")

8. How many principals have heard the following rejections

from high schools? These communications are authentic — and continue to flow:

"If he is not one of your best boys, forget it."

"It is not that we don't want him — he is a nice boy. He just won't fit in here. It wouldn't be good for him."

"He only made out between tov and beinoni (good and average). He won't make it here."

"He did well on the bechinah. He is a good boy. But I have only two openings and I am holding them for two superior boys."

The Excuses for Exclusion

The case histories cited can be reinforced with many more such stories, to constitute substantial anecdotal evidence that our schools are excluding children for a variety of reasons, along the full continuum of their career, from grade 1 through high school:

Children who require special attention because they are "different" for reasons of foreign birth, weak background, or physical handicap; children who suffer learning disabilities; and children who do not measure up to the higher academic standards to which a school aspires.

Of course, schools may feel that they have justification for each case of exclusion or expulsion. But it is my contention that with extra measures of compassion and determination, these objections can be overcome. Moreover, I believe that schools have a responsibility toward these children in spite of the objections. In fact I would suggest that yeshivos that refuse to make room for all types of children may be accountable for such treatment.

The major arguments against accepting weak children into a yeshiva, and in defense of easing out those with difficulties, is that by accepting and keeping such children, a school lowers its standard. This need not be the case.

A yeshiva can maintain high standards, regardless of how it caters to the needs of the slower students, as long as the brighter *talmidim* are challenged.

In our yeshiva, for example, we have ב"ה many hundreds of *talmidim* striving for excellence and graduating into the mainstream institutions of today's yeshiva world. Yet we find it no contradiction to our mission to have a Resource Center, with five full-time teachers working with mildly learning-disabled children. Indeed, the weaker children are gaining significantly. The sad part is that we are inundated with requests on a daily basis from parents of children from all walks of life and yeshivos; but we cannot accommodate them all because our capacity is saturated. Accommodations for them should be made closer to home. Why should the 8-year-old son of a widely respected *Rav* be forced to *schlep* from another borough for 1½ hours every morning to our yeshiva and 1½ hours home every night on a city bus, often with unsavory bus-mates?

With this special program in effect, our stronger students become even better students — not only in *middos,* but academically, as well, for they rate favorably with students from the so-called "elite" institutions.

Schools also plead lack of space, lack of equipment, and other explanations based on economic considerations. Should an endowment come their way, these yeshivos would probably find the means to accommodate students with special needs — even to the point of hiring private *rebbei'im.* Perhaps the initiative must come from concerned individuals, or the community as a whole. After all, the yeshivos are communal institutions, and generally are responsive to communal expectations. Moreover, they receive support from the broad community, and can be expected to carry out the community mandate; to teach all children Torah as long as it is within the realm of the possible.

Let us bear in mind that at least one of every ten boys, and a smaller percentage of girls, are born with learning disabilities. Certainly not all children are born with superior intelligence. But we, as a community, have accepted the concept that our schools are for the superior children. Even worse, many or most of our parents insist on the fiction that their own children are superior, with the result that their children do not receive the sort of help and attention that would benefit them, because the classes are targeted for a level beyond their capabilities. And those schools that are flexible enough to permit learning-disabled and slower children to stay on their rolls, often leave these children to vegetate in their classrooms and become the class dummies or "nebs" — because the *Ribbono Shel Olam* did not bless them with the high degree of functioning intelligence that the other children in the class have.

Not in Our High School

When we speak of Mesivtos and Bais Yaakov high schools refusing applicants, we are not discussing youngsters who have even slightly strayed off the well-defined *derech* — the boy with the so-called "bummy" appearance, or the girl who has learned her street smarts. Most high schools will not touch them! We are referring to the boy who looks like a *ben Torah*, acts like a *ben Torah*, but cannot handle all the *Tosafos* in the ninth grade. Do the "better" *yeshivos* agree to accept him? They do not. And the girl who is academically weak will often be forced to settle for a high school out of her immediate neighborhood.

And then there are those high-school students (usually boys) who are advised to go elsewhere for the next year because of learning difficulties — not those who are disruptive because of emotional problems. It is all too common that in our day, adolescent *bachurim* and even elementary-age youngsters are told to leave their respective yeshivos, sometimes even for minor infractions. One yeshiva head says that it is his policy not to retain any boy who is sent to him more than once a year for disciplinary reasons; he is too busy running the institution to be distracted.

Contrast this with the fact that the late Ponovezher *Rav* would never expel a *talmid* from his yeshiva for any reason unless he first consulted with the Chazon Ish. This certainly makes us wonder about the comparatively cavalier approach in some of our yeshivos. Remember, the Ponovezher *Rav* had at his side in the yeshiva such great leaders as Rabbi Eliyahu Eliezer Dessler and Rabbi Chaskel Levenstein; and yet he would never ask a *talmid* to leave Ponovezh without the consent of the Chazon Ish! His reason, he stated, was that he deemed the question to be *dinei nefashos* — a matter of life and death, and for such a decision he needed the consummate *poseik*.

The time-honored approach of the *gedolim* of yesteryear has always been not to expel a *talmid* unless he has a definite, clearly identified detrimental effect on other *talmidim*. How many children are *mechallel Shabbos* today because of this new policy to "transfer them out if they do not fit our educational standards"! Let us remember that the nonstudent or yeshiva dropout in the traditional European community had a safety net of religious Jews, functioning in a decent, self-contained social setting. Even as a comparative illiterate, the dropout had a place and was not in danger of straying from a life of Torah. Today, however, any child not in yeshiva will *ipso facto* be destined for spiritual, and possibly social, disaster.

⇨ A Source of the Problem

A major portion of the guilt lies with parents who insist that their children not attend a school that accepts average or below-average children. What objection could they have to weaker children in the same school building? Status? That is simply another word for "selfishness." There is another factor, and it is not a matter of deliberate malice.

Yeshivos and families are both subject to external considerations that affect how they view and carry out their roles. Competition is one of them. *Baruch Hashem,* our major population centers enjoy an abundance of Jewish children with parents who want superior results in their Torah education. This applies to boys and girls almost equally. The performance of a school is generally measured by academic results, by how well its students perform at the Shabbos table, and by how they are ranked in the higher academies of America and Israel. Parents also demand a rarefied environment that is free of improper influences. So it is common that parents, justifiably, inquire as much into the quality of the parent body and general *hashkafah* of the school and its families as they do into the curriculum.

Since schools compete for students, it is only natural that they will seek to satisfy the "consumer."

The general trend is clear. Not only do most yeshivos seek better students, the *rebbei'im* and teachers cater to them. The inevitable result is that the middle and lower end of a class — and every class has such a mix — are not receiving their due. And parents? They are thrilled with the prestige of being in the elite yeshivos, having the renowned *rebbi,* seeing the notebook crammed with *chiddushim,* witnessing their son on the fast track to the Jewish equivalent of Harvard and a marvelous *shidduch.* That the picture is illusory doesn't matter. Most people don't know; the rest don't care.

The result is that the entire community is in a trap. Yeshivos are not doing what they know they should be doing, parents are not receiving what they expect, and uncounted numbers of children are not receiving a proper *chinuch.* Those *in* the yeshivos, at least, can feel a measure of satisfaction — but those who suffer the most are those who are denied admission to schools or who, if admitted, are virtually ignored because they do not receive specialized attention.

Parents in search for success in their child's growth should bear in mind the *zechus* of *Toras Chessed* — similar to that of Rav Preida — and demand of our yeshivos that all children feel welcome. Then, with G-d's help, they will witness true *hatzlachah* with their own children.

The intention of this article is not to elicit letters-to-the-editor pointing out that here and there institutions do cater to the weaker *talmid.* There are some exceptional *mosdos* that do. Rather, this article is an appeal to the vast majority of mainstream institutions to open their hearts and classrooms to those members of the *chareidi* population that are now locked out. Do not be afraid to be the first one. It did not hurt any yeshiva to house a P'TACH class, or to engage special *rebbei'im* and teachers to provide special attention to children with special needs.

⤖ Solutions

All of our children deserve the chance to become true *bnei Torah* and *bnos Yisrael*. There are solutions to the problems. But first, what the solution is NOT: We must *not* set up ghetto institutions for children of average or slightly lower intelligence except where absolutely necessary. By perpetuating the myth that these children do not belong in regular classroom, we are labeling them for life.

The viable solutions may be as follows:

For the children who cannot fit into a regular yeshiva classroom:

1. Encourage self-contained classrooms (such as P'TACH) in all regular institutions for those children who need a full day of individualized attention. Ensure that these children are mainstreamed for any class that they can handle. Certainly make sure that they *daven* (where appropriate), eat, have recess, and so on, with the rest of the school, and function as an integral part of the yeshiva, unlike the experience of some P'TACH students who are made to feel by the mainstream yeshiva as if they are less-than-welcome guests.

2. Set up programs for children who attend special schools such as Chush or Lexington School for the Deaf to be integrated with *chaveirim* in their own communities — e.g., organize a *chavrusa* program where regular *talmidim* can tutor these children in their free time. The experience is uplifting and inspirational *for the tutors*. Or: Form a second-track small class for them.

For the children who can fit into a regular yeshiva classroom:

1. Every elementary school should have a Resource Room for all those children who cannot cope with particular areas of study. Engage professional staff for both *limudei kodesh* and

limudei chol to bring the children up to par. If learning problems are dealt with at the Pre-1A or first-grade level, they will not mushroom into bigger problems later, and often will disappear altogether. The big argument will be: finances. If you — the school, the administration, the parent body — really recognize the problem as your own, you will find a way. If funds cannot be raised, pass the costs on to the affected parents who — in most instances — will be happy to find a way to raise these funds so their child can attend a regular yeshiva.

OR

2. Run a two-track system where less is demanded of the B-class. At the high-school level, children who cannot handle the workload will thrive in a two-track system. But this works only if the *menahel* does not make these children feel that they are different and inferior.

There are about twenty yeshiva high schools within a 100-mile radius of New York City. If each of these yeshivos were to open a B-class every four years (meaning five such classes per year), they would be able to work with 125 new children every year within the regular and normal framework of the system. By the time these children graduate from high school, most of them will have caught up with the classmates in the A-class and maybe even surpass their level through their *hasmadah* and the individualized attention they will have received.

In short, as individuals we all do our utmost to live up to our birthright as *rachmanim, bayshanim, v'gomlei chassadim* — merciful, humble, compassionate people. Let us open our *mosdos haTorah* so that all children of *Klal Yisrael* — *Bnei* and *Bnos Yisrael* — will have the opportunity to learn the Torah that was given to us at Mount Sinai. Then we will truly be able to say, "*Torah tzivah lanu Moshe morashah Kehillas Yaakov* — Moshe commanded us the Torah which is the inheritance of *all* of *Klal Yisrael*." Just as we have always been a compassionate people, it would behoove us to go out of our way to have our Torah institutions do the same, teaching and personifying the true *Toras Chessed*.

When Children's Learning Handicaps Are of Our Own Making
The Early Placement Syndrome

Rabbi Yitzchak Kasnett

⇝ Working With the Learning-Disabled Child...

DURING MY SEVEN YEARS AS THE COORDINATOR OF THE P'TACH Yeshiva Rabbi Chaim Berlin program, I spent my days (and many evenings) with youngsters exhibiting a variety of learning disabilities — auditory, language, memory, visual and/or motor in nature. In the P'TACH program, the student's learning disability is identified through comprehensive psychoeducational testing. The teachers then develop plans for working with the child, projecting goals for each child to pursue as he or she begins his or her (hereafter "he... his") process of remediation. In addition, the student is taught to relate to his weaknesses in a positive manner, externalizing them as a part — and *not* the whole — of one's self. With a healthy self-image, the student can make great strides in achievement — and usually does.

Indeed, P'TACH and Yeshiva Rabbi Chaim Berlin's joint program succeeded in graduating over 90 percent of the seniors in the P'TACH program with regular high-school diplomas, including one young man who became the valedictorian of his mainstream class after having spent two years in P'TACH.

⇢ ...And the Bright Early Starter

Surprisingly, a child with learning problems placed in a contained classroom can be far more assured of developing his or her potential for a successful future than many children in mainstream classes who are not learning disabled at all. Throughout my years of psychoeducational testing in my private practice in Brooklyn, I have found a statistically relevant and troublesome profile appear over and over again: Many of the children referred for testing were encountering difficulty with their schoolwork, yet they exhibited no evidence of a learning disability. Anaylsis of the data recorded during the testing sessions,[1] however, did reveal a disturbing, yet interesting source for their difficulties.

Simply, they are too young for their class placement and lack the emotional, neurological and/or social maturity to succeed in a highly structured learning environment.

In each case, the child scored at the average, or above-average, level for his age-appropriate placement, but each skill area became devaluated one or two steps when viewed in terms of grade-placement norms. Thus, the child will score at the average level for full-scale cognitive functioning for *age* norms — that is, his skills in listening, interpreting visual information, short-term memory, visual-motor integration, reasoning, and language is equal to others of his age group; yet he is often found to be functioning in these same skills at the low-average range for *grade* norms. Had this child entered the school system one year later, he would most probably function more than adequately in the lower, but more logical, class placement. The children found to suffering from this "temporal" learning problem may well end up with an environmentally generated learning disability, and

---

1. Among the other tests, I use the Woodcock-Johnson Psycho-Educational Battery as the mainstay of my testing tools — one of the best diagnostic tests of its kind, with an excellent level of test reliability and validity. The test itself produces a voluminous assortment of scores, including distinct assessments of all skills for both age and grade placement, and it is at this level of analysis, the comparison of age and grade norms, that the source of difficulty challenging these children is most dramatically revealed.

quite possibly with severe behavioral and emotional adjustment problems as well, as they fall further and further behind. Worse yet, the school generally does not provide them with a structure to help them externalize the impact that their failure and frustration can have upon them. They identify as losers.

A Widespread Problem

This is a widespread problem, for many of our yeshiva students start their educational careers one year earlier than do most children in the public sector (where students contend with only one curriculum). Thus, while the student may be placed in fourth grade, his or her test profile will appear at the average (and above) for third grade *age* norms, with deficits of varying degrees for expected levels of proficiency at the child's *actual* fourth grade placement. There are many reasons for these early placements (some with acceptable rationale, others without), the exploration of which is beyond the scope of this article. At some future time, however, a comprehensive yet practical set of guidelines for early placement should be developed.

This article is meant to raise the consciousness of our parent body, so they will become more cautious when considering early placements, until appropriate guidelines are available. These placements should be made with thorough consideration for the child's overall levels of social-emotional, language, memory, motor, and sensory development, and not merely by convenience or well-intentioned hopes.

In addition, it is important to remember that time spent in school is taken from time spent at home. Every child requires quality time with his parents, time that is translated into the subtle and consistent transmission of confidence, integrity and self-respect, which become the foundation upon which this young life is to be built. Realize that the special moments you invest in your child when he is young become memories that remain for a lifetime, and will most probably become the blueprint for his own attitude and conduct with your grandchildren in the future. These special moments are forfeited when the young child is in school.

It would be beneficial for the schools themselves to adopt some criteria for early admittance so as to alleviate some of the lowered functioning that surfaces from the third to fifth grades. This is the period when discrepancies appear, for the schoolwork in these grades demands more sophisticated levels of comprehension and skill integration. In the primary grades children often resort to substitute tactics to cover up for deficiencies; for instance, they may remember the brief text printed on a page from having heard it read aloud several times. In the intermediate grades, however, these compensatory strategies become overrun and no longer work effectively.

⟻ The Age Advantage

The widespread existence and the seriousness of this phenomenon (distinct from the true learning-disabled child) in the greater school population was recently supported by the published results of a study[2] completed in Israel, reporting "that students were more successful when they begin school at age six, rather than five." The research findings reported that of the 104 Israeli 5- and 6-year-old first graders participating in the study, the older students scored higher on their achievement tests, were more accepted by their peers, and had a stronger self-image than their younger peers. In addition, their teachers rated them as adjusting better to school. While there is no reason to assume that Israeli schoolchildren are different from their American counterparts, or that yeshiva children mature at a different pace than *mamlachti* school-children, it is in place to cite the opinions of two experienced American elementary-school yeshiva principals, which corroborate the Israeli findings. I thus invited Rabbi Yehudah Frankel, *menahel* of the Mirrer Yeshiva K'tana, and Rabbi Shlomo Klein, *menahel* of the Yeshiva K'tana of Yeshiva Rabbi Chaim Berlin, both of Brooklyn, to comment on the issue of early placement.

---

2. *Journal of Genetic Psychology,* Vol. 149, No. 4, 12/88.

Some Suggestions

IN LIGHT OF THE RESEARCH AND DISCUSSION PRESENTED IN this article, it appears that (until the age of admissions is raised or standardized by the yeshivos) it would be to the benefit to this group of children to follow the recommendations below:

1. Suggestion to the Parents: A careful evaluation of the child's development and an assessment of his or her social-emotional needs should be completed before deciding on early placement. To this end, there are several good Early Childhood Screening instruments available, including informal evaluation by a competent learning specialist.

2. Suggestion to the Yeshiva: Develop internal administrative mechanisms to request and review screenings of early placements (upon application and not after acceptance) to identify those children who may be at risk for this early-placement syndrome. Certainly a comprehensive questionnaire concerning the child's readiness could be developed (some already exist) to be completed by the parent with the standard enrollment forms. Should any doubt then exist concerning the child's readiness, the yeshiva could request further testing (as mentioned above) before admission is finalized.

In this manner, both the parents and the yeshivos can be spared the burden of intervention at a later and more critical time in the child's development; of greater importance, the child himself could be spared what might be many years, if not a lifetime, of failure, self-doubt, and lost potential.

A Teacher's List of Do's (not Don'ts!)

Mrs. Rochel Leah Frankel

◆━━ **Clear Concern**

TALMIDOS ARE INFLUENCED BY THOSE THEY BELIEVE CARE about them and are concerned for their welfare. If we are to make a difference in a student's life, we must make it clear that her well-being and success is our goal.[1] All those in the field of *chinuch habanos* are here because they care. We know that, but it is not enough for *us* to know; our students must know it, too.

> *Sara Laya left the office in a huff. The very fact that the principal could say this to me, she thought, shows that she doesn't even know me or care about me. She doesn't begin to comprehend who I am. All she cares about is the "school's name."*

It may come as a surprise that the advice offered was rejected. Not because it wasn't sound advice. Not because it didn't hit home. But simply because the student felt that her well-being was not the issue. Even when there is obviously no personal motive, the student must be made aware that all you seek is *her* benefit. When a student threw me the line, "You only care about the 'school's name,'" I turned to her and said,

---

1. *Rambam Hilchos Dei'os* 6:7.

"What is a school? A school is not a separate entity, a monolithic monster. A school is made up of individuals, *yechidos*. If every girl has a good name, a *shem tov*, then the school has a good name. So all I am concerned with is you." With that, we sat down to address the issues at hand.

Even when a *talmidah* knows that you care about her and that her success is your number one goal, there may be times when she feels you could not possibly understand her. Perhaps she thinks you cannot relate to her situation since you appear to be too *frum*, mature, smart, or different from her. Putting yourself in her shoes, conveying an understanding of her struggles or difficulties, can prevent such a situation.

⚞ Understanding Their Struggles

A very glum and dejected Tali sat before me. "It's no use. I give up. I will never be a real Bais Yaakov girl. I just am not like the rest of you." I inquired how she felt she differed from "us." "Oh, just that you are all so good, being tzeniusdig seems to come naturally to you. Do you know what an effort it is for me? What a constant battle it is?"

"Welcome to reality Tali," I said. "No one has it easy. Each person faces difficulties on her level. Each of us has our own struggles...."

A little glimpse into the daily tug-of-war all students face was all she needed to realize she was as "normal" as the rest. Even more so, she needed to realize that teachers also have their own struggles.

Taking the time to understand a student's personal struggles can also diffuse a potential situation.

Fraidy sat before me, defiance oozing from her every fiber. Her remark was out of line, but how was I going to explain that to her effectively? "You must be very upset about something to have answered the teacher like that," I finally said.

She looked up at me in surprise. "How did you know that I was so upset?!" I explained that both she and I knew that chutzpah was unacceptable, and as such, she must have lost herself. We discussed the source of the problem and some potential solutions. I pointed out that her remarks had not helped solve her problem. On the contrary, they had given her another problem to deal with. We both agreed that chutzpah was uncalled for even when one is upset, and left with a line of communication and understanding open for the future.

Explain It in Their Terms

There are times when a student is convinced of the truth of her case. She sincerely feels that a teacher is wrong, she knows a *Rav* who disagrees with school policy. It serves no purpose to lock horns with her. No one wins in such a situation. It is as though she wears a sign proclaiming: "My mind is made up, so don't confuse me with the facts!" Listen to her. Let her have her say. I didn't say I agree with her. Then very gently use her own argument or logic to point out flaws in her conclusion.

> *Rina politely informed me that she would no longer be able to sit in Morah L's shiurim. Even her parents agreed with her that this teacher was just not equipped to discuss the subject involved. She was so narrow minded and not in sync with the school's policies. I heard her out. I commented on how difficult it must be for her to sit in class and take notes in a class given by a teacher she clearly disagrees with. I commended her on her high grades in the subjects taught by that particular Morah, and then calmly turned to her and said: "So you don't like the fact that Morah L is so narrow minded and intolerant in the lessons she conveys?"*
>
> *Rina bobbed her head in agreement and said she felt the teacher lacked tolerance.*
>
> *"And what about your lack of tolerance for Morah L?" I asked. Of course she had never thought of it from that perspective. Needless to say, she continued to attend the shiurim and became an active participant in the lessons.*

⟸ Know Your Students

If there were a golden rule for teachers, it would be: Know your student. Of course I know her, you might say; she's the one who is always disrupting in class, the ringleader, the non-performer. These all may be true, but who *is* she?

Students do not function in a void. They are members of a class, but they are also daughters, sisters and friends. They bring all sorts of "baggage" to school in their designer backpacks. We must diagnose the issues involved: the social predicament of the student, her home situation, her personal shortcomings, her areas of strength. All these factors directly influence her growth and accomplishments.

> *Liba was not the best of students. Though the teacher put in much effort, she still did not produce laudable results. One semester, her grades took off. Immediately, the teacher had doubts as to Liba's integrity. Not long after, it was back to the old test scores. This only served to bolster the teacher's suspicions.*
>
> *The truth of the matter was quite different. Liba had a very difficult home situation. For that short time, things had changed dramatically and with the change her ability to concentrate and study improved. Unfortunately for Liba, the change did not last.*

⟸ Teach by Example

All students crave guidance and direction. When it is properly given, they are receptive and responsive. If we do not provide the direction, they will take their cue from other sources. When giving guidance to our *talmidos*, it is important to remember that *hashpaah* (influence) is caught, not taught. Each time we stand up in front of a class, we are living examples as to what is expected of them. We refer to this as role modeling. The problem is we are likely to think of it as just that; a modeling job. You show up at the job site, properly attired, pose for the necessary time and take off the costume/attitude upon leaving. There is nothing further from the truth. When teaching impressionable young minds and souls, we never know what will make the greatest impression. It may surprise you to know that it is not always the difficult *meforash* that you deliver with great skill that has the strongest impact on a girl and changes her focus, but rather the reaction you had to a challenging class situation.

> *We were on a school Shabbaton in the mountains. Many staff members and their families had come along to add ruach to the experience. There were inspiring speakers and thought-provoking lectures. Surprisingly, upon our return to school, one girl said that the thing that had the most impact on her was the exchange she overheard between her teacher and her son. It had taken place Shabbos morning as they prepared to go to shul. The boy had been up for some time and had been helping out in the kitchen with preparations for the Kiddush. As a reward, he had received some cake which he promptly fed to himself and his shirt. His mother said to him, "You can't go to shul like that. It is not kavod." This the girl could not get over. It changed her whole approach to kedushas beis haknesses and tefillah.*

⟜ Praise: The Magic Tool

Praise is so valuable a tool, I often wonder why it is underutilized. It is not expensive, does not require much effort, and produces the most amazing results. We must be truthful when we praise. Praising a girl for doing so well when she is failing will more likely produce a snort rather than the desired effect.

Every student has some good qualities. Focus on it and build the rest to match. A very good example of this type of praise-induced change is one I use in parenting. The scenario: a (very) messy bedroom. The advice: Find one spot in that mess that is neat. Focus on it by saying, "Let's get the rest of the room to match that shelf/drawer/corner."

> *Tzila was having a hard year. Although she had done well in the past, her current marks were not reflecting her capability. A teacher was detailed to speak with and*

motivate her. Upon perceiving that there was interest in her accomplishments, Tzila began to put in more effort. As soon as it was noticeable, I went over and complimented her on her improvement and informed her that the teacher had told me how well she was doing and how impressed she was with her determination. You should have seen Tzila float out of the office as though on a cloud. Slowly, her effort expanded to include other subjects as well.

⇥ Stressing the Positive

People thrive on praise. It creates a desire to repeat the action that brought about the praise, initiating a cycle of success. As teachers, we must incorporate praise into our very being. It must reflect a positive attitude towards people and life.

Positivity is a key ingredient in *chinuch*. The receptivity of a student hinges on positive presentation. Most students do not reject the ideals taught in principle. Their rejection is due to the manner in which they are conveyed. This is with regard to classroom discipline, school rules and procedures, and, most importantly, *Torah hashkafah*. Stress the beauty of Torah. דרכיה דרכי נועם – show how Torah enhances our lives.

This is especially important when conveying sensitive issues such as *tzenius*. It is vital that *bnos Yisrael* realize that they are *bnos Hamelech*.[2] Just as a princess never feels her crown is a burden (though it is quite heavy), but rather wears it with great pride, so too do we view *tzenius* as our badge of honor.

> *Chedva asked me one day to show her where in the Torah it says not to wear a certain style of dress that we had prohibited. I knew that she was aware that this is not a "d'Oraysa," and was looking for a loophole. I asked her if she knew why this type of dress was created. She answered immediately, "To attract attention." I asked her why she would want to wear something that was created for that specific purpose, since she was*

---

2. *Tehillim* 45:14.

such a refined girl. "No, no! I would never wear that, I just wanted to know."

⟶ Signs of Trouble

All the above Do's are in the preventive category. When we establish an open line of communication, and understanding, we can solve many a problem before it gets out of hand. Were we to succeed, many a tragic situation would be prevented. Yet, the problems do crop up — in part, because we are not the only caregivers of this child. There may be a home situation that may not complement all the positivity you radiate, or some other situation beyond your control. You will be sensitive to changes (even subtle ones) in a *talmidah's* behavior if you have this type of relationship.

What to look for:[3]

Changes in scholastic achievement: One of the more obvious signs of a student's disenchantment is a marked drop in grades. It is often interesting to note that she may maintain her average in the *limudei chol* department. Perhaps this is due to the fact that secular subjects do not demand certain behavior, are basically theoretical, and do not tend to contradict her desired lifestyle.

Dress styles: Another symptom is change in mode of dress. When a girl begins to adopt a new dress style – i.e., more casual, less careful of *hilchos tzenius*, trendy – you must keep an eye out. Also common is the lack of *Shabbos*-type of dress on *Shabbos* and *Yom Tov*.

Negative relationships: Note any change in her circle of friends and acquaintances, or improper relationships. These point to a new type of behavior and interests or lack of attention and affection.

Cool speech: Watch for trendy talk. Every generation has its own catchphrases and lingo. A student who suddenly begins talking differently is obviously trying to fit in with a

---

3. The following are only a partial listing of the more common symptoms to watch for.

new crowd. Perhaps she is remaking her image so as to fit in with more "cool" students.

Lack of eye contact: A student who is not feeling good about her actions will suddenly begin avoiding eye contact. You will only note this if you had a relationship beforehand. This is due to her feelings of embarrassment. She knows you would not approve of her behavior.

Challenging questions: A student begins stridently challenging and confronting you in class on issues of *hashkafah*. These issues had never bothered her before, but now she is hotly debating every topic you raise.

You know you have a problem on your hands, or perhaps the makings of a problem. The student displays one or more of the above signs. What to do now?

⟞ What to Do Now

When as a principal or teacher you are confronted with a problematic situation, take the time to fully investigate the issues. Be sure to ascertain the precise nature of the problem. Do not get confused and treat symptoms in place of the root causes.

Keep in mind that there are no "one size fits all" *chinuch* tips. What worked for one may not be the solution for another.

Beware of "fishing" for information. It is not wise to confront a girl before you have the facts. It is more worthwhile to wait a little longer until you have all the information than to confront her and have it wrong. Students tend to focus on the part that you got wrong and conveniently forget about the true issues you raised.

Always give her a chance to explain. Appearances are deceiving and second-hand information can be garbled. It is also an opportune time to express disbelief: "I just could not believe the information presented to me so I am coming to verify it with you."

Show disappointment that a girl with her ability could behave in such a manner. She will work to regain her standing in your eyes.

Focus on the bad behavior, not the bad person. When a student is labeled "bad" (or *chas veshalom* worse), she no longer feels a need to strive for improvement, because she is bad! Like a self-fulfilling prophecy she lives up to her reputation.

If the behavior warrants punishment, care must be taken to present it as a consequence of her actions. This is not a personal struggle. It just follows the rules of cause and effect. *If you misbehave or break rules, there are consequences.* Keep it free of emotions.

Celebrate minor accomplishments so that she can continue on to major ones. Any small improvement is cause for rejoicing. Remember, this is all about direction. Is the student in a growth mode or *chas veshalom* intent on self-destruction? She may not look or dress the way you like, but note the minute improvements.

> We had agonized for a long time over the dress code for the Shabbaton. Baruch Hashem, most of the girls looked wonderfully fine and aidel. It was obvious that each of the girls had tried, on her level, to bring along her finest ensemble, although some still fell short of our expectations. Monday morning, back at school, I addressed the student body. I told them how proud I was of each and every girl. I commended them on their sensitivity, and said, "For everything you brought along, I know there was something you left behind." One mother called to say, "My daughter appreciated your understanding of how she agonized over her choice of clothes."

The most important thing a *mechaneches* can do is *daven*. *Daven* that your *talmidos* accept what you teach them. *Daven* that they see the beauty in Torah. *Daven* that they not fall prey to temptation. *Daven* that they improve if *challilah* they have stumbled.

The day will come when we will no longer need address these issues. כי מלאה הארץ דעה את ה' כמים לים מכסים — the beauty of Torah will be apparent to all.

Shabbos, Yom Tov, etc.

Pivotal Precepts in the Building of Our Nation

My Father's Kittel

Pivotal Precepts in the Building of Our Nation
With Shalom Bayis at the Cornerstone

Rabbi Zev Cohen

IN PREPARATION FOR PESACH, WE ARE REQUIRED TO DEVOTE time and effort to reviewing the relevant *halachos* (laws) of the festival. In the process, not only do we become more keenly aware of detailed requirements of the specific *mitzvos*, we can gain insights that may have far-reaching implications in how we lead our lives.

For example, the requirement to drink *daled kosos* — four cups of wine during the *Seder* — is of such significance that the *halachah* even requires a destitute person who relies on charity for basic necessities to sell his very last shirt, or to sell himself into servitude, in order to procure the wine necessary for this *mitzvah*. The same far-reaching obligation applies to the acquisition of candles for the *mitzvah* of lighting Chanukah *neiros*. There are those who seem to be perplexed as to what the Talmudic source of these laws might be.

↦ The Importance of Publicizing the Miracle

At first glance, these two *mitzvos* share the common theme of *pirsumei nissa*, publicizing miracles experienced by *Klal Yisrael*. The four cups of wine commemorate the process of the creation of the Jewish people, while lighting the *menorah* proclaims the miraculous survival of the soul of the Jewish nation. When we publicize the miracles of our exodus from

Egypt through the drinking of the four cups of wine, we affirm our desire to be counted as members of *Klal Yisrael*. We triumphantly raise our cups and proclaim that we are forever thankful to Hashem for the miracles that facilitated for us the unique privilege of becoming His people. So too, on Chanukah: with the lighting of the *menorah*, we publicly thank Hashem for the miracles He performed that enabled us to remain His people. Both of these *mitzvos*, along with their statements of belonging to the *Klal*, brook no excuses. Men and women, young and old, rich and poor, even the destitute — all members of *Klal Yisrael* — must participate in the *daled kosos* and the lighting of the *menorah*.

In regard to expenditures for performing other positive commands — even those of Torah origin, such as *tefillin, succah, lulav* or *shofar* — a person is only obligated to spend 20 percent of his assets to ensure the fulfillment of the *mitzvah*. Why, then, in regard to the aforementioned *mitzvos* are we obligated to spend *all* of our resources? It would seem reasonable to assume that it is the *pirsumei nissa* factor in these two *mitzvos* that makes them so unique. Publicizing both the creation of the Jewish people and the spiritual survival of the nation would seem to elevate these *mitzvos* to special status.

➣ Making Choices Among Mitzvos

It would follow, then, that when a person of limited funds is called upon to perform one of these *pirsumei nissa mitzvos* as well as another *mitzvah*, the *pirsumei nissa mitzvah* takes precedence. Therefore, on *Seder* night a person who has only enough assets to purchase either wine for the *daled kosos* or *matzos* is required to buy the wine. Similarly, on *Shabbos Chanukah*, he is required to use his limited funds for the purchase of *ner Chanukah* and not for the purchase of wine for *Kiddush*.

As we often find in *halachah*, however, there is an exception to this rule. The *Gemara* (*Shabbos* 21b) declares that if on Friday night-Chanukah a person has funds for only one candle, it should be used for *ner Shabbos* and, surprisingly, not for the special *pirsumei nissa mitzvah* of *ner Chanukah*. The *halachah* follows the same ruling with regard to giving priority to the purchase of *ner Yom Tov* on the first night of Pesach, over buying wine for the special *pirsumei mitzvah* of *daled kosos*.

The glaring question is, why do the *Shabbos* or *Yom Tov* candles take precedence over the established supremacy of the *pirsumei nissa mitzvos*? The *Gemara* offers a remarkable answer:

> Rava says, "It is simple to me [i.e., I need no textual proof]. In a contest between acquiring a candle for Shabbos and a candle for Chanukah [when there is only money for one of the two], ner Shabbos comes first, mishum shalom beiso — because of peace and harmony in the home."

In other words, if we were to ask which *mitzvah* in the *Shulchan Aruch* necessitates the primary expenditure of funds, the unequivocal answer would be *ner Shabbos* because the light promotes *shalom bayis*. This is so obvious to the *Gemara* that it does not even need to bring a proof.

⤏ A *Halachah*-Based Priority

It would be in place to draw attention to the implications of the *halachah* we just reviewed, and perhaps reassess how we tend to spend our money so that it be in accordance with *halachah*. As we have seen, a *mitzvah* that promotes *shalom bayis* actually takes precedence over *mitzvos* that are public declarations of thanks for the creation of the Jewish nation and its survival: Without *shalom bayis*, we cannot have a Jewish nation. We must take a good hard look, then, at how much time, money and energy we invest in building, maintaining and strengthening *shalom bayis* in our own homes and in our communities. *Shalom bayis* should assume a prime place in our lives, without any exception or loopholes.

While this article is not meant as a medium for rendering halachic decisions, it is not out of place to suggest some guidelines. For example, when one is faced with a choice of how to spend "top dollar" on various *mitzvos*, or whether to devote precious resources to the enhancement of *shalom bayis* through various means, such as shared quality time, buying that special gift, conscious consideration of one's spouse's feelings or sensitivities (no matter how irrational they may seem), or resorting to professional counseling, may I suggest that *shalom bayis* should definitely take precedence?

Shalom bayis is not merely something to "wax Rabbinic" about at *Sheva Berachos*. *Shalom bayis* is real and it is vital. *Shalom bayis* is complicated. And it is crucial to one's well-being. We all know couples in pain, couples whose *shalom bayis* is lacking. There are dedicated *rabbanim* and mentors, as well as highly capable professionals, who are skilled in helping others with their *shalom bayis*. And then there is the Yitti Liebel HelpLine (which is also available for people outside of New York City). We cannot afford to wait until the eleventh hour to seek assistance, or to advise others to do so. We cannot hide behind the excuse of shame, because this is not shameful. It is a problem that can plague almost anyone; it must be dealt with, and it can be overcome.

Delay in receiving help can be extremely damaging. As a *Rav*, I have witnessed the corrosive effects it can have on the couple; as a *Mashgiach*, I have seen its devastating effects on the children. *Chazal* say that a husband and wife, through their hard-earned *shalom bayis*, can merit the *zechus* of having the *Shechinah* dwell in their home. Like any other *zechus*, it takes work. Like any other *zechus*, it cannot be taken for granted. *Shalom bayis* takes work, continued work. It takes work throughout our lifetime. And where effort alone does not seem to bear fruit, one should seek help.

When I was a bachur in Lakewood, a story circulated which we all flippantly repeated but could not really appreciate at that stage of our lives.

A yungerman had shown Reb Schneur Kotler a beautiful esrog for which he had paid a small fortune. The Rosh Yeshiva commented, "You would have done better to have bought your wife something special for Yom Tov."

A friend's *esrog* can be borrowed, a friend's *shalom bayis* cannot

My Father's Kittel
Rabbi Myer J. Schwab

THE PROPHET *YESHAYA* (CHAPTER 30) REFERS TO THE NIGHT of Pesach as *"Leil Hiskadesh Chag* — The night when the holiday assumes its holiness." A special *kedushah* is relegated to the *Seder* night, more than on all other *Yom Tov* evenings of the year, one that seems to approximate *Kol Nidrei* night itself.

The *Taz* and *Magen Avraham* both mention the *minhag* (custom) of the father of the house wearing a *kittel* (white robe) at the *Seder*. The reason for this is not quite clear. Some say it is related to the "king's vestments" — white garments worn by royalty, and thus worn by us this night when we are all thought of as royal offspring of the King. Also, the *Taz* says it is to be worn *shelo tazuach daato* — so that one does not become too lighthearted at a time of joy, which is also a time of great seriousness.

My father [Rabbi Shimon Schwab] told us that wearing a *kittel* was not his father's *minhag,* but he adopted it for the importance that it signified to him. We understood that importance to be the *kittel's* framing our father and focusing on him as the transmitter of the *mesorah* as he fulfilled the *mitzvah* of *"Vehigadeta levincha* — And you shall tell your son" on this holy night.

The atmosphere at our *Seder* table was thick with an intense *kedushah*. We all sang the *Kiddush* together, with my father leading in his bell-clear, melodious, tenor voice in an atmosphere of heightened *kavanah*. The "reading" of the *Haggadah* that followed echoed the ancient *niggun* of *Gemara*-learning. He melodically punctuated the text, hinting at its inner meanings. My father's *perushim* (commentaries) on the *Haggadah,* the time-honored *nigunnim,* his heightened anxiety for the proper fulfillment of the *mitzvos* of the night — capped and gowned in white, totally immersed in his *avodas Hashem* (Divine service), he transported us to another time and another world. It was an experience as uplifting, moving and transforming for us as was witnessing the *avodah* of the *Kohein Gadol* on Yom Kippur for those who were present to see it.

Still vivid in my mind is that *Seder* night of almost 50 years ago when, after a few cups of wine, we children started to become a bit giddy. Our father, still a young man, took hold of the lapels of his *kittel* and sternly proclaimed in a loud voice: "In this *kittel* I will be buried! We are now in the midst of a great *avodah* of *Leil Pesach*. This requires *yiras Shamayim* and no laughter or jokes."

He then quickly resumed his pleasant demeanor and the *Seder* continued. For us, however, that moment put the *kedushah* of *Seder* night in its proper perspective — forevermore.

Belief in *Yetzi'as Mitzrayim* — the Exodus from Egypt — is the foundation of our *emunah,* our faith. It follows, then, that the night of Pesach is the prescribed time for the *chinuch* of that fundamental conviction, the time when parents should respond to the commandment "And you shall tell your children." If our children are to be ready, eager, and willing to accept the *mesorah,* the atmosphere must pulsate with the energy of pure *emunah,* emanating from the story of Pesach.

Among its various messages, the *kittel* symbolizes to one's children the father's unspoken, but powerful, message that "If tonight were my last night on earth, and — prepared as I am in my *kittel* — I were to take leave of you for good, I would tell you these truths with which I die. These *mitzvos* of *matzah* and *marror* are not just 'nice traditions'; these stories that we relate are not just 'tales and legends of an ancient people.' These are fundamental beliefs by which I lived my life and with which tonight, I am willing to go to my grave."

To us, this was the meaning of our father's *kittel!*

How potent an opportunity this night affords for *chinuch* and for the transmission of our *mesorah*! Pesach is that *Yom Tov* which galvanizes our *emunah* in Hashem. To transmit *emunah*, we must also be a bit of an *uman* (artisan) — a gifted storyteller, as my father was; vividly describing and acting out the events of the exodus, to make them alive, vital, and real for the children, conveying not a dry story, but a most exciting one that can leave an everlasting imprint on the children.

The Pesach *Seder* can be a high point of our children's *chinuch* so that all that follows during the year will draw from the inspiration they receive on this *Leil Hiskadesh Chag* — that night which is permeated with holiness.

Meeting the Needs of Special Children

A Parent's Agony

These Children Are Ours

A Special Visitor

Reflections of a Parent

A Parent's Agony

Anonymous

OUR COMMUNITY PRIDES ITSELF FOREMOST WITH HOW WE take care of our most precious asset — our children. As true as this is, I am afraid that there is one group of children that are being woefully neglected. Our regular children get an education that can't be duplicated in the secular world. Each yeshiva tries to outdo the other as to how much material our little geniuses cover in one year. The competition between yeshivos is fierce as to who will produce more future *Roshei Yeshivos*.

Our handicapped children are being well taken care of. There is HASC, Mishkon, P'TACH and a variety of other programs in which we can all pride ourselves.

Then whom am I talking about? Children who don't fit into the mold of the perfect child. I know this from personal experience. I must therefore remain anonymous.

My youngest child had slight neurological problems in infancy which left him with labored speech and clumsy movements. He has above-average intelligence as verified by I.Q. tests given every few months due to his condition. His *middos* are second to none.

When the time came to register him, I had no idea that there would be a problem, as he was a sibling of very successful older *talmidim*. I thought the policy of the yeshiva was clear;

that siblings get priority. Having developed what I thought was an open relationship, I was very frank about my son's situation. I really didn't think that yeshivos judge children according to their athletic prowess. At the interview, however, I was coldly told to go to a special school. I then walked through Boro Park in tears wondering that, if a person in *chinuch* cannot accept him, how would the average person?

Now came the catch-22. Since he was so bright, Special Ed had a hard time accepting him, but with a lot of coaxing they finally did. Having been told that his application would be held in the yeshiva for the next year, I waited in vain for a call to be reinterviewed. It never came. I thought it was a mistake, so I called the yeshiva and was told that his folder wasn't in the file and registration was closed. This, mind you, was in the month of December!

I was frantic. Didn't this child deserve an education? Why can't he be given a chance? The door was closed in my face so quickly that I couldn't even explain anything about him. Now I had to start a renewed search for a yeshiva, but how can this be done at such a late stage? Since he did have a slight problem, I refused to put him in a "factory-style" yeshiva because I knew that he would get lost there. I looked for a yeshiva with a good name. After hitting a few dead ends, I finally was granted an interview for a Tuesday morning. Not mentioning he had a problem, I held my breath.

We walked in at 9:30, and the grilling started. How much can you test a 4-year-old? One, two, three hours. There was no end in sight. At the end of the interview the principal looked at me and said, "We would love to have him, but tell me, is there something you are not telling us?"

I told him what the problem was and he looked at me with disappointment. He was upset, so I told him that the reason I didn't say anything beforehand was that the yeshivos had taught me to be devious. Had I told him the truth, he probably wouldn't have given him an interview. He looked insulted, but I really didn't care. I finally had my precious baby in a good yeshiva.

People in similar situations seem to gravitate to each other. From these people, I've learned several important things. My opinion of the "factory-style" yeshiva has mellowed somewhat. They tell me that their children's classmates have been wonderful and have learned to show respect to a challenged individual.

However, it still doesn't mean that a large yeshiva is good for these children who can easily get lost in the crowd. People will argue that these children belong in a special program. Doctors and psychologists disagree, saying that this can only further damage the child's self-esteem. Functioning in a regular program makes them feel like everyone else, and they also see what is expected of them in the real world. These children need to be accepted. A child does not need a special program because he needs three extra minutes to have a sentence rephrased.

It seems as though the yeshivos are throwing away our most cherished gifts. Luckily, my son is bright. What happens to a child like him who is only of average intelligence? Why should a good education be reserved for our gifted? Are our yeshivos telling us that a klutz of average intelligence does not deserve a quality education? Beside cheating that child, we are also cheating our other children by teaching them that anything less than perfection is deserving of scorn. Their *middos* will definitely suffer. They must be taught to be *bnei rachmanim* and must learn tolerance. Every yeshiva must teach *gemillas chassadim* and it must start in the front office.

These Children Are Ours
Rabbi Abraham J. Twerski, M.D.

WE MUST ALWAYS BEAR IN MIND THAT, AS RAV SAID, "TO deprive a child from learning Torah is to rob him of his heritage." We are dealing here with two groups of children who are entitled to their Torah heritage and we must see to it that it is theirs.

One group consists of learning-disabled children, who can be of average intelligence and even of superior intelligence. They are faced with one or more problems that interfere with their ability to learn. When these are resolved, these children can function at a fine and even outstanding level.

Another group of children are referred to as developmentally disabled, or mentally retarded. These children are handicapped in that they do not possess full intellectual capacity. But they, too, have the ability to learn. Lest one make the fatal mistake of writing off these youngsters, saying that they have no responsibility as Jews, and thus we in turn have no responsibility to teach them, one should take note of a *teshuvah* (halachic responsum) by the late Rabbi Moshe Feinstein, wherein he ruled that these are youngsters who have every obligation of Torah and *mitzvos* and that it is incumbent on us to teach them.

We must see to it that these children are indeed taught Torah and are united with their heritage.

In the articles that follow, the authors deal with children suffering from both types of these disabilities. Rebecca Amster describes the problem of educating children suffering from learning disabilities. Mr. and Mrs. Gerald Tauber share with the reader the ordeal and the rewards of bringing up children suffering from Down syndrome, while Dovid and Leah Greenwald tell of the challenges and gratification that are theirs after opening up their hearts — and their home — to such a child.

A Special Visitor
Dovid Greenwald

⇒ Chaim? or Christopher?

MY WIFE AND I FIRST NOTICED THE ADVERTISEMENT ONE night during the summer. A picture of a small boy accompanied these pleading words:

My name is Chaim, but soon it will be changed to Christopher, chas vashalom. I'm living in Saint Mary's Residence for Children, because no Jewish family will take me. Everyone at St. Mary's loves me and takes good care of me. They are hoping a Jewish family will adopt me.

But there is no Jewish family. Some of the families who visit St. Mary's would like to adopt me and the State will make me go to one of them if no Jewish family wants me.

Maybe I look a little different and learn a little slower because I have Down syndrome. That doesn't make me forget I'm Jewish and how much I loved going to Shul, singing Zemiros, and wearing my Kipa.

Please help me! *Contact Ohel Children's Home and Family Services.*

We read and reread the advertisement and seriously began to consider Chaim's plight and our personal situation. Like most people, we had never considered adopting a child. Nevertheless, we felt we had the ability to expand our family circle, at least temporarily. We knew very little about the services of Ohel Children's Home and even less about Down syndrome children, but we became determined to see if we could help Chaim in some way.

Upon contacting Ohel, we ascertained that while an adoptive home was being sought, they had also been actively searching for a foster family for Chaim in the interim. The court would certainly be more patient with Chaim's case if he were living in a suitable home, rather than in a hospital. Of course, Chaim's life would be far richer in a home with a father and mother, sister and brother, and the *ruach* that only a Torah home can provide.

Could we assume the responsibilities of foster parents and, in Chaim's case, could we deal with a Down syndrome child? Our primary concern was the impact on our 6-year-old daughter and our 4-year-old son. We were honest with them about Chaim — the effects of Down syndrome and the need for a family to care for Chaim until a permanent home could be found.

Before Chaim joined our family, we took the children to visit him. We encountered a warm and cheerful child. He told us about an Uncle Moishe concert that he had been to and about a circus that he had seen at Camp HASC [Hebrew Academy for Special Children]. The kids could relate.... True, he could not express himself fully or comprehend completely, BUT he could enjoy himself and participate on his level.

Three weeks later, Chaim joined our family. We had braced ourselves for a tough beginning. And, as with most children, he was initially upset at having been placed in a strange environment. However, the warmth with which our children welcomed him —sharing their toys and including him in their activities — made him feel like a member of the family. That night my son insisted on sleeping right next to Chaim so that he should not be lonely or afraid.

Quite honestly, we had not received much encouragement from our parents and friends in this venture. They were afraid for us. Perhaps it would have a negative effect on our personal lives. But, ב"ה things have gone smoothly, and our relatives and friends, and our children's friends, have also warmly accepted Chaim.

The first time my wife took Chaim to meet my mother was when my mother was sitting *shivah*. They entered a room filled with women. Chaim pointed to my mother and asked excitedly, "Are you my Bubbie?" And at that moment she became his Bubbie.

⤖ Have Our Lives Changed? Definitely!

Have our lives changed? Definitely; and being attuned to these changes, keenly observing each member of the family for positive and negative effects, is a vital part of being a successful foster family. Sibling rivalry, jealousy and illness are some of the things that need to be addressed. Taking in a foster child may place additional strains on the course of daily living. For example, it took weeks of meetings with psychologists, school committees, and paperwork before Chaim was properly placed in school. He began school in mid-October. Also, Chaim requires more visits to doctors than our other children, and special medication before each meal.

True, there is more work, but there is also more *nachas* because of Chaim. We *shep nachas* from his developmental growth and from his contentment since he has come to live with us. Six-year-old Chaim came to us in diapers; as a result of his being in a proper home environment, he cooperated fully and has been trained.

Saying *berachos*, participating in *Kiddush* and *Zemiros*, listening spellbound to *tekias shofar*, dancing with a little *Sefer Torah* on Simchas Torah, Delighting in a *Shabbos* or *Yom Tov* visit to Bubbie and Zeidie — this is the Chaim that we have come to love.

Our children have learned many important lessons because of Chaim. Their understanding and appreciation of this *mitzvah* is deeper than we expected. On Rosh Hashanah, my daughter announced, "It's a good thing we took Chaim before Rosh Hashanah." Obviously, she could sense the magnitude of this *chessed*, and it made her feel good. Many *middos tovos* — such as *chessed*, *rachmanus*, *savlanus*, and *ahavas Yisrael* — have been strengthened within all of us as a result of this experience.

More on the Background Story

Until now, we have shared our story with you. Now for some of our comments, based on our observations. During the past year alone, twenty-four special children — Jewish children — were turned away by Ohel due to a lack of foster homes and an even greater lack of adoptive homes. These children will generally live their lives with non-Jewish families and Christian agencies. It is particularly sad that many of these children are Down syndrome children, as the parents are aware at birth of the child's handicap and believe that they will not be able to cope. We have learned, however, that these children, like Chaim, have a real ability to feel acceptance and rejection, love and pain.

When, due to extenuating circumstances, parents cannot care for their own child, others should assume this responsibility. Some people may be unaware of this unique opportunity for *chessed*. Others may feel unqualified. But you don't need a degree in special education or psychology to be successful foster parents. Ohel will provide the necessary professional support services. The key, for the parents, is knowing how to give love and be loved, and remembering that each *Yiddishe neshamah* belongs in a warm and wholesome Torah home.

For those who cannot assume a full-time undertaking there is also a need for families who will invite a special child to their homes, for a shorter period of time — a *Shabbos* or *Yom Tov* — providing a respite for the parents. Additionally, community members can participate in and support programs which enhance the lives of these special children, and at the same time lighten the load of their parents. For example, Chaim attends a Sunday-morning program, staffed by wonderful volunteers in Monsey; Chaim enjoys this program immensely, and looks forward to it all week. *Lekavod Parshas Vayeira,* he brought home his arts-and-crafts project: *ohel shel Avraham Avinu.* At the *Shabbos seudah,* his face glowed as he stood and displayed his *ohel.* Our children were so pleased that Chaim, too, could have a turn at *parshah* time. They helped him sing his song about Avraham waiting for guests, welcoming everyone through the four doors of his tent. May we be *zocheh* to have all of our doors always open for all of our children.

Reflections of a Parent
Ephraim Milch

⇒ Euphoria and Joy — Interrupted

THE WEEK OF *PARSHAS VAYEITZEI* 1987, MY WIFE GAVE BIRTH to Sheryl, a little sister to our 15-month-old son. Excitement, euphoria, happiness and joy — the miracle of birth. Yet, those feelings were suddenly interrupted (I use that word purposely) with the doctor's statement that our precious daughter had Down syndrome and possibly a severe congenital heart defect.

Indeed, as a parent of a child with Down syndrome, the struggles and challenges, fears and frustrations center around the physical infirmities that our child must overcome or learn to live with before she can even attempt to reach the classroom or playground. Perseverance, commitment and a unique temperament are critical to parent and child, in order to cope with the higher incidence of ear infections, eating disorders and often life-threatening heart defects. These concerns and difficulties deflect the parents' attention from other less apparent problems — the low muscle tone, late physical development and mental retardation. There is pain in knowing our child will always struggle and still never attain what most people take for granted. But the pain is more intense when our child lies at the *akeidah* of an operating room or intensive-care-unit and we wait for G-d to say: "Do not stretch out your hand to the child," so to speak, to grant her survival.

⚷ Groping for Understanding

Down syndrome (trisomy 21) is a genetic accident; indeed, medical science cannot identify a cause or reason why any specific child is born with Down syndrome. Accordingly more than other disorders, it is one of those rare situations that point directly to *hashgachah*. G-d decided that this child should be born with this specific handicap and G-d decided that our family is where this child is destined to be. The child comes to this world with its own soul and its own mission for reasons we do not know. At the same time, G-d surely has complex plans, which often call for creating specific familial and community relationships, in order to test, purify and bless each of us.

We lack clarity of vision, a prophecy that can inform us what G-d has in mind and what path we are to follow to best serve Him. Instead, G-d sends us the directions by way of life's "turn of events" which, with the help of the interpretation and guidance of our Torah leaders, can lead us to our eventual goal — a goal we do not fully recognize until the trip is over. Our family portrait obviously required a child with Down syndrome. If that child is removed from the picture, then the entire picture and all those in it cannot accurately reflect what G-d had intended. I am a different person as is each person who had been touched by a child with Down syndrome. That is what G-d intended. There could be no other way. As the Chazon Ish wrote in *Emunah U'Bitachon*, *emunah* is the trust and realization that everything that happens is determined by *hashgachah* — decided by a loving Father. There is no fate or chance. *Bitachon* is living with this realization.

A couple in their early 20's does not give much thought to an event like this occurring to them; accordingly, one cannot be prepared with any answers. Yet, G-d provides the strength. He does not guarantee that we *will* be successful in raising such a child. He does guarantee that we *could* be successful, by providing us with the potential to properly manage the situation.

⤛ Negotiating the Rough Spots

In attaining the achievements, we pass through a series of rough spots:

Can I love this child or grandchild as I do the others? The question itself presents fear and pain. The answer lies in seeing and holding the child. Love of parent to child and child to parent quickly replaces the feelings of doubt and aspects of rejection. Human love transcends the experience and allows us to develop an all-encompassing bond with this child, as with any child, a bond that cannot be severed, despite moments of difficulty. To hold and to care for; positive emotions surface and continue to assert control.

We stand outside the operating room of Children's Hospital, our daughter undergoing open-heart surgery, and we realize through the heart-throbbing tears and desperate prayers that the love is forever present and that the parent-child attachment cannot be severed nor described. Through a most trying experience, G-d has reassured us of the love and commitment that He knew we had and we, as human beings, needed to recognize.

This cannot be happening to me, or my child, or my grandchild. Parents and grandparents awake together to face G-d's complex world as never before experienced. Perhaps we previously deluded ourselves that life presents such situations only to others. Perhaps we refuse to accept imperfections or human limitations.

To a great extent, family members take their lead from the parents of the handicapped child. When the grandparent sees strength and stability in the parents, he, too, develops the courage and guidance necessary in such a situation.

There are also moments, particularly early on, when the

pain is so great that we lose self-control and dare ask, "Why me?" G-d is surely aware of our belief and trust despite the confrontation.

We face challenges and, of course, our reactions are human. G-d does not demand a uniform response. We are tested because we are human. Because we are human, we react individually. Some people grapple alone with the pain, questions and fears, and find meaning and strength on their own. Others find comfort, encouragement and answers by opening themselves and sharing with others... Some will cry longer. Others will question harder.

⇒ Better Than Reuvein? Or Worse?

"Why me?" Am I worse than Reuvein, that G-d has decided to punish me in this world? Am I better than Reuvein that G-d is sending me direct punishment in this world, and treating me to something better in the World to Come? If a child with Down syndrome is G-d's way of pointing out the failure of the "me" generation to properly give as parents, have I been a parent long enough to have failed in that area that G-d must punish me? If G-d is *not* punishing, but looking for "special" parents, have I been a parent long enough and acquired the maturity, extra sensitivity and special caring to deserve and properly deal with such a child? If we are being challenged, to question is normal. To feel the pain is normal. It is our task to come up with the responsive action.

⇒ Seeing the Beauty in the Test

Our struggle to deal with our child is our private *akeidah*, and we continue to refer to the original incident to better understand what is expected of us:

Avraham awoke early in the morning. G-d had called, and he was ready to respond. Yet, obviously he harbored doubts, or it would not have been a test. Who accompanied Avraham and Yitzchak to the *Akeidah*? *Chazal* tell us: Eliezer, Avraham's chosen servant, who later was trusted to select a wife for Yitzchak, studied with Avraham and, indeed, walked up to his neck in water in order to travel to the *Akeidah*. Yishmael, as well — the son of Avraham, who underwent circumcision at 13, and now traveled the same course to the *Akeidah* as Eliezer. At that point, say *Chazal*, Avraham compares them to a donkey. The greatness of Avraham and Yitzchak that distinguished them from Eliezer and Yishmael was their ability to see the Cloud of Glory hovering over the mountain, while the others saw only a hill. Eliezer and Yishmael recognized that this mission was a calling from G-d. They trusted and believed. But they failed to see the potential in the event ahead.

The key to transcending mortal shortcomings is not to dwell on the questions of "Why?" and "How come?", and instead to pray to G-d for the strength to ask, "What can we do?"; to see the mountain and the enormous potential that this child has to serve G-d as does any child, in his or her way. Once again, *emunah* and *bitachon* slowly reassure us and human love helps provide the needed strength. The questions, although perhaps not completely answered, no longer seem so pressing.

⇨ Advancing Toward the Future

A person with Down syndrome is a complete Jew and is obligated as all people to serve G-d to his or her full potential. We have the responsibility to educate her in Torah and *mitzvos*, and because she is no different from you or I, she will enter the community of Israel at the age of 12 and will assume all the obligations of an adult. Having a handicap does not diminish a person's human status. To the contrary, each *neshamah* is placed on this earth to perfect itself; a *neshamah* placed in a *guf* with limited faculties obviously has fewer weaknesses requiring perfection. The Chazon Ish would stand before those children with limited mental capacity and note that they are particularly holy and pure.

Through it all, one continues to live with dichotomies. Tears emanate from the pain and frustration; tears emanate from joy and happiness. Tears flow from being overwhelmed by the moment; tears flow from the love and concern of others. Helping hands of family and friends at a difficult time are so important — their just being there, suffering in our difficult moments and rejoicing in our happiness, dreams and hopes, friends who not only presented a shoulder to cry on but who cried themselves. And some tears are shed in intense moments of prayer — alone, man and G-d.

We seek answers, to explain the past; G-d continues to provide solutions for the future. A world of sophisticated medicine and special education continually affirms the Hand of G-d and His greatness on earth, and we benefit from the selfless dedication showered on individuals — indeed, our daughter who but a few years ago society ignored.

Sheryl provides us with a continuous lesson in true parenting. It is difficult, as a parent, to live vicariously through a child with Down syndrome, to dream that she will live out your unfulfilled dreams and carry on your hopes after you have passed on. The joy is in the achievement, the communication — at whatever level — of each child as himself or herself. The greatest proof of our humanity is in the noncomparing love we can show for our children and for each other. At the same time, she provides abundant love in all directions. She showers us with more satisfaction, more love and more personal growth than we could ever hope to instill in her. As Dovid *Hamelech* wrote in *Tehillim*, "The stone which the builder rejected has become the chief cornerstone."

Dealing With Problem Situations

Short Term Gifts (a SIDS kid)

An Open Letter to My Questioning Friends

Intensive (Care) Reflections

When Crisis Looms

Short-Term Gifts
Rabbi Avrohom Y. Stone

THE *DAF YOMI* TAPE PLAYED IN THE BACKGROUND, BUT I hardly noticed it. Gathered around the dining-room table was my *Daf Yomi shiur*. As they had done in other instances, they had moved their study of the daily page of Talmud to a local house of mourning, as a merit for the deceased. Only this time it was different. This time, it was my dining-room table they were sitting at. And it was I who was in mourning.

My family sat in the living room on small chairs, low to the ground. In the same spot where we had celebrated her birth with a festive *kiddush* just three and a half months earlier, we now sat *shivah* for my baby daughter, Shoshana Devora ע"ה. The "sweetest little baby in the world," as I had often called her, had gone in for a nap while being watched by the baby-sitter, never to awaken. A perfectly normal, healthy baby had died suddenly, for no apparent reason, and the slightly imperfect world of our family had been cast into indescribable sadness and unbearable pain.

Many of the people who walked through our doorway to comfort us in our time of sorrow were themselves extremely disturbed by what had occurred. After all, this is not something that is supposed to happen. To our eyes, death is reserved for the sick, elderly and infirm. Innocent, healthy little babies are not supposed to die. Yet, surprisingly, by the last days of the *shivah*, I found myself much more at ease, much more untroubled, than many of those who were coming to offer us strength.

The death certificate states that Shani died of SIDS, a totally not understood phenomenon. Perfectly healthy babies die in their sleep, without so much as a hint that there is something wrong. The general practice in such cases which, with the help of many caring individuals we were able to avoid, is for the medical examiner to perform a full autopsy. All of the child's vital organs are removed and they are subjected to every manner of test known to medical science. In the end, absolutely no problem of any kind is found with them. The reason for the death is totally inexplicable to the doctors and researchers. However, since it happens about 4000 times a year in the United States, they gave it the name of Sudden Infant Death Syndrome, or SIDS It's only a fancy way of saying: "We don't know why, we can't explain it, but since it happens with frequency, it must be something."

As we sat in the emergency room that evening — arguing with medical examiners and judges, dealing with the *Chevra Kadisha*, deciding on a place to bury her — our lives suddenly shattered in pieces around us, I shared with my wife one comforting thought: "At least we had been spared a lifetime of guilt and torment. Since there was no apparent cause, there was nothing we, or anyone else, could have done to prevent it."

The next morning, waiting for the Medical Examiner to release the body so that we could make a funeral, a thought that crossed my mind the night before came back to haunt me. "Why," I asked myself, "if she was perfectly healthy, did she have to die? There was nothing wrong. She wasn't the least bit sick. How in the world could this happen?" It was, to say the least, a very disconcerting question, and one I feared would haunt me for the rest of my life.

Strangely enough, it is in the seemingly inexplicable and incomprehensible nature of her passing that I am able to find true solace and comfort in Shoshana's death. We are so used to analyzing and explaining nature that, when presented with an event that contradicts all that we know and understand to be true, we throw up our hands in exasperation and find ourselves at a loss. Yet, it is in exactly those situations where the truth should be most clear. The only possible explanation is that there is a G–d Who runs the world; that everything that occurs is only because He wills it to be so; that life and death are completely in His hands; and that, whether it agrees with nature or not, He is the One Who determines exactly how long a person will live and the amount of time they will have on this earth.

On the certificate issued by the medical examiner, on the line stating "cause of death," the doctor will write: SIDS On my copy, however, I would simply write: *G-d runs the world*. He had determined that she would only live four and a half months. When she reached that moment, her life ended, just as He had planned. The seemingly random nature of her passing was not random at all. Rather, it was exactly as He had decided it would be from the very beginning. Her life simply ended because that was all the time she had been given.

I thought back to a time almost a year before. During the third month of her pregnancy with Shani, my wife had experienced an incident which was a cause of great concern. We wound up consulting a high-risk obstetrical specialist. After studying the results of the ultrasound examination he had administered, he sat facing us behind his desk, his manner ominous. "The situation is serious," he had told us then. "There probably is only a 50-50 chance that the baby will make it." His facial expression, however, said that the baby didn't have a chance.

My wife contacted a well-known *tzaddik* and asked that he give us a *berachah*. The message was relayed to him, and his response gave us some degree of hope. His words: "The baby will be *zara chaya v'kayama* — the baby will live and survive."

Much to everyone's surprise, most of all the doctor's, the baby's situation began to improve dramatically. Repeated ultrasounds showed that the threat to the viability of the pregnancy had decreased markedly, and after four weeks, my wife was allowed to leave her bed and resume her normal daily routine. In my mind, however, the same fear overtook me every single day: Maybe she'll lose the baby.

Ultimately everything turned out all right. On June 24, 1997, at 5:50 in the morning, my daughter made her appearance in this world. She was of perfect weight, perfect size; perfect and healthy, in fact, in every way imaginable. The kind of child that every parent hopes and prays for. There were no deformities; no abnormalities; no imperfections of any kind. Just a beautiful, huggable, adorable infant, with at least three chins and cheeks that took up most of her face. If you looked in her eyes, you could tell that there was intelligence there, too.

She was the kind of baby that everyone could love, and love her we did. With seven older brothers and sisters, it didn't take long before they were arguing over her and fighting to take care of her, holding her, playing with her, and loving her.

And what would Shani do? She would sit there in her swing, or lie on her blanket on the floor, her huge cheeks sitting on three chins, a serious look on her face, until she realized you were looking at her. Then, your attention would be rewarded tenfold, as her entire face would erupt in a huge smile, and a look of love and adoration would fill her eyes. When you spoke to her, she would make noises back, and you sensed there was something wonderful she was trying to tell, or she snuggled comfortably in your grasp. That was the situation from the day she was born until the moment she passed away.

Suddenly, so suddenly, it all ended. Sitting in the hospital, trying to absorb what had occurred, there was one point that my wife struggled to come to terms with. "How could it happen?" she sobbed. "Didn't we get a blessing from the *Rebbe*? Didn't he say that she would be '*zara chaya v'kayama*,' a living and surviving child?"

I can't pretend to speak for this wonderful *tzaddik*. But, to be honest, I don't understand the question. Is there any other way to characterize my baby's life? The term "*chaya v'kayama*," living and surviving, implies that the child will be healthy and strong, able to survive. So she was. There was never any sickness, never any pain. She was strong, happy and healthy and she survived. For as long as she was destined to. Until, and including, her last breath.

One of the women in our community, a person who knew Shani and was truly heartbroken, sat in my kitchen and put to me the question that shadowed her every thought. "Rabbi," she asked, the pain coming through in her words, "how can Hashem let such a bad thing happen?"

I'm far from able to even begin to fathom the Divine plan in any circumstance, and certainly not one which so deeply affects me. But, in my mind, there was, and is, only one true way to respond; that it isn't bad, and nothing happened. Something just ended. As it had clearly been meant to end from the beginning.

And how can you call it bad? If a person lived seventy, eighty or a hundred years, and everyone who knew that person found them a source of only love and happiness; they themselves knew no suffering, only the adoration and love of others; when such a person would die, how would we feel? Certainly, there would be the hurt and pain of losing such wonderful human beings, and they would be missed dearly. But, reflecting on their life, would you feel sorry for them? Would you feel an ounce of regret for the beautiful, perfect world they had known and created? I ask you, then: Does it really make a difference whether it's meant to be 135 years or 135 days? In terms of good and bad, I just don't see how you can call something so special, so wonderful, so beautiful, "bad." It's hard to call it good, because it hurts too much. But you can't call it bad.

That Wednesday morning, during the last few hours we were to have her, when things were still good and the sun still shone, I wanted to make my wife feel even better about our baby. You know how it is. With the hustle and bustle of a large family, and the extra demands of an infant, you sometimes forget how special they really are. As my wife held Shani, and my little baby's face erupted in her trademark smile, I pointed at her and told my wife — "That's our miracle baby. This is the baby who wasn't supposed to be here."

She was a free gift from G-d, a gift that, perhaps, at one point I was never meant to receive. What bothers us so is that the gift was for so short a time.

There is a story in the *Gemara Berachos* that I had learned with my *shiur* a few days before Shoshana died, that keeps running through my head. It tells of how the Sages, for various reasons, decided to remove Rabban Gamliel as the *Nasi* and *Rosh Yeshiva*. Looking for a replacement, they settled on Rabbi Elazar ben Azaryah. When they offered him the position, he consulted his wife, who asked him a pointed question. "What do you need this for? How do you know that they won't throw you out tomorrow, just as they threw Rabban Gamliel out today?"

I had explained Rabbi Elazar ben Azaryah's reply as follows. "And if they do remove me? So what if I occupy the position for only one day? Does it mean that it has no value? Absolutely not! From that day on, my whole outlook on life will be different and improved. Everything will take on new meaning. I'll know what it feels like to be the *Nasi*, the *Rosh Yeshiva*. From that one day, I'll have memories that will last a lifetime. Everything I look at will be from a different perspective, a more meaningful one, because of the moments I served in that capacity. Are you saying that, just because an experience won't last forever, it means that it has no value? That, since I might have to give it up, I should never know the experience in the first place? That it won't be worth every second because it will have to end? *Chas veshalom!* Heaven forbid!"

I feel exactly the same way about my baby.

G-d gives us many gifts in life. Some are long term; others are short term. Each child is a precious gift from Him. I sincerely hope and pray that the seven gifts he has given me, and the ones that will, G-d willing, come along, will be long-term ones, for 120 years. But the eighth gift He gave me was a short-term one. And she was a gift that I really thought I would never have. So what should I do? Should I sit here and be angry, and complain to G-d because He cheated me? Or should I sit and be grateful for every single day of the free, short-term gift He bestowed upon us? The first day we had her was wonderful, and it didn't necessarily ever have to have happened. So too, the second. And the third. And the 135th. They were all wonderful, special days that, at one point or another, I didn't think would ever be. The challenge for us is not whether we will be angry with G-d or harbor complaints against Him. The challenge is whether we have the capacity and ability to appreciate every special moment He gave us. Guess what? We do.

During the weeklong period of mourning, Shani's playpen remained in its place in the corner of the living room, her toys inside it. Her swing stayed in my study, and her crib still stood in our bedroom. Some of the people who came to console us, especially some who had lost children the same way we did, were upset. They felt that it must be too painful for us to see those items. If they felt that way when their own child passed away, that's all right. Everyone deals with this in the way that's best for them. I, however, didn't feel that way. I know that her things will eventually have to be put away. But she did live. She was a part of our family, a part that was adored more than anyone can imagine. And she continues to be a part of us.

When I shared my thoughts with someone else who had lost a child, he looked at me, shook his head, and said, "You have a lot more faith and belief than I did." I think he's mistaken. It's really not a question of faith or belief. Just look at the facts as I have related them. Look at the before, the during, and the end. Turn them upside down, twist them around or do anything else you wish to them. And then you tell me. Is there any other way to understand this story? Isn't it obvious that this child was meant to be here for only a short time, and that the time she had was special and wonderful? On top of that, we almost didn't get her. If you can find any reason for problems or complaints, please enlighten me. Because I only see reasons to be grateful. Abundantly grateful.

One of the hardest parts of our loss is explaining all this to Shani's brothers and sisters. The baby that they had loved so much had been taken away from them. They each had their own private, personal relationship with her, and each one grieves deeply, but differently. There are many different meals being served in our house these days; no one is eating the same lunch. I try to help them deal with it as positively as possible. I tell them to imagine if G-d would have gathered the whole world together and said, "I have a special little girl I need someone to take care of and love. But, I have to tell you in advance — I'm only going to give her for four and a half months. Who's willing to take her?" Knowing now how special she was, and how much she meant to us, would we have ever let anyone else even try to get her? Imagine if, a year ago, He would have looked into the future and seen how sad we are and how much we miss her. What if He would have decided that it's not fair for us to feel so much sorrow; so, to spare us, He was going to give her to some other family? All of my children agree. We wouldn't want to have missed her for anything in the world.

One of my youngest, not yet old enough to fully comprehend what has occurred, asked me the other day, "Why did Shani die?" I told her that Hashem had a special little girl whom he had to send down to live. However, she was so special, and He would miss her so much, that He couldn't bear to be apart from her for long. So, He was only going to send her away for 135 days. She didn't want to be away from Him either, even for so short a time, but He told her she had to go. As a consolation, He promised her that He would find the very bestest, the very lovingest, the very specialest family, who would love her and hold her and take the very best care of her. Together, they looked down at all the families in the world, with all the brothers and sisters, "and," I asked her, "guess which special sister they found? Can you guess who that family was?" She broke into a smile as wide as the room, and proudly pointed at herself.

Perhaps we might just get through this all right, after all.

This is not to say that we aren't hurting. Believe me, we are. For my wife, the evenings are hardest. For me, the mornings are my time to cry. Strangely, as the days pass, the pain seems only to intensify and I miss her more and more. If your heart goes out to us, if you want to share our hurt, if you want to take a part of our sorrow over how much we miss her, we won't object. Pain shared is pain lessened. But if you wish to help us deal with the seeming injustice of it all, the apparent unfairness of it all, please don't bother. For, while we will always grieve and there will always be pain, there will also always be gratitude and appreciation. For having gotten something that we thought we would never have. For a lifetime of happy memories condensed in four and a half months. And for having merited to receive the most special short-term gift we could ever have hoped for — Shoshana Devora, the sweetest little baby in the world.

An Open Letter to My Questioning Friends
From That Mother of the Boy on Crutches

Dear *Reb Yid* (or *Rebbetzin Yiddine*),

YOU DON'T KNOW ME, AND I DON'T KNOW YOU. WE WILL probably never meet again, so I am writing you this open letter in the hope that you will see it and know how I feel. It just might give you some food for thought in the future.

This morning on your way home from *shul*, you passed my house just as two of my children were boarding their schoolbus. You stopped and spoke to me. My parents taught me to have *derech eretz,* and seeing a respectable-looking person, old enough to be my father, I felt compelled to stay and answer you.

You had noticed that one of my children boarding the bus has only one leg, and you wanted to know what had happened to him. Now, logic would dictate that there could be only three possible answers to this: (a) He was born like this, or (b) he lost it to an illness or (c) injury. Whatever the reason, it is done already and cannot be glued back on! So why ask? Another thing my parents taught me was not to stare or point at people, and *never* ask personal questions of strangers, as this may cause them pain or embarrassment, *chas veshalom*. However, I am certainly not ashamed of my son, so I answered you very simply that he had lost it to an illness.

This should have been enough for you, but apparently you needed all the details — when it happened, the exact location, etc. Again I answered your questions, even though I could see no purpose behind them other than idle curiosity. But, true to my upbringing, I could not act with disrespect. (To be perfectly honest, had you been an old lady with a funny-looking hat, I still would have felt compelled to treat you with *derech eretz*.) You then needed to know how many doctors we had consulted and if they all really felt that an amputation was necessary. I told you which *Rebbe* we had consulted and which prominent surgeon he sent us to. I even explained to you the unusual details of the case that made this course of action absolutely necessary.

Did this satisfy you? Of course not. You still had to know why I didn't seek yet ANOTHER opinion. (I wonder if you meant another *Rebbe* or another surgeon.)

By now, my friend, you had certainly gone beyond the bounds of common decency.

I'm certain that at this point even my parents would have given me permission to close the door on you and terminate the conversation. But you see, by this time, I felt that I had to justify myself. After all, what kind of mother WOULD allow her son's leg to be amputated unnecessarily? And what kind of stupid people would make such an important decision based on one man's say-so? I had to make you understand that it was unquestionably *bashert* and that we have to believe that it was for the best.

Attitudes and Such

I am sure that some people reading this will be saying, "Oh, she just has a poor attitude. She shouldn't take things so personally." But you can't get much more personal than to question a person's decision-making ability, especially where her children are concerned. As for "attitudes," permit me to tell you: Some time ago my son was in a grocery store and an old man asked him a question about his condition, which my son calmly answered. The man then asked my son if it was all right that he asked him (a little too late, I would think). My little boy answered that people are always asking him such things and that he understands that they do this because they care about him and want him to get better. I am very proud of the way this 5-year-old handled the situation; I don't think we have any attitude problems here!

Perhaps you feel that I am overreacting to one person's curiosity. But you see, *Reb Yid,* although we don't know each other — I MEET YOU MANY TIMES A DAY. Sometimes you are wearing a long *rekkel,* sometimes a sports jacket, sometimes a windbreaker. Sometimes you have on a *Chassidishe* hat, sometimes a suede *yarmulke.* You may appear as a man or a woman; sometimes old, sometimes young. Your accent and vocabulary vary, but I recognize you just the same. Occasionally I get lucky and meet your brother. Even though he doesn't know me, he will stop and tell me that he once knew someone who went through the same thing and is now grown and married, with children. Then he will wish me *nachas* from my son and go on his way — without asking any personal questions or questioning my judgment or abilities. He always brightens my day and I am happy to meet him.

This is not to say that I don't want to answer any questions. On the contrary. I am always happy when friends and acquaintances call to ask how my son is doing. There is also a time and place for giving out information. My son has explained to all of his friends and classmates exactly what was wrong with him. He has showed them his prosthesis and explained how it works, adding, "This is just until *Mashiach* comes. Then I get the real one back."

What I really object to is being expected to give a complete *din vecheshbon* to every stranger who demands it. Would you ask a childless couple if they are really sure that they cannot have children? Would you ask an older single person if he is really trying to find a *shidduch?* Would you be insensitive enough to ask a *baal teshuvah* how it really feels to eat pork? (On second thought, considering some of the articles I have read recently, I'm very much afraid that you just might!)

⇨ Guidelines for Greeting the Handicapped

The Torah obligates us to judge our fellow Jews in the best possible light. After speaking with you, I am sure that you are not cruel by nature. Nor would you willingly cause another person such pain. Perhaps you never had the benefit of parents who taught you to deal sensitively with other people, as I have. Maybe, like many people, you just don't know how to react to handicapped people when you encounter them. If that is the case, here are some guidelines. If you follow them, you can't go far wrong:

1. Don't stare, but don't avert your eyes either. Being invisible is worse than being stared at. A pleasant and a cheerful "Good Morning" is always nice. (Note: This works well with nonhandicapped people also.)

2. Don't ask personal questions. Just don't! The exception here is if you need information for some practical reason. I am often approached by parents of children who have been diagnosed with illnesses similar to that of my son. I am more than happy to answer any question they may have (no matter how personal) and to help in any way that I can. I also belong to a support group for parents of children with life-threatening illnesses. The purpose of this group is to meet other people in the same boat and give *chizuk* to each other. This is not the same thing as asking questions out of idle curiosity.

3. If you see a person in need of assistance (handicapped or not!), by all means offer to help. The person then has the option of accepting or refusing your help. If the person refuses, smile politely (see #1 above) and keep moving. Some people derive immense satisfaction from accomplishing a difficult task alone. If the person accepts your help, ask first how you can best be of assistance. Sometimes what YOU feel is needed may not be appropriate. Never assume that you know what needs to be done without asking first. I do not refer here to holding open a door for someone loaded down with packages. I refer here to something like lifting my son up steps — he can do it perfectly well himself, and you could

An Open Letter to My Questioning Friends / 327

startle him, causing him to lose his balance. Always ask first.

One final thought, *Reb Yid*. You mentioned that you were compelled to stop me because it hurt you to see a Jewish child like this (trust me — it hurts me more than it hurts you). You are not a bad person, *Reb Yid*. On the contrary. This compassion for another's suffering is what marks you as a child of Avraham *Avinu*. I would not have it any other way. The next time you see my child, or any other person in unfortunate circumstances, by all means feel for them. Experience their pain. But don't take it up with me. I am not the one responsible. Take it up with *Hakadosh Baruch Hu*. He is the One responsible for everything that happens in this world. Perhaps if enough people will talk to Him, He will rectify the situation by bringing *Mashiach* speedily in our days.

Intensive Reflections
From Parents of an Eight-year-old in the I.C.U.

Ephraim Milch

⇒ The Risks of Confidence

WHAT STARTED AS THE COMMON COLD OR FLU, AND most of the time would have disappeared in a week or ten days, this time developed into something worse. We take for granted modern medicine and the luxury of antibiotics. There are risks that come with such confidence. Occasionally we are reminded of the blessing of good health and the importance of G–d's role as the *Rofeh Cholim*— Healer of the sick. Indeed, it was not that long ago when flu season was dreaded and epidemics were frequent. Perhaps we are more unsettled by tragedies and difficulties and less prepared to withstand the challenges than previous generations because generally we do not have it as hard.

Whether it is health issues, anti-Semitism, or poverty, we become complacent, expecting a tranquil, prosperous life, only to be shaken out of our slumber when the expected does not occur. In the past, a person expected less and thus appreciated more. Today we expect more, and are disappointed more often. We lack the appreciation and joy that one should feel at living in such times. Times when there is freedom to live as Jews being denied very few of the opportunities that all Americans have. Times when children are expected to survive pregnancy, be born healthy and live to be *zekeinim* (elderly). Like the Jews of the desert born after the manna was an actuality, we forget that there is no entitlement. Occasionally we are reminded of the reality and that we have much to be thankful for.

⇥ Home Immediately, or With Parents at Her Side

Our daughter expressed her desire to go home immediately and, if unable to do so, that we not leave her side. Otherwise, she reacted most positively to the entire ordeal. A combination of maturity, trust, security and naivete. But even the slightest discomfort to one's child is too much for her parents. Did she comprehend the severity of the situation? I hope not. Her actions and words constantly reminded us how much we mean to her. I hope we properly conveyed how much she means to us.

Standing in the intensive-care unit, one perceives G-d's presence. There is an uninterrupted line of open communication. To pray; to praise. I count my blessings as I pass each bed. One feels G–d's tears as He shares the experience. If G–d accompanies man into exile, how could He not accompany the patients in a pediatric intensive-care unit? Innocent, wholesome, trusting children fighting with the angel of death. Kids who just the other day were playing ball, laughing with friends, taking their first steps or saying their first words suddenly lie motionless where every second is a gift. Each case defies explanation. Diseases they did not ask for. Drunk drivers they did not want to meet. Somehow their parents and family assume top importance.

We received support, strength and love from family and friends, which I hope will instruct us in becoming better parents and friends and, thus, better people. One is likewise moved by the dedicated professionals. Professionals rising to the occasion. Most important, the enormous example set by the patients themselves. Where do they get the strength and courage to battle the odds? And for those conscious, how do they maintain their optimism and the ability to interact with others? No lessons, no preparation, yet little children are asked to confront life's greatest difficulties and to face man's greatest questions. And they prevail.

⇒ Insufferably Alone or Strongly Connected

The tragedy is insufferable when one is alone. Connection to others is critical. There is vertical connection over time from creation to redemption, all part of a master plan. If all is connected, there must also be horizontal connection over space between people and in community. To be alone is to be abandoned. Every visitor, every phone call, every card makes a difference—nonintrusive, just being there. It has impact for the moment and forever.

We noticed and appreciated. Some people have a way of keeping other human beings' feelings and problems on their own mind. To put it simply, they are people who truly care. They don't preach it, discuss it or learn about it. They just do it.

It is often those who are most busy, yet find the time for a visit, a phone call or a note. Even merely a kind word when they see you on the street. *Me, my life, my thoughts are important to you. I matter.* One cannot underestimate how important those feelings are. Calls from friends, relatives and even *Roshei Yeshiva* from near and far. As Rabbi Aharon Kotler said, "You can't be involved with *Klal Yisrael* if you are not involved with the individual." Busy with communal concerns, national issues and their own personal responsibilities, yet time for one more person and his needs.

⇒ A Break for Home

I go home — to kiss and hug the other children. For a brief moment, one stops worrying about neatness, and a not-so-perfect report card, a forgotten homework assignment. That perspective doesn't last long, but every now and then we need to reevaluate our priorities, appreciate life for its opportunities, and cherish the truly important things like health and love. There will be time later to scream about the magic marker left in the dirty laundry.

One learns so much about the character, depth and precious nature of one's children at times like this. "I can't sleep because I miss my sister." "The only Chanukah present I want is for her to come home." The hug and smile between patient and sibling when they see each other cannot be captured—except in our hearts. As parents, we comfort and reassure the children, whose fears and concerns cannot be ignored. They naturally and unknowingly reassure and comfort us, as well.

When our daughter first returned home, her brothers and sister were overly sensitive—sharing and caring. It was, however, but a few hours before the special treatment ceased and they were back to their usual selves. Isn't that the way it's meant to be?

⌁ Bonding Through Shared Vulnerability

At the hospital, the mutual vulnerability of the patients' families gives rise to a bonding. Personal stories normally withheld are shared among each other. We are reminded that everyone has their own package of difficult experiences, some having passed, others ongoing. Even those seem to have passed always remain with us. Memory can be a blessing or a curse. But without it, our life has no meaning. Our past defines us and connects us. We are often unaware of what others are contending with, that there is likely a good explanation for their seemingly inexcusable behavior. They are preoccupied with matters they wish not to reveal; matters that consume their complete attention.

And yes, despite the lack of time for each other, the bond between husband and wife grows. It is G-d's way of picking up the difference. The emotional intensity draws you together. But equally significant is the love that comes from watching a spouse as she exhibits love that only a mother can display for a child. The pain is shared as if the umbilical cord were still attached. Decisions are made that may not be the most rational or in the best interest of the entire family. But they are made out of love and from a bond that need not be explained or justified. It takes time to accept those maternal decisions and maturity to appreciate them. In the end, these decisions reflect the unique nature of the family unit, the mother's central role, and why family is the most critical unit for the survival of Judaism and all of civilization.

When Crisis Looms
Dr. Aaron Twerski

⇒ Should Problems Arise

SHALOM BAYIS, SUCCESSFUL MARRIAGE, AND DIVORCE ARE in a sense topics more appropriate for discreet discussion in the privacy of one's living room than for the pages of a magazine, dealing as they do with sensitive and delicate matters — especially as we address what happens when marriages face enormous stress and we contemplate the sad reality of divorce.

As is well known, the non-Jewish world has an enormous divorce rate and while we are more than a few steps behind them, we have nonetheless been affected by the general trend, and it is time for us to face the music: There are significant problems in marriages within the Torah world.

When marriages begin to get stressful, we should, by right, tell couples that at the first sign of difficulty, they ought to seek help. It is advice that will probably not be listened to. But what is tragic is that even when the situation gets undeniably bad — even when it verges on crisis — even then help is not sought. Couples continue to live with the difficulties and, what is worse, inflict irreparable damage upon each other and themselves, because they refuse to seek help.

There are *rabbanim* with great sensitivity who are able to help, and do so with unusual effectiveness when they are consulted. Should the situation require professional counseling, these same *rabbanim* will refer those in need to competent religious marriage counselors. There is a myth afloat that counseling will not help, and that when a couple does go for help, the result will be a patched-up marriage. Even in those cases where it is true, it is better than the alternative. Every day that counseling is needed and is not sought is a day that the underlying problems of the marriage are not being dealt with. Furthermore, the hurt and the damage that people are inflicting upon themselves in that stressful period are being compounded day by day, and often much of it cannot be undone.

The Role of the Family

When a marriage is in trouble, there is a very specific role for family and friends to play. It is basically a passive, silent one; and it is seldom honored. The *Shulchan Aruch* has some harsh things to say about *lashon hara* and *motzi shem ra* (gossip and slander) and yet, as a rule, when marriage problems surface, they become a subject for public discussion in all their forbidden detail. At the outset, parents themselves peddle it — first and foremost, to other members of the family, to brothers and sisters, to uncles and aunts, complicating the situation enormously.

I recently was attempting to coax a couple into counseling. Between Wednesday, when I met with the husband, and the following Monday, when he came back to me, something intervened. There was a family clan meeting, and the clan — the brothers and sisters — took the situation apart. From that point on, I was no longer dealing with an individual and his wife, but with the Capulets and the Montagues. Once the clans were in conflict, I could no longer reach anyone.

There is yet another evil that even surpasses the damage of *lashon hara*. A marriage is first and foremost a private arrangement between two people. The chapter in *Shulchan*

Aruch dealing with marital relations is entitled *Hilchos Tzenius*, which means "Laws of Privacy." That title speaks volumes. When the privacy of a marriage becomes compromised and other actors in the scene — brothers, sister, aunts, friends — become involved in discussion, the privacy is destroyed. Even if the marriage is eventually restored, the sense of privacy that once surrounded it is lost. Unfortunately, tidbits are whispered on the avenue, which should never have been said in any instance in public. Yet one hears such talk constantly. Once people have the information and talk about it, it becomes a formidable task to attempt to put the marriage back together again.

Nobody's life is a bed of roses. Just as every individual goes through stressful times, so does every marriage have its moments of stress. Marriages can take a lot of pressure, and still survive. But they can only take it within that context of privacy. I hereby issue a plea to every parent, and to every uncle and aunt, and to everyone who is sought to be drawn into marital conflict: Stay out! And see to it that the people who can act constructively do act. A marriage in trouble is not an acceptable subject for discussion on the avenue or in the *shtiebel*.

⤝ Parental Involvement: Positive and Negative

Parental involvement can be a serious problem, indeed. In my experience in helping others, a very large percentage of marital problems are parent instigated; and those that are not, are parent complicated. There are, of course, occasions when parents can act responsibly with their own children.

When my father was suffering from his terminal illness, he called me into his room and asked that I serve as scribe for his personal will. Among other matters that he instructed was that we, the children, not name our children for him. I was taken aback and told him, 'You know, don't you, that we shall not follow these instructions." But he was not dissuaded. He turned to me with considerable emotion and said, "How many times have I witnessed battles over which name to give a child. What should be a time of joy turns into tears of a '*veibel.*' Spare me that kind of *nachas.*"

My father passed away. Many years went by and none of the children had a name for him. And then my father-in-law was *niftar* while my wife was pregnant The baby was a boy. There was no controversy. My father had seen to it that he not be the cause of family discord. Parenthetically, a year later another son was born to us. This child does bear my father's name. Having already fulfilled his will, I was certain that he would have had no objection.

There are creative roles for parents to play, but they are narrow, and they have to be used with great care and with great wisdom.

Dealing With Divorce

When the situation has deteriorated so irreconcilably that divorce seems inevitable, a new host of issues must be discussed: custody, visitation, child support, yeshivos, education — the gamut.

In seeking a dispute-resolution mechanism — that is, a method for resolving the dispute [I put aside the halachic question of going to court because I do not know of any halachic *hetter* for going to a secular court] — I would like to expose the myth that there exists an institution called "family court" where family issues are resolved. True, there is a place called family court in every major city in America. But it is not a good dispute-resolution mechanism. The legal process is long and protracted. Often the lawyers are the only ones that stand to gain anything out of the process. The opposing parties who invest so much emotion and resources into the battle are rarely satisfied. Wives all too often have little to show for their paper victories. Recalcitrant husbands who must be pursued for payment of child support or alimony often escape the clutches of the law. And although the situation is better today than in the past, collection of child support and alimony is still a vexatious problem. By the same token, husbands learn that court orders for child visitation are easily frustrated by a wife determined to deny those rights to an estranged spouse. Courts cannot do for parties that which they refuse to do for themselves. If they insist on being deadly adversaries, the courts are in no position to monitor their daily behavior to one another.

As for the role of the lawyers, they are good at adversarial relationships, because that is what they're trained to do. I know, because that is the way I teach them. They are not trained to be mediators or marital counselors. Some lawyers are particularly gifted at negotiation and mediation but for the most part they cannot resolve the fundamental tension which lies at the core of divorce actions.

Popular wisdom has it that the *din Torah* route somehow ends up being unfair. My experience has been otherwise. In fact, *batei din* that deal with family law problems are staffed by fine, *ehrlicher rabbanim* — men of integrity who do their utmost to deal with the issues honestly, conscientiously, and in a manner consistent with Torah principles.

A Plea to the Principals

Issues relating to divorce settlement cannot be resolved in an adversarial atmosphere — whether the venue be a court of law or a place of *din Torah*. I often tell couples, "You have a great fight going between you. But the resolution of your problems has got to be here, at the table."

The marriage created conflict — irreconcilable conflict. Yet one aspect of the relationship between the ex-husband and ex-wife will remain constant, and that is the children. Parents are going to have to deal with each other on matters that relate to the children for quite some time, and they would be wise to put aside all their disagreements and ill feelings to work things out as best as possible.

Massive studies that are in the midst of being conducted demonstrate that the key factor in the psychological damages inflicted on children in a divorce is not economic deprivation, not the personalities of the parties, not their level of education, not the frequency of visitation, and not even custody. The most significant factor is the inability of the parents to deal with each other vis-a-vis the children, in a nonadversarial relationship. This is a sure indicator that we must teach ourselves to mediate these problems in a civil manner. Given a choice, one should certainly go to a *Rav*, invite him to "please sit with us and mediate," instead of relying on a non-Jewish judge to resolve in court which yeshiva his kids will attend. To do otherwise is insanity.

Of course, some situations are extraordinary. There are some that are nonnegotiable and others that take on a course of their own. In the vast majority of situations, however, people — not circumstances —have turned divorces into clan fights, into a contest where the primary issues are *kavod* and ego. Popular wisdom has it that you can arrive at a multi-million-dollar settlement in a divorce action, but you may not be able to settle who gets the dog. In this case, popular wisdom is absolutely on target.

⤖ Tefillin and Esrog and Shalom Bayis

My father told me the following story a number of times. He had heard it from his father, whose primary source was the Rebbetzin of the Chernobyler *Maggid*:

The *Maggid* owned a pair of *tefillin* with *parshiyos* (parchment) written by Reb Efroyim *Sofer*. (The *Baal Shem Tov* would list the order of *sofrim* — scribes — in *Klal Yisrael*, saying, "Ezra Hasofer, Nechemiah Hasofer, and Reb Efroyim Sofer.") Reb Efroyim's *parshiyos* were of unusual quality, and were worth a fortune of money. Now, the Chernobyler *Maggid* lived in dire poverty, and from time to time his Rebbetzin would remark, 'Why don't you sell the *tefillin*? I would then have enough money to live for five or six years!" The house lacked sufficient food, the children weren't clothed properly for the cold winters. Yet it never dawned on the Chernobyler *Maggid* to sell those *tefillin*.

One year after Yom Kippur, however, the *Maggid* was extremely dejected, for he did not have a *lulav* and *esrog* for the approaching festival. The *Maggid* was staring out the window and noticed a stranger walking by with a *lulav* and *esrog* in hand! The *Maggid* ran out and asked him, "Where are you going to be for *Yom Tov*?"

"I'm not going to be here. I live in another city."

The *Maggid* pleaded with him to stay in Chernobyl, but the man replied, "Rebbe, my family is in the other city, and I can't stay."

Finally, the *Maggid* said, "Sell me your *lulav* and *esrog*. There are no *esrogim* to be had this year."

"I'll have to take one hundred rubles for the set," said the stranger.

The *Maggid* asked the man to wait a few minutes. He took his *tefillin* with Reb Efroyim Sofer's *parshiyos*, sold them for one hundred rubles, and bought the *lulav* and *esrog*.

His Rebbetzin later entered his room and found him with an expression of great joy on his face, in stark contrast to his previous despair. When asked what had taken place, the *Maggid* told her the entire episode. The Rebbetzin later related that in her mind she reviewed all the bitter winters that she and the children had suffered, the many times that they had gone hungry and shivered for lack of clothing. Out of her great anger she grabbed the *esrog* and threw it to the floor, breaking the *pitum*, rendering it unfit. At first, the *Maggid* was silent. Then he said, "Listen, *Ribbono Shel Olam*, I have no *tefillin*. I don't have an *esrog*, either. What does the *yeitzer hara* want? He wants me not to have any *shalom bayis*, either. That he will not accomplish!"

One of the *Chassidic* rebbes who heard this story from the Rebbetzin remarked, "I understand why the *Maggid* never wanted to sell Reb Efroyim's *tefillin*. And I understand why he sold the *tefillin* for the *esrog*. But where he got the strength of character not to lose himself is beyond me."

May I suggest that the value of *tefillin* is that it is used for a *mitzvah*, and so is an *esrog* precious because it is used for a *mitzvah*. *Shalom bayis* is no less a *mitzvah*. We must learn to take this area of life — in all its glory and even in all of its misery ח"ו — and put it within the confines of Torah. Violation of *lashon hara, hotzaas shem ra,* and betrayal of *tzenius* are deadly enemies to the *kedushah* — the sanctity — of marriage. When problems arise, they will not be solved on the avenue, over the telephone wires, or in the courtrooms; they must be solved by people, realizing that ultimately their obligations are to themselves and their children, as prescribed by the Torah.

Combating Negative Influences

The Jewish Home Under Siege

From Station to Station

"Plastic Frames"

Affluence or Attitude

Landmines Along the Information Highway

The Time for Perfection Has Come — Are We Ready?

The Gift

The Jewish Home Under Siege
Fighting Off The Forces of Cultural Assimilation

Rabbi Shimon Schwab צ"ל

↬ A Historical Perspective

INVASIVE INFLUENCES THREATEN THE SANCTITY OF OUR COMmunity. We may take comfort in that, as a community, we number some six million Jews in the United States. Less than 7 percent of them, however, consider themselves Orthodox. As such, then, we Torah Jews are a group under siege, with the vast majority of our brethren estranged from our heritage, undergoing a spiritual holocaust of catastrophic proportions. Let us bear in mind that this is not happening under some atheistic dictatorship, but right here in the United States, within the framework of a benign democracy with full religious freedom for all. Nothing should play heavier on our minds than the concern over how to save our lost brothers and sisters from oblivion, and bring them back into the fold.

The classical case of thoroughly assimilated Jews are the *Misyavnim* of the time of the Chanukah miracle — the Hellenists, who worked hand in hand with *Yavan* (ancient

---

1. The Greeks were not always characterized as evil. In the time of Alexander the Great, when Shimon *HaTzaddik* was the leader of the Jews in Israel, Greece was living up to the *berachah* bestowed by Noach on its progenitor, Yefes: "*Yaft Elokim layefes...* May G–d extend Yefes' [boundaries] but He will dwell in the tents of Sheim"

Greece), helping them carry out their evil designs.[1] Jewish collaborators were highly influential, politically and socially, and propagated the slogan: "We have no share in the G–d of Israel," ח"ו, with full cooperation of the Greeks.

Ultimately, of course, the oppression of *Malchus Yavan harshaa* collapsed together with its Hellenist collaborators, and the Jews were treated to a glorious display of Divine miracles, which spelled a decisive victory of light over darkness — a victory without which *Klal Yisrael* would no longer exist ח"ו.

⇒ A Contemporary Counterpart

We have, in our time, experienced seventy years of a similar, almost-fatal *gezeiras hashmad* in the former USSR. We are also aware that Soviet oppressors included quite a few *Misyavnim* — the so-called *Yevesektsia,* who outdid their non-Jewish Communist comrades in their merciless suppression of religion and belief. And we also are witness, in our day, to the total bankruptcy of the system that they initiated. At the same time, we see how the grandchildren of those *Misyavnim* of seventy years ago are coming back in droves to the *chadarim,* to the *beis hamidrash,* in keeping with the prophecy: "And the sons will return to their boundaries." However, let us beware of a gross mistake. The atheistic power structure of Communism has not collapsed. Only

---

(*Bereishis* 9:27). During this glorious era, Hashem granted the Greeks special wisdom, imbuing them with a keen sense of beauty and esthetics, opening their minds, as it were, to acquire scientific insights into nature. The ancient Greeks developed important discoveries in mathematics, astronomy, medicine, and government, and *Chazal* considered it befitting that the beauty of the Greek language dwell in the "Tents of Sheim" — a reference to the *Makom Hamikdash*. But then came a transition period when the glorious Greek empire gradually turned into *Malchus Yavan harshaa*, as their preoccupation with the pursuit of this world's pleasures eventually brought them to the worship of the animal aspects of the human body. The long-term result was a cultural atmosphere that fostered artistic projections of fantasies of the *yeitzer hara* — a fascination with physical lust in all its various aberrations. This was followed, historically, by the cruel persecution of the *kedusha* (sanctity) of the Jewish way of life, beginning with the prohibition of *Shabbos* observance, *Rosh Chodesh* and *mila*, subsequently developing into a *gezeiras hashmad* — aimed at totally alienating the Jews from Torah and *mitzvos*.

in the former USSR can one behold the miracle of *yispordu kol poalei aven* — the disintegration of the perpetrators of evil. But in China, for instance, with its population of one billion souls, Communism is still very much alive. The *malchus harshaa* there is still in full control.[2]

Hakadosh Baruch Hu endows us with the ability to think, and so we come to recognize that just as we are witnessing the total defeat of the former *Misyavnim* in Russia, the same will happen eventually to the *Misyavnim* in whose midst we are now living. We are only *mispallel* with our entire heart that the downfall of our *Misyavnim* shall come mercifully, peacefully, without any evil befalling them; rather, we hope for a complete reversal of their stance, initiated by our modern-day *chalutzim* — the steadily developing army of *baalei teshuvah* — who are finding their way back to the *Ribbono Shel Olam* before our very eyes.

So here we are, drowning in almost a bottomless swamp of assimilation. The vast majority of our people are fast losing their identity as Jews, and they are aided and abetted by our modern-day *Misyavnim,* self-appointed spokeswomen who hasten the process of radical spiritual extinction ר״ל.[3] We are all aware that "in those times, in these days," the victory was won not by human strength and ingenuity, but by *mesiras nefesh* and *kiddush Hashem barabbim,* which made our forefathers worthy of extraordinary Divine inter-

---

2. Why is China flourishing while the USSR has disintegrated? For us Torah Jews there is one simple answer: In contrast to the USSR, China never interfered with the observance of Torah and *mitzvos.* In China, they never closed yeshivos and *chadarim.* In China, they never prohibited *shechitah, milah, mikvah,* and so forth. The reason, of course, is simple; there were no Jews for the Chinese to persecute. Certainly, one day, China's downfall will come, in Hashem's own time, when the *Malchus Shamayim* will be revealed in the world. But in Russia, which had unleashed a spiritual war to the finish against millions of Jews, there is today a state of political chaos bordering on anarchy, and the once powerful leaders of this accursed country are now begging for financial handouts from capitalistic European and American governments for their hungry citizens.

3. Just two examples: The majority of all Jewish marriages are mixed, bringing together Jews and gentiles, performed jointly by Jewish and gentile *galachim.* Furthermore (please forgive my lack of delicacy), gay and lesbian synagogues and clergy people are being legitimized, and given full recognition in the *Misyavnim* media. All this is shadowed by the almost total indifference of the Jewish establishment.

The Jewish Home Under Siege / 347

vention, providing us with a light which still guides our steps. If we but have the courage, the commitment to *emes* and love of Torah, to follow the Torah leadership of our generation, we too can merit an overwhelming victory over the forces of darkness in our time.

⤖ Self-Examination, to Merit "Yeshuos"

We would like to be worthy of such *yeshuos,* but this calls for some painful self-examination. Instead of returning to our practice of whipping, again and again, the dead horses of Reform and Conservatism, let us take a close, candid look at ourselves. This must also take precedence over our protestations against the outrageous proclamations of the more militant "centrist" leaders, who in any case seem to be deaf to our cries of protest.

The *halachah* states that an *avukah* — a torch, which is a combination of many wicks, like the candle we use for *havadalah* — is unfit for the pre-Pesach search for *chametz;* a single flame, coming from one wick, is more suitable for a close search. Similarly, our own spiritual inventory to determine whether we are truly worthy of the *nissim* and *yeshuos* for which we are *mispallel* calls for a private self-examination, by pinpoint illumination, quite apart from the public, fiery responses to the constant public attacks against *kavod haTorah* and basic *emunah* in *Misyavnim* newspapers and journals. Let us first make a *bedikas chametz,* so to speak, in our own homes, so as to sweep out any traces of assimilation from our own private corners. Otherwise, we may ח"ו not merit the enormous *siyata diShmaya* — Divine assistance — which we need so desperately to withstand the onslaught of the twofold dangers that threaten our physical and spiritual existence. Perhaps it is because we unknowingly harbor the germs of assimilation within ourselves, that we have not been too successful in convincing others to change their wrong ways and attitudes.

⤖ A Declaration of War

It is my conviction that the most subversive influence is the presence of television sets in our homes. Unfortunately, a great many of otherwise Torah-observant Jews, whose children are enrolled in yeshivos and Bais Yaakov schools, are regularly *kovei'a ittim le* television, night after night, and they do not see anything wrong with it. We must face the incontrovertible fact: Television is a dangerous object of the first magnitude. When the set is turned on, the Jewish home, which is supposed to be a *mikdash me'at* — a miniature sanctuary — loses this distinction, because the *Shechinah* is no longer present from that moment onward.

Some decades ago, when television was in its infancy, some people considered it harmless because no hint of filth or smut was allowed on the screen. Actually, programming was not so harmless even then, primarily because it was a cause for widespread *bitul Torah* for men; in addition, it was a medium for slowly and gradually introducing non-Jewish concepts, foreign ideologies, as well as non-Torah modes of behavior into the minds and hearts of the viewers — men, women and children alike.

Television leaves a much deeper impression than reading a newspaper or a book does. Sitting in front of the screen, you no longer think for yourself; the thinking is done for you. You simply absorb, uncritically, whatever your eyes see and your ears hear. The assimilatory influence of television is thus much more insidious than that of other media, when our critical faculties are in full function.

⤖ A Wide-Open Window to Immorality

All this was already true years ago. But today, how blind can one be not to realize that television is a wide-open window, letting into our homes the foul odor of the immoral and amoral atmosphere that prevails outside? The full range of *avodah zarah, gilui arayus* and *shefichas damim* have free entry into the Jewish home, and drive out the *kedushah*. For instance,

Jewish "children" curious to witness a Catholic mass on December 25 in a cathedral need but turn a knob, and — presto! — indelibly imprinted onto their young, impressionable minds is a form of foreign worship, in which they participate as enraptured onlookers. But not every child is going to sit through the seasonal pageantry. So one just turns the knob a bit more, and is treated to a potpourri of murder, torture, sadistic violence, spilled blood — the whole ugliness of crime, with all horrid details graphically displayed. And then one turns the knob a little further. This time, we are exposed to an explosion of *pritzus* and *znus* (promiscuity and licentiousness), normal and abnormal, the whole arsenal of the *yeitzer hara,* in full realistic color. Fascination just might give way to revulsion, so we'll turn the knob again, and now we may see a harmless advertisement for a new product. But watching the commercial, one is again subjected to a lethal dose of *pritzus,* which penetrates deeply into the core of a sensitive Jewish *neshamah.* Gone is the sense of shame, gone is the sense of *bushah* — our precious legacy from our forebears. Nobody blushes anymore. No wonder the newest fashions, which violate basic considerations of modesty, gain entry into our homes without too much resistance!

By the same token, the mind becomes poisoned ever so slowly by an emphasis on power, wealth, and the relentless pursuit of gratification of the senses. Slowly, even seeds of doubt in the veracity of *emunah peshutah* may be creeping into us, creating a blasé attitude toward the sanctity of Hashem and His Torah.

The excuses are well known, and worn out:

Some programs are very educational, others only deal with science, or politics, or sports, or finances, and so forth. But we all know that the same information is available on the radio or in the newspapers, without exposure to the filth that is projected on the screen. In brief, a television set is just as harmless as having a loaded gun in the house. Sometimes it may not go off, but the risk is one of life-threatening proportions. How else can we explain the paradox of *frum,* faithful, Jewish wives and mothers, with modest coverings on their heads, sporting the latest fashions, which were created by famous designers to arouse the *yeitzer hara*? The nobility of Jewish daughters is likened to *bnos melachim,* and the concept of *tzenius* in clothing was not only meant to protect females from embarrassment, but also to protect males from *hirhurim ra'im* (indecent thoughts).

The outrage of television is closely related to pornographic cassettes, easily available in video stores. These stores have been aptly described as "*Pis'cha shel Gehinnom* — the Gateway to Gehinnom." Enough said What are we men and women going to answer when we will have to give an accounting of our lives and our actions one day before the *beis din shel maalah* — the Heavenly Tribunal? Let us identify Agudath Israel of America with the banishing of television from the *frum* community! Imagine how many hours of *kiruv rechokim,* how many hours of *askanus be'tzorchei tzibbur,* how many hours of *ahavas chessed* this will gain for us! And imagine for a moment the newly found light of *kedushah* that will illuminate the *mikdash me'at,* resulting from the darkening of the TV screens in the Jewish homes!

⇝ Needed: Patience, Diplomacy, and Courage

We must admit that it will require an abundance of patience, a strong dose of good taste, and a good measure of consistency to overcome potential hurdles which might emerge by considerations of *shalom bayis.* One must proceed with respectful caution rather than take a sledge hammer and smash the box into smithereens. The first step is to just turn the set off. Should somebody insist on turning it back on, leave the room. All that counts is the firm resolve not to watch under any circumstances. Eventually it will fade out of your life by itself. But our community must go on record that we have *declared a war against* television, that we are extending encouragement to all those who will do without the sights and sounds of a decaying civilization in their homes, and will continue to grow in the spirit of *maalin bekodesh ve'lo moridin* — one must endeavor to grow in sanctity rather than backslide.

The Jewish Home Under Siege / 351

We may be few in number, we may be weak in influence and power. But in the world of *nissim,* political, military, financial and economic strength does not count. Purity and devotion to Torah do. These past few decades, Agudath Israel of America has made such impressive progress that it borders on the incredible — due to its commitment to Torah values, not because of numerical or financial strength. But to belong to the few calls for courage. There's a natural tendency within all of us, even in Orthodox circles, to want to be part of the mainstream. People would rather follow the rule: "Look and think as the others do." Nobody wants to be pointed out as an exception or an extremist or to be labeled a fanatic. Far from fanaticism, our pride stems from the fact that we do not deviate from G–d's Torah; we are Torah Jews, living in consonance with the *Shulchan Aruch.* We are guided by *daas Torah,* the *psak halachah* of our *gedolei Torah,* who are themselves the faithful *talmidim* of the *gedolei Torah* of yesterday, and so on, upward, generation to previous generation, back to Sinai. We may be a minority, but we take deep pride in that ours is a very forceful and very idealistic minority, inspired with *mesiras nefesh* for *emes,* and driven by compelling dedication to *harbatzas haTorah,* with a keen sense of love and *achrayas* for *Klal Yisrael.* Being that kind of minority, we live with the *bitachon* that Hashem will let us ultimately be victorious.

From Station to Station

Akiva Davidsen

CALL ME A FANATIC. "AN EXTREMIST," PERHAPS. GO AHEAD. I won't blame you. I might even join you. What I've done warrants a designation of that sort. And yet, I wouldn't want it any other way.

Allow me to explain. Today marks three months since I last listened to the radio. That's right. No news. No sports. No music ("light" or any other kind). No talk shows. No commercials. No public service announcements. No traffic and weather together — or separately. In short — no static. No noise. Just quiet. Quiet at home. Quiet in the office. Quiet in the car. Quiet.

Quiet? Quiet in New York City? Can it be? Can the noise really vanish? No. Not entirely. But it can be filtered. And it can be productive. AND entertaining. And stimulating. And pleasant.

⇒ The Genesis

My "discovery" of this most dramatic utilization of my *bechirah chafshis* (free will) came totally without warning. It was *Shabbos Shuvah* and the words leaped out of his *drashah* (sermon), not unlike a "special bulletin" interrupting a "regularly scheduled broadcast." "Isn't your time and attention worth more than whatever is blaring on the radio?"

For some reason, I took the question seriously, though it was probably meant rhetorically. I took it personally, not philosophically. "Isn't it?" I asked myself. "Do I really gain much, or anything, from the decibels of drivel being aimed at my eardrum, medulla, wallet, and *neshamah*?"

Can life possibly proceed without knowledge of immediate and detailed reports and analyses of every idiosyncratic phenomenon of every sector of the globe?!

Will I cease to exist without political acumen, disaster tolls, investment expertise, Rush Limbaugh, tips on tree pruning, current hockey injuries, Frank Perdue, the eminent SHADOW TRAFFIC, and the ever-so-exalted FIVE-DAY FORECAST? I had to find out.

In the Beginning.....

I began immediately after Shabbos. "One day at a time," I told myself. "Let's see what develops."

The project intrigued me almost immediately. The first thing I noticed was how much radio I *used* to listen to. Not really listen, perhaps, but *on* nevertheless. "Background noise," we call it. As if my effervescent, never-docile family didn't provide enough background noise. And yet there I was, instinctively, even habitually, on "day one," reaching out for the magical "on" switch.

"*Vatishlach es amasah*," I thought. Pharaoh's daughter, Bisya,[1] *lehavdil*, also extended her arm in instinctive fashion, to save the abandoned and crying infant and future savior of *Klal Yisrael*. Had she allowed logic to invade her intent, explains Reb Chaim Shmulevitz, the great distance between her and the cradle in distress would have certainly precluded any attempt of rescue. But Hashem performs miracles when our instincts are so pure and well intentioned. A helping hand was transformed into an extension of Providence that altered history forever.

My outstretched arm had far less imposing ramifications. Mankind, as we know it, would not be eternally transformed

---

1. Yes, Bisya is the correct pronunciation. See *Divrei Hayamim I* 4:18.

by my experimental abstinence. But if we are true believers of *bishivili nivra ha'olam* (the universe was created for me), "my world" might never again be the same. Perhaps Hashem had a meager miracle available for these private times, too. Slowly I drew my hand back — and smiled. Insignificant? I think not.

⇥ Out of the Closet

The days went by and the experiment continued. After four days, I revealed to my wife my "silly" little foray into the world of isolation. I wanted to be sure it was real. She didn't laugh. It was real.

Information infiltrated. News entered via *The Wall Street Journal*, the only newspaper I can bring into my home without blushing—not AM or FM. Music was selected from tapes—some long buried. Weather reports arrived with alarming accuracy, for a change — I opened my window. Insights and analyses were now gleaned from speeches of *gedolim* (Torah giants), both current and past; recorded and live. And the hockey injuries continued to mount—I can only assume.

Slowly I confided in friends — carefully selected. Most of them were surprised. "Not even TRAFFIC REPORTS???"

Some showed concern. "You didn't make a *neder* (vow), I hope."

A few were jealous. "It won't last, you know."

No one required oxygen.

One supporter suggested a goal, to reinforce my resolve. "Hold out at least until *Hoshana Rabbah*," he said (two weeks from the start). A new rendering, perhaps, to "*Kol mevasser, mevasser v'omer*" (The voice of the herald heralds and proclaims).

Yom Tov ended, but the static blackout was showing fresh legs. Not unlike the recovering compulsive smoker who eventually discovers that his body no longer craves nicotine, I, too, was doing fine, thank you. I noted no more episodes of instinctive radio "outreach," and less and less curiosity about events that very recently seemed indispensable and spellbinding. My challenging enterprise was actually getting easy. "*Haba l'taheir mesa'yin oso*"(*Shabbos* 104a). Those that come to be purified receive special (heavenly) assistance.

⟜ The Home Stretch

The human species is a creature of habit. We become so accustomed to doing things in a certain way that we frequently do not consider that there might actually be alternatives. When this *hergel* (regularity) sets in, we become more robot than man, and our daily routine becomes just that—routine. The *Navi Yeshayahu* (29:13) refers to this phenomenon as "*mitzvos anashim melumadah*," the practice of *mitzvos* in oblivion. But the same holds true for everything we do, whether they be *mitzvos* or otherwise. We tend to forget *what* we are doing and *why* we are doing it. It is then that man becomes an actual prisoner, locked into a system of habitual behavior that dictates virtually every step he takes and fastens him to a gestalt of trancelike conduct.

On a recent visit to *Eretz Yisrael*, I was fortunate to have taken a tour of the current excavations being conducted on the southern side of the *Har Habayis* (Temple Mount). While ambling down the numerous steps that meander their way through *mikvaos* (ritualariums) and ruins, I couldn't help noticing that each step of stone seemed to vary from the previous one, both in dimension and in depth. Negotiating the hike down was rendered rather cumbersome by the inconsistencies in the construction. "Lousy architect," I quipped with irreverence to our tour guide.

"Not at all," he responded.

"Quite the contrary," he added. "Have you ever heard of the concept of *mitzvos anashim melumadah*?"

I understood. The Temple contractors, with their keen wisdom, realized that even something as sacred as a visit to the *Beis Hamikdash* was in jeopardy of becoming routine to many, especially those who came often. (Notice the similarity between the words "*hergel*" and "regular"?) Constructing the steps in unequal proportion would compel the visitor to concentrate and reflect on each and every step he took into the *makom kadosh* (holy place), and think about why he was there. Brilliant.

⇢ Crashing Through the Clutches of "Hergel"

Many of you are, in all likelihood, a lot like me. A radio addict, by habit. You cannot imagine life without it. The media itself has ingrained in us the concept of the "requirement" to know "all the news, all the time." But crashing through the clutches of *hergel* can have extraordinary effects on one's *tzelem Elokim* (G–dly image) [see *all* the major *sifrei mussar*]. And the venerable radio could be a great place to begin that assault.

Yes. Reason must prevail. *Sheviras hamiddos* (breaking one's habits) need not require that you flee any department store that happens to be playing a radio on its sound system. Nor must you hang up on your travel agent whenever he places you on "hold."

And yes. There are more important issues for us to grapple with—as a People, in our communities, in our families, and even in ourselves. But our Torah society has already made huge strides in the antitelevision campaign, and clearly every elevation of *kedushah* can only help.

So call me a fanatic. Go ahead. But first try it for a week. Or maybe just a day. If you find quitting difficult, beware. You just might be hooked on radio.

One final note of caution: Tuning out your radio could become habit forming too. For me, the habit is three months and counting.

So give away those twenty-two minutes; you could get back your world.

From Station to Station / 357

Plastic Frames

Anonymous

PLASTIC FRAMES FOR EYEGLASSES CAN BE PURCHASED FOR as little as $3. Wire rims seldom go for less than $40, even at the cheapest store in Brooklyn. For years my son begged me for wire rims claiming that all the boys in yeshiva make fun of him because he has plastic frames.

My health insurance policy will fund prescription glasses once every two years per family member. When his turn came around, since it did not cost me anything, I allowed my son to get wire rims with the understanding that in the event of breakage, the lenses would be popped into plastic frames again. Two months later, my son got off the bus from yeshiva with his glasses in his pocket, in pieces. As per our agreement, he did not expect me to buy him wire rims. However, he would not accept plastic frames under any circumstances, insisting that everybody would make fun of him. He used his entire life savings to pay for his new wire rims by himself.

Until last night, I did not believe my son. He is a good student, good in the classroom and at recess. He is a clone of his classmates. He is not the type of boy normally targeted to be picked on. He cannot recognize me from a distance of ten feet without his glasses, yet he has gone to school without them when his only choice was plastic frames. Until last night, I thought he was saying that boys made fun of his plastic frames only as a ploy to get him to purchase his personal preference of wire rims. Now I know I was wrong and he was telling the truth all along.

Long after he and the other children had gone to bed, my son came out of his room and asked to talk privately with my wife. He seemed very distraught. At first he could not even speak. He tried to retreat and told my wife it really was not important and he didn't want to talk after all. Finally he began — three boys in his class (whom my son would not name), who all attend the same exclusive summer sleep-away camp (which my son would not identify), have been ridiculing him in an extremely vicious manner. On a daily basis they have been criticizing him for the following "faults":

- My son has never been to a sleep-away camp;
- he does not know whether he will be going to sleep-away camp this coming summer;
- his new, black, low-top sneakers were purchased at a local discount shoe store;
- his new winter jacket is identical to the jacket of a student who has severe learning and behavior problems;
- his clothing is not up to par;
- his family does "stupid" things together during their summer vacation;
- other "faults," all fabrications, were cited with regard to myself and my wife;
- finally my son is being ridiculed because last year, for a period of three months, he wore prescription glasses with plastic frames.

My son's classmates took note and remembered the plastic frames on his glasses from over a year ago. My son was not making it up. I must beg his forgiveness for not believing him.

Now I understand why my son never invites a friend over after school. What if a "friend" were to see a crack in the plaster of the house that we RENT!?!

Now I understand why my son wants me to wait in the car instead of entering his classmate's palace of varnish and crystal. What if the classmate sees dust on my hat !?!

Now I understand that the word "*treife*" applies not only to food, television, vulgar speech and immodest clothing, but also to the sick, materialistic priorities so effectively handed down and imbibed by the sweet, innocent *neshamos* of our children.

The *menahel* and the *rebbei'im* of the yeshiva are in no better position than I to stem this rampant tide of materialism. Full-tuition parents are very unlikely to ever recognize or acknowledge this problem. Their sons are not going to be targeted and ridiculed for wearing glasses with plastic frames or for not knowing whether they are going to attend sleep-away camp. They are not likely to believe that their son would ridicule a classmate the way my son has been ridiculed. Who is going to inform them of these improprieties and inquire about their roots!?!

The innermost sanctum of *Yiddishkeit* in this world is located in *galus*. While the shadows of falsehood that darken our lives may not be erased until the coming of *Mashiach*, it is our responsibility and constant obligation to reach for increasingly higher levels of *kedushah* in our lives. My son has gained from this ordeal. He has experienced the value of silence. By ignoring their barbs and not answering back, he was able to decrease their frequency and intensity. By withholding the identity of his "friends," he has learned to be careful about someone else's honor, even though they were so disrespectful to his. By being on the receiving end of cruel and bitter verbal assaults, he may remember the pain and be less inclined to inflict the same upon others. He has seen that while "having" may seem quite appealing, the material gifts that Hashem bestows upon us can be quite dangerous if we use them in a careless and destructive fashion.

As I write these words, my son sits in yeshiva growing in the lessons he is learning from his *rebbi* and from his classmates.

Old enough to know how to choose my battles, I have decided to sidestep this one. Instead of trying to change the tone of an entire yeshiva, I have been searching for one populated with students from less-affluent families. Perhaps I can begin by examining the frames on their glasses?

Affluence or Attitude
Rabbi Shimon Finkelman

⇒ A Matter of Fashion

My REACTION TO "PLASTIC FRAMES" WAS, PREDICTABLY, one of pain and sadness. Pain for the student who has to endure the ridicule of his misguided classmates, and sadness that such episodes can actually occur in a yeshiva. Not that I was surprised. The unfortunate truth is that to some in our community, clothing, glasses and the like are far more than a necessity of life.

In the world at large, the pursuit of fashion is both a means of achieving status in one's social circle and of drawing attention to one's presence. Both ideas are contrary to Torah. The Torah extols the attribute of *hatzne'a leches,* serving Hashem without fanfare; to draw attention to oneself through manner of dress is to tread the path of self-glorification and to shun humility, a most precious and elusive trait.

From a Torah viewpoint, the problem is far deeper. For a woman, the overriding factor in dress should, of course, be *tzenius.* The concept of *tzenius* encompasses not only hem, necklines and sleeve length, but, equally important, the concern that one dress in a refined and "quiet" manner, one which does not cause heads to turn in one's direction. For those to whom "being in fashion" holds importance, this is a definite problem. In the words of the Manchester Rosh Yeshiva, Rabbi Yehuda Zev Segal:

> Let us think for a moment: Who are the designers of these fashions and what guidelines do they use in originating their designs? The designers are secularists and more often than not are immoral. Their goal is to design a style that will attract the attention of men. In other words, these styles are a direct contradiction to the attribute of *tzenius* that is the hallmark of Jewish daughters (Inspiration and Insight, vol. I p. 298).

With regard to *bachurim* who show excessive concern over their appearance, Rabbi Segal began by citing a Midrash:

> R' Ami said: "The yeitzer hara does not walk on the 'side streets' [among the humble and modest who are not overly concerned with their outward appearance — Maharzu]; rather he walks down the 'main thoroughfares' [after those who are concerned with their appearance]. When he sees someone fingering his eyes, fixing his hair, and adjusting his step, he says, 'This one is mine!'" (Bereishis Rabbah 22:6).

[The Rosh Yeshiva continued:]

> "There is no question that a ben Torah must have a neat and clean appearance — but Heaven forfend that he seek to be 'in style,' clothing himself in the latest fashion designed by the gentile world. Nor should a ben Torah be so concerned with his appearance that he preens himself before a mirror, carefully combing every hair on his head. It is in regard to those who engage in such practices that Satan says, "They are mine!" (Inspiration and Insight, vol. I p. 214).

It would be sad enough if the problem of the students who ridiculed their fellow classmate over his out of-vogue clothing and glasses was limited to that of poor *middos*. Given the above, however, the problem encompasses much more;

though they may spend much of their day in front of a *Gemara*, their behavior is, in fact, reflective of an outlook which is not at all rooted in Torah.

◆═ Root of the Problem

The author of "Plastic Frames" concludes by saying that rather than attempt to effect a change in his son's yeshiva, he is, instead, searching for one whose students come from "less affluent" families. Certainly, the problems which his sons encountered are more likely to be found among "rich kids." As stated in the opening chapter of *Mesilas Yesharim*:

> *Thus, man is actually placed in the midst of a raging battle, because all situations he will encounter in this world, whether good or bad, are actually tests for a person. A person may be tried by poverty on the one hand, or by wealth on the other, as Shlomo said, "Lest I become affluent and deny G–d or I become impoverished and steal" (Mishlei 30:9). A person is thus caught in a battle from the fore and from the rear. If he is victorious on all fronts, he will then be the adam hashaleim, the "complete man," who will succeed in uniting himself with G–d ...*

Surely the percentage of yeshiva students to whom fashion is important is higher among the affluent. Whether or not one should purchase the latest suit from Pierre Cardin or the newest Dior silk tie is more of a test for someone with money, who can easily afford to satisfy his tastes and who is more likely to feel a need to compete with wealthy neighbors who dress this way.

It is untrue, however, to say that this problem exists only among the affluent. There are many yeshiva students from affluent homes who dress rather simply, and there are many from nonaffluent homes to whom manner of dress is a major issue. The most crucial factor is not the size of the parents' bank account, but the way in which they raise their children.

And certainly, the example that parents set, in manner of dress, as well as in other areas, will have a profound influence on their children.

◆◈ Prince for a Day

Chinuch habanim, child rearing and education, is an ongoing process, every day at every hour. There are certain occasions, however, that are milestones in a child's life and when proper *chinuch* is especially crucial. Surely there is no more important occasion for a boy than when he becomes *bar mitzvah.*

Several months ago, a former *talmid* of mine, now in eighth grade, met me in the corridor of our yeshiva and excitedly informed me that he would be becoming *bar mitzvah* that night. I told him, "You should know that tonight you will not be the same person that you are now. Now, if you will join nine men, a *minyan* will not be formed; tonight, you can be the tenth member of a *minyan,* and in so doing bring the *Shechinah* into our midst."[1]

"*Zohar Chaddash* states that R' Shimon bar Yochai held a *seudah* on the day when his son, R' Elazar, became *bar mitzvah.* When asked to explain the reason for his great joy, R' Shimon replied that on that very day, his son received a *neshama kedoshah,* sacred soul. R' Shimon sat his son beside himself, with sages to his right and left, and said, "Sit my son, sit. Today you are holy and your lot is with that of holy people."[2]

How unfortunate that for many, the spirituality of the moment is overshadowed or at least tempered by the hoopla of the event, beginning with the donning of *tefillin* for the first time a month or so before the *bar mitzvah.* Aside from the magnitude of the *mitzvah* itself, donning *tefillin* for the first time should signal the beginning of intense spiritual preparation for the *bar mitzvah,* akin to the message sounded by the first blowing of the *shofar* on *Rosh Chodesh* Elul. For some,

---
1. See *Berachos* 6a.
2. Cited in *Sefer Matan L'Bar Mitzvah.*

this milestone, like the *bar mitzvah,* is marred by that most familiar *simchah* creature — the camera. As one more *Yiddishe neshamah* is binding his mind and heart to the sacred words hidden inside his *tefillin,* lights flash. Couldn't the picture-taking wait until after *Shacharis*? Would it not be an important lesson for life to say to one's child, "The *tefillin* are so *heilig* (sacred) and wearing them is so special, that we don't want anything to interfere with your concentration when you put them on for the first time. The pictures can wait for later."

Then, of course, there is the *bar mitzvah seudah.* One need not throw a "big bash" to send his son the wrong message. Once, I attended a rather plain *bar mitzvah* at which a slide show was presented, showing the "star of the show" at his best from birth to *bar mitzvah,* certainly not a lesson in humility. A *bar mitzvah* is a time to show a boy not who he is, but who he can become.

It has become "fashionable" in some circles to hand out party masks at *bar mitzvah* affairs, turning the dance floor into a masquerade — accompanied of course, by "Jewish" disco music and fancy footwork. What will the *bar mitzvah* boy take home from such an evening, aside from gifts? The significance of his entrance into halachic manhood will probably be lost in a sea of glitter.

It is up to parents to determine whether their son will see his becoming *bar mitzvah* for what it really is — a major spiritual milestone and transformation. If this message is not imparted, and in its place, the boy perceives his turning 13 as little more than his chance to be in the spotlight, then a golden opportunity may, *chas veshalom,* become a negative experience.

Simply Beautiful

Some years ago, a *talmid* of mine from an affluent home became *bar mitzvah.* The *seudah* was held in a *shul*-basement catering hall; plastic and paper goods were used. It was the plainest of affairs. Toward the end of the meal, the father spoke. The gist of his message was: "I could well afford a more elaborate affair, but I felt it unnecessary. Instead, I calculated the difference and have written out a check in that amount which I would like to present now to the *menahel* of my son's yeshiva."

Later, when I expressed my admiration to the father, he responded, "I was very uncomfortable making that speech. It seemed as if I was patting myself on the back. But I felt that it had to be said."

On another occasion, I attended a *bar mitzvah seudah* of a boy who also was from a well-to-do home. Had the father been a *melamed* or a *kollel* fellow, the affair could not have been more simple. (I might add that this boy is not a flashy dresser.) There were about sixty guests, aside from the *bar mitzvah's* classmates. The highlight of the affair was the boy's completion of all six orders of the *Mishnah*. The father wept with tears of joy. It was a beautiful evening. Most important is the lasting impression that such an evening surely had on they boy.

On the other hand, when parents place undue emphasis on the style of the *bar mitzvah* boy's hat and the rest of his outfit, on the way his hair is cut, on party decor and other foolishness, then the child has learned: What is important is not who I am on the inside, but who I appear to be on the outside. It is such a child who will quite possibly become clothes conscious and might even taunt a classmate who dares to be seen wearing plastic frames.

Landmines Along the Information Highway
What Every Jewish Home Should Know About the Dangers of the Internet

Yoseph Herman

⊷ Welcome to Modem Country

THE PERSONAL COMPUTER (PC) IS TAKING THE SECULAR world by storm. As it passes from the offices to more and more homes, many fine Orthodox Jewish families that would not dream of owning a television now proudly display their PC. To the outside world, the home PC is largely an entertainment medium. To our Torah community, however, it provides not only a means of word processing and managing home finances, but a powerful potential source of income. We all know of *kollel Yungeleit* who are supported by incomes associated with computers. So when we see little Yankele or little Rochele playing with the computer, we are thrilled. After all, computer literacy is essential for today's and tomorrow's jobs. So what if Yankele wastes some time on an inane computer game? He is on the way to acquiring vital job skills in the safety of his home, without having to enter any university, with all its attendant risks.

Yet are we aware of the fact that the same universities, which have never been trendsetters in moral decency, are now rising in alarm? That they are setting up safeguards to protect their students from the unimaginable levels of moral depravity that can be accessed by anyone today through the use of computers? A person sitting at a computer can access filth far worse than available through television. He can communicate interactively with people whose sick minds should require that they be locked up for the sake of public safety. He can view pictures that even Times Square newsstand vendors dare not display. He can do all this without his parents or *rebbei'im* ever suspecting the sewage that is penetrating his mind. This article is being written to alert *rabbanim, mechanchim* and parents to the dangers of the Information Highway in general, and the Internet in particular.

The dangers we are mentioning here are not inherent in the isolated home computer. Once someone attaches a "modem" to this computer, however, this feature allows the computer to link into computers all over the outside world, using the telephone lines. It is that link to the Internet that opens the channel to the vast world of information that exists. Most of that information is valuable or harmless. Much of it, however, does not belong on the computer screen of any decent person. This article will explain what the Internet is, what it can do, the types of information access that are available to computers equipped with modems, and possible defenses against the pitfalls.

The Internet

When President Clinton began his administration, he introduced the term "Information Highway" to the American public. This would be a vast electronic network that would allow information to flow at great speed, substantially increasing America's competitive position in the world. The ideas sounded attractive. Soon people discovered that there already is such a highway in existence, the Internet. With this new awareness, there began a continuing stampede by the masses to find and mount the "entrance ramps" to this vast Information Highway.

The Internet was born over twenty years ago.[1] At that time the U.S. Defense Department was looking for a way to link

---

1. Ed Krol, *The Whole INTERNET, User's Guide & Catalog,* 1992, O'Reilly and Associates.

together all the computers doing military research into a network in such a manner that should an enemy bomb-attack knock out part of it, it would not be crippled in its entirety. That evolved into the idea of tying together large numbers of individual computers in such a way that they can still communicate with each other regardless of whether individual computers are added to or missing from the network. The military effort evolved over the years into today's Internet. However, it is important to appreciate the significance of the starting philosophy. Anyone can link his computer to the Internet, whether it be a scientific laboratory, a government agency, a university, a business organization, or a depraved individual or group. All these and many other groups comprise the Internet community. To join, one does not fill out applications, does not pay dues, is not answerable to any supervisory agency. The only requirement for your computer to be a part of Internet is that it conform to established computer-related standards (and provide a fee to a service provider who could not care less what you do with your computer connection). Today's television has maintained whatever moral standards prevail because there still is some authority that exercises some supervisory control over it. Imagine how much lower television could sink if all the policemen were removed from it. That is the Internet.

Anyone with $1000 to $5000 can buy a computer, link it to the Internet and offer from his computer any information at all to the international community. In early 1994, there were 3.2 million reachable computers on the Internet.[2] The explosive growth of Internet is evidenced by the fact that there was an 81 percent increase in such computers over the last year alone! Our little Yankele or Rochele only needs a modem costing under $100 to add to the home computer, an inexpensive special computer program to talk to the Internet and a subscription fee of about $10-$20 per month. With these, he or she can access over the telephone line many if not most such computers, and sample the information that they offer.

---

2. M. Strangelove, *How to Advertise on the Internet,* 1994, Strangelove Internet Enterprises.

Most denizens of the Internet are not perverts. Most functions of the Internet are justified on constructive grounds. We will try in the following sections to explain the major services that the Internet offers and how these can be used for valuable functions. We will also demonstrate how they can be and are being subverted towards unsavory ends, and how difficult it is to marshal defenses against the problem areas.

⟶ Services Provided by the Internet: Benefits...

Most of the services available to the users of the Internet are not objectionable. Nevertheless, it is generally agreed that most of the data that flow along the Information Highway today involve indecent information. This we will discuss later. Let us first consider the second most popular use, electronic mail or E-mail. Every user of a computer who has access to the Internet is assigned a unique address. Anyone on the Internet can send a message to anyone else anywhere on earth. This is done by typing a message into the computer and directing it to the address of the recipient. There is no additional fee for this message service. When the addressee connects to the Internet, he is automatically informed that there is a message waiting for him, to be read at his convenience.

There is a much more personal version of this E-mail facility, called "chat." This is the computer version of having a group conversation. Any two individuals, or many people from all parts of the world, can each be sitting at his or her computer. Each in turn can type in some information, which will be printed out on the screen of every other participant. This allows interactive discussions and debates.

The Internet can transmit not only printed text, but also pictures. All such information can be stored in digital computer form in computer files. This allows one user to connect to any other computer and look at the contents of the files stored there, whether they be words or pictures (unless blocked from doing so by the creator of the file).

These facilities can be combined for legitimate uses. People seeking information on topics from agriculture to zoology[3] can connect to the appropriate computer and find pertinent data. There are sets of tools that help in locating the exact information needed. One can access the weekly grain-export files of the U.S. Department of Agriculture, for example. During the recent national elections, Internet users could follow the election-return progress in California, on a minute-by-minute basis. The potential benefits of this system to international business are just beginning to be understood. Suppose that I am situated in New York and am a small importer of certain lines of toys. Until now I may have received a few catalogs or seen a few salesmen with a limited selection of toys and prices. With Internet, toy manufacturers in Hong Kong, Taiwan, or anywhere can put a computer on the Internet. They can store their latest catalogs on the computer, complete with pictures. From New York, I will be able to scan tens or hundreds of catalogs. I will be able to do my price and delivery negotiations using E-mail and use electronic bank-fund transfers to handle the payment. The Internet can now give small businessmen the competitive advantage that only the large players enjoyed heretofore.

...And the Flip Side

What happens when these powerful communication facilities are used by people with sick minds? The same computer that can hold a toy catalog complete with pictures of toys can and often does hold indecent or perverted literature — and pictures. The Internet Yellow Pages[4] is a book that contains 359 pages of listings of information available on the Internet. Of these, a relatively small fraction is devoted to unsavory matters. Some of those listings, however, would make one's hair stand on end. Some of the topic names cannot be printed in a family magazine. Some of the less-offensive sounding of these subjects

---

3. H. Hahn and R. Stout, *The Internet Yellow Pages,* 1994, Osborne McGraw-Hill.
4. Ibid.

include six pages of offerings called "Bizarre" including a group devoted to "Tasteless Topics," plus headings called "Cyberpunk," "X-Rated," or "Drugs." It is not hyperbole to say that our Yankele or Rochele can have their mind permanently maimed by the worst that man can produce, some of it in the form of pictures in full glorious color.

In a simple experiment I conducted while doing research for this article, I used an Internet search feature to find for me references containing the words "drugs." It produced a variety of suggestions involving legitimate medicines. After about two minutes of searches, however, I was looking at a selection of newsletters produced by groups dedicated to the propagation of the use of illegal, mind-altering chemicals.

The business community is not slow in capitalizing on the weakness of people. In the book *How to Advertise on the Internet*,[5] there is a chapter describing how to make money from the business of indecency. It even gives examples such as where, for a fee, an individual can connect to a live person over the Internet. It is advising its readers on how to take advantage of the lack of decency constraints on the Internet, to devise advertising that really catches attention.

We are not finished. One of the features of Internet is the "Newsgroups." As originally envisioned, a newsgroup is a gathering of people with the same interests who send E-mail messages to a central bulletin board. Everyone who subscribes to such a newsgroup (cost free) would see all of the messages that are sent. Thus, for example, there are newsgroups for nuclear physicists, for individual hobbyists, or virtually any topic of interest to anybody. These newsgroups allow discussions, debates and general communications between people of similar interests. Anyone can start a new newsgroup. With a simple computer command I can accept or reject the offer to subscribe to each newly formed newsgroup. If I accept, then I will automatically receive each day all the notes that anyone addressed anywhere in the world to this newsgroup.

---

5. M. Strangelove, *How to Advertise on the Internet*, 1994, Strangelove Internet Enterprises.

An example of the constructive use of such services (although strictly speaking not a newsgroup) is Project Genesis, run by Rabbi Yaakov Menken, who uses the Internet as an outreach medium to do *kiruv* work. He offers regularly dispatched items on the *parshah* of the week, on *shemiras halashon,* the daily translation of the *Halachah Yomis* portion of the *Shulchan Aruch, Ramchal,* and many other valuable items. On the other hand, each morning, as I connect my work computer to the Internet, I get a listing of the latest offerings of newly formed newsgroups. A sickening portion of these titles are oriented to distasteful topics. These newsgroups will guarantee that the participant is kept up to the latest perversions unleashed on the Internet.

The future promises to get worse. On one hand, new computer programs are coming out with increasing frequency, with the purpose of making the task of accessing the Internet as easy as possible. In another area, research is concentrating on perfecting video conferencing on the Internet. Ideally that would allow two businessmen an inexpensive way to use television cameras coupled to the Internet to hold face-to-face conferences from locations across the world. At the same time, this opens even more offensive opportunities to spread a smut on a personal and powerful basis. That technology is not yet perfected or pervasive. Once it is, the Internet will sink to even greater depths as interactive moving pictures of all sorts will proliferate, complete with sound.

⟜ Other Potholes on the Information Highway

Thus far we have concentrated on the indecency aspects of the Internet for two reasons. First, these dangers are of particular concern to the Torah-oriented home. Furthermore, it is true that most of the services available on the Internet are legitimate, as mentioned above. However, those who have measured the total amounts of actual information zooming over the communications lines between computers have determined that by far, most such transmitted information is in the indecency category. It seems that the staid businessman, who would die of embarrassment if he were seen purchasing questionable literature from a Times Square newsstand, feels free to indulge in the same or worse in privacy.

The Internet offers a much greater variety of dangers, however, as indicated by a growing number of newspaper reports. International police are just now waking up to the fact that international criminals, hate groups, and terrorists are turning to the Internet as a relatively safe and fast method of communicating with each other, free from the usual controls such as law-enforcement wiretaps. Additionally, it should not take too long for a Jew participating in a multiparty "chat group" to receive a vile torrent of anti-Semitic hate messages, if it is discovered by the others that he is Jewish. It seems that the thin veneer of civility that makes overt anti-Semitism unfashionable is stripped away by the anonymity of the computer terminal, and the inherent Jew-hatred of the typical *Eisav* comes barreling down the Information Highway. Further, digital versions of a wide variety of frauds are beginning to separate the naive users of computers from their hard-earned money. Trusting children have given out their addresses and other vital information to those only too eager to prey on the innocent.

How Can We Protect Our Families? — Part 1

The only way that we can protect our families with any certainty is to forbid any family member to access the Internet from our home or anywhere else. This aspect will be discussed further in the next section. Here, however, we will discuss the details of the options available to one who wants to use the Internet, but wishes to install safeguards as a protection from the dangers outlined above. It is important to comprehend these options in order to understand the degree of such protection available today, such as it is, and what can be developed in the near future.

For someone to roam the Internet from his home PC, the following three elements must be added to that PC:
- a modem to allow the PC to communicate over the telephone lines.

- a special computer "interface" program that can "talk the language" of the Internet.
- a service-provider utility that provides the actual connection to the Internet.

Historically, five service providers have evolved that, over the years, have made available, for a fee, many of the services now being offered more broadly over the Internet. It has been possible to use a modem to dial a local phone number anywhere, all over the country, and access these services. These are now expanding their facilities and are in varying degrees offering gateways to the Internet. The five service providers are CompuServe, America Online, E-World, Delphi and Prodigy. Probably, the easiest way to get on the Internet is to open an account with one of these services. Once you have your modem, they will provide the other requirements, the connection to the Internet, and the interface or program to communicate with the Internet.

In response to the growing interest in Internet, many other local providers are now offering a more basic service, one that has only one function, to allow the PC owner to connect his modem to the Internet by dialing a local phone number.

New Internet interface programs are being offered to the public in an increasing variety. In addition, there is Microsoft, the company that is producing the popular "Windows" program that most of today's PCs require to perform their various functions. Microsoft has already announced that the next version of this Windows program, due in late-1995, will contain an Internet interface program. Therefore, by the end of 1995, most PCs will have available stored in their computer programs that will allow users to access the Internet merely by adding the modem and subscribing to a service provider.

In principle, the vast power of the computer-information processing technology should be able to be mobilized to provide a credible defense against the widely perceived perils of the Internet. In practice, the use and abuse of the Internet has exploded so rapidly that the defenses are lagging far behind. It is difficult at this stage to predict what defenses will eventually develop. However, a brief survey of what is currently available or envisioned will be attempted.

The five service providers, CompuServe, America Online, E-World, Delphi and Prodigy, have always exercised forms of self-censorship for the Internetlike services that they had been providing. They are now starting to extend these to cover the connections that they are providing to the Internet. For example, at the time of this printing, America Online has "Parental Control Features" that allow parents to block their children from accessing entire facilities of the Internet, such as instant messages, chat rooms, or public computer conferences. Concerned parents will probably find these five companies at the forefront of offering more forms of such censorship.

For those who purchase their own interface program, it will probably also be possible in the near future for a parent to instruct the interface program to block access to all features that have certain keywords as part of their names. It is unknown at this time what parental-control features the forthcoming Microsoft Windows package will have. That is the package that will be available on most PCs by the end of 1995.

Whatever censorship feature the parent chooses, its effectiveness at this point is very questionable. Most children are more familiar with computers than their parents. Even if effective parental-control features are developed, will the average parent have the ability to make certain that it is used to its full power? Furthermore, it is difficult to conceive how one can block information sources that have names that one did not anticipate when these safeguards were being programmed.

↦ How Can We Protect Our Families? — Part 2

This article was written to alert the Torah community to dangers to our spirituality that most of us would not have dreamt of in our worst nightmares. The Internet is a far greater threat than, say, theater or television. Our Yankele and Rochele can explore the depths of Internet, usually without the supervision of the unsuspecting parent who may think that they are learning computer skills. It is very easy to push a single computer button to make the questionable Internet display disappear whenever someone approaches. A second push of the button will bring it back as soon as it is safe. Without the safeguard of shame, what keeps a person from getting caught in the trap?

The easiest solution to all the problems outlined in this article would be to ban PCs or at least modems from the Jewish home. Without modems, there cannot be any connection from the local PC to the Internet. The Jew in *galus,* however, has traditionally supported himself and the community institutions by excelling in business. It is becoming increasingly apparent that much of tomorrow's commerce will flow along the Information Highway. If we exclude the Internet in its entirety from the Jewish home, are we not placing the current and future Torah-observant generations at a serious competitive disadvantage in national and international commerce? We could, of course, mandate that the Internet be allowed in the Jewish office for business purposes only, but not in the home. One of the advantages of the computer is that business can be conducted from home — for example, by the housewife supporting her husband in *kollel.* In addition, the home computer allows us to provide vocational training to future businessmen, without need for formal higher education.

If it is agreed that some access to the Internet is desirable, then the question is how to draw the line allowing our families access to the good parts while avoiding the unsavory parts. A related question is whether it will ever be technically possible to draw such a line effectively. Today that cannot be done.

Protecting our homes from the dangers of the Internet requires guidance from Torah authorities. Working groups of technically knowledgeable people should be formed to monitor this rapidly exploding field and provide data upon which our leaders can form their recommendations. These Torah leaders should then issue guidelines to allow us to protect ourselves and our children from the landmines along the Information Highway.

The Time for Perfection Has Come — Are We Ready?

Dr. Aaron Twerski

The crown jewel of our Torah existence — the family — is undergoing serious stress. The tensions need to be identified and steps have to be taken to reduce them to manageable levels. It is time for serious introspection.

⟻ Conflict, Crisis and Confusion

OUR CHARGE IS TO DETERMINE HOW THE JEW CAN SERVE as a vehicle for *k'vod Shamayim*, i.e., how our daily lives can enhance respect for G–d and His Torah. It is often instructive to understand a concept from its negation. The clearest and most manifest expression of *chillul k'vod Shamayim* arises when Jews worship idols. Of such magnitude is the sin that a Jew is required to sacrifice his life rather than commit idolatry even under coercion. When the Jewish nation first sought to violate this cardinal sin with the creation of the Golden Calf, the Torah relates that they "gathered onto Aaron and they said to him, 'Come, let us make for us gods that will lead us'" (*Shemos* 32:1). *Rashi* notes that the Talmud was struck by the term *"yeilchu lefaneinu"* (lit. *they will lead us*). The Hebrew word *"yeilchu"* is plural. The request should have been for a singular god that would replace Moshe *Rabbeinu*. The Talmud explains that the Jews sought not one, but many gods: "*Elohus harbei evu lohem.*"

Why a multiplicity of gods? Upon reflection, one can discern a profound lesson about Jews: We either worship one G–d and fulfill His will, or we are pulled in a multiplicity of directions. One source of idolatry will not suffice.

The lesson is clear. When we suffer *pizur hanefesh,* when we are torn in many different directions, it is a sign of deep and serious trouble. A Torah Jew's life must be focused. It must reflect the unity that inheres in the service of One G–d. When we sense that we owe allegiance to a multiplicity of goals, it is time to step back and ask ourselves: Are we still loyal to Hashem and His Torah or do our conflicted lives give evidence of a deep internal division that is inconsistent with the basic tenets of our faith? My own sense is that we are the most stressed-out generation of American Jews in recent memory. Internal stress, conflict and confusion of purpose have become staples of our daily existence. It has begun taking a serious toll on our mental health and that of our children.

I cannot claim to have conducted a scientific inquiry but anecdotal evidence provides more than a little support for my thesis. For example, discussions with those knowledgeable about the sale and dispensing of pharmaceuticals in areas of heavy *frum*-population concentration in New York reveal that prescriptions of tranquilizers, antidepressants and a whole range of soporifics are higher than they should be. Psychologists, mental-health therapists and social workers confirm this observation. It is not that these drugs are being needlessly dispensed; rather the need for them has escalated.

Perhaps even more disturbing are the observations of professional educators. I have heard from several principals and *menahalim,* as well as a random selection of *rebbei'im* and teachers. They all perceive a decline in performance of entering classes in the past several years. They find more children that are distracted and not able to focus as well as compared to previous years. In some schools, gross academic benchmarks confirm the learned intuition of the professionals. Most of these sources admit to being genuinely puzzled as to why the changes are occurring, but there is little disagreement that something is amiss.

I am neither a sociologist nor psychologist. My analysis need be taken with a grain of salt. I would be remiss, however, if I don't share with you insights gained from discussions over the past several years with a broad range of people from all spectra of the Torah community.

⇒ Those Who Make It, Those Who Don't, and Those Who Make It and Don't

Earning a livelihood has been the topic of considerable discussion and concern to us. It is not merely a societal problem that is tangential to living in a Torah community. The mounting costs of yeshiva education for large families present awesome and often crushing burdens on parents. Concomitantly, inadequate salaries for *mechanchim* and burgeoning class size compromise the ability of teachers to teach with peace of mind and the potential of children to learn in an atmosphere where they are not lost in the crowd.

A sophisticated readership does not need to be told that these are not merely a desideratum which can be wished away. They are matters the *Shulchan Aruch* addresses. They are tied to inexorable halachic imperatives. How does our community cope with these responsibilities? For the sake of simplicitly, I will break down our community into three groups. Each is faced with stress that takes its special toll in a Torah-centered community. The wealthy or the "haves," for the most part, meet their financial obligations to family and community with relative ease. Our community, however, has almost no old-line families of wealth.

We are a post-holocaust community. We have no analogues to the Rothschilds, Fords or Kennedys. Our wealth is mostly first- and, at best, second-generational. It is heavily entrepreneurial. It is thin, fragile and tenuous. There is little margin for comfort.

A second category of well to do are professionals who have been highly successful. Once again, these are self-made persons whose income is almost solely dependent on their outstanding individual skills and continuing performance, which is highly demanding both intellectually and emotionally.

Our "haves" are for the most part extremely stressed out. They keep long and grueling hours at work. When they return home, the cannot shuck their worries and responsibilities and park them at the door. The tension level in the home is often extraordinary. Faced with large families and community demands on their time, many of them do not cope well. What passes for communication with children is often polite banter but no real talk. The family is often an unwelcome distraction from what has become an all-consuming involvement with business and profession. Their personal commitments to Torah learning and spiritual growth are sorely tested, and they find themselves torn between unyielding demands on their time and energy. It is little wonder that they swallow tranquilizers and that their children appear more distracted and unfocused than yesteryear.

Even more distressing is the lot of our so-called "middle class." I have dubbed this group as "Those That Make It and Don't." This hard-working middle class may be earning anywhere between $50,000-$85,00 per year (either single- or two-income earners). With large families and multiple tuitions, however, these families are choking. They may be in the top 10 percent of American wage earners. Bill Clinton may think they are doing well, but the reality is that the financial pressures are most unbearable. As the children become older, each family begins facing the day when they will begin marrying off their children. And they often do not have the foggiest notion of how they are going to manage the expenses of a *chasunah, matanos,* let alone the desire and need to help the children in the early years of *kollel* life. They can barely make it through the month — without facing extraordinary expenses. Something has to give, and it does. The tensions of debt, feelings of inadequacy, and social pressures to earn more and work yet harder take their toll.

> *Recently, a father who fits the above paradigm was chatting with me. He said, "Please, don't take this the wrong way. But, you know, I have days when I'm envious of my Italian neighbor who earns $500 per week. He comes home to his 1.8 children and his wife, and he is a hero. The children attend public school. He lives modestly, and he fulfills all his obligations to society. I earn three times that and I'm a bum. I'm a bum for the tuition committee, an inadequate wage earner for my wife and children, and am slightly above the status of a schnorrer in the community. And now when I think of marrying off my children in the next ten years —I have nothing but nightmares.*

It will not surprise you to learn that this fine *ben Torah* is on antidepressants and tranquilizers. He has richly earned the right to them. And if the younger children of such folk begin demonstrating diminished performance in school, it is no mystery as to why.

Finally, we have those who do not make it. They are at least spared the agony of unrealizable expectations. Unless they have some special status in the community as that of an outstanding *talmid chacham,* however, they face the ignominy of poverty. The simple truth is that we are wont to place the "have-nots" in the *schlemazel* category. Stratification based on wealth is pernicious and sinful. It is totally foreign to Torah values. but I have heard all too many times about one or another that *ehr iz nisht kein balabatisher yunger maan.* Badges of shame are not worn without cost. They too contribute to the never-ending cycle of depression and feelings of worthlessness. Children whose pride as members of a family so tarnished cannot always be expected to easily don the requisite pride so necessary to a healthy ego and to strong scholastic performance.

It is not my intent to proclaim that we live in a state of disaster. The values and beauty of Torah homes provide a multitude of strengths to deal with these problems. We have a deep heritage for survival under adversity and it serves us well. If we seek to ameliorate and correct problems, however, they must be sharply stated. Overstatement is not warranted, but understatement would lull us into inaction. And act we must.

⚯ The Social Calendar

If our mental diversion and inattention at home were not sufficient, we have an added dimension that impacts upon our family life. We are all too often physically absent from home. Our social calendars have become so crowded that we have come to dread our social obligations. Several weeks ago, I attended a funeral, ר"ל, one morning. A relative whom I encountered told me that after the funeral he had to attend a *bris*, to be followed on the same day by a *Tennayim*, a wedding and a *Sheva Berachos*. Although this is unusual for one day, it is not unusual at all to be booked solid night after night for weddings, *bar mitzvahs*, engagements, parlor meetings, PTA's, *tzedakah* parties, lectures, etc.

A principal of a fine yeshiva recently told me that the two months of the year that are the most tense for the students are the very months when parents are absent from home almost every night. January and June are examination months. They are also the prime wedding season. From any of us, however, the phenomenon is to limited to two months of the year. It has become a staple of our lives. We are just way too busy and distracted. There is too much electricity coming over the wires. If we are not careful, we shall give birth to a new generation of latchkey children. Parents will be home for them when they come home. But if parents must leave night after night to fulfill social obligations, the children will be sorely neglected. The constant tension of having to leave by a certain time, dressing for the event, rushing homework and supper, all exact costs.

We need more quiet in our lives. We need it for ourselves and we need it for our children. We need to be at home both physically and mentally more, a lot more, than we are at present. Are there practical steps that can be taken to reduce the psychic drain that has become the bane of our existence? To this challenging question I now turn our attention.

⇒ Some Modest and Not-So-Modest Proposals for Change

Before offering any suggestions for reducing the tensions, a disclaimer is in order. My proposals will not deal with the issues of *parnassah* in general or the problems of increasing the earning power of members of our community. That is a topic worthy of serious discussion, in and of itself. But the problems outlined above will not be alleviated by marginal increases in wealth. And truly significant increases in earning power are not in the offing. We cannot and should not expect to produce a middle class with an average earning power of $150,000 per year.

What can be done is to find ways to reduce expenditures. We have established that one area that cannot be cut is tuition. We are already operating our yeshivos on shoestring budgets. General modesty in lifestyle is certainly to be encouraged. But, to be fair to our middle class, the general lifestyle is relatively modest. The cost of housing is determined by the market. Unless we are to open up a broad new neighborhoods in areas where housing costs are demonstrably less, we face fairly stable fixed costs. One area of our lifestyle must, however, undergo serious reevaluation. The cost of *simchos* of all kinds must undergo sharp and significant downsizing.

The reasons are many. First, it is the one area of our lives where we can realize significant savings without impinging on basic lifestyle. Second, with the increased size of *frum* families, the total financial and psychic burden is crushing both for those who make the *simchos* and for family and friends who participate in them. Third, we can no longer close our eyes to the opulent Jewish *simchos* that constitute such obvious conspicuous consumption that they disgrace us all.

- *Bar mitzvahs* are a good place to start. There is no reason that *bar mitzvahs* should not be limited to close immediate family. For the most part, they can be done at home. Where that is impossible, a small *shul*-hall will do just fine. For *Kiddush* in *shul*, a *lechayim* is quite sufficient. Several *Chassidishe* communities have mandated such *takanos* (ordinances). They work beautifully. The entire cost is in the $1,000 range.

- The entire constellation of *simchos* attendant to marrying off a child needs serious restructuring. *Tennaim* should be done at home.

    Formal parties, from *Lechayim* to *Vort* to actual *Tennaim*, constitute a huge financial drain. They are purely an American invention. In prewar Europe they were unheard of.

- We must find ways to drastically cut the cost of the *chasunah* night itself. Unless tough *takanos* are put in place, we are bound to continue the present system. We invite many friends and relatives because we are obliged to do so. They are obliged to come because they have no alternative. The inviters would be happy to forgo the formal full *seudah* invitation because they are unable to afford the cost. The invitees would be pleased to forgo attending the entire *seudah* because the cost of the present and the baby-sitter amount easily to $100 for the evening. Both would be happier with an invitation to *simchas chassan v'kallah*. Without formal and binding limitations, however, sense of obligation mandates that the invitations be made and be accepted.

    With burgeoning family size, *b'li ayin hara*, invitations to even immediate family can take on sizeable proportions. For some families, married first- and second-cousins number in the hundreds. Once again without some formal limitations, cutting costs without creating conflicts simply cannot be done.

- The cost of *Sheva Berachos* needs to be sharply diminished. Catered meals on four or five successive nights can run anywhere from $4,000 to $10,000 for the week — excluding *Shabbos*. It would be quite sufficient to have the *chassan* and *kallah* and parents for dinner and invite a small group of friends for *Birchas Hamazon*.

Takanos with teeth could reduce expenditures enormously. Saving in the magnitude of $20,000 and more per wedding event — i.e., *Tennaim, Chasunah, Sheva Berachos* — are easily realizable. For families with eight to ten children the total amount saved is staggering. Include the debt service on borrowed money to fund these affairs, and the savings are even more impressive. Finally, consider the psychic toll of friends and relatives who look bleary eyed after a week of mandatory attendance at *Sheva Berachos*. We really must rein ourselves in.

- The need for *takanos* extends to *seudos* of *bris milah, pidyon haben* — indeed, to all *simchos* that are part of the ordinary Jewish life cycle. Putting this entire aspect of our lifestyle in order will, when added together, have a significant impact on the quality of life for all of us. Modesty, true *tzenius,* could become fashionable.

"But I Really Can Afford It"

Whenever the issue of *takanos* is raised we hear a hue and cry from some quarters. *Why should we have to restrict ourselves from more lavish simchos if we can afford them? Let the rich make opulent simchos. And let the others scale down in accordance with their abilities.* Many people of substantial means strongly support the institution of *takanos*; however, the argument on part of the naysayers is stated so frequently and with such vehemence that it needs rebuttal. The primary source of the rebuttal come from *divrei Chazal.* The Talmud (*Moed Katan* 27a-b) relates:

> *Formerly, it was the practice to convey food to the house of mourning, the rich in silver and gold baskets and the poor in baskets of willow twigs, and the poor felt shamed; they [Chazal] instituted that all should convey food in baskets of willow twigs to uphold the honor of the poor....*
>
> *Formerly, it was the practice to bring out the rich for burial on a dargesh, i.e., an ornamental bed, and the poor in a*

> plain box, and the poor felt shamed; they [Chazal] instituted that all should be brought out in a plain box to uphold the honor of the poor.... Formerly, the expense of taking the dead out to burial fell harder on the next of kin than his death so that the dead man's next of kin abandoned him and fled, until Rabban Gamliel came forward, disregarded his own dignity and was brought out to his own burial dressed in simple flaxen clothes.

On a similar note, the *Mishnah* (*Taanis* 26b) relates:

> *Rabban Shimon ben Gamliel said: "Israel had no days as festive as the Fifteenth of Av and Yom Kippur when the maidens of Jerusalem would go out dressed in white garments that were borrowed so as not to embarrass one who had none."*

As the Talmud relates, on these days *shidduchim* were made. And *Rashi* notes that the wealthy maidens were forbidden to wear their own clothing lest they embarrass girls from poor families who had no suitable garments of their own.

Takanos of this sort have a long and honored tradition in Jewish life. The famed *Vaad Arba Haaratzos* established standards for *simchos* of all kind. The well to do simply had to conform for the greater needs of the *Klal*. To allow for discretion leads us where we are today. The slope is far too slippery. The pressure to conform to the more honored status is too great for mortals to resist. It is interesting that today when we see an elaborate non-Jewish funeral cortege, we react: "That's so *goyish*!" It was once very Jewish. No longer. When non-Jews look at our elaborate weddings they say: "That's so Jewish!" Enough. We need to embrace the "*hatzne'a leches im Hashem Elokecha*," and declare it to be the norm for Jewish life.

Are We Prepared to Listen?

The issue of *takanos* for *simchos* has been on the agenda of the American Torah community for many years.[1]

---

1. See "Community Controls on Extravagance: Is It Time To Revive Them?" — *JO* '71.

Most recognize that they are an absolute necessity. Why have they not been mandated? Some point the finger of blame at the *gedolei Torah* for not *sua sponte* issuing a proclamation setting forth the standards. I place the blame on ourselves. Until recently, I believe we were not ready to listen. And our leaders for good and plenty reasons did not wish to issue decrees that would be honored mostly in the breach.

But, why have we not been ready to listen? Why have the *gedolim* been so reticent to take us on? My own sense is that they sense in us a cynicism incompatible with the kind of *emunas chachamim* necessary for a true allegiance to Torah. On matters that affect our lifestyle, too many of us are quick to question every perceived inconsistency that may appear to arise, and charge hypocrisy to salve our own sense of guilt.

When I was a youngster, my father constantly cautioned me against falling prey to cynicism. On numerous occasions he told me that when our matriarch Sarah banished Yishmael from the house of Avraham, her predicate for doing so was that in her view Yishmael was the quintessential cynic. My father interpreted the *pasuk* in *Bereishis* (21:9): "And Sarah saw Yishmael and son of *Hagar Hamitzris* who was born to Avraham *metzachiek*" — to mean that she saw him scoffing. Sarah concluded that she could not raise her son Yitzchak in an atmosphere where everything sacred was subject to daily cynicism. It was destructive and antithetical to fundamental Torah values.

There is a famous Yiddish saying: *Azoi vee es kristelt zich azoi yiddilt zich*. Loosely translated, it means that Jews pick up quickly on non-Jewish attitudes and traits. The cynicism of the non-Jewish world has spilled over to the Torah world. And our generation has developed cynicism into a fine art. Ours is a generation without heroes. We are far too ready to take cheap shots at Torah leaders and to disregard their edicts. If they are on occasion silent or their words are muted, it is because they realize that we may well treat their pronouncements with disdain. The dictum of *Chazal*, "*Kesheim shemitzvah lomar davar hanishma kach mitzvah shelo lomar davar she'eino nishma*" (Just as there is a *mitzvah* to speak when one will be listened to, so is there a *mitzvah* not to speak when one's words will be disregarded), must be taken into account. If we truly want direction from *gedolei Yisrael* on the subject of *takanos*, we will have to communicate to them that we are prepared to put our scoffing aside and abide by their decision.

Purging ourselves of cynicism would do wonders for us all. Let me share a very moving story with you:

> *Reb Chaim Tchernovitzer, the author of the Sidduro Shel Shabbos and the Be'er Mayim Chayim, was one of the great Chassidic masters. Reb Chaim's kedushah on Shabbos was beyond human comprehension. It was said that from the time he left the mikvah Erev Shabbos until the conclusion of Shabbos, he stood a head taller than he was on a regular weekday.*
>
> *In the city of Mosov lived a famous scoffer — "Herschel Mosover." He was blessed with a fine mind and an acid tongue that he used to heap scorn on all that was holy. He was most entertaining and whenever he would take up residence in the marketplace, he would be quickly surrounded by idle folk who would enjoy his repertoire of fun-making and cynicism. No one and no subject was off limits to him. He was prepared, if the spirit moved him, to poke fun at the greatest of the great and holiest of the holy.*
>
> *Hershel Mosover was a businessman and his travels once brought him to Tchernovitz. As was his custom, he went to the marketplace and before doing business he was quickly surrounded by people seeking to enjoy themselves at the expense of others. On that day, Reb Chaim set out to collect tzedakah from the businessmen in the marketplace.*
>
> *From afar Reb Chaim noticed Hershel Mosover and decided to avoid him. Why present Hershel with yet another opportunity to scoff at the Rav of the town? But Reb Chaim came into Hershel Mosover's line of vision. Hershel called out gruffly, "Rebbe, kumt aher!" (Rebbe, come here!) Reb Chaim disregarded the call, but Hershel would have none of it. "Rebbe, kumt aher!"*

Seeking to avoid a scene, Reb Chaim walked over to him. "Rebbe, what are you doing here?" Reb Chaim answered softly that he was out collecting money to redeem a family that had been thrown into prison by the poretz (nobleman) of the town for nonpayment of rent for a long period of time. The family was starving and freezing in the cold wet dungeon. Hershel Mosover asked, "Rebbe, how much money do you need?" Reb Chaim responded, "I need fifteen hundred guilden."

Hershel opened his purse and emptied it of its contents — fifteen guilden, a fortune of money. Everyone was waiting for Hershel Mosover to snatch the money back and make a joke out of the whole matter. A minute passed in silence. And then another. Finally Reb Chaim turned to Hershel and said, "Hershel, how should I bless you? — May you henceforth taste the true flavor of Shabbos!"

Hershel returned home to Mosov penniless. At first he was ashamed to admit to his wife and children that he had squandered his fortune. Ultimately the story came out. The anger of his family knew no bounds, but what were they to do? The deed was done. Hershel returned to his place of honor in the marketplace of Mosov and resorted to his old ways. Things continued continued normally until Thursday afternoon. Hershel began feeling unwell. He went home and tried to lie down but rest eluded him. Shortly, he was up and about, dancing and clapping, "Shabbos, Shabbos, Shabbos." Friday his ecstasy increased. He had to be peeled off the wall. Shabbos itself was beyond relief. He could find no rest, dancing and singing, "Shabbos, Shabbos, Shabbos." And then Shabbos passed.

Sunday morning, the old Hershel was back to himself. But when Thursday arrived, the scenario of the past week repeated itself. Several weeks followed this sequence. His family then learned from him of Reb Chaim's berachah. They decided that they would have to accompany their father to Tchernovitz and seek the recision of the berachah so that their father could exist as a normal human being.

The Time for Perfection Has Come — Are We Ready? / 391

> When they came to Tchernovitz and made their request, Reb Chaim told them that it was not possible to rescind the berachah, but he could make it possible for Hershel to withstand the kedushah of Shabbos kodesh: "Leave him with me for a while and you will see that he will be fine."
>
> Hershel stayed on with Reb Chaim and became his disciple. When he eventually returned to Mosov, he was no longer the same Hershel. So lofty had he grown in avodas Hashem that Chassidim who could not make the trip to Tchernovitz would travel to the Rebbe Reb Hershel of Mosov to experience the kedushah of Shabbos that one felt in the presence of Reb Chaim Tchernovitzer.

For one moment in his life, a scoffer put cynicism aside. He was able to act with the compassion of a *Yid*, and became an *ish kadosh*. If we can put aside the cynical attitude that so pervades society and listen with open ears and even more open hearts, we can realize real change in our lives. If we insist on placing our own imprimatur on the *takanos* — if we first ask, *"Ma kasuv bo?"* — we shall never receive the direction we so sorely need.

The time for action and acceptance has come. We must — if we are to survive, both spiritual and physically — reorder our lives. *Takanos* are not a panacea. But they are an important start. And we must begin somewhere.

The Gift
Dina Smith

A MAGNIFICENT GIFT! AN EXPENSIVE, FABULOUS GIFT! MY uncle, who always enjoys showering us with gifts, overdid himself this time. He presented us with a brand new Windows 95 computer fully loaded with dozens of programs (only educational, at my request). My home went through a total transformation since that gift arrived. The once boisterous and disarrayed house became quiet and neat, as the children ran down to the basement each day to experiment and enjoy this new wonder machine. Peace reigned. I happily would complete my work and cooking in a children-free kitchen.

One day as I went to the basement to check on my little angels (I haven't called them that for three years), I felt an involuntary shiver go down my back. There they were — all five of them crowded around the computer watching the oldest play an educational game. The king on the computer looked mad as he ground his teeth. My son had answered another math example correctly, enabling him to walk off with one more of the king's treasures. "Boom Boom" went the sound, as my son clicked the mouse at the tree, discovering yet another treasure.

My little Ephraim stared in fascination. His big blue eyes had shown similar fascination when he looked at the *Aleph*

Beis and licked the honey in the *cheder* at his *upsherin* a few weeks earlier. I wondered to myself: Will the *Aleph Beis* still hold the same magic for Yossie? Or will they have to compete for his interest over the colorful animation of the computer?

I stayed on. I watched more. Different programs were put on. I observed silently how they spelled words correctly. (My children were probably too engrossed in the computer program to realize my presence.) "Spell dance," demanded the computer, and so they did. D-A-N-C-E. "Right on," complimented the hidden voice behind the speakers. Then, rewarding their efforts, a ballerina (in a sleeveless, short tutu) performed a dance for them! Word and picture association, it's called, I remembered. This is education in 1998!

⇥ I Should Be Thrilled, But —

I couldn't watch anymore. I returned to my quiet kitchen and dialed my older sister (and advisor). "I should be thrilled the kids are busy," I lamented, "and yet something about these programs disturb me. Until now, I built my home exclusively with *kedushah*, not permitting anything alien to seep into my *mishkan me'at*, my miniature sanctuary. Is this any different? Are the designers of educational programs sensitive to offensive gestures, dress or mannerisms that their cartoon figures are feeding into the minds of my pure, young *kinderlach*? Do I want them to say 'right on' or to wiggle like the cartoon figures, or to experience the violence of taking someone's treasure or shooting down objects? Perhaps I'm overdoing it, making a big deal over innocent animated games that are simply part of the contemporary American scene."

I paused as I awaited the sage advice of my sister. She replied: "Dina, listen to your gut feeling. If you feel something is wrong, it probably is below your standard and you should put a stop to it." She remembered hearing a similar idea on the topic of *tzenius*. If one is in doubt about buying a dress because perhaps it's not in perfect harmony with standards of *tzenius*, then let her stay away from it. In other words, follow your instincts.

"But," I wailed, "what about my neat home and the quiet working time I gained with the kids busy with the computer?"

My sister sounded surprised. "I don't think you'd accept that as an excuse to let the kids watch TV. When something is wrong, convenience never enters the picture. Besides, throughout our history, drawing on *mesiras nefesh* in raising children has only had beneficial results."

No more had to be said. I was convinced.

I'm sorry, though. If you thought I was going to offer you my computer, it is not available. We are still using it, and printing away. We create beautiful cards to cheer older relatives and to wish friends happy birthday. The kids made striking Chanukah posters to decorate a party. As far as the standard programs, they might not be so terrible, but for my kids I want only the best!

Postscript

The day after I had spoken to my sister, I told my five-year-old that I don't want him to play a particular program anymore. "Why not?" he asked.

"Because I don't like it," I answered.

To this he innocently replied, "So don't look!"

Maybe that was the problem till now. I wasn't looking.

Dropouts

An Ounce of Prevention

Dealing with the Dilemmas of Kids At Risk

Where Responsibility and Love Intersect

The "At-Risk Child":
Early Identification and Intervention

Buying Time

Consequential Conversations
(Without Being Confrontational)

An Ounce of Prevention
Rabbi Yakov Horowitz

⇌ Reaching Today's Underachievers Before They Become Tomorrow's Dropout Teens

WE ARE FACED WITH A CRITICAL PROBLEM, ONE THAT WE must address as a society. There is a spiritual underclass that exists in our community—dropout teens. This group of teenagers has no defining prerequisites, they come from every type of home, and every income level. These are children that we as *mechanchim* (educators), parents, and indeed society as a whole have failed to reach. In Monsey alone, there are dozens of such boys ages 16 and above who are in no yeshiva setting at all. We bump into them at the mall, and we catch sight of them through the plate-glass window of the pool hall. In the greater New York area there are hundreds. And their numbers are growing. Rapidly.

On analysis, only a small percentage of these boys (and girls) have extenuating circumstances that may have contributed to their difficulties. Some come from very trying home situations. Others of a more intellectual bent have serious *emunah* questions that ר"ל led them astray. The vast majority, however, have but one thing in common. They have never felt successful in yeshiva. Shuffling from class to class, or worse yet, from school to school, their frustration grows to intolerable levels. Parental pressure increases; they often feel incredibly inadequate compared to their siblings; their self-confidence shrinks and often disappears. When they attempt to assert themselves at home or in school, it is often in awkward and inappropriate ways. This leads to more rebuke, more slings and arrows attacking their already low self-image.

This downward spiral continues until the child reaches eighth grade, and the harrowing search for a mesivta begins in earnest. After a rejection from the local mesivta, the parents frantically begin to research yeshivos geared to the underachieving student. For some, the search ends there. For others, their parents fear that this type of yeshiva places a stigma on their son. Hopefully the child is accepted to his second (or third) choice of yeshiva high school. If this does not happen, this sensitive teenager is forced to admit to his peers that he has no idea which yeshiva will accept him. While his classmates are excitedly making summer plans, he is in limbo regarding his status for *Elul Zman*. By the time his parents have placed him in a yeshiva, his self-image has suffered yet another body blow.

If this trend does not reverse itself in ninth or tenth grade, new dynamics enter the equation. A driver's license. Work. A social life. Suddenly this young adult, who has never been made to feel valuable or appreciated before, is told what a wonderful job he does, how charming he is, etc. At this point we have entered a new phase in the struggle for this *Yiddishe neshamah;* a very difficult uphill battle.

A Call to Action

Two *rebbei'im* in Monsey, Rabbi Aaron Milstein and Rabbi Shammai Blobstein, have heeded the call of the local *rabbanim*, and have formed a wonderful series of nightly *shiurim* geared to such young men and their specific needs. To call this program a success would be an understatement. The *shiurim* are generally well attended and sparked by much genuine enthusiasm. Most important is the opportunity that presents itself for these *bachurim* to bond with a *rebbi*. Many times these *shiurim* are followed by heart-to-heart conversations with the *rebbi* lasting well into the night.

A monumental difference exists between our "drop-out teens" and those of the secular world. A specific "*shelo asani goy*" is in order. While the external trappings of these boys are not those of the average *yeshiva bachur*, there is a genuine thirst for spirituality in these young men. What is astounding is the devotion these *bachurim* have for their *rebbei'im* and for each other. Many times the boys themselves approach one of the *rebbis*, offering to contribute to the rent money for the facilities that they use. Every wedding of one of the group is celebrated with great *simchah* by all. They have developed a remarkable sense of unity that cuts across the greatly divergent backgrounds from which they come.

The secret to the success of this program is that the dedicated *rebbei'im*, all volunteers, follow a simple set of guidelines; one that can be instrumental in making our own contact with these youngsters successful. Don't be judgmental or condescending. Speak to them with respect. Don't comment on their appearance. Never, ever attempt witty cracks or humorous lines at their expense. Just accept them for what they are; nice kids going through a difficult time.

⤖ A Childhood Squandered

The most bittersweet feeling when observing this phenomenon is: Why couldn't we have reached these *neshamos* five or eight years earlier, and avoid all this heartache? Each "client" represents so much strife within the family, so many sleepless nights for the parents, so much turmoil and pain within the boy's psyche, so much unrealized potential for growth; indeed, a childhood squandered. We must collectively examine this situation carefully and search for meaningful changes that we can implement to reverse this frightening trend.

Each situation, taken separately, lends itself to a logical explanation. When viewing the broad picture, however, it becomes glaringly obvious that something is very, very wrong. About one child you'll hear, "Of course he rebelled; look at how strict his parents are." Yet regarding another *bachur* in the same situation, you hear, "Growing up in such a permissive environment can only lead to total *hefkeirus*."

"I begged his parents not to spoil him like that" versus "Are you surprised that he ran off to work? Look at how poor his family is!" "Could you imagine the pressure he feels growing up with such a *chosheveh* father?" versus "Like father like son — he never had a role model at home. What do you expect?"

It is intellectually dishonest to dismiss this situation as anything other than what it is — a crisis in our *chinuch* world.

↬ Searching for Causes

What, then, has changed so dramatically? For one thing, the moral level of the secular world at large has been in an unrestrained free fall for many years now. In the 14 years that I have been teaching eighth graders, the decadence they are exposed to has increased not incrementally, but exponentially. And it shows. Even those who do not have a television set at home cannot shield their children from the relentless barrage of *tumah* (abomination) that permeates every facet of secular society. Anyone involved in *chinuch* will tell you that today's *tinokos shel beis rabban* (schoolchildren) face monumental *nisyonos*. Despite our best efforts, we cannot completely shield our children from this onslaught.

What we must address is a problem about which we can do a great deal to remediate. Throughout the past generation, we have been, *Baruch Hashem*, raising the expectation level of what our yeshiva system should produce as a final product. *Yeshivos gedolos* are not merely satisfied with graduating a group of young men who will attend a *shiur* and support their local yeshiva. Our goal is to graduate *baalei battim* who can give the *shiurim*, and *yungeleit* who have the ability to become the *Roshei Hayeshiva*. We as *mechanchim* are rightfully thrilled by this development. Our yeshiva-educated parent body demands it, and we eagerly do everything in our power to accede to their requests.

⇒ The Crescendo of Taunts

The harsh reality is that a substantial percentage of our children simply cannot keep up with these demands. Try as they may, many of them are unable to meet these higher expectations. As we ratchet up the tension level and raise the bar to encourage them to hurdle to greater heights, many of these children crash into the bar time and time again. Broken hearted and discouraged, they simply stop trying and seek fulfillment elsewhere.

> *The haunting story of Elisha ben Avuyah-Acher comes to mind. Acher had sinned and the door to teshuvah was closed to him. He heard a Bas Kol, a heavenly voice that proclaimed: "Shuvu banim shovavim chutz m'Acher." The voice informed him that all were welcome to do teshuvah except for him. His response was "Hoyil....lishani behai alma." He replied, "Since the option of teshuvah is not available to me, I will at least derive pleasure from this world," and he ר״ל returned to his path of aveiros.*

These sensitive young men are misreading our well-intentioned messages to them. They are not hearing our calls to improve, they misconstrue the pleas of their parents to better their lives and enrich their future. All that keeps reverberating in their ears is the never-ending shout of voices that pierce their hearts: "We don't want you in our classroom, in our yeshiva, in our mesivta, in our home."

⇒ Searching for Solutions

It is not my intent to offer broad solutions to this complex problem. For that we defer, as always, to our *gedolim*. I would humbly like to share with other *mechanchim* some of the methods that—combined with *tefillah* and *siyata diShmaya* — I have found to be helpful in these situations.

• Convey to your *talmidim* again and again that each of them has a contribution to make to *Klal Yisrael*. We all had classmates who struggled in yeshiva and became outstanding adults. Share some anecdotes with some of the weaker *talmidim* in a private setting. This past year, when I had quite a few *talmidim* who were not learning well and were very frustrated, I was speaking to the entire class about overcoming adversity. A *talmid* respectfully asked me, "What do you know about difficulty?"

I immediately responded, "You obviously never met my eighth-grade *rebbi*."

When the laughter subsided, and I saw that he was not satisfied, I softly informed the class that I had had a speech impediment — stuttering — as a child and I had to go to therapy to correct this problem. They were shocked. They also didn't believe me. I told them to think back carefully and remember that during a difficult piece of *Gemara* I often let my guard down and stutter a bit. It made such an impression on them that several parents called that night thanking me for sharing my infirmity with the children, and what a *chizuk* it was for their son to know that their *rebbi* had to overcome shortcomings of his own.

• The Parent-Teacher Conference affords an important opportunity to review the accomplishments of the *talmid* with his parents, and discuss areas that need improvement. It has its limitations, however. The conference is generally conducted in December, after much of the *zman* (semester) has passed. There is precious little "quality time" for a serious, protracted discussion of the situation. Most of all, the most important element of this dialogue is missing — the *talmid*. (This brings to mind the proverbial story of the Rabbi who conducted an appeal for *Ma'os Chittim*. When asked by his wife how successful the appeal was, he replied that he accomplished half of his intended goal; all the poor people were now willing to accept the money. All that remained for him to do was to convince the rich people to contribute the funds.)

Three years ago, I experimented with a new technique for helping *talmidim* who were not learning according to their ability. The week after Succos, I invited the parents of one such *talmid* to my home and requested that their son come along. We scheduled the meeting for late evening, when their younger children (and mine) were sleeping. We spent approximately a full hour discussing many issues pertaining to the *chinuch* of the *bachur*. The improvement in the boy's learning was remarkable.

Since then, I have been doing this with all *talmidim* that are not performing at their level. I have yet to conduct such a meeting and fail to see a dramatic improvement in the boy's attitude and learning.

• We teachers must stop the destructive habit of obtaining a scouting report on our *talmidim* before the new *zman* begins. There is no valid reason for doing this. One would have to be superhuman not to let negative information taint the way we treat the incoming class. Speak to many of the teenage "problem kids." You will hear this refrain again and again: "I was never given a fair chance after my first bad year." There just might be some truth to it. How many times have we heard the warning,"Watch out for —" ? In the spirit of fairness, let us imagine that we were told negative information about the best *talmid* in the class without the prior knowledge of what a *masmid* and *lamdan* he is. Picture the scenario. This young *talmid chacham* raises his hand the very first day to ask a splendid *kushya*. The *rebbi* hears warning bells. ("They were right about this kid; he's starting up already!")

"Put your hand down."

"But I have —"

"I said put your hand down!!"

"But *rebbi*, you misunderstand —"

"I WHAT?? OUT!!!"

It is critical for a *rebbi* to have certain information about his *talmidim* before the year begins, to ascertain which students require more sensitive handling. If a child has a sick parent or sibling ר"ל, or if the child comes from a broken home, etc., these facts must be conveyed to the *rebbi*. When a new group of *talmidim* enter the classroom, the first thing that the *rebbi*

An Ounce of Prevention / 405

should tell them is that he knows nothing about them, and that he has no interest regarding their past performance.

- Parents, teachers, and other authority figures at times hold up children for embarrassment or shame in front of classmates, siblings, or friends ("Do you really know '*Oleinu*' by heart? Without a *Siddur*? Come, let's all hear your marvelous memory at work!"), leaving emotional scars and feelings of anger that can smolder for years. Not every sin must be uncovered. Words of admonishment that are offered with love and understanding, respecting the child's feelings and need for privacy, will be received accordingly.

- A dress code is an integral part of the structure of any yeshiva. Indeed, it is often a defining element in the school; as such, the yeshiva has the obligation to enforce these rules vigorously. When the child runs afoul of these guidelines, however, it can be a source of great conflict between a *talmid* and his *rebbi*. I strongly suggest that if it becomes obvious that these violations are not isolated incidents, but rather indicate a rebellious pattern, it would be appropriate for the administration of the yeshiva to step in, and time for the *rebbi* to exit gracefully.

A *rebbi* cannot afford to squander all of his political capital and enter an adversarial relationship with a *talmid* over the length of the child's hair, size of his yarmulka, etc. To be sure, parents must assume responsibility and support the yeshiva's position. Without this crucial backing, the yeshiva will find it quite impossible to resolve this situation painlessly.

- Within a heterogeneous group, much can be done to accommodate the educational and social needs of the *talmid* who is encountering difficulty.

    1) Tests can be a source of great stress for the underachiever. On a temporary basis, it is often helpful to allow the child to be tested on a small portion of the material covered (one *blatt* out of four; until *Sheini* in *Chumash*). Insist on perfection for that amount. After you have built up his self-confidence, he will be able to be accountable for larger amounts.

2) If a *talmid* is absolutely unable to read the *Gemara* or *Chumash*, perhaps assure him that in the short term you will not call on him to read publicly. Or better yet, give him a short piece to prepare, then call on him to say this piece. He will be grateful to you for caring about his feelings and his *cheishek* (ambition) to learn will increase tenfold.

3) Another helpful idea is to allow the child to take notes during *shiur* and then use them during the written exam. Insist that they must be *his* notes only; don't allow him to copy from any other boys. You will be training him to be focused and involved in the daily *shiur*.

Much tact is needed to avoid incurring the envy of the other students. One way to deal with this is by reserving the top echelon of report-card grades for those who do not resort to any of these aids. Generally speaking, the other students will respect the fact that you are dealing gently with their peers. You also will be teaching them a valuable lesson in *derech eretz* and tolerance.

To Track or Not to Track

There has always been a heated debate among *mechanchim* whether larger yeshivos, those that have two classes or more in each grade level, should "track" the *talmidim* (grouping them according to ability) or not. Those who disagree with the tracking method cite two valid reasons:

1) The presence of *talmidim* who excel in their *limudim* (studies) give average performers a goal to aim for. Indeed, lack of boys that are "*shtieging*" could lead to lowered expectations, resulting in weaker children not even performing in accordance with their limited abilities. Additionally, the presence of a stronger group of *talmidim* is often a positive influence in terms of *yiras Shamayim*—they daven better, etc. To deprive weaker *talmidim* of this positive peer-pressure is unfair and undermines their future. Why should we compromise the goals of these *talmidim* just because they find learning difficult?

An Ounce of Prevention / 407

The often quoted *p'sak* in this matter is from Rabbi Aaron Kotler, who advised *menahalim* and *rebbei'im* alike not to remove weaker students from the class, and they will, with the passage of time, integrate with the other *talmidim* and remain devoted to Torah and *mitzvos*.

2) We do not live in a Utopian society. The brutal reality is that these children become labeled as soon as they are placed in a slower track. They feel inadequate, no mesivta will take them, they will become second-class citizens. *Menahalim* fear a bruising battle with each parent who is informed of the decision to track their son.

⟜ Rethinking the Issues

Perhaps the time has come to rethink our opposition to this system. Let us address the two above-mentioned factors. First the educational concerns:

We will begin with the *p'sak* of Reb Aaron. As explained to me by Rabbi Yehoshua Silbermintz, who discussed this issue personally with Reb Aaron, the *Rosh Yeshiva* was addressing a totally different situation. The question posed was: "At what point does the yeshiva/*rebbi* have the authority to ask a disruptive child to leave the yeshiva/classroom?" To which Reb Aaron replied that if the presence of a *talmid* is so detrimental to the general *chinuch* atmosphere by his conduct or by introducing *tumah* into the minds of others, the yeshiva has the right, indeed the obligation, to remove him before he harms others.

The next question posed was what to do with a boy who casts a pall over the classroom—not by disrupting, but by his lack of effort or inability to keep up. In this context, the poignant *p'sak*, "Let a weak *talmid* remain and listen," has little bearing on our discussion.

Even if there were a direct *p'sak* regarding this issue of tracking *talmidim*, I would suggest that the dynamics of today's situation, as described above, would dictate that we ask our present-day *gedolim* to reassess this difficult situation for us. This is not ח"ו to question the previous *p'sak* or to doubt the far-reaching vision of our *gedolim's daas Torah*. Due to the more elevated nature of our mainstream classes, however, it is entirely appropriate that we ask the *she'eilah* again.

⇒ On Track in General Studies

Afternoons, I serve as the General Studies Principal at Yeshiva Bais Mikroh in Monsey. The children are tracked according to level in secular studies. During May '95, grades 5 and 7 took the Iowa Tests, a battery of standardized tests. The results confirmed what I had long suspected. Many of the boys who were below level in reading and spelling were above average, even brilliant, in math. Others who were strong in reading found math difficult. I restructured grades 6 through 8 to permit students to be in the "A" track for math and "B" track for all other subjects; or vice versa. This move involved a great deal of effort. After carefully reviewing each child's report card to be certain that my placements were sound, I called all parents of children who were to be affected. Before the teachers left for the summer, I requested their evaluation regarding all of their students.

The result? Many boys now thrive in classes they can keep up with; many bright boys who were bored in the lower math class are now excited to be working at their level. Discipline is less of a factor, and I certainly am more familiar with every student and his progress. In fact, two eighth graders in the "B" track for Language Arts are currently in an accelerated "Regents Program" in math — no small accomplishment.

⇒ Some Implications

I do not advocate departmentalizing *Limudei Kodesh*. Torah is handed down from *rebbi* to *talmid*. It is difficult enough to maintain the proper *kesher* (bond) with 25 *talmidim*, let alone 75. We can, however, structure our classes to create homogeneous groups so that the underachieving student can be educated *al pi darko*. This would also alleviate the very real problem of bright *talmidim* who in the mainstream classes are developing poor study habits and are becoming frustrated at being forced to endure long stretches of *chazarah* (review) and "down time" between the new *inyanim* (topics) of *Gemara* that they so quickly and eagerly devour. Which brings us to the social issue —

Without question, it is hurtful for a child to be informed that he belongs in a weaker class. However, this temporary discomfort will pass. Children adapt to all situations. This cannot begin to compare to the ongoing pain of knowing you are not growing, the agony of that walk to the *rebbi's* desk to pick up your test paper, the dread of being called on to say the *Gemara* during the *farherr*.

The major difficulty is getting the parents on board. I firmly believe that parents will be willing partners in this endeavor if we can convince them that these changes are for their son's benefit and not to alleviate a problem that the yeshiva has. If they are still unhappy, we must have the courage of our convictions. Our job is to decide what is in the child's best interest and then to act. We cannot be in the position of reacting to the polling data regarding the popularity of a decision on such an important issue. The parents only want what we want: a happy, motivated, well-adjusted child. When they witness their child's progress, they will agree that we made the correct decision.

⇥ A Rewarding Challenge for the Right Rebbi

A word to those *rebbei'im* who might have the inclination to teach a tracked class geared to the underachieving *talmid*: By all means, do so! If your *menahel* is opposed to the idea, plead with him to try it just once. You don't need any special training. You need to love your *talmidim*, and believe — truly believe — that there are no bad children. Your *talmidim* will pick up on this feeling and give you their utmost. It will be the most rewarding experience of your *chinuch* life.

Yes, you will miss that delightful feeling of starting a *Beis Halevi* and watching the brilliant *talmid* jump up and finish it for you, all the while giving you that 100-watt smile. Your successes will be very small at the onset, but they will without question grow as the year progresses. Most of all, that wonderful feeling of knowing you turned a young man's life around forever will be yours for the rest of your life.

You must be made aware of the drawbacks of teaching a class such as this. You will be genuinely sad when the year ends — you'd love to have just a bit more time to polish the diamond that you discovered and washed so very carefully. You will worry about them — long after they have left your class — in a way you never thought you could. You will find yourself calling their present *rebbei'im* to plead with them to have a soft touch with your *talmid*. Every *bein hazmanim*, as soon as the boys return home from yeshiva, they will drop in to say hello. Former *talmidim* will call you every Friday afternoon to wish you "*A gutten Shabbos.*" Every Purim, until they go off to *Eretz Yisrael*, or get married, they will be at your home with *mishloach manos*. You see, you aren't becoming a *rebbi* of theirs; hopefully you will become **the** *rebbi*, the one they will remember for the rest of their lives.

Dealing With the Dilemma of Kids-At-Risk

An Interview With Rabbi Shmuel Kamenetsky

IN THE COMPLEX, CONFUSING FIELD OF DEALING WITH CHILDREN at risk, the heart often says *no* while the mind says *yes* — or the reverse. One yearns for objective yet compassionate guidance, cognizant of the various pressures and trends in contemporary society, capable of a response that encompasses Torah values, and sees beyond immediate demands, to long-term implications.

We have selected several questions that deal with the entire phenomenon of children at risk in the Torah community, and submitted them to Rabbi Shmuel Kamenetsky for comment. Rabbi Kamenetsky is the *Rosh HaYeshiva* of the Talmudical Yeshiva of Philadelphia, chairman of the *Nesius* (Presidium) of Agudas Yisroel of America, Rabbinic Advisor of Agudas Yisroel's Project YES, and a member of the Rabbinical Administrative Board of Torah Umesorah, the American Society for Hebrew Day Schools.

I. *JO:* As parents struggle to balance their concern for their troublesome children who are at risk, and their more conventional children, a question can arise: Is there a point when a child is "sent out of the house," a point where tolerance and *savlanus* must be sacrificed for the sake of protecting siblings?

Rabbi Kamenetsky: As a general rule, a child who does not conform to family standards in religious conduct and general decency must still be included as a member of the family, living under the same roof. This should apply as long as the child exhibits respect for his or her parents.

Once the line is crossed, however, and the child is consistently defiant of parental authority, the child's presence in the house can have a destructive effect on siblings. Under such circumstances, rabbinical guidance must be sought as to whether an alternative place of residence should be considered for the "difficult" child – not as an act of banishment; to the contrary, he (or she) is still a member of the family, but as a measure of protection of the other children. If at all possible, the substitute home should be with a relative or close friend.

II. *JO*: Besides the explosive growth of the *yeitzer hara* presence in the home – vividly conveying vulgar, immoral, illicit images, via TV, video and the Internet – is there any explanation for the fact that the number of *chareidi* children on the fringe – and beyond – has exploded in the last several years, far more than anything Torah Jewry in America has experienced since World War II?

Rabbi Kamenetsky: One need not go beyond the corrosive effects of the entertainment and information media in search of a source for recent destructive trends. Even homes that do not harbor such media can suffer from corrosive seepage from the general marketplace of ideas and values.

Another factor, however, is also at work: the extraordinary emphasis on luxurious living that has engulfed our society. Among those who have already attained their desired level of "good living," many seem to become completely involved in self-indulgence and the trappings of affluence; others, who have not yet realized their dreams, focus their hopes and their efforts on doing so. In either case, people are losing their sensitivity to spiritual matters, and their sensibilities are becoming dulled as they become immersed in material longings and pursuits.

If such is the *Zeitgeist*, should we be shocked if children go astray and abandon Torah life?

One must add yet another factor. Because of the extraordinary growth of the Torah community, schools are overcrowded, and not every child receives the attention he or she requires to develop properly. Many children do not realize their potential, and some simply slip between the cracks. Growth in numbers calls for equal growth in personnel and individual attention.

III. *JO:* Are there legitimate grounds– academic, financial, or religious – for a school to expel students? How far is the responsibility of a school to an individual errant student *lehachziro lemutav* (to lead him back to Torah)? When can a student be considered a *rodeif* (a spiritual "life-threat to others"), and how can that classification be applied?

Should parents heed their children's requests to transfer to a "less *frum*" school as a means of stemming the downward descent of the teen?

Rabbi Kamenetsky: A student's failure to maintain minimum academic requirements of his school does not constitute grounds for expulsion. Should it appear that he could gain more in another school, the parents should be encouraged to transfer him, but he cannot be forced out.

Inability to make tuition payments is not a basis for expulsion of a student. After all, every school does turn to the community for financial support, and the schools, in turn, have their obligations to the community's children. Other means for making up the deficit must be sought.

When a child does not conform to the school's code of conduct, a careful, painstaking evaluation must be made in regard to the degree he/she disturbs the class or is a detrimental influence on other students. Of course, the child's *rebbi* and teachers must be included in making this evaluation. This extremely sensitive matter has been described as *dinei nefashos* – a life-and-death decision – and deserves to be weighed accordingly.

Parents may be reluctant to yield to their child's request to transfer to a school with less-restrictive standards, but should the child conform to the more-liberal school's policies, he/she will be a member of good standing of an Orthodox society.

This can be preferable to being a nonconforming student in a school of higher standards.

IV. *JO:* Can the various schools in a community be held accountable for difficult children; or can each school, individually, simply shrug off kids-at-risk by claiming: "We're just not equipped to deal with your child. Try elsewhere."?

Rabbi Kamenetsky: Once a child is enrolled in a yeshiva or Bais Yaakov, the school carries responsibility for his/her development, and cannot shrug off this assignment or arbitrarily pass it on to others. Before enrollment, however, the individual school has no obligation to accept a child it is not equipped to teach. When a child with difficulties is not yet registered in a school, the community at large – or the schools of the region – do have an obligation to insure that all boys and girls being graduated from the eighth grade have a place to learn, and either create a facility or program to accommodate them or set up a system of assigning them to the participating schools.

V. *JO:* Does the *Rosh Yeshiva* have any additional comments to make on the topic?

Rabbi Kamenetsky: In *Eretz Yisrael*, the yeshivos and Bais Yaakov schools are ahead of our schools in many ways, in the way they deal with kids-at-risk. For example, Lev L'Achim sponsors a free telephone help-line for high-school-age boys and girls: *Lev Shome'a* (the Listening Heart). This has proven to be an extremely effective source of guidance and support system for young teens attempting to work out their problems. This specific program, among others, should have a counterpart – a free-access 800 number, if you will – in America.

Where Responsibility and Love Intersect
A Rosh Yeshiva's view of "Kids at Risk"

Rabbi Shloime Mandel

CHILDREN ARE THE GREATEST BERACHAH GRANTED TO A human being. Children are our link to eternity, a touch of immortality granted to us by the supreme immortal Being, *Hakadosh Baruch Hu*. When Rachel *Imeinu* was faced with barrenness, she begged Yaakov *Avinu*, "*Havah li banim v'im ayin meisah anochi* – Grant me children or I am dead" (*Bereishis* 30:1). Life is not worth living for Rachel *Imeinu* if there were no one through whom she could perpetuate those values that she held dear and that she lived for.

And yet, sometimes this great *berachah* does not turn out the way we expect it to. Then the plea emerging from our lips cries out, "*Im kein lamah zeh anochi* – If this [child] be so, why should I go through this?" (ibid. 25:23). When Rivkah *Imeinu* suspected that her child would be traveling down a path of alien worship, those were the words that she uttered. Today this cry has become a chorus, a chorus of parents wondering what went wrong. How did this great *berachah* – this gift worth more than life itself – *im ayin meisah anochi* turn into *lamah zeh anochi*.

There is no foolproof guarantee that a child will develop properly by virtue of growing up in a beautiful home.[1] Children

---

1. See commentary of Rabbi Moshe Feinstein in *Darash Moshe*, in regard to Yitzchak *Avinu*'s fathering Eisav even though he himself had been brought up in the home of his extraordinary parents, Avraham and Sarah.

cannot be raised on autopilot, on the assumption that they will "inherit" the proper values from their parents and grandparents. "*Chinuch* left to chance has no chance." How then do we create a generation where *all* our children are inculcated with Torah values, knowing right from wrong and acting accordingly?

Though our schools have a great impact upon our children, the influence of the home is still the greatest determinant of children's future. All elements in our homes have to be in harmony with each other, like one orchestra. You cannot preach one approach, and practice another.

Children will not grow up with a commitment to *kedushah* when videos, Internet, magazines, television — and today, even newspapers — bring the most unacceptable experiences and concepts into our homes.

Two summers ago, I had occasion to call the home of a bachur learning in a local mesivta. His parents were still in the mountains. When he answered the phone, I could barely hear him as the noise level was so high. "Excuse me a moment," he said, "I have to turn down the volume on the video."

Irony of ironies, his parents were shepping nachas from a hundred miles away because their son had gone home early to begin mesivta!

⟜ The Art of *Tochachah*

Perhaps the most difficult and important art to be mastered by both parent and *mechanech* is that of *tochachah* (reprimand). While we must rebuke our children when they do wrong, we must do it with obvious love in our voices, our faces and our gestures.

Shlomo *Hamelech* advises us that "Hashem chastises the one He loves" (*Mishlei* 3:12). One must emulate the *Ribbono Shel Olam* when exercising the responsibility of *tochachah*. Not only must the words be laced with love, they must be based on love, and resonate with love.

The elderly Rabbi Tarfon posed a question in *halachah*, which was brilliantly resolved by the much younger Yehudah ben Nechemiah. A smile crept onto Yehudah ben

Where Responsibility and Love Intersect / 417

Nechemiah's face, and Rabbi Akiva turned to him and said, "Yehudah, you smile with satisfaction for having shown the elder that he's wrong. It would greatly surprise me if you were to live long" (*Menachos* 68).

The *Shitah Mekubetzes* states that there is a word missing in the *Gemara's* text. Rabbi Akiva actually prefaced his comment with "Yehudah, Yehudah." It would appear that just as Hashem's repetition of a name – "Avraham, Avraham" at the *Akeidah*, and "Moshe, Moshe" at the Burning Bush – was meant to convey love,[2] so too did Rabbi Akiva want to express love and caring for his disciple by repeating his name before delivering his strong rebuke (see *Rambam, Hilchos Dei'os* 6:7). This implication is especially compelling, coming as it does from Rabbi Akiva, who lost thousands of disciples for their not having conducted themselves with mutual respect. Thus Rabbi Akiva said in effect, "Yehudah, I love you. How could you do something like this?"

> *I and a number of baalei battim had a meeting before last summer with several teenagers in the neighborhood – basically kids from "heimishe" backgrounds who have been involved in almost everything, including drugs, immoral conduct, etc. They asked the boys several questions, among them the very legitimate query, "What are you doing for the summer?" As one of the boys was about to answer, the questioner interjected – "Pot?"*
>
> *The boy later said to me, "I know I'm a piece of garbage, but did they have to advertise it in public? Maybe if he would have told me that I am a 'tayere Yiddish kindt' but fell and hurt myself, and he wants to help pick me up and think about the summer, I would think differently about myself. My problem is that I think of myself exactly as he said it."*

We must recognize that our children feel bad enough about failing. We must preface our rebuke with an outpouring of love, and deliver our *mussar* with an arm draped lovingly around the child's shoulder. Caring, love, and recognition of

---

2. See *Rashi, Bereishis* 11:22.

a child are of utmost importance, and many times are crucial to what may transpire years later. This lesson must be absorbed by parents and *mechanchim* alike.

> *A number of years ago, a yungerman who had been a talmid in our yeshiva for a short period of time approached me with a special request. Could I see to it that the rebbi he had had in our yeshiva receive $100 extra every month, without his knowing from whom the money is coming? I agreed, and he has continued to do so until today. I didn't ask him any questions. Recently, he revealed his reason: "All my life, my parents and the yeshivos I attended treated me like a nobody – always finding fault with me. No warmth, no love. This rebbi made me feel like a mentsch, caring and feeling for me. In my mind, he stands out with glowing warmth, and I will never forget him."*

A major pitfall to avoid when giving *tochachah* is inserting our own personal agenda. "Yaakov/Rivkah, do you know how you embarrass me? I'm ashamed of what the neighbors think!" "How will we be able to do *shidduchim*?"

A parent called me saying that her husband doesn't want to bring their son to the bungalow colony because he wears one of those flashy shirts that are not so acceptabe. He actually wanted to leave their child in the city rather than be "shamed" by his mode of dress. The child must feel that you are looking out for his/her benefit when giving tochachah, not for your own. Tell the child, "Yankele, I love you. You are a ben Olam Haba. Stop and think: Is this how a ben Olam Haba would act in this situation?"

Everyone's Obligation

One cannot give up hope and must pursue every available avenue to turn a child around. He/she is a *Yiddishe neshamah* lost or gone astray, waiting to be retrieved. A former *rebbi*, counselor, friend or neighbor who has a good rapport with the child can be engaged to strike up or rekindle some kind of relationship with him/her. We all have a responsibility to do our utmost to redirect the struggling, straying *neshamah*.

> *A yungerman approached me not long ago with a perplexed look on his face, followed by a question on behalf of his friends:* "We found out that you have been very involved with a group of boys who dared break in and desecrate the yeshiva. If anyone should be upset with them, it is you. How and why do you sacrifice so much time and effort on their behalf for over a half year?"
>
> *I took off my watch and asked him if this $25 watch were lying on the ground, lost by one of these terrible boys – on drugs, mechallel Shabbos – what would he do? He looked at me with puzzlement, and said,* "I would track him down and return it to him." *When I asked why, his wonder and dismay were even more evident,* "What do you mean? I have an obligation of hashavas aveidah!"
>
> "A lost $25 watch is hashavas aveidah and a lost neshamah is not hashavas aveidah?"

⚯ Who I Really Am, Who I Need to Be

The parents of one boy who had seemed hopelessly lost received a letter from his *Rosh Yeshiva*, informing them that their son is a true *nachas*. This *bachur* wrote the following note: "I really don't know how to say it, but I feel like I just learned who I am. I need time to develop myself into who I really need to be. I've set certain goals for myself: I put on *tefillin* everyday, I try to have *kavanah* as to what the words mean. I learn two times a week; I wish I could learn more, but it's hard. I'll get there someday. I plan to get somewhere in life."

A member of the family told me that his mother never stopped *davening* and never gave up on him. She told him that she believes in him, and that she still loves him.

To a great extent, the fault lies in ourselves. We can blame friends, outside influences, the yeshiva system, but basically, it is *we* who must mend our ways if we want to stem the tide that threatens to overtake so many among us. How can we prevent the blessing we plead for, "*Havah li banim, im ayin meisah anochi,*" from becoming "*Lamah zeh anochi?*" By removing the "*anochi*" – the self-centeredness – from being the primary focus of our relationships with our spouses, we can create *shalom bayis,* so essential to nurturing *Yiddishe neshamos.* By taking the "*anochi*" out of our *chinuch* and the reprimands to our children, we can build a relationship based on mutual love and trust. By taking the "*anochi*" out of our attitudes towards yeshivos, we can place responsibility where it really belongs. By abrogating the "*anochi*" and prostrating ourselves in *tefillah* before the *Ribbono Shel Olam,* we can all be *zocheh* to the true *Yiddish nachas* that we long for.

The "At-Risk Child": Early Identification and Intervention

Dr. David Pelcovitz & Rabbi Shimon Russel

I. Background

IN RECENT YEARS THERE HAS BEEN AN UNFORTUNATE increase in the number of adolescents from *frum* families who have been seriously disruptive, rebellious and defiant. Their parents desperately try to understand the source of their adolescent's problems, which may involve a serious reduction in religious observance, use of drugs or alcohol, refusal to abide by parental rules and/or school truancy. Unfortunately, by the time the situation has grown to such major proportions, it is far more difficult to deal with than had the problem been caught while the child was younger. The purpose of this article is to address some of the ways that parents can identify if their child is at risk for developing such serious difficulties. We will also present some strategies for intervention.

It is critical to recognize that the cause of serious conduct problems in children can rarely be attributed to a single source. Experts in child psychology usually ascribe such difficulties to the interaction of numerous factors such as temperament, poor peer influences, problematic parent-child interactions, and poor self-concept engendered by repeated academic and/or social failures. An understanding of how these factors can place a child at risk for conduct problems can be an important first step in prevention.

II. Risk Factors

⟶ Temperament

EVEN AS VERY YOUNG CHILDREN, DIFFERENCES IN BASIC temperament are evident. While one child can be even tempered, sleep well, and, in general, pose very little in the way of challenge to his or her parents, another child can from infancy on show signs of a difficult temperament. Numerous studies have documented the kind of temperament that places a child "at risk" for later conduct problems. The intense child with a high activity level, distractibility, negative, irritable mood, and difficulty with changes in routine is at greater risk for developing behavioral difficulties than a more placid child. Such children often lack flexibility and have a low frustration tolerance.

Of course, as the *Rambam* makes clear in *Hilchos Dei'os*, biology is not destiny. A child with a difficult temperament can be helped to learn to channel his intensity for good purposes. Parents of such a child, however, should be aware that if they find that the negative in their interactions outweighs the positive, they should seek help in learning how to deal with the special challenges presented by such a child. Relatively short-term efforts when a difficult child is young can prevent a problem from developing that is far harder to deal with when they reach adolescence.

⟶ Oppositional-Defiant Disorder

It is not at all unusual for children to go through stages where their behavior is mildly defiant or disruptive. In one of the largest studies ever conducted of behavioral difficulties in children, researchers found very high rates of disruptive behaviors in typical children between ages 5 and 9. For example, 46 percent of the thousand boys in this sample were described by their teachers as at times disruptive, 26 percent were found to be disobedient and 30 percent as occasionally "hyperactive." What differentiates the child who is at risk for more serious and sustained rebelliousness is a pattern of frequent negativistic, hostile, and defiant difficulties that last for at least six months and causes significant impairment in their ability to function well at home, in school or with peers.

This pattern of behaviors, which is called "oppositional-defiant disorder" by mental health professionals, is characterized by some or all of the following: frequent loss of temper, argumentativeness with adults, an active defiance or refusal to comply with adults' requests or rules, repeated attempts to deliberately annoy people, a tendency to blame others for his or her mistakes or misbehavior, and indifference or resistance toward the performance of *mitzvos*. Such children are also often described as touchy, resentful and easily annoyed by others. They may respond to anger at others by becoming spiteful or vindictive.

This pattern of disruptive behavior is most likely to be found in children born with difficult temperaments. These children are also more likely to have parents who are inconsistent, punitive, or neglectful. A child with symptoms of oppositional-defiant disorder is at risk for developing into an adolescent and/or adult with more serious conduct problems.

⇒ Repeated Academic Failure

Another factor that places children at risk for serious conduct problems is that of the child who feels himself or herself to be a failure, relative to his peers because of school failure. Children with learning disabilities, particularly those with significant reading problems or language disorders, often experience repeated academic failure. These children are at risk, at least in part, because the poor self-concept which these difficulties typically engender can make them more vulnerable to negative peer influences.

Childhood Depression

Depression in childhood often takes a different form than it does in adults. In addition to depressed mood, difficulties with concentration, and altered sleep and appetite, depression in childhood may also present in the form of irritable and aggressive behavior. The seriously depressed child can be at risk for later behavioral difficulties. Research shows that many adolescents who develop conduct or drug problems had prior bouts of depression as children. As depressed adolescents, they may turn to drugs as a form of self-medication.

The Role of the Parent — Factors in Alienation

What family characteristics are associated with children who are defiant? Researchers have consistently found that a parental discipline style characterized by high levels of yelling, lecturing, criticism and punitiveness or infrequent expression of unconditional love are associated with a drastically increased chance that a child will be noncompliant and rebellious. Of course, this doesn't mean that child misbehavior should be ignored. On the contrary, children with difficult temperaments need even more limits and structure than more easygoing children. The key in dealing with such children is to find the balance between *"s'mol docheh veyemin mekareves"* — setting limits with one hand while providing an atmosphere of love and warmth with the other.

There is an intriguing series of studies on the effects of stress on parenting. Parents who succumb to the myriad of time and financial pressures, which are all too common in our community, are more likely to exhibit parenting practices that are associated with fanning the flames of rebelliousness. Research has documented that parents who feel powerless in their lives are more likely to harshly chastise their children, engage in coercive disciplinary practices and focus on the negative while failing to recognize positive behaviors in their child. Such parenting practices are an almost certain recipe for the exacerbation of behavioral difficulties in at-risk children.

Perhaps the most important stressful situation, which can impact significantly on parenting, is marital difficulties. Children exposed to frequent fights between parents are at risk for a variety of behavioral problems. These children learn from their parents that the way of dealing with frustration and anger is to lash out at others. The parents in families with high levels of marital distress are also more likely to engage in inconsistent discipline, a major risk factor for childhood behavior problems.

Finally, since approximately half of mothers who are in a distressed marriage have been found to be suffering from significant levels of depression, it is important to understand the interaction between parental depression and the development of conduct problems in children. Since irritability is often a component of depression, depressed parents are more likely to respond to misbehavior in an unproductive, emotional manner. Furthermore, the pessimism inherent in depression makes it more likely that there will be a focus on the negative in the child's behavior. Such children may come to think that they can't win since any efforts at improvement are squelched when their depressed parent fails to recognize these attempts.

◈ Reactions and Judgments

While reacting overemotionally to defiant behaviors in children can exacerbate their behavioral difficulties, the other side of the coin — not dealing with behavioral problems — is equally dangerous. Furthermore, when parents are unable to give their child a sense of consistent love and attention they may place their child in danger of turning to acting out peer groups as substitute sources for unconditional love and acceptance. Lack of family cohesiveness, insufficient parental involvement, and failure to adequately supervise a child are among the most commonly cited contributors to childhood hostility and defiance. For example, one study that followed children from early childhood to adulthood found that parents who connected to their children by spending time with them, having discussions, and caring enough to supervise their activities with friends were far more likely than other parents to raise children who were well behaved and respectful.

Notwithstanding the above, we urge parents, friends and *mechanchim* to recognize that often times, poor parental treatment of the situation was the result of the problems and not its cause. Remember, "*Al todin es chavercho ad shetagi'a limekomo.*" It is impossible to imagine the fear and pain felt by parents, as the crisis develops within their home, and how that fear can cause even the best parents to err in their judgment of and reaction to their children's behavior. The more supportive and nonjudgmental friends, family and *mechanchim* are of parents going through a crisis with a child, the less the parents will feel ashamed and embarrassed, and their ability to deal with the situation will be enhanced.

III. Interventions:

Identifying the Problem

ONE OF THE MOST EFFECTIVE INTERVENTIONS FOR THE problem of at-risk children is to identify and treat the problem that places the child at risk as early as possible. If, relative to peers, your child is more aggressive or non-compliant, assessment by a qualified mental-health professional should be considered.

This does not necessarily mean that regular counseling will be recommended. Recommendations can range from a single meeting, where the counselor will provide guidelines on how to deal with your difficult child, to ongoing sessions, which will combine parenting guidance, individual sessions and consultation with the school. As noted earlier, since marital conflict or parental depression can increase the chances of minor behavioral difficulties in your child becoming major, it is important to deal with these problems, as well. This is clearly a situation where the best way to help your child is to get help for yourself.

⤖ Family-based Interventions

Dealing with children calmly but firmly is at the heart of effective prevention of serious behavior problems. Consequently, understanding the source of parental emotionalism is crucial. Perhaps the greatest contributor to excessive anger at children is the tendency to assign blame for the child's misbehavior either to one's self or to the child. A belief on the part of the parent that their problematic child is acting that way because something must be wrong with their competence as a mother or father can increase the chance that a parent will respond emotionally and unproductively. It is human nature to respond to feelings of incompetence and powerlessness by lashing out at others – in this case, the child. Unfortunately, such an emotional response typically yields the opposite of what is called for. The solution feeds the problem and the situation is exacerbated in a manner that makes it more likely that the child will misbehave in the future.

Special sensitivity is therefore demanded of *mechanchim*, who often are in the unenviable position of regularly pointing out to parents their children's problems. It is critical that in doing so they not make parents feel even more incompetent than they already do.

Similarly, if the parents view their child's behavior as willful and a reflection that there is something seriously wrong with their child's *middos*, this too will fuel a counterproductive emotional reaction. In contrast, if the parent views the problematic behavior as stemming from a biological predisposition rather than from a deliberate, or lazy behavior, then their response is far more likely to be calm and productive in helping their child's behavior change.

The following interventions can help minimize defiance in at-risk children:

• Try to anticipate which situations are most likely to trigger rebellious behavior by learning the patterns behind your child's explosiveness. Parents might find it useful to keep a diary of a typical week in your family's life. The diary would note each episode of misbehavior in your child, with a particular emphasis on what the trigger was for each incident. Eventually, a pattern should emerge which should allow you to anticipate which situations are most likely to elicit explosive or noncompliant behavior. Parents often find that use of distraction, empathy or logic, which typically are ineffective once the child has lost his temper, is far more likely to be effectual if the situation is caught before their child loses control.

- Recognize that while you may have no immediate control over your child's misbehavior you do have significant control over the consequences. At-risk children do best when expectations at home and in school are clearly spelled out and consequences are immediate, consistent and calmly implemented. It is equally important that positive behavior be consistently recognized and reinforced. A number of helpful parent-training books are available (e.g. Greene, R., *The Explosive Child*; Clark, L., *SOS Help for Parents* [second edition] Parents Press), as are parenting classes. It is crucial to keep in mind that should behavioral difficulties increase in frequency or severity, consultation with a child menta-health professional should be obtained.

- Consider carefully which battles are worth fighting. If the parent-child relationship is dominated by frequent fighting, it is often very helpful to make a list of which behaviors must be dealt with immediately and which can be safely ignored. For example, ignoring verbal bickering between siblings and letting them work out minor differences by themselves frequently reduces the frequency and intensity of sibling fighting. Of course, any issue involving your child's safety or the safety of others must be dealt with immediately.

Anger Control Strategies for the Child

Children who are at risk often need help in being taught the necessary skills needed to control their anger. Seriously consider seeking professional help to learn how to teach these skills to your child without antagonizing him/her further. Teaching the "right" skills with the "wrong" attitude always fails.

⌫ School-Based Interventions

1. Close cooperation with the school is necessary to diagnose and remediate any learning difficulties. Early identification of language problems, learning disabilities or attention-deficit disorder is crucial. If difficulties are suspected, evaluation by specialists in these areas should be conducted as early as possible. With early intervention there is a greater chance for success.

2. Consider having a tutor/mentor for a child experiencing academic failure. This person can provide the dual role of helping the child cope and improve academically, while at the same time serving as a mature sounding board to help guide the child through difficult relationship issues.

IV. Conclusions

EARLY IDENTIFICATION AND INTERVENTION IN DEALING WITH children who present with significant oppositional and defiant behavior in childhood can prevent them from developing into more serious difficulties in adolescence. Most children and families are resilient. Thus, taking a proactive approach in dealing with behavioral problems when they are more easily manageable should *B'ezras Hashem* spare us from having to deal with rebellious and alienated adolescents.

Buying Time

Rabbi Michoel Levy

THE PHONE RINGS. HE'S BEEN THROWN OUT OF YESHIVA. You're told to come and get him. While driving there, you wonder, "What now?" Maybe you saw it coming, maybe you didn't. Now he's in a new yeshiva. It's been quiet for a few months. He likes his new yeshiva; at least he says so. But you can't rid yourself of that nagging feeling that it's a matter of time before the phone will ring again. A few months later it does.

Now he's home. The difference is that now you are receiving an abrupt introduction to a son you don't know. Instead of arguing about his homework, the battle rages about smoking, his new wardrobe, and why he must be in before 4 a.m. His old friends are gone. They've been replaced by a different set. They look scary to you. Going to *shul* Shabbos morning, *tefillin, tzitzis* are all things of the past.

HELP!

You're at a loss. The slightest comment or question you pose is met with an explosive and angry response. Everything you try backfires. It seems that anything you try to prevent him from doing only causes him to react in an even harsher manner, accelerating his descent. "You don't own me, it's my life and I'll do as I want" is the immediate response to anything and everything.

His siblings are scared, embarrassed and confused. What happened to him? You're not sure yourself. Can't everything go back to the way it was? Can't he just be the regular yeshiva boy you once knew?

The answer is no.

The moment you understand that *the child you see now* is *who he is now*, and you are now parenting the child you're looking at, not the one you knew, you've started the long journey toward saving your son.

⇥ Not Knowing Why

Something must have happened at some point that caused this. The possibilities are endless. Something at home, school, with friends, a learning disability, emotional problems, any of these or a few combined may have precipitated these events.

Don't try to torture yourself over where the fault lies. In the early stages, it's almost impossible to know. Although your child has formed a list of grievances in his mind about the how's and why's, it is safe to assume that he himself has no idea what caused him to change his mindset so dramatically. He may know he's unhappy; but lacking emotional maturity, he does not really know why.

Most boys in their early teens, while possessing many aspects of physical maturity, lack emotional and mental maturity. Your son doesn't know whether he is coming or going. He acts on impulse and emotion. He doesn't need a reason. Perceptive – yes; bright – maybe; mature he is not.

Half the process of retrieving the boy you once knew is time.

When he reaches the age of 18, 19, things will have gotten clearer to him. His outlook will change. He matures mentally. He begins to realize that his life is his and that his decisions will affect himself more than they will affect anyone else.

Time must pass to reach this stage. You must buy this time. The rates are steep. How the time is bought will determine much of what your son will think and want out of life when he gets to this stage. Everyone settles down eventually. But when the dust clears, what kind of person will you see? It all depends on how you buy time during your child's adolescence.

↢ How to Buy Time

For starters, it is wise to find someone with whom your child can file his complaints. A psychologist, a family member, or a family friend may detect something that has been overlooked. Sometimes breaking the fall is as simple as that. Even if the child uses this person to get at his parents, you can only gain more understanding by hearing another point of view.

When buying time, structure is the key. Take it in any form it comes; work, school, gym, *chavrusa*. The ultimate structure is high school. If the yeshivos he has attended have not quite worked out, but he still expresses a desire to go to a more lenient school, a school that does not necessarily have the same *hashkafos* as yours, do not reject it out of hand. Ask *daas Torah*. Do not get caught up in appearances. It may save your son's life.

Sometimes sending him away to a foreign place will give him a fresh start and less cause to rebel. *Eretz Yisrael, however, should not be an option before he is 17 years old.* He will not utilize his freedom to his benefit and it might ruin any chance of his gaining from this experience in the future.

If he shows an interest in *anything* – employment, computers, sports – grab a hold. Create some sort of schedule out of it. Never lose sight that even if every course you try fails, you have not failed. With each school and job that he tries, you are buying time — time, which will bring you closer to your goal of getting him through his adolescence. If there are younger siblings at home that are being adversely affected, or the open confrontations with you have reached the impossible stage, try having him live with a relative or family friend to give both of you more space. Even so, it is absolutely essential to let him know that you're not writing him off. Make him understand that although you love him, he is not the only consideration in your family picture.

Don't pressure or impose. Don't draw artificial lines. Trying to prevent him from doing things he's already accustomed to will only foster more rebellion, and is counterproductive to maintaining your relationship with him. And the key is to work on maintaining the best relationship possible during this tumultuous period. Discuss things, keep open the channel of dialogue.

Do not attempt to change things back to the way they were. You cannot. *He* must do it himself.

Turn the other cheek whenever possible. The more you ignore those little things (dress, language, etc.), the less shock value they have, and the greater likelihood that he will tone them down a bit. At the end of this trying period, you want to see a young adult who, although he has not followed the lifestyle of his parents, has only good feelings for who they are and what their lifestyle represents. Then, when he embarks onto this new period of life, he may want to try out his old lifestyle once again.

⤖ Phasing Back Into Yeshiva

The yeshivos that work with teenagers at risk employ many different methods. The common denominator of all these strategies is that the boy develops a new concept of what a *rebbi* is. *Rebbi shmuesses,* "chills," plays ball and teaches Torah in a language he can relate to. In general, *Rebbi* is one of the boys. He makes it clear that you can be perfectly happy, content and "cool" while living a strictly Torah life.

The yeshiva in this role does not necessarily change what is going on in the boy's head, nor does it curb all his activities outside of the yeshiva. But it does provide a strong alternative to those activities. Learning with "the rabbi" may not be hangin' out with the boys, but it's up there in the ratings. And if the boy maintains this commitment to yeshiva, then ultimately he will still identify himself as a yeshiva boy. This identification is critical when he reaches 18 or 19 and looks to make decisions.

Every boy is different, and so are his circumstances. Every single case must be weighed differently. The activities of some teenagers are more harmful (illegal) than others. Some of these problems must be treated in a professional facility. The concept of buying time, however, applies to all teenagers at risk. Implementing different methods of buying time is part of *gidul banim* for some of our children. After all is said and done, *tzaar gidul banim* is a reality for all: less painful for some, excruciating for others.

Let us never forget that, come what may, these teenagers are part of *Klal Yisrael*. With a little *siyata diShmaya*, the time we buy will ultimately result in keeping them there.

Consequential Conversations... Without Being Confrontational

Rabbi Aharon Kaufman

The following conversation is not fictional. Nor is it alone, or unique in any way. This excerpted conversation, and many others virtually identical to it, have taken place between the author of the article and today's teenagers. An exchange that the reader can scan in a matter of minutes may well have taken an hour or two, and then some.

"WHAT ARE YOU GOING TO TELL ME THAT I HAVEN'T heard before?" is his question. It resounds with years of bitterness and harsh exchanges, and carries with it the crushing weight of someone who has given up.

"I'm going to tell you how you can maximize your pleasure and happiness in this world," is my calm reply.

This is a surprise to him. "How are you going to do that?" he asks disbelievingly.

"You're a rabbi, what do you know about fun? I'm already doing things that make me happy."

"Fun and happiness have nothing to do with each other."

The shock power of an idea lies in its originality. People so naturally equate fun with happiness that a conscious assess-

ment of that fact is never actualized. In fact, they are two separate interactions with the pleasures of life. They have absolutely nothing in common, and are even chronologically inaccessible to one another. Fun is something you have while you are doing something. Happiness is what you experience afterwards. Fun is temporary; it does not stay. As soon as the stimulus that caused it is gone, then the fun is gone. Happiness — true happiness — is a deeper emotion that abides for much longer. Happiness can last for long years after the stimulus is gone. Many rich and famous people have all of the money and toys that bring them fun, but they are incredibly depressed, lonely, and miserable.

"Well, I *like* having fun, okay?" he interjects. "I like enjoying myself."

"So do I. I have pleasure every moment of my day."

" I thought that pleasure is *forbidden*," he says, drawing out the word. "I've yet to meet a rabbi that believes in it."

"You have now."

Pleasure is by no means negative. On the contrary, it is the aim of human life. Judaism instructs us how to squeeze the most pleasure out of life. The limitations that the Torah places on us are actually for full maximization of pleasure. There are many fun things that actually destroy the very ability to enjoy life. They suppress the very capacities of potential enjoyment, and they shape a person to settle for far less than they are actually capable of. A line of pure Colombian cocaine might give someone a rush of fleeting pleasure, but afterwards so much sense and feeling is lost, and indeed even scarred permanently, that in balance the gain is no gain, but an unparalleled loss. If people are enjoying themselves at present, but they are headed toward disaster, what is the present enjoyment really worth? It is the pleasure of a man who enjoys the breeze coming through the open window of his car as he drives it off a bridge.

Pleasure that does not extend beyond the moment is really an accelerated process of degeneration.

"So you're going to tell me how to find pleasure and happiness," he says. The disbelief is still there, but he is listening.

"Well, in order to find happiness, we have to know what we're looking for," I point out with a smile. "What is happiness?"

He shrugs. "Friends," he offers.

"Are you happy hanging out with your friends?" I ask.

"I guess so," is his response.

"Are you *happy*?" I ask again. "When you go home after spending a night out with your friends, and when you wake up the next morning, are you happy?"

He considers that, then shakes his head. "So what would make me happy then?"

"A genuine relationship," I tell him.

"Like what?"

"You tell me."

He thinks, and then after a moment of reflection he says, "A *meaningful* relationship." I motion for him to go further, and he adds, "With a family, I guess. Eventually with a wife and children."

He's hit the nail on the head. Meaning. Meaning and purpose bring happiness. When people have no reason for being, when they feel that there is no real difference in whether they exist or not, they can never be happy. The only think that they can have is fun, and that fun is always temporary, bringing with it only a brief period of time where one covers the pain in his heart with a mask of forgetfulness.

The interesting paradox of many teenagers is that they frequently deny their own family, while their goal is to have one. They value family as precious, even if they cannot actualize those relationships. They yearn for what they cannot articulate, they desire what they cannot verbalize.

"When you have a *real* friend," I tell him, "you gain happiness from that friendship, not just fun."

"What's a 'real' friend? Aren't all my friends real?"

"Tell me, do your friends care about you, or do they just care about spending time with you? And similarly do you really care about your friends, or do you just care about spending time with them?"

"What's the difference?"

"You tell me."

After thinking for a while, he says, "I guess if I cared about someone then I'd be willing to give him something of mine, but if I just enjoy spending time with him then I'd be taking from him."

He's right again. Real caring involves giving, not just from yourself, but of yourself. If you really care about your friend, you will not limit your time spent with him/her to only things that you both enjoy. Such friendships come and go, because similar to fun, they are transient in their very nature. That friendship is based on the event, not the person. If our friendship is based on each other, then it lasts as long as we last.

It's amazing how quickly friends can come and go. Many people are always looking for new friends, and have no stability in their acquaintances. When you have a deep friendship, you do not need to look for more. Only a thirsty man desires water. Only someone who is dissatisfied with what he has will go on to seek more.

"How many giving friends do you have?" I ask gently.

He fidgets, and does not face me directly. A long silence passes, one that speaks loudly. Finally he says, "Not many." A longer silence. "Not any at all, really."

"Who were you friends eight years ago?" I ask.

"People in my class," he shrugs.

"What were their names?"

"Their names?" He searches. "Um, Boruch, I think — I don't know!"

"You know," I point out deliberately. "You'll be doing this again ten years from now. The tragedy of life is that who you are at 30 is because of your friends at 16. Except at that point you can hardly remember their names. Do you still want to be the person you are now when you are 30? Or 40? Or even 70?"

"No." The fear in his reply is evident.

At this point I shift the momentum of the conversation, and I quickly ask him, "Would you like your children to be just like you?"

This time the answer is quick and instinctual. "No way!" Then he realizes what he has admitted to. He's not happy, and he is far from what he would really like to be. At this point he looks me in the eye and says, "So now what?"

He doesn't know it at this point, but he is already back on the *derech*. *Derech* simply means "the way," and not "the end." He is willing to listen, and he has begun to search.

"Now let's discuss your future," I tell him.

"What future?" he almost laughs.

It is at this point that I feel his pain the strongest. In that bitter laugh is his lack of hope, his lack of self-esteem, and his inarticulate cry for understanding and acceptance. He wants someone to show him the way out, but he does not really believe that someone can.

"Why are you denying your future?" I ask him. "Your future is the strongest future in the world! You and I are equal in terms of future. In terms of the past we may be different, but the future is vast and open for both of us."

He shakes his head, not letting himself believe. "I've heard that before. I've heard that four-letter word *potential* so many times that I'm sick of it! You don't know anything about me! You don't understand! Nobody does!"

"The problem is not that nobody understands you," I say, looking into his eyes. "The problem is that you don't understand yourself. Seek to understand yourself, and only then to be understood."

"What are you telling me?" he demands. "I know who I am. This is me! For better or for worse, this is what I do!"

"Is what you do coming from you?" I ask him. "Is it coming from inside you, and as a result of your own choice? Or does it come from outside pressures — from what you see in the movies, or your 'friends'? How much of what you do is your own choice, and not the result of programming from the best advertising men on Madison Avenue? If I move your hand for you, did you choose to move that hand? Is that really you?"

Most people's lives are not self-dictated, because first we make our habits, and then our habits make us. The strongest chain around a man's neck is the one that he does not see.

"You're telling me that I'm controlled?" he asks aggressively. "I'm a free man! In yeshiva they control me! When I'm out of yeshiva, it's my own choice, and I picked it. I'm in control."

I answer him clearly. "The Torah demands one thing from you above all else, and that is to think. Madison Avenue demands one thing above all else as well. They want you to stop thinking. Choice — real free choice — is when I can clearly see both options, and I can clearly think about both paths. How much about the Torah do you know that you can really say that you made this choice?"

If you are not a thinking person, then you are not aware of your choices, and therefore you are not aware of the consequences of your choices. You may not realize it, but you are blindly following the dictates of a society that is only interested in what they can get out of you. Billions of dollars are spent in this country on getting people to make choices without thinking. If you truly want independence, don't opt to deal with the world by blocking out your ability to analyze.

Usually they disagree with the fact that they don't know what it means to live a Torah life. A casual questioning of Tanach, biur tefillah, Jewish History, and philosophy shows them how deficient they are in their comprehension of the life that they want to throw away.

"You're making me think too much!" he complains.

"I'm not making you think," I tell him. "You're thinking yourself."

He rolls his eyes. "So I have no past, I have no friends, I have no understanding, and I have no life." He throws his hands up into the air. "So what am I supposed to do? What future could I possibly have?"

"Listen and you'll hear."

We must grasp the fact that happiness comes from meaning, and meaning comes from struggle. True happiness will involve some pain. Struggle involves pain. Conquest and accomplishment of that struggle brings happiness. In short, nothing worthwhile is ever easy. What every person needs to know — child, teen, and adult alike — is that avoiding pain means avoiding accomplishment. Torah is the guide to this accomplishment.

When a person does nothing meaningful with his life, his neshamah senses it, and the pain that the neshamah feels is depression. Depression is the shadow cast by the soul's sitting still and not growing. The easy "solution" to this depression is the quick fix of fun, be it movies and television that take away one's cognizance, or drugs that take away one's very sense of feeling. The real solution is to get moving, to have growth and accomplishment as part of one's life. And you can't get moving if you don't know where you are moving to.

Goals that will bring a person to fulfillment and happiness are true, growing relationships with people, and a true, growing relationship with Hashem. A good home, children, and a solid commitment to growth are the destination of a good life's journey.

Are there obstacles? Are there challenges? Of course there are. Overcoming the challenges is what causes growth. They define the struggle. And in fact the challenges, the things that seem to cause tears frustration, and anguish, are the cause of the greatest joy. To overcome the obstacles is to make oneself stronger. Viewed in this manner, the dreaded stumbling blocks become welcome stepping-stones.

It is within your ability. All of those aforementioned obstacles are not reasons why you can't, they are reasons why you can. The interesting paradox is that the more obstacles there are to a goal, the more possible it becomes, because its effects will last all the longer! You past is not a stone around your neck, it is the wall you are shoving yourself away from to gain momentum. Those faults and failures are behind you, and your determination is ahead of you. To go ahead with your life is your decision. To stay behind is the decision of others.

The conversations that follow — excerpted from longer exchanges, as the previous ones were — took place six months after those recorded above.

"Was it worth it?" I inquire.

The glow on his face has already answered my question for me. "Yeah," he says. Then he reflects for a bit. "Actually, I even enjoyed the tough parts," he adds. Further thought. "Wait a minute, I enjoyed them more than anything! I wonder why that is?"

"It's because the joy of the accomplishment is already felt when you are struggling." I explain. "The struggle gives you confidence, because if you can fight, then you can win."

"But whey does it need that struggle?" The bourgeois mentality of early-21st century life is hanging onto his mind. "Why can't it just be instant? You know, upload it?"

"Why is it so good to get something instantly?"

His eyebrows suggest that I have just wondered aloud as to why you can't swim to the moon. " 'Cause I don't want to wait!" he exclaims. "Why shouldn't I get it now?"

"What on earth do you ever get 'now'?"

"What?"

"What is there in this life that's instant? There's nothing gotten instantly."

"Of course there is!"

"Name one."

"Instant coffee, instant soup, battery jumps —"

"The coffee was grown, ground, refined, cooked, freeze-dried, packaged, shipped, and marketed. The soup company did the same. Both are indexed on the S&P 500. The centuries of sweat and grind that went into the factory that produced the batteries for the cars would take a full week to detail. None of that is instant."

"But it's instant for me!"

"And is that a good thing?"

He claps his hands to his head. "And tell me," he begins in a voice that contains an edge of exasperation, "why shouldn't it be? I like a quick fix."

"Because you didn't produce it," I point out. "What you produce yourself is of far more value to you than what you are given. If you don't believe me, check into a nursing home, and sit in a bed all day hooked up to machines that eat for you, breathe for you, and live for you. But you won't. Why? Because you would be miserable there. You, and me, and every other person on the planet were not meant to receive instantly."

"Where do you get that from?"

"There are givers and there are takers. There are those that produce, and those that receive. The receivers are never fulfilled, only satiated. And even that satiation is only a temporary one. They are never happy. The producers are the happiest people in the world. If you cooked something yourself, it tastes better. If you grow it and develop it yourself, you have a wonderful successful feeling even before you sit down to eat it!"

"So I am not supposed to consume at all?"

"You have to consume to some degree, but only on a maintenance level. Your mission in life, the primal cause of your existence, is to be a producer!"

"How do you know that?"

"If not, why did your old lifestyle feel so hollow?"

Isn't it odd that unlike the majority of the animal kingdom, particularly insects and reptiles, that are born fully functional, the human being, the elite of all creation, is born deficient? He is hardly a person at birth, but merely animated matter. Then slowly, very slowly, his senses begin to develop. He turns, craws, walks, talks, and he continues to progress incrementally until his senses and concepts mature. The first twenty years of his life are spent becoming merely functional!

The explanation of his singularity is that it is precisely because man is paramount, strictly because he is born in the Almighty's image, he is born incomplete. Man was granted the divine and unique opportunity to become a meaningful partner in his own creation. He gives birth to himself in a way, as he forms his own self by expanding and developing all of his life, shaping his own destiny. Every person, every event, every step we take, no matter how feeble it may seem, is of cosmic importance. Man's reach exceeds his grasp.

Since I have the mission to create myself, and to produce my life, I cannot be happy in a role that is not mine. Man was meant to produce, not merely be produced. That is the underlying truth of Tzelem Elokim. G-d produces and man produces. A man that cannot produce, is not a man. There is no such creature. A man can produce. There is no man that cannot act in the image of G-d and produce. There is such a thing as a man who can produce, but does not. Those people have their own designation. Unhappy.

"That's a great thing, but not everybody can live like that."

"Of course they can."

"Look, you've already got it, you're a Rabbi! You can control your mind. I have no attention span, I think I'm —"

"Please don't say those three letters to me," I beg. "You'd think that ADD was the bubonic plague the way it spreads."

He laughs. "Okay, but I don't have the self-control I need."

"Yes you do."

He looks at me with suspicion. "I do?"

"Yes."

"No I don't!"

"You have the self-control that you need, not the self control that someone else needs. Understand something clearly. A person is not build overnight, but a person who is building overnight *will get built*. You were brought into the world for this purpose, and that purpose is waiting for you, stretching out to take your hand."

"I don't know — "

"I'll prove it to you. You have self-control and concentration, and you have the willingness and ability to listen to the intricacies of rules and regulations, and limit yourself by them."

"Really?" His tone is extremely dry. "And where do you see that?"

"Do you play sports?"

"Yes, but — oh."
"Exactly. Do you play pool?"
"Yeah, sometimes."
"Are you good at it?"
"Absolutely!"
"When have you ever won a pool game without concentrating?"

You wouldn't play sports without rules and regulations, because that's the whole game. When you examine it, it's the rules and regulations that make the game. That is the game itself. A game without them is not a game. You find the game enjoyable because you know that the rules are there for you. Since you clearly see what the rules are for, and how they help you, you do not even begin to think about them as limitations. Rather, it's the opposite. You see them as things that set you free.

Mitzvos are the rules and regulations of life. Torah is the guidebook. You, my dear, are the active participant. Seek out a rebbi or an older bachur to mentor and coach you along.

Throughout life we all make investments of various kinds. However, the most important investment you can ever make is in yourself. And the greatest end result that you can make of yourself is that which happens to be the definition of a ben Torah; a purposeful person, a creator, someone doing something magnificent with their life, dealing with eternity. Failure to do so, no matter what the reason, will result in a little less of you, which is an irreplaceable loss. It's your failure if you allow it, but it is also your success if you succeed. Yes, you can give me a thousand reasons why you can't develop into that ben Torah, but there is one reason why you must. Because that is you and your mission in life.

Afterword

Basic Principles of Parenting

Postscript

"Hereby Resolved..." A Father's Resolutions

Afterword
Basic Principles of Parenting
Rabbi Shlomo Wolbe

Introduction

CHINUCH (EDUCATION) IS A MISSION OF THE HIGHEST PRIORITY, a mission whose success guarantees the continuity of the Jewish people and its Torah. *Chinuch* is also a responsibility assigned to every father and mother, and one cannot excuse oneself from it, saying, "This isn't my job." Furthermore, *chinuch* is a task that parents naturally long to perform; from deep within themselves, parents yearn to educated their children properly.

Even though education is a natural yearning and responsibility, it is also a deep wisdom. It cannot be mastered after a bit of casual consideration or by depending on one's hunches. Parents and teachers cannot rely on their God-given intuition alone and assume that is enough and everything will turn out all right.

Today few people realize that *chinuch* of children is an art that requires study and attentiveness. Unfortunately, often even teachers working in the field lack this awareness. In order to educate children properly, we must understand what education really means. We must organize and define all the different components of our standard educational methods, identifying which actions are really educational, which have nothing to do with *chinuch*, and which are the antithesis of *chinuch* and even produce undesirable results.

Sometimes we use methods that are counterproductive because we assume that they contribute to the educational process, but further investigation – especially keeping the long-term in mind – actually reveals that these techniques hinder education. We must carefully examine and define all the components in this third category of educational methods, understand why people might mistakenly think such actions work, and then see why they really are anti-educational.

Finally, even after careful study of all the components of education, we hope and pray that Hashem will be satisfied with our efforts and grant us success.

Age Appropriateness

CHAZAL ESTABLISHED THAT A CHILD HAS STAGES. DURING childhood, the child passes from period to period. We must recognize these periods *and relate to them at the appropriate time*.

From the words of *Chazal*, we see the seriousness of *chinuch*, and the seriousness of precisely timing our *chinuch* efforts to match the child's stages of development.

Parents must recognize more or less the period the child is passing through during his maturation, and they must *match their demands to his ability in every period*. If they ask more than the child can do – i.e. when the child is not yet sufficiently mature to understand what his parents want from him – this is terribly damaging educationally.

In this presentation we are not trying to define these periods. That belongs in a separate discussion. Rather, we are focusing on the essentials of *chinuch* according to the Torah.

We will now offer several common examples of inconsistency between the child's ability and the requests made of him.

Often we don't relate sufficiently to the child's play. For the child, play is a serious matter. Rabbi Yisrael Salanter used to say: When a child plays with a piece of wood in the bath, and he pretends that it is a ship, if we take the piece of wood away from him he has the same experience an adult would have if a real ship of his sunk. For the child, the piece of wood is like an adult's ship. When an adult interferes in a child's play, he steals something from the child.

Certain errors are widespread and are accepted as norms. For example: People demand that their children sit at the Shabbos table throughout the meal, even though the meal can extend for an hour, 90 minutes, or sometimes even longer. A young child can't sit quietly for so long. He needs to frolic. If we force him to sit through the entire meal, we are compelling him to do something far beyond his ability, and we need not explain how destructive this is. The intention is good: We want to build. But for the sake of building, we push the child beyond his ability; and children can't be built with demands that are beyond them. Ultimately, such demands damage the child. The damage is especially serious when the demands are made of young children, since even the smallest interference at the time of planting can produce serious aftereffects.

Customized Education

PARENTS NEED TO RECOGNIZE THEIR CHILD'S UNIQUE character. No two children are alike. If parents don't know this, and therefore they assume a child possesses potentials that he doesn't, the *chinuch* and efforts they invest in their child won't match the child.

"Educate a child according to *his way*; even when he grows old he will not depart from it" (*Mishlei* 22:6). If I want to educate a child, I must contemplate and examine what this particular child's way is.

It is obvious that a banana plant needs different care than an apple tree. If I raise a banana plant and an apple tree, and provide both of them with identical care, at least one of them won't grow well, and perhaps neither will! The same is true of children. I must discover the child's traits and take them into account.

Personal Example

PARENTS' GREATEST RESPONSIBILITY IS TO SERVE AS AN example. Every child naturally wants to identify with his parents and imitate them. If their personal example is good, and if the relationship between the parents and the child is healthy, a warm and heartfelt relationship, then a boy will naturally want to be like his father, and a girl will naturally want to be like her mother. One of the most important essentials of *chinuch* is personal example. If parents demand of their children things that they themselves aren't doing, they risk corrupting the children entirely.

Self Improvement

WITHOUT GOOD *MIDDOS*, IT IS IMPOSSIBLE TO EDUCATE. IF a person doesn't work on himself – on his *middos* – he cannot be an educator.

In the book *Minchas Shmuel*, the author quotes his *rebbi*, Rabbi Chaim Volozhiner, saying, "Today, harsh language won't be accepted." If we express ourselves harshly, people will not listen to us. People can only hear soft, nice words. "And someone whose nature is not to speak softly, and who angers quickly when people don't do his will, is exempt from the *mitzvah* of *tochachah* (rebuke)." This is the *psak* (halachic decision) of Rabbi Chaim Volozhiner: An angry person cannot give *tochachah*.

The *mitzvah* of *chinuch* is anchored in the *mitzvah* of *tochachah*. It seems that an angry person is exempt from *chinuch*. However, one cannot exempt oneself from *chinuch*, since ultimately a father remains a father. Therefore, we have no option but to control ourselves. More than 140 years ago, Rav Chaim ruled that one should not use harsh language. How much more so today must we avoid harshness, especially with children. Harsh words and actions accomplish nothing. The opposite is true: Harsh words and actions damage. We have no option but to use soft approaches. What should be done when the child doesn't listen? We must express our demand and re-express it until the child listens. This is the wisdom of *chinuch*: to know how to speak and when to speak.

Consistency

GENERALLY, THERE IS NO NEED TO MAKE A LOT OF DEMANDS of a child. However, we should not compromise on what we have demanded. If parents see that they must demand something of the child, and they demand it, then they should not back off. They must get the child to accept the demand. Of course, this must be done wisely, in such a way that obviates the need to spank the child or yell at him, but which nevertheless gets the child to accept the demand.

False Goals

PARENTS OFTEN UTILIZE PURPORTEDLY EDUCATIONAL techniques which, in reality, don't have the slightest connection to their children's education. At the root of these behaviors are selfish, egoistic motivations. Sometimes the parents are driven by completely corrupt traits, traits that the parents would never consider displaying in their relationships with other adults. However, we may exhibit these very traits in our relationships with our children and consider them acceptable: jealousy, hatred, pursuit of honor, anger, conceit, etc., and especially a desire for control. Parents often want to control their children: "The child is under my authority, and I have the right to exercise unconditional power over him."

Here are a few examples of corrupt traits in action.

❧ Jealousy

If I see that the neighbor's child provides his parents with more assistance than my children provide me, I feel jealous: "Why doesn't my child help more!?" If later I force my child to help more, it is possible that I am not being driven by educational theory – by a deep understanding of my child and what is appropriate for him – but by a simple jealousy of my neighbor.

⇌ Honor

If guests visit, I want my child to greet them nicely and behave pleasantly – not necessarily for the sake of my child's growth, but so that I can elicit compliments from the guests on my superb childraising expertise. Then *I* feel good.

⇌ Anger

I feel anger whenever someone violates my will. When it comes to children, there is plenty of opportunity for anger since children often don't behave as we would like.

There are many similarly unpleasant traits that we express in our relationships with children. However, we conceal all these bad traits with the excuse that our behavior is "necessary for educational purposes." If out of anger I strike my child, I might excuse myself saying that it was "educationally necessary." If out of jealousy of a neighbor I make demands of my child, I can fool myself into believing that this too is "educationally necessary." If I want to boost my image in others' eyes through my dear child, and therefore, compel him to act in a particular fashion, this too I can justify as "educationally necessary." In short, exercising total control over my child for entirely selfish motivations can be justified as an educational necessity.

Parents often deceive themselves into thinking that their primary concern is their children's education, when their motivations are really selfish. The net result of this self-deception is that we don't see the child for who he is. We see the child as our property. We think that his purpose on earth is to benefit us, the parents. This is not to say that parents don't feel a responsibility to care for their children. They do. However, too often they do with their children whatever they please. What happened to the principle that we should "Educate a child according to *his way*"? Sometimes parents egocentrically assume that "*his way*" means *their way*. Others recognize that their child has a unique "way" but don't respect it. They think that he should abandon *his way* and adopt *their way* instead.

Prayer

The most primary parental obligation is to pray for one's children, and this obligation begins even before the child is born.

We can never pray enough for our children. The obligation is infinite. Our Sages also prescribed no particular petition. There exists only the opportunity to pour out our hearts in prayer, and so we must do, each of us composing our own personal entreaty. Our words should address the moment's needs and concerns.

The concept of praying for our children and their education is so important that one might argue it is the single most important principle of *chinuch*. It is self-deception to think that the *chinuch* and growth of our children to be great in Torah and excellent in *middos* is in man's hands, our hands. The matter depends on Hashem. Indeed, Hashem deposits the children in our hands, and we must fulfill our obligations. But we must pour forth a lot of *tefillah* before Hashem for the deposits with which He has entrusted us.

Postscript
"Hereby Resolved"
A Father's Kabbalos [1]
Dr. Jerry Lob

I WILL REMEMBER THAT I AM YOUR *TATTY* (FATHER) AND THAT I love you.

I will remember that you are a child.

I will find ways to show you that you are loved. I will say, "I love you," more often and I will express it in other ways as well, perhaps with touch, tone of voice, smile, look on my face, and by giving of my time.

I will not degrade you, laugh at you, ridicule you in any way.

I will say, "I am sorry," when I'm wrong.

I will criticize less and focus more often on the positives in you.

I will look for the big picture, keep perspective, keep my eyes on the prize, the prize of a loving, caring, joyful relationship with you.

I will remember that you are fragile, that my words and tone of voice can damage and slice through you, that you are soft even when you act hard. I will not be fooled when you act uncaring. I know different and I will remember.

---

1. Note: While a *kabbalah* is a commitment to Hashem, I've chosen to phrase these *kabbalos* in the intimate, from me to my child(ren), in a way that may have more impact on me. To be sure, there is an awareness of Hashem as witness to these resolutions.

I will tell you directly and assertively when I disagree with you, but not in a rage, and not with sarcasm, and with no eye rolling.

I will not hit you, no matter what. I will remember the words of Rabbi Shlomo Wolbe, that in this era it is prohibited to hit our children, that it will lead to their hatred. And the words of my *Rebbi,* the *Rosh Hayeshiva* Rabbi Yitzchok Feigelstock, that in this generation we need to follow the *derech* of warmth, no hitting.

I will smile more to you. I will smile more, period.

I will be attuned and more open to feel joy about you, to revel in your very existence. And I will display this joy more often.

I will respect you. I will respect your feelings, your need for space and privacy. I will respect your dignity. I will respect your opinions and your decisions, though at times I may overrule them (in your younger years).

I will be more patient. I will be more patient. I will be more patient. I will think often of Hashem's *middah* of *erech apayim* (slow in anger).

I will set appropriate boundaries for you, for your safety, for your growth, for your *ruchniyus,* and I will not shirk my responsibility. And I will remember that it's OK for you to be upset with me. I do this out of love.

I will remember that you are a work in progress, not a finished product, and while your pronouncements may sound secure, confident, finished, they're not. I will patiently wait for you, with anticipation and some trepidation, through your journey.

I will be less concerned with *kibbud av,* and more concerned with *kavod habrios* (you are my most precious *briyah*) and I will remember the *Mishnah* that *kavod* comes to those who give it to others.

I will choose my battles and try to remember that the battles themselves are not personal, but part of the miracle of your growth. And I will learn to bite my tongue more.

I will be more loving to Mommy and always respectful to her. I will remember the look on your face when I've said something hurtful to her. I will make more effort to bring joy into our family, to bring to our home a spirit of song.

I will remember that no matter your age, you still look to me (as I look to my father), and what is important is not so much the information I impart to you, but who I am to you.

I will not take revenge when I am hurt. Even if you have intentionally hurt me and even if I am so angry, so very angry, I will not respond in kind. I will remember that I am the parent and you are the child. I will try to find quiet and calm. I will not give you the silent treatment, either. I will ask for your apology, but I will not take revenge.

I will laugh more. I will be on the lookout to laugh more with you. At times I will try to laugh at myself.

I will remember the sparkle in my father's eyes when he saw me or introduced me to others, the sparkle that spoke more eloquently than words of his pride. And I will sparkle for you.

I will play more with you. I will give you your own time with me every day even if only for a few minutes.

I will learn more with you. And I will try to make this time warm and joyous and not full of tension and anger.

I will be determined to be proud of you. I will see your inner beauty, not your grades or how you look, but your *neshamah*, your goodness, your kindness, your unique strengths, skills, and talents. I will remember that each child is different and may have a different *derech*. I will love you because you are, not because you do. And not because of what you give to me.

I will attempt to bring more joy into *Shabbos* and *Yom Tov* and into *Yiddishkeit*. I will remember that it is my *simchah* in Torah and *mitzvos* that will draw you to them, my enthusiasm that will generate yours, and it is my love of Hashem that will deepen your love of Hashem.

I will take an interest in your life. If you share it with me, I will feel joy in your joys and sadness in your sorrows. I will not make light of your reactions. I will take you seriously. I will be available for you and will be respectful if you choose not to share.

I will not look at you with disgust. I will not call you names. You are my child.

I will not try to break your spirit. I will try to embrace, celebrate and guide your spirit.

I will not ignore your suffering. I will put aside my work and my tiredness and my *chessed* work and even my learning to be there for you, whenever you need me. You are my most important *mitzvah*.

I will look deep into myself and remember how painful childhood and adolescence can be, and I will honor you and support you. I will not abandon you when you need me most, even when it feels like you are pushing me away.

I will have more fun with you and I will remember that our shared laughter and love brings the *Shechinah*.

I will remember that I am your *Tatty*, and that I love you.